The Moffat Road

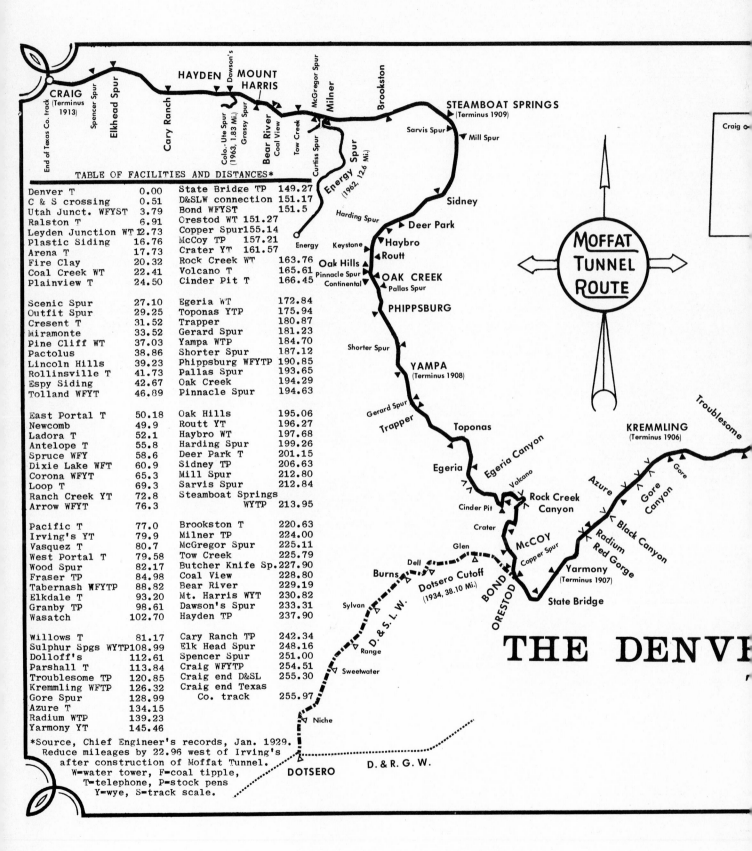

MOFFAT TUNNEL ROUTE

THE DENVE[R]

TABLE OF FACILITIES AND DISTANCES*

Station	Mileage	Station	Mileage
Denver T	0.00	State Bridge TP	149.27
C & S crossing	0.51	D&SLW connection	151.17
Utah Junct. WFYST	3.79	Bond WFYST	151.5
Ralston T	6.91	Orestod WT	151.27
Leyden Junction WT	12.73	Copper Spur	155.14
Plastic Siding	16.76	McCoy TP	157.21
Arena T	17.73	Crater YT	161.57
Fire Clay	20.32	Rock Creek WT	163.76
Coal Creek WT	22.41	Volcano T	165.61
Plainview T	24.50	Cinder Pit T	166.45
Scenic Spur	27.10	Egeria WT	172.84
Outfit Spur	29.25	Toponas YTP	175.94
Cresent T	31.52	Trapper	180.87
Miramonte	33.52	Gerard Spur	181.23
Pine Cliff WT	37.03	Yampa WTP	184.70
Pactolus	38.86	Shorter Spur	187.12
Lincoln Hills	39.23	Phippsburg WFYTP	190.85
Rollinsville T	41.73	Pallas Spur	193.65
Espy Siding	42.67	Oak Creek	194.29
Tolland WFYT	46.89	Pinnacle Spur	194.63
East Portal T	50.18	Oak Hills	195.06
Newcomb	49.9	Routt YT	196.27
Ladora T	52.1	Haybro WT	197.68
Antelope T	55.8	Harding Spur	199.26
Spruce WFY	58.6	Deer Park T	201.15
Dixie Lake WFT	60.9	Sidney TP	206.63
Corona WFYT	65.3	Mill Spur	212.80
Loop T	69.3	Sarvis Spur	212.84
Ranch Creek YT	72.8	Steamboat Springs	
Arrow WFYT	76.3	WYTP	213.95
Pacific T	77.0	Brookston T	220.63
Irving's YT	79.9	Milner TP	224.00
Vasquez T	80.7	McGregor Spur	225.11
West Portal T	79.58	Tow Creek	225.79
Wood Spur	82.17	Butcher Knife Sp.	227.90
Fraser TP	84.98	Coal View	228.80
Tabernash WFYTP	88.82	Bear River	229.19
Elkdale T	93.20	Mt. Harris WYT	230.82
Granby TP	98.61	Dawson's Spur	233.31
Wasatch	102.70	Hayden TP	237.90
Willows T	81.17	Cary Ranch TP	242.34
Sulphur Spgs WYTP	108.99	Elk Head Spur	248.16
Dolloff's	112.61	Spencer Spur	251.00
Parshall T	113.84	Craig WFYTP	254.51
Troublesome TP	120.85	Craig end D&SL	255.30
Kremmling WFTP	126.32	Craig end Texas	
Gore Spur	128.99	Co. track	255.97
Azure T	134.15		
Radium WTP	139.23		
Yarmony YT	145.46		

*Source, Chief Engineer's records, Jan. 1929.
  Reduce mileages by 22.96 west of Irving's
  after construction of Moffat Tunnel.
     W=water tower, F=coal tipple,
       T=telephone, P=stock pens
       Y=wye, S=track scale.

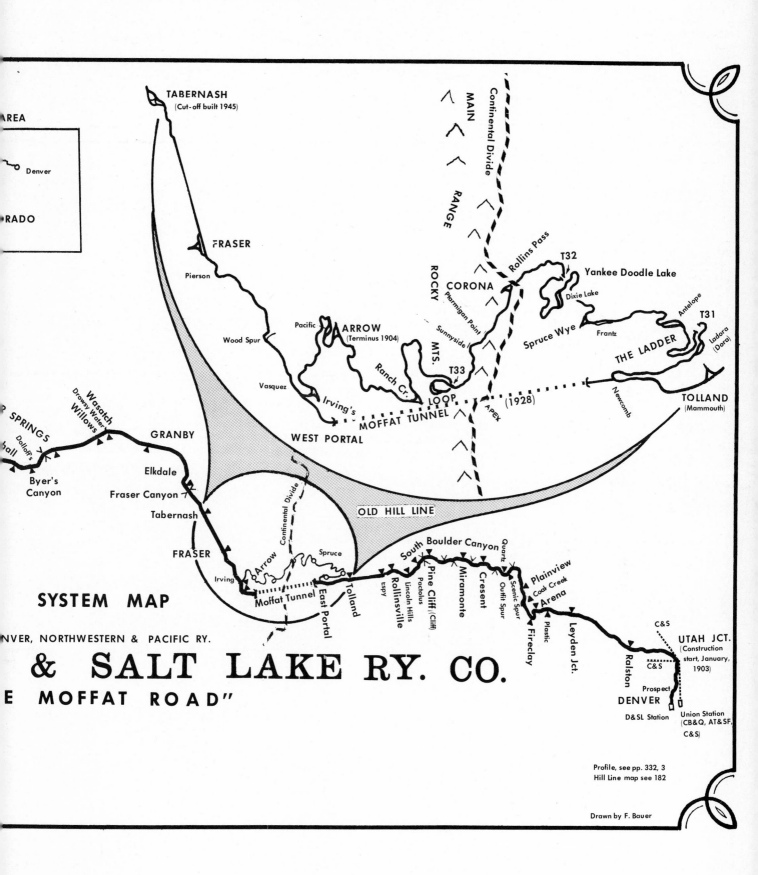

AREA

Denver

RADO

TABERNASH
(Cut-off built 1945)

FRASER

Pierson

MAIN

Continental Divide

RANGE

ROCKY

CORONA

Rollins Pass

T32

Yankee Doodle Lake

Dixie Lake

Ptarmigan Point

Spruce Wye

Frantz

Antelope

T31

THE LADDER

Ladora
(Dora)

Pacific

ARROW
(Terminus 1904)

Sunnyside

MTS.

Wood Spur

Ranch Cr.

T33

Vasquez

LOOP

Irving's

(1928)

APEX

Newcomb

TOLLAND
(Mammouth)

MOFFAT TUNNEL

WEST PORTAL

SPRINGS

Wasatch

Drowsy Water

Willows

GRANBY

hall

Dolloff's

Byer's
Canyon

Elkdale

Fraser Canyon

Tabernash

FRASER

Irving

OLD HILL LINE

Continental Divide

Arrow

Spruce

Moffat Tunnel

East Portal

Tolland

South Boulder Canyon

Quartz

Pine Cliff (Cliff)

Pactolus

Lincoln Hills

Rollinsville

Espy

Miramonte

Cresent

Outfit Spur

Scenic Spur

Plainview

Coal Creek

Arena

Plastic

Fireclay

Leyden Jct.

C&S

UTAH JCT.
(Construction
start, January,
1903)

C&S

Ralston

Prospect

DENVER

D&SL Station

Union Station
(CB&Q, AT&SF,
C&S)

SYSTEM MAP

NVER, NORTHWESTERN & PACIFIC RY.

& SALT LAKE RY. CO.

E MOFFAT ROAD"

Profile, see pp. 332, 3
Hill Line map see 182

Drawn by F. Bauer

The Moffat Road

Edward T. Bollinger

and

Frederick Bauer

SAGE BOOKS

THE SWALLOW PRESS INC.
CHICAGO

Dedicated to Alan Swallow, author and publisher, for his daring new conception of books and for making possible a multitude of works on the Rocky Mountain West.

Sage Books are published by
The Swallow Press Incorporated
1139 South Wabash Avenue
Chicago, Illinois 60605

Some Moffat relics posed against the background of the original Denver, Northwestern and Pacific blueprint of the line around Yankee Doodle Lake: In the rear, a–Certificate of Beneficial Interest for ten shares of D. & S. L. Railroad stock, 1913; plan of 50-thousand gal. D&RGW water tank used on the Moffat, 1939; train order hoop used at Kremmling until the introduction of CTC with D.N.W.&P. train orders found at Sulphur Springs during dismantling of the station (both courtesy J. N. Barnes, Jr. Arvada):

In second row, publicity postcards issued by the Moffat when postage was one cent, and back of them a piece of canvas from the cab of malley 210 wrecked below the Loop; switch list, and billing for loaded car at Oak Creek, 1912; 1888 form from the Denver, Utah and Pacific which road preceeded the Moffat and partially completed the tunnel at Yankee Doodle Lake (courtesy Tiv Wilkins, Boulder); D. N. W. & P. completion report on laying of the corona coal chute spur, 1913.

In lower row, fragment of glass of beautiful amethyst color from 60 years exposure at Corona; D. & S. L. Railway Table of Distances 1929 from which maps in this book were constructed; back of the Table, a unique Moffat rail anchor which prevented slippage of the rails downhill against the ties under the weight of trains; souvenir postcard booklet of the James Peak route through the Moffat Tunnel; contract between the Colorado-Utah Construction Co. and the D. N. W. & P. for the original roadway work in 1902; switch lock and key from the Fraser baggage room (courtesy J. N. Barnes, Jr.); and telegraph insulator from the Hill. All from F. Bauer collection.

Preface

In an earlier work, *Rails That Climb,* I attempted to present the almost unbelievable story of privation and courage endured by the men of the Moffat Road. Furthermore, I had hoped to open some closets filled with the skeletons of intrigue against Mr. Moffat. But those closets are sealed forever. A step through a shallow grave, however, made Fred Bauer and me determined to write this book, a task which has taken five years. Farrington Carpenter, a Colorado attorney, called the story *"The Rape of the Moffat Tunnel."*

This work is not the record of all past history. This is the record of the opening chapters only of a terrific battle for a route west of Denver which the Rio Grande is fighting even today over the Ogden Gateway and over a detrimental ownership of the Western Pacific. The Rio Grande route is so economically favorable and the company so effectively organized as to place competitors in an unfortunate position.

Readers may note a similarity between *The Moffat Road* and *Rails That Climb.* This is natural because they are, after all, a record of the same railroad. As compared with the former work, however, *The Moffat Road* has more than three hundred additional pictures and maps, and much additional detail on the Moffat Tunnel, the Dotsero Cutoff, the many shorter tunnels, wreck stories, and the more recent history after the D.&R.G.W. integration. Important additional information is provided concerning Moffat's desperate attempts to secure financing, the Moffat Tunnel steal, an explanation of the Denver and Salt Lake's failure to build the Dotsero Cutoff, and an evaluation of the Freeman administration of the Denver and Salt Lake.

I am grateful to Fred Bauer, electrical engineer in charge of vehicle electrical engineering with the Ford Motor Company, who is co-author of this work. He has done a magnificent job in telling the thrilling story of the construction of the Moffat Tunnel. He shared the load of this work, running into apparent blind alleys in seeking facts and pictures of the Air Brake tests. He digested everything written on the construction of Dotsero Cutoff, as he did in making a study of the construction of Cascade Tunnel compared to the Moffat Tunnel, one a private, the other a public, enterprise.

Fred kept my interests in this subject going when the desert journey had me stalled.

Together we take great pleasure in presenting so many pictures and maps from our collections. We have included some pictures which the falling snow flakes blur. This is how our vision was blurred in such storms in Middle Park for years. We are sorry that the reader cannot feel the bite of fifty degrees below and the weariness of snow shoveling with a slide above you ready to let go. There are other pictures that were taken and we could not find, some burned and destroyed by unappreciative relatives. There are subjects that the reader will desire to know about that we do not have space for. Indeed, the reader might have discarded some things we wrote about to make room for those other matters!

We are pleased to present the pictures of L. C. McClure, for these are the ones that fascinated me as a boy and gave me the desire to know the story behind such high mountains and great snow.

We wish to acknowledge the kindness of J. B. Culbertson above all others. Joe was in earshot of more of the history than any other living man. He was the first, middle, and last Chief Dispatcher. And then he went to work for the Rio Grande as Chief and was so valuable that they kept him on to the age of eighty. He read and checked this manuscript, so that there would be no lap orders. He slowed us down as we took some curves, and he asked us to make time other places.

All students of history owe the retired office engineer of the Moffat, Ed Sunergren, a very great debt for his appreciation of historical material, which he tried to preserve. His respect for older engineers made his twenty-four years as a railroad engineer richly endowed with stories of the original survey parties. He read proof for us in addition to guiding our search.

To Jackson Thode, Rio Grande research analyst and president of Rocky Mountain Railroad Club, for criticism and proofreading we say thanks.

To all the men of the Moffat Road and the Rio Grande who have been so interested and helpful we say thanks for giving us their patience and their pictures, and to President G. B. Aydelott for his insight that history should be accepted whether we like the facts or dislike them.

Appreciation is given to Agnes Wright Spring, State Historian, for her help and encouragement; to the Western History Department of the Denver Public Library, Alys Freeze, Opal Harbor and James Davis, for assistance in research; and to Mrs. William North for her work in research; to Ernie S. Peyton, for his copies of ICC wreck investigations. In addition, the writing of this book would have been impossible without the seemingly limitless reference materials in the Detroit Public Library where publications of the 1900 era popped forth within minutes. The depth of the bibliography is testimony to the storehouse of information available.

Photographs and other information were furnished by a number of people, and we have tried faithfully to credit them where the prime source was known. Mr. Henry C. Ritchie, Archivist of the City of Schenectady, was especially helpful in finding Alco builder's photographs.

In giving our thanks to others, we cannot do justice to our closest helpers, critics, and Girls Friday—Geraldine Bauer and Alice Bollinger. Their understanding has made us persevere.

One special problem must be mentioned: the spelling of the Denver Northwestern and Pacific Railway Company. The initials D.N.W.&P. were almost universally used, suggesting the spelling Denver, North Western and Pacific. Our appendix materials give authority for two other spellings, Denver Northwestern and Pacific, and Denver North-western and Pacific. In this book we have not attempted what has been called a tedious consistency, since all of these variants have historical backing.

Make no mistake! The writing of a book such as this is labor, albeit a labor of love. Such a venture does not have profit as its prime objective. This book is written in the hope that after reading it the reader may have a better insight into the minds of men who have done some real pioneering in Colorado. We hope it inspires the reader to seek the high country . . . to drive over Rollins Pass and to be inspired by the mute timbering which still remains.

The Moffat story is a true American epic: high hopes, frustration, defeat, but eventual success over almost hopeless odds. Books have been written about abandoned railroads, long forgotten. Not so this one. We wrote this volume to record the history of a railroad which is now successful and which constitutes the backbone of one of America's great traffic arteries.

Second Edition Preface

The National Association of State and Local History gave the first edition of this book its highest honor when it gave the *Moffat Road* the Award of Merit on August 24, 1962.

We have taken the opportunity in the Second Edition to introduce a system map on page 5, a drawing of the first Utah Junction office on page 13, a "slip bill" on page 54, a new research on page 62, a tribute to Henry Swan on page 115, a photo of the sixtieth anniversary of the first train to Corona on Devil's Slide Bridge on page 220, the same anniversary at East Portal with Joe Culbertson on page 306, a 1909 train order on page 341, and a D.N.W.&P. lantern on page 359.

We express our appreciation to Rio Grande Trainmaster Jerry McCall for catching the illustrious Mr. McClure's errors of tunnel numbering. On the other hand, we regret having lost a correction given by an unknown individual for the account of the meeting of the East and West Tunnel crews of the pioneer bore, as given on page 197.

We ask a question: Was the Moffat Road Steal too hot to comment on closer to Denver than Salt Lake City? Or is it that such fast deals are an unfortunate part of life, and men just growl and pay the cost dumped on them?

Finally, we hint that the old poker game against Dave Moffat's superior route is not over. The Union Pacific would like to close the Denver Gateway to the Rock Island. But the man who holds the Moffat Route cards is capable and is backed by a top crew that crowds the line with more, real fast freights.

Above all, we say thanks to Enid Thompson and her staff at the Library of the State Historical Society of Colorado; Maxine Benson, acting State Historian; the *Rocky Mountain News;* and Mel Shieltz, their head photographer.

Ed Bollinger and Fred Bauer

Table of Contents

Tables

Table of Illustrations

Table of Illustrations

A Thwarted City and a Great Man

The twentieth century slipped into Denver just as quietly as the zero cold slipped down from the nearby peaks and penetrated deeper into the ground, looking not in vain for water lines to freeze. Denver was held in check. Could she be called a city? Discouraged and weary from the freezing out of her best enterprises, Denver's hopes were going to sleep like an exhausted mountaineer caught in a storm.

Denver had been a logical place to locate a cotton mill. Her virile men had built a railroad into Texas to bring in the cotton. But the mill did not have a chance, even though the West Coast market was near. Reason—it cost twenty to twenty-five per cent more to ship cotton goods from Denver to the West Coast than from New England to the West Coast by rail. Why? The men who controlled the New England mills controlled the railroads to the north and south of Denver that reached the West Coast.

Denver had been a logical location for a woolen mill. Here were the hills where the sheep grazed, those mountain hills. But when the product was completed, the freight rates were higher for Denver shippers to the West Coast than from New England.

General Palmer had run up against the same men when he erected his steel mill in Pueblo. Iron and coal were close at hand. But still closer were the hands of the owners of the Pittsburgh steel mills. They controlled the rates on steel.

Several giants had been at war with one another over controlling American industry through the railroads. These men had worked out an uneasy truce by declaring spheres of influence in which they

Utah Junction. In this unpretentious building train orders for the D.N.W.&P. were created by Joe Culbertson. The trainmaster kept his records and examined men for his crews. There was a small freight room as well as an office for the agent. Since this junction with the Burlington and Missouri River Railroad was north of Denver, few passengers boarded the train here though many employees did. The artist and Museum Technician of the State Historical Society, Roy Hunt, drew this picture from a description Mr. Culbertson gave. *The drawing is used by permission as it was drawn for the 1967 Winter issue of the Historical Society's* Colorado Magazine.

ruled supreme. Colorado enterprise suffered most from the spheres controlled by Harriman and Gould.

Coloradans also contended with the Rockies which were by far the highest and roughest through their state. Slim gauge roads had squeezed through the narrow confines of canyons and clung to the steep walls of mountains to reach gold and silver camps that could only exist with the help of cheap transportation.

Denver's 17th Street at turn of century. Seventeenth Street bankers had opened mines by building narrow-gauge roads into the most rugged mountains. These men had given in to the Wall Street giants who had said "No" to Pueblo becoming the Pittsburgh of the West, cotton mills in Denver, and any direct rail route West. Citizens were quick to tell Eastern tourists how much harm Eastern financiers had done to their dreams. The twentieth century found Colorado's great men past the age of adventuring. Why risk what you had gained in a lifetime? But there was another David seeking the right stone for his sling shot. He was determined to develop northwestern Colorado and build a direct route West. *W. H. Jackson photo.*

The first transcontinental line should have gone directly west of Denver. This route had proved superior through the years. But the initial challenge was too great for her builders. So Colorado had not only been by-passed to the north by the Union Pacific, but also she had lost a main line that could have developed industry at an early date across the state.

A second route reached Salt Lake more by accident than thanks to original design. This was the Rio Grande, which had started for Mexico, lost Raton Pass to the Santa Fe, and turned west at Pueblo to serve mining interests but gradually wandered west.

The map shows that Denver was off the main lines. The Union Pacific connection was made several miles east of Denver and a hundred miles north. The Rio Grande was equally as roundabout to the south.

The Union Pacific had decided to use the low passes and great valleys of Wyoming. Her engineers were willing to fight the terrible blizzards of that route rather than contend with construction west of Denver.

This is easy to understand, for not only was the Front Range higher here, but it was also so steep and rugged that it snagged the clouds into dropping their precious moisture in the form of tons of snow. The winds swept the heights clear, leaving passes thirty feet deep with snow.

Nevertheless the very steep walls of these towering mountains spoke of a superior route that could be established by piercing the Front Range with a tunnel and slipping down the valleys and canyons which were protected from the sweeping blizzards by range after range of mountains.

This every great engineer and many lesser men knew.

Harriman and Gould were among those who feared what would happen if this route was opened. So they set out to discourage every attempt to build it.

Colorado had not lacked great men. The western half of the state had challenged men to grow great to conquer. But the empire builders had grown weary of the battle; with their wealth, they could now be content. This New Year's night, all but one man slept well. This man refused to have an easy conscience over Denver's defeat. He still was determined to unlock the resources of northwestern Colorado by a short line to Salt Lake and the coast.

A Thwarted City and a Great Man

The man who would not be frozen out was David Halliday Moffat, Jr. He was born in Washington-ville, New York, on July 23, 1839, where he attended school until twelve, when he became a messenger for the New York National Exchange Bank. One year later he followed a brother to Des Moines, Iowa, and in several years he became bank clerk for A. J. Stevens and Company. However, at sixteen he thought a fortune could be made in real estate at Omaha, where the Pacific Railroad was to start. So delayed was this venture that he lost all he had made. Meanwhile he was given the Bank of Nebraska to liquidate. He was able to do this without loss to anyone.

Hearing the persistent reports from Colorado that gold had been found in Cherry Creek, he formed a company with C. C. Woolworth of St. Joseph, Missouri. They raced to what is now Denver to open, in a log cabin, a stationery store whose wagons were faster than the U. S. Mail, bringing in Eastern papers that were sold at a premium. He pitched into the life of this community serving as postmaster for a while and becoming the first telegraph operator.

A crisis developed because the Union Pacific turned down the Colorado survey; merchants moved to Cheyenne, and miners gave up with no hope of transportation. Moffat emerged with such proved leadership in helping Evans promote the Denver Pacific to reach the Union Pacific at Cheyenne, that

he was honored by having the first locomotive named the "D. H. Moffat."

He was first of all a financier. His mine holdings finally included one hundred investments. But to be a miner you had to be a railroad builder. This he did from his office as cashier, and later as president of the First National Bank. He used his business judgment and leadership in incorporating and serving on the boards of directors of a host of railroads: The Boulder Valley, The Denver and South Park, and the Denver, Utah and Pacific, which located the route later used by the Moffat.

Moffat became a king maker. He considered the character and enterprise of a man's collateral on which the man could build his business or open his mine. His losses were above average but his gains were still higher.

No better choice than Moffat could have been secured for the presidency of the state's largest railroad, the Rio Grande. He recognized that Colorado's greatest need was to be served by a transcontinental route. So he initiated surveys that cost $106,374 in an effort to shorten the Rio Grande or locate directly through the Divide. When the New York board members could not see the need of a branch to some promising mining area, he built the line on his own. He recognized the narrow gauge as a mistake, and made the change to standard gauge. The earnings of the road he wanted to put back into line improvements. The Eastern board, however, wanted these for profits. At this time he resigned, denying that this was the reason, but

Horse changing station at Idlewild in Grand County. Sixty miles west of Denver, Grand County was isolated. She was waiting for news of a railroad to justify the running of the first telephone wire over Berthoud Pass down to Idlewild. Moffat's announcement to build west sent these men to string the first wire. *Art Weston photo.*

Page 15

The hogback of the front range west of Denver. West of these lakes a 2.6 miles tunnel could pierce the Divide at an elevation of 9,900 feet. or a 6.2 mile tunnel could be located at 9,030 feet. James Peak in the background. *McClure photo.*

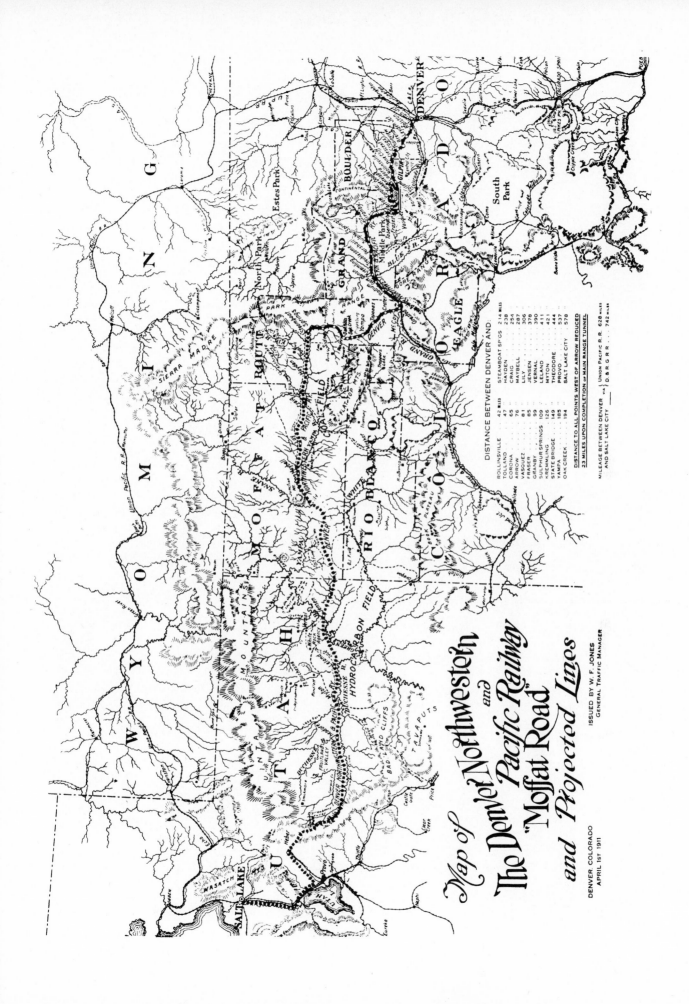

David H. Moffat, Jr., 1885. *State Historical Society of Colorado.*

Chesapeake Beach Engine No. 4. Little did this engine dream that she was destined to leave the cadets in trim dress at Annapolis and go to work on a construction train in the Rockies for David Moffat. *Alco photo.*

historians believe that he felt that the Rio Grande, with absentee control, could not solve Colorado's need for main line transportation.

Through forty years he backed the establishment of every railroad, save the Colorado Midland, including the line to Fort Worth, Texas. Yet Denver remained a quiet little tourist community decidedly of white collar interest—denied at every turn the hope of becoming an industrial metropolis that could unlock the tremendous mineral resources, together with lumbering and agriculture, in the western part of the state over the rugged Divide.

The new century slipped in, finding Moffat the mining king of the state, the banker who had saved from bankruptcy many of the state's foremost builders. He was the state's wealthiest man. No one was better able to retire than Moffat. He still owned the "Gold Belt" (Florence and Cripple Creek). Men of his success were establishing universities, endowing libraries, and buying pipe organs. Moffat only once indulged in this. He gave the church in Washingtonville, New York, an organ, for here he had gone to Sunday School. He also gave a library to this village. His passion was to develop the northwestern part of Colorado.

He sent young men East after the turn of the century to find financing for an interurban electric of slim gauge limitations to serve Arvada and the

Leyden coal mines. He hoped that this line could be pushed up the foothills and through the canyons to the Divide where it could slip over and down to Hot Sulphur Springs. But this was a plaything compared to the work Moffat had been doing. With men in the field following up his great interest of the years in piercing the Divide, he dreamed of the low freight rates that Harriman denied them to the West Coast. To Moffat the Sherman Anti-Trust law had proved unable to handle the giants. The efforts of the Interstate Commerce Commission had proved helpless without sufficient legislation. Moffat did not look for help through legislation.

On July 18, 1902, he wired his boys Hughes and Evans in New York to stop promoting the electric line. What he announced in Denver shook Harriman, who never dreamed Moffat considered himself as daring as a certain other David he had heard about in Sunday School. Moffat was going to build a steam road to Salt Lake and the coast. Moffat was well informed by costly and thorough investigation of the vast resources to be tapped. He was sure of his facts and knew that intelligent investors would recognize a good investment. He would pour his fortune into the idea of piercing the Divide at the narrow hogback, fifty miles west of Denver, and then

Page 19

down valleys protected from the wintry blizzard by the high walls of mountains; he would build an all time main line through the Rockies.

He did not underestimate the power of the giants, but he did overestimate the courage of men who were openly restless with Gould, Harriman, and others. He did not know Colorado's businessmen had grown weary in the battle and were content, nor did he reckon with the folly of little men who see green grass in other states. So far his judgments had been sought and his decisions respected by men who pulled together. Moffat was no man's fool.

The name of his new road was Denver Northwestern and Pacific Railway Company.

The Honorable John Evans, Territorial Governor of Colorado, 1862. He took a liking to the youthful Moffat soon after the lad arrived in Denver. His grandson, another John Evans, is now chairman of the D.&R.G.W. Board. *State Historical Society of Colorado.*

Plans into Action

To build and to operate a railroad west of Denver in 1902 was almost as daring as to fly to the moon sixty years later. This the people of Denver knew. The Divide was fifty miles away. Its *base* was almost four thousand feet higher than Denver; those fifty miles to the base of the Divide were piles of rugged mountains left by the Almighty's great ditcher. There was only one way to get through to the base of the Divide, and that was to creep through the canyons that the centuries of melting snow waters had cut. Wagon roads had to avoid the narrowest places in the canyons by great detours of painful mountain climbing which wearied teams before they reached the crest. Then dropping down to the creek bed again meant miles of tortuous braking of the wagons. Logs and stumps were chained behind wagons many times. This was disheartening to the traveler, for he knew he had again to climb the entire lost elevation to arrive at the base of the Divide which was called the Front Range.

Slim-gauge railroads had found their routes through the narrow canyons thanks to heavy blasting. But they operated in constant fear of the canyon closing in on them or floods carrying out their right of way in one ugly hour.

Into this country Moffat had sent T. J. Milner, chief engineer of the narrow-gauge interurban, to find a route west for the extension to Hot Sulphur Springs. Capable locating engineers had headed parties and had worked several months under the personal direction of Moffat. The line to the base of the Divide had been located; lines were being run on both sides of the Divide.

Grading had actually begun on the swell west of Denver at Rocky Flats up into the mouth of Coal Creek Canyon. This creek afforded a grade a little steeper than two per cent up to the beginning of the creek. From here a long tunnel of 6,000 feet was to be bored with a slightly adverse grade to carry the line to South Boulder Park in order to avoid the more rugged confines of South Boulder Canyon.

With the announcement that Moffat was going to build a steam road came the announcement that the Rocky Mountain West's greatest locating engineer, H. A. Sumner, would be chief.

The grading located by Milner was immediately stopped on Coal Creek. Since this was to be a short line west, a most extensive survey for a route was justified. The small number of parties was increased. This road was to be standard gauge. Financiers were unfavorable to any grade over two per cent. Possessed with his personal experience of the ill-fated Colorado Railway as well as knowledge of the previous surveys, Sumner sent his engineers into South Boulder Canyon and one party back to Coal Creek to see if a two per cent grade could be found. He was fortunate in having some men who had worked previously on the Colorado Railway survey.

Friends of T. J. Milner felt that he had received an injustice. As the survey lines were established, it became evident that the South Boulder route would need thirty short tunnels. Their combined length challenged the proposed 6,000 foot Coal Creek tunnel. It was easy to say Sumner was prejudiced and no better than Milner. Thus, H. A. Sumner added to this difficult technical problem the problem of resentment. He set out to overcome this handicap with every inch of his Christian gentleman-like character.

Young fellows filled with all the ornery devilment of their youth discovered the true stature of their chief as they occasionally rode horseback beside him and received, in offhand remarks, hints as to how to become top locating men.

To keep up the morale of the crews was not easy. Men were forever climbing over loose rocks, only to find themselves pushing through scrub pines or underbrush. The air was so thin that the sun blistered the lad who took his shirt off. Sudden hail storms turned the innocent looking clouds into enemies, and hours were spent by men miserably wet with no return of the sun. Gasping discomfort chilled one's enthusiasm for the beauty of the country, in the thin air above timberline.

There was a fear of not achieving the grade physically in this high country. If one failed, another job was hard to find. In addition, there would be the long walk back over the steep Berthoud Pass wagon road.

The first night on the job came with some men too exhausted to drag themselves to the cook tent for supper. Morning found the young men almost too weary to get up for breakfast. Some lost out as they dragged too slowly cutting stakes or holding the rod. Day in and day out the struggle was a battle of one day at a time for two weeks, then a man began to be thankful for the veteran's jokes that made life easier.

When one became strong enough to enjoy living, there was no town or even crossroad store to buy tobacco, or by chance to meet a girl. Homesickness ate in a man's heart. The evening campfire was welcomed as some plucked on the banjos or sawed on their fiddles. Resentments of the day melted away as they sang by the firelight and played impossible jokes on one another.

If the food was not good because of a delay in supplies, the party chief found a resentful crew. Cooks had to be ingenious in keeping meat from spoiling without ice, or from being stolen by mountain bears or lions. Meat had to be in the shade in the day time, a particular problem above timberline where one had to make his own shade.

The instrument man knew the tragedy of losing a screw which could not be replaced in less than a week's time. Locating engineers had to have a seventh sense, enabling them to look over the mountains and to see the two percent grade favorably placed, so that weeks were not wasted running down impossible or costly lines.

To the lad who had not been to college it was clear that experience was not enough. Some youths even dared to study engineering late at night by candle light and an I. C. S. course. This was a great opportunity, the great adventure of Colorado—the building of a main line west.

Moffat was the red blooded man who had become the wealthiest man in the state. It was not through craft in cheating others, it had been in daring decisions intelligently worked out. The name David Moffat meant success if there was to be success. Those who belittled him established their own reputations for "sour grapes."

David Moffat immediately appointed H. A. Sumner Chief Engineer. No better man could have been found, for he had solved locations in Colorado that no other man had solved. His experience included the vast work that had been started directly west of Denver by the Burlington sponsored Colorado Railway that had failed for financing because of the locomotive engineers' strike in 1880. Moffat had given him the job of locating a shorter route for the Rio Grande up South Platte Canyon. This effort had been halted by the eastern directors. Many former Main Range Tunnel surveys were available for his use. Years later Arthur Ridgway, Chief Engineer of the Rio Grande (brother of Amos Caryl Ridgway, the first General Manager), said of Sumner's route, "Between Denver and Toponas is the most successful route through the most difficult country ever built in all of America." *Sumner family picture.*

A strategy took shape in the Denver office. The line to the base of the Divide had to be quickly yet correctly established. It looked as if thirty tunnels would have to be started through the ribs of South Boulder Canyon to avoid curves too tortuous. This was to be a main line, not a branch to tap some mining community. These tunnels had to be contracted for and under construction with some access roads built so that machinery and supplies could reach the Divide. Only then could the proposed main range tunnel get under construction.

Against this race for time came the threat of the first winter. Snowshoes had been ordered for parties that had to remain in the field to complete the main range tunnel study. But the snowshoes were lost between the state of Maine and Denver. Or could this be the hand of the enemy pulling every conceivable dirty trick of war?

August waned. Indian summer came with a reprieve from the snows. Storms came and melted. But the weather after Christmas made the struggle ugly. With stiff fingers the topographer drew his maps at night by kerosene light. Field books were translated into intelligible writing, and errors were caught. Cross hairs of transits were double checked for accuracy.

H. A. Sumner heard party chiefs complain of competent men whose personalities clashed. One had to be tops in human relations to make the team click without jeopardizing morale.

Then there came the missing of personal possessions, such as a beautiful gun. It was clear that there was a thief in this party. Whispering did not build up morale. Weeks went by. The man was clever. Suspicions were put on innocent men. Then came the day the sheriff was summoned to take the man to prison. This meant bringing charges and taking time off for the trial.

All the time the locating engineer had to be figuring out the problems that the contractor would have and be ready with sensible solution.

Contractors interested in bidding on the Tunnel section were aghast at the problems. No steam shovel could be moved in to any of the tunnel sites. How could such an inaccessible country be let out for construction without modern machinery? But a contractor of mountain experience quietly said that he had not seen any place that a mule and cart could not go.

It would be hand drilling in hard granite. It would be springing those holes so that powder could be poured into them. It would be careful blasting, picking, and shoveling.

The Chief Engineer had an exacting General

To reach the west side of the Front Range (Continental Divide), survey parties rode the stage from Georgetown over Berthoud Pass and down to Idlewild. This was the horse changing station. The wet spring snow was still clinging to the trees the day one of the boys took this picture, a few minutes after the stage dropped him off. He now had to find his way up to the Jim Creek campsite of the survey party he was joining. Jobs were scarce, survey work was coveted, but could he last it out? The thin air caused him to wonder as he struggled over the rough mountainside trying to please the party chief. In two weeks his breath was coming easier at ten, eleven, and twelve thousand feet, and he would soon be moving with almost the ease of the bear. These were the lonely hours fighting homesickness out in the Moffat Road wilds, as he sang around the evening campfire or listened to the Spanish American war being fought over again. *Art Weston photo.*

Manager, A. C. Ridgway, to deal with. This man, the son of a great railroader, always seemed to growl that the proposed line was too high above the stream or too near flood waters. His father had been called "Old Tige." This son had bull dog tenacity and some obstinacy. He had cut his teeth under a remarkable father battling blizzards, weary men, and forgotten orders. The necessity for better location, protection against spring-time floods and rock slides, as well as the grind of training men to handle air brakes on the steep mountain grades of the Rio Grande was always in his mind.

Moffat naturally selected such a man as his general manager knowing that together with the Rocky

The office tent of the party chief, where field notes were translated into maps, and important discoveries were recorded in a diary together with the human interests of the day. The surveyors brought their fishing poles along and a target pistol as well as the glass plate camera which took this photo. The summer proved too short to finish the work. This tent continued to serve as the office even in 40° below weather. *Art Weston photo.*

Mountain West's greatest locating engineer he would be well advised. These two men had to report on the one greatest expense of the Denver Northwestern & Pacific—the Main Range Tunnel. Apparently every great engineer and railroad promoter who had considered crossing the Front Range in this area had taken a tunnel for granted.

T. J. Milner had left in his plans the suggestions that a switchback line be thrown over the hog back at the tunnel site so that machinery, materials, and men could work from both ends and thus halve the time of construction.

H. A. Sumner admitted the switchback would be practical for such limited freight operation. But he desired to have a temporary main line that could

be used for the three or more years while the tunnel was under construction. Sumner knew that with such a line over Rollins Pass he would be able to build the road clear to the coast. When the tunnel was completed the heavy transcontinental traffic would be ready to use the Main Range bore.

Ridgway surprised everyone by being unfavorable for a tunnel at that time. He said Rollins Pass was just a matter of power. He had his eye on a new type of power, the mallet. For a fraction of the cost of becoming involved in all the unforeseen questions of drilling a long tunnel, sufficient powerful locomotives and rotary plows could make operation possible. To understand Ridgway's advice we must recall that up to this time railroad men in the Rocky Mountain West just could not conceive of tunnels over a mile long. To be of any help at this high altitude a tunnel would have to be 2.6 miles long to get under the worst effects of winter storms.

H. A. Sumner also warned that in any long tunnel the unforeseen was to be seriously considered. Nevertheless, he considered the tunnel a necessity.

Moffat could delay the decision on this tunnel until the rails reached the 9,930 foot location. For this was December 18, 1902. Five months had gone. Sumner had accomplished the impossible. He was fully satisfied to recommend the line, call for bids, and on this day let the bids.

Moffat went to New York to see how serious Harriman's opposition was. It was already apparent that many investors were being intimidated by this giant. Moffat had faith that men would stand by promises made previously. And Wall Street was not the only source of finances. In Boston there was money, and Moffat knew that there was more than enough capital held by men who would rejoice to see the bully Harriman held at bay for just once. Besides the East, there were England and Europe where investors were looking for new world enterprises. The Rio Grande had its start with capital from Wales.

Ridgway left Sumner to needle the contractors to get into the mountains and start their tunnels while he went to the drafting rooms of locomotive works to get the power he had talked about. Also he had heard that the Chesapeake Beach Railroad to Annapolis was going to electrify. They should have some good passenger equipment to be thoroughly checked as only Ridgeway could check.

So Sumner assisted the contractors and exhorted them to begin construction of the thirty tunnels up the South Boulder Creek line. Ridgway had been favorable to this line, for he was an operating man who appreciated the steady two per cent grade in contrast to the T. J. Milner line up Coal Creek which had a detested 6,000 foot tunnel and an adverse grade as it made its way into Boulder Park. A steady grade meant the most efficient use of helper engines. That this tunnel district is through a very difficult mountain terrain is evident by the fact that every surveyor and operating official since then has asked why Sumner did not use the Coal Creek survey.

Among those who tried later to reroute the line

Finally the snow was four feet deep. With only four pair of snowshoes for twenty men, the work became an ugly battle against the elements. Frantic efforts to find the other snowshoes went on through the winter. They were lost somewhere between Maine and Denver. In the spring they were found in a Boulder freight house with the shipping tag lost. The instrument man risks frost bite to his fingers to set the instrument. The party chief lets the boys keep a puppy who made this field trip. This picture was taken several miles above Fraser, which later became famous as the ice box of the nation. One became rugged, or one went home. *Art Weston photo.*

in this difficult terrain, to avoid the many tunnels, was the brilliant W. C. Jones, Chief Engineer of the Moffat of later years, who came to the conclusion that H. A. Sumner knew what he was proposing, and Ridgway's brother, who as Chief Engineer of the Rio Grande when it began operating over the Moffat, concluded that this was the most practical location well carried out in the most difficult country in all of America.

It is easy to see why the contractors were slow in getting on their locations. Tunnels under a thousand feet had been sublet to enterprising Swedes. These men used their brawn to hand-drill fourteen foot holes and spring them with dynamite so they could take larger charges. They usually sprung these holes three times. The third time the holes were large enough to hold sufficient powder to lift granite out of the entire tunnel opening. When the horses and men were led back from hiding, picks

The locating engineers rode this stage into Middle Park leaving crews high in the hills and mountains to the left seeking locations for the Front Range Tunnel as they considered what lay ahead in Fraser River Canyon, Byers Canyon, and Gore Canyon. This is two miles south of Fraser on highway 40 of today. *Art Weston.*

were swung and shovels heaved the muck into carts which were driven to dump the rock and build up the fills. The worst hazards of this work were delayed charges, which sometimes exploded, blinded, even killed the men.

In such remote locations the snows of winter did not encourage men to stay on the job. They slaved all day and struggled all night to dry out their clothing.

Sumner had recommended and secured a construction line telephone to keep him in constant touch with his contractors at all points. This was the first time a telephone line had been built for such use.

By February 1, 1903, 187 men were clinging to the sides of South Boulder Canyon, drilling tunnels. Later 3,800 men slaved long hours. Donkey boilers

were brought by cart into this country and pipe lines dropped hundreds of feet to water to make possible the use of power drills in several of the longer tunnels. At Tunnel 10 five electric drills were put to work; at Tunnel 16 Leyner air drills chiseled away at the hard rock; at Tunnel 30 a steam plant made possible steam drills. Gas engines proved to be too temperamental at this early day to furnish steady power.

But the building of this railroad is not measured by listing the modern machines used nor is the story told by adding up the cost in dollars. It comes by feeling tired at night, as tired as only strong men can be, then to have to go out for some more wood. It's your turn tonight! Loud voices of men turning to a bottle, the dice on the floor as men try to make better wages with Lady Luck—all speak of the slaves men have been.

Leaking roofs on bunkhouses as the snow piles high on the roof and the ice forms; a new cook who is not so good; a delayed wagon bringing supplies and the monotony of the same beans; the smell of cheap coffee; the heartache of being away from home and loved ones—these all are a part of building a railroad. Youth's thrill of the romance of being away from home is gone! The arguments of men who can't get along with themselves or anyone else, the piercing night air, the cold, the days one is sick and not at work, that feeling of longing, the continual grind of working harder to keep up—all make a picture that no plush-seat recliner can ever understand.

To understand H. A. Sumner, listen in on that primitive phone in the evening as the field engineer reports. "Tunnels 19 and 17 are in trouble. The ground is still slipping. The top of the timbering has bent one inch, even two inches some places. Tunnel 17 continues to have a pressure on one side, but farther in the pressure comes from the other side. The rock is decomposing as the air hits it."

Next morning A. C. Ridgway asks for a report from H. A. Sumner to see if he is on the ball, for Ridgway has eavesdropped on the line the night before.

Sumner knows this, for he is a gentleman and has friends while Ridgway is a difficult man who has enemies. Holding his composure, the chief recommends giving up two tunnels. To do this the minimum curvature had to be sharpened and the line detoured to avoid the tunnels.

The contract had been an expensive one—just $78,323 a mile. This was three times the cost of construction elsewhere on the road. Sumner's bypass over Rollins Pass was very cheap—a little over $20,000 a mile.

The name of David Moffat was magic. Good men respected him. George Barnes, a conductor on the Rio Grande, had been given as much as two thousand miles of narrow and standard gauge mountain lines to supervise as Trainmaster. Barnes needed no invitation to head for the Moffat. With no trains to operate, he was sent to Lincoln to buy some extra gang cars.

Ridgway found plenty for Barnes to do. He put him to work installing the first switch. Then when power was needed and the two new moguls were

Construction was dependent on the location of the line so that an unseasonal snow dare not stop the men as they worked in the loneliness of this wilderness country. So ingenious were the pioneer ranchers or mail carriers that they made their own snowshoes by steaming the ends of native pine boards for many hours. Today we call them skis, but to these boys they were snowshoes. If the Moffat line had not been favorably located, the Rio Grande would not be operating through Moffat Tunnel today. The surveying of a line either made or killed any proposed mountain railroad. Improvements could always be carried out later only if the total adopted location was practical. H. A. Sumner magnificently summarized all the known work of other efforts and recommended the route which is protected from winter's storms. This was not realized until Moffat Tunnel could be built. *L. Van Buskirk photo.*

not out of the locomotive works, Barnes was conductor for the borrowed Burlington and Missouri River Railroad engine that made the first movements on the Moffat—such as moving rails up to the rail bending machine that was to strengthen rails by cold bending for the sharp curves on the two per cent. The Irishmen who laid these rails got $2.00 a day in the year 1903.

Engines 20 and 21 arrived in July, after missing the July 7 honor of moving the first cars. These powerful six-wheelers were admired even by Union Pacific men. They cost $12,996.50 and $13,501.61, respectively. By September 28 enough track had been laid that it was felt worthwhile to run a special up to the heavy earth swell at present day Rocky Flats where a giant S was being dug by a steam shovel. Engine 21 had the honor and was considered a "most powerful mogul." Ridgway kept quiet. This engine was just half the engine that would appear when freight was to be moved. Old Maud, a new mallet type, was proving herself on the Baltimore and Ohio, and Ridgway was going to have the biggest locomotive in the world on the Moffat.

Opening a tunnel in South Boulder Canyon, 1903. Contract for the tunnel section was let December 18, 1902, five months after the announcement of the Moffat Road. Thirty tunnels of varying lengths had to be rushed to completion, so that the construction train could reach South Boulder Park for the assault on the mountains. These tunnels were high up on the wall of South Boulder canyon which was only reached by trails. Hand drills, powder, and supplies were carted in. The rock was blown out after painfully slow hand drilling. Steam, electric, and air drills were tried. *Art Weston photo.*

The men and teams that had been removed from the blast area return to load carts and haul out the rock. Meanwhile the slow process of hand drilling new holes began. Unfortunately efficient steam shovels moved only on rails. Only a cart could reach this rugged country, or a daring engineer on a spring wagon. Sub-contracts were let to hardy Swedes for various tunnels. The men lived in tents and hastily constructed log cabins. Powder blasts occasionally came from incomplete firing of the many holes when a worker struck the spot with a pick. Blindness or death lurked there every day. *Art Weston photo.*

Nearly all the tunnels had a curve in them like Tunnel 6. Some tunnels were entered and left by curves. Long before these rails were laid, the telephone line was stretched from the office out into the field so that contact could be established with the engineers and contractors and their needs met. The telephone in construction use was a first on the Moffat. *McClure photo.*

The road climbs through colorful Rainbow Cut and Tunnels 2 to 7 before swinging out to the left high above South Boulder Canyon. The railroad hired the illustrious McClure to make photographs of the spectacular beauty of the line to lure tourists and picnickers. McClure was trained by none less than the West's greatest photographer, William Henry Jackson.

Soon the construction train was unloading steel for the modern 60-foot-high steel trestle to carry the Moffat for 265 feet over Coal Creek. Then the day came when the work train laid the track through Tunnel 1. From here on there were twenty-seven tunnels in twenty-four miles. The country demanded one or more trestles for each tunnel.

The second winter of the Moffat found construction men trying to remain in the thin air of 11,660 feet grading the Rollins Pass line. So needed was this grading and blasting open of cuts and digging of two little tunnels that H. A. Sumner authorized the increase of wages from $2.00 to $3.43 a day. There were days when the beauty of high altitude sunshine ended suddenly in a blizzard. And there were sunny hot days when the thermometer dropped a degree a minute after the sun had set, and suddenly the whole world was black with darkness.

Frostbitten hands and toes, smell of men who had no water to take baths, and whiskey, the ever present remedy for frozen men, was the story of this winter. *The Denver Post* might arrive with its

Page 31

Through the ribs of the front escarpment the line was built. Tunnel 7 was very short. *McClure photo.*

caption " 'Tis a privilege to live in Colorado," but the men would only sneer.

Spring never comes in the Rockies. The snow melts and people get spring fever and then comes a weepy wet snow with the smear of mud and clay. So it was on June 23, 1904, when enough track was laid for a train to reach Mammoth (today's Tolland). Investors and prospective investors and anyone who wanted to follow Moffat's example and buy a ticket could be on the first passenger train movement on Time Card One. But that day men took slickers, for it rained and was cold. Several days later Thomas Doane, chief engineer in charge of building the Hoosac 25,081 foot long tunnel, arrived to advise Moffat. If this tunnel had cost $14,000,000 in 1875, what would the proposed Main Range tunnel run into before its total cost was added up?

Tom Doane turned to Moffat after walking down the mountain, "You have a hard proposition, but

Up at Mammoth (Tolland) the right of way was constructed with a great deal of human brawn, wheeled scrapers, pig noses, carts, and powder. A steam shovel would have come in handy in the heavy cuts, but until thirty tunnels had been blown open and trestles thrown across streams, no shovel could be brought in because shovels moved on rails only. *W. I. Hoklas collection.*

The rail bender. Moffat employees spoke with pride saying that this was the only rail bender in the world. A cold steel process was used, springing the rail until it was stronger. This machine was also used to bend old rail and I-beams for tunnel reinforcements. This photo was taken at the east end of old Utah Junction Yards just prior to the Rio Grande removing the shops to make way for the modern North Yard. Those in the picture are king snipe Ed Harrison (left), Bert Schneitman, B & B foreman (center), and Ed Bollinger (right), one time D.&S.L. gandy dancer. *Ed Bollinger photo.*

you will have to have that tunel. It will likely cost $4,000,000."

Moffat replied, "I will have to get help. I have already sold my tramway stock and water stock."

Who would help Moffat? Already one Coloradan, Walter Cheesman (who was worth enough to build this tunnel himself), had pulled out on Moffat from blue blood jealousy. Harriman had managed to prevent anyone from giving Moffat help in the East.

Almost single handed Moffat stood with enough money to bore that tunnel, but not to lay the rails down into Middle Park several miles below.

Moffat had to make his decision. Boring the tunnel was postponed for another six months. Could Uncle Dave stretch that $4,000,000 to get the rails into the coal fields of Oak Creek? Could he break the fear of Harriman? Would men he had rescued in panics and failures remember him and come to his help? Sixty-four-year-old Moffat was faced with the most cruel battle of his life. His engineers were meeting all kinds of trouble ahead as overnight every valley through which they were thought to build was bought up by some never-before-heard-of power company.

Little did the public realize how hard pressed Moffat was. The newspapers continued sensational stories about a $15,000,000 steel mill that was to be built at Utah Junction just out of Denver, and the fight to get into Union Station. Men talked but hardly believed what they talked about. It was just something to say, "Moffat's Shortline Threatened." What the public saw was train Number One running in several sections to Mammoth where people had a four-hour recess to picnic and explore the luck of a fisherman or the joy of picking wild flowers.

Ties and rails were laid by the Roberts Track Laying Machine which was leased for this work. Note the ties coming up an endless conveyor of rollers. Rails were handled the same way. Steam was furnished by a steam line to the first locomotive. This belt conveyor idea stretched back to the tie and rail cars. The track laying train is approaching Plainview. *W. I. Hoklas collection.*

The line was spectacular to see. Compared with the slim-gauge lines with their sharp bends, this was a very impressive main line which continually went through the mountains and not around them. The grocers had their picnic specials. Parson Uzzell loaded three long trains with his congregation and all their friends, the Woodmen had their day, and the Baptists of Denver remembered the orphans with a Special.

What equipment did the Moffat have that summer? In March two husky fifty-seven-inch driver consolidations Numbers 100 and 101 arrived. A month later passenger Engine 300, a sixty-three-inch ten wheeler had arrived. A bargain was secured in ten passenger cars from the Chesapeake Beach Railway; these were numbered 700 through 708, and

800. Also two fairly new high stepping passengers Numbers 3 and 4 had been purchased with the knowledge that when the shops were built their wheels would have to be trimmed down decidedly, so that they could be of use on the two per cent. These engines were renumbered 390 and 391. One furnished steam for the Roberts Track Laying machine and was assisted by one of the six-wheelers. However, when the construction train hit the four per cent tunnel-by-pass over Rollins Pass the 390 was good only for steam for the Roberts Track Laying machine. Hoggers questioned if she could move her tall slim drivers on that grade.

The construction train continued to crawl higher

The long tedious day's work begins as the men carry ties ahead from the track laying machine while others get up energy to handle the next rail. The frosty morning will give way to the torrid heat of noontime, when men would desire to remove their shirts. However, the thin air would let the rays blister them. *W. I. Hoklas collection.*

Way car 10002. This early construction train crew of Paul Brown, Frank Spaulding, and engineer Bob Bishop prided themselves in this new way car with wooden frame and ladder like steps. Above the cupola was one of the latest marks of a modern railroad, the boxlike signal by which they could talk to the front end. Because these men were away from home, not only days but weeks at a time, their caboose became a second home where they fell to sleep when exhausted, learned to cook while the train rolled and rocked on new track, and had an occasional game of cards. For a half a century men fought to retain their second home as *their* home. *A. Clarke photo.*

No longer racing 80 mph, Chesapeake Beach 4 Spot has been tailored down to mountain climbing with small wheels. She is handling the tie train, but her crew seem proud of her. She is still polished clean by loving hands. *A. Clarke photo.*

Engine 391. Chesapeake Beach Engines 3 and 4 were re-numbered 390 and 391. Original drivers were so big the engines could hardly take themselves up 4% grade; so the drivers were cut down. Years later they were used on work trains and handled the Saturday evening "Fisherman's Special." This Special left Denver at 1:00 P.M. for Sulphur Springs; return arriving Denver 8:00 A.M. Monday. During the week, Monday through Friday, they handled the two-car Nos. 3 and 4 between Denver and Tolland. Miramonte got most of the travel because financiers, etc., had summer homes there. The piping visible over the engine bell extending to the cab and the main driver furnishes steam for the track layer-hose on tender. *Denver Public Library Western Collection.*

Needle's Eye tunnel. Ballast had not yet been laid on this fresh track through Tunnel 32. Today cars can drive through here over the forest "highway" from East Portal to Winter Park. *H. Eno photo.*

into the land of thin air and silvery lakes. The men talked about how many Burlington cars had been rented for the last picnic specials. Finally the rails were laid around a gem of all lakes—Yankee Doodle. The men looked high above them to the place on the mountain where they would be laying rails in a few days. Tunnel 32 was up there just 700 feet straight above them.

That night an official overheard the Irish track layers complain that every stream and lake had been fished out by the engineering parties and contractors. When H. A. Sumner heard about this, he recommended that the railroad stock all the streams on both sides of the Front Range so that the picnic

Construction train on Coal Creek Trestle. The grading of the first twenty miles leading to the tunnel sections began the next spring. As the grade approached Tunnel 1, two large steel structures had to be erected, this one over Coal Creek and the prior grading of T. J. Milner up Coal Creek. The two powerful Engines 20 and 21 hauled the construction train. These new engines were the pride of the line.

specials would be even more popular next summer. He also issued orders that around all stations and places of beauty care should be taken to protect the scenic wonderland.

Several days later the rails were laid through Tunnel 32, which was nicknamed Needle's Eye. The men now shivered as they looked below at Yankee Doodle Lake. "Watch your step!" and then the man rolled and slid 700 feet to the track below. And unbelievable as a novel, they saw the man climb to his feet and begin walking the long weary miles around the four per cent to go back to work on the construction train. Those Irishmen were tough!

There were only two miles of track to be laid now before the rails would be 11,660 feet at Rollins Pass. This would call for a celebration. But in these two miles the track had finally to stick to the wallpaper-like wall of North Boulder Valley. To do

this two trestles were laid on the wall. This time no man slipped down. The place was called very appropriately Devil's Slide.

A name had to be secured for the station at the top of the world. A new timetable was being prepared and names were needed. Naturally the Chief Dispatcher was concerned about the schedule and from this man, J. B. Culbertson, came the name Corona; this to Joe meant "Crown of the Mountain."

Looking again at the map, Joe suggested that the terminal of the road eleven miles down the other side should be called Arrowhead. "See the track goes around the town like an arrow."

Who was Joe Culbertson? He was a man like George Barnes, who was to become part of the Moffat legend. These two men, dispatcher and conductor, preached safety. Every man that went into

Engine 300 above Arena. Engine 300 has arrived from the Schenectady plant and is now ready for her trial run. If a rail fan had existed in those days, he would have asked the fireman to get off his seat and throw on some coal to dirty up the sky. The tunnel smoke deflector is seen on the stack. *Photo from Buckwalter Collection, State Historical Society of Colorado.*

June 23, 1904, proved to be a rainy day at Mammoth when the very first scheduled passenger train pulled in. David Moffat bought his own ticket that day as a hint that important people could contribute to the success of the much desired line. Note men wearing top coats. *Denver Public Library Western Collection.*

Train No. 1 crosses Boulder Creek. Engine 300, smoke deflector down, stops on trestle over South Boulder Creek to have her picture taken before going into Gato (Pine Cliff of today) with Chesapeake Beach passenger equipment which made up the first passenger cars. *Photo from Buckwalter Collection, State Historical Society of Colorado.*

train service was examined by Culbertson. Culbertson was a little fellow who had come over from the Burlington. Between these two men the remarkable safety record of the road was begun and carried on. In this time the Moffat road handled its passengers so carefully that no one was ever hurt enough to be able to sue the road.

Naturally George Barnes was conductor on September 2, 1904, when Engine 300 pulled three cars up to Corona. From here the people looked west into Middle Park where the rails would be laid next spring. They also looked west to range after range of mountains which spoke of the rugged country through which this short line was daringly being surveyed. But as thrilling as the day was, a warning came before noon of the next day. A blizzard burst upon this pass so hard that the bridge carpenters

had to quit their work on the snow shed for a time, not once but twice!

Just what kind of a pass was this going to be for the line until the Main Range tunnel was built?

In this above timberline work, lightning struck down a track layer and he was buried by the right of way. There were eleven miles of track to be laid to Arrow. Winter was at hand. Men were leaving. They had enough of the thin air and temperamental high country weather. Soft fills had to be shored up. A trestle was built over the Loop which was a mile around. And then once in Tunnel 33 under the Loop someone noticed that the timber was native soft pine, not durable fir.

The Loop was an engineering wonder to rival the famous Georgetown Loop. The line circled a mountain, crossing under itself in an unceasing slope down into Middle Park valley.

"Sure, why waste the money?"

"Next spring the Main Range tunnel will be started!" was the answer.

By the time the rails were laid into Arrow the crew had almost fled. Cattle were already in the stock pens at Arrow. Ranchers were anxious to avoid the hard drive this time of the year over any of the passes. Yet at Arrow it was a magnificent Indian Summer day, September 24, 1904. News again spread quickly. Regular train service will begin October 21. Of course, the cattle were shipped out before, as well as cars of lumber from the neighboring mills.

What did Arrow look like? Well, she was not down on the floor of Middle Park where the headwaters of the Fraser River flowed. Ranchers looked up to Arrow just two miles above Berthoud Pass wagon road. The enterprising railroad had spent good money to get a wagon road down from Arrow to Berthoud Pass road. Contractors would be using this road.

However, Indian summer returned to Arrow, which was only 9,585 feet high. Carpenters were trying to get buildings up. The ranger was trying to find out who was selling booze in the national forest. Contractors were looking for ties. The woods were alive with the song of the axe. Some men were hewing out ties with a double-bitted axe.

There was one way to sell liquor legally in the National forest: incorporate the town. Before the year was out, Arrow was incorporated; also the enthusiasm was such that pressure tank gasoline street lights of the boulevard variety were ordered. A

This picture of Sphinx head rock tells quite a story. Engine 100, a heavy, small-wheeled consolidation, has just hammered out of her stack more than enough smoke and soot to overflow Tunnel 30, leaving everything on the engine miserably dirty. Above the oil headlight can be seen the elk horns that engineer Billy Rush placed to designate his engine, which he so carefully babied. She is just crossing the former grade of the ill-fated earlier efforts of the Denver Utah and Pacific which the Colorado Railway had taken over. They had not thought of going through this cliff but around it thanks to their narrow-gauge ability to kink the route and thus save many tunnels. Note that the trestle across South Boulder Creek is covered with ballast to discourage sparks from setting it on fire. In 1959 the Rio Grande relocated the creek at this point, so that the earlier grading is obliterated. *McClure photo.*

DENVER AND MAMMOTH.

Station Numbers	WESTWARD — SECOND CLASS		WESTWARD — FIRST CLASS 3 Passenger Leave Sunday Only A.M.	WESTWARD — FIRST CLASS 1 Passenger Leave Daily Except Sunday A.M.	Miles from Denver	TIME-TABLE 1 — JUNE 23rd, 1904. STATIONS AND SIDINGS	Miles from Mammoth	EASTWARD — FIRST CLASS 2 Passenger Arrive Daily Except Sunday P.M.	EASTWARD — FIRST CLASS 4 Passenger Arrive Sunday Only P.M.	EASTWARD — SECOND CLASS		Car Capacity
0			9.00	8.10	0	D DENVER DN	47.36	5.45	5.45			
					0.90	B. & M. CROSSING	46.46					
					1.50	ARGO	44.96					
					2.40							
3			9.25	8.35	3.60	D UTAH JUNCTION UJ (D. N. W. & P.)	43.76	5.20	5.20			T. S. R. Y. 0 ● 44
					3.66							
7			9.32	8.42	7.26	RALSTON	40.10	5.11	5.11			45
					6.02							
13			9.43	8.53	13.28	LEYDEN JUNCTION JN	34.08	5.05	5.05			Q 56
					4.90							
18			9.55	9.05	18.18	ARENA	29.18	4.53	4.53			4
					6.63							
25			10.12	9.22	24.81	D PLAINVIEW PA	22.55	4.36	4.36			0 . 37
					7.11							
32			10.36	9.46	31.92	CRESCENT	15.44	4.13	4.13			
					5.33							
37			10.59	10.09	37.25	GATO	10.11	3.53	3.53			44
					4.90							
42			11.11	10.21	42.15	ROLLINSVILLE	5.21	3.42	3.42			37
					5.21							
47			11.25	10.35	47.36	D MAMMOTH MN		3.30	3.30			T. S. R. 0 ● Y34
			Arrive Sunday Only A.M. (2.25)	Arrive Daily Except Sunday A.M. (2.25)		47.36		Leave Daily Except Sunday P.M. (2.15)	Leave Sunday Only P.M. (2.15)			

Between Denver and Utah Junction, all Trains will be run on the Time-Table and subject to the Rules of the B. & M. R. R. CO.

Eastbound trains are superior to trains of same class in opposite direction. (See Rule 81.)

At meeting points between trains of different classes, the inferior train must take the siding and clear the superior train at least ten minutes, and must pull into the siding when practicable. If necessary to back in, the train must first be protected as per Rule 99 unless otherwise provided.

Trains running in same direction will keep not less than fifteen (15) minutes apart between Plainview and Gato, and not less than ten (10) minutes apart on other portions of the line.

Train No. 2 will wait at Mammoth until Train No. 1 has arrived.

Train No. 4 will wait at Mammoth until Train No. 3 has arrived.

community hall was talked about, money raised for it. Water was carried from Arrow spring at twenty-five cents a pail. A town well was considered on this knob protruding from the mountain.

During the winter lively times gave the community a boom town name. Girls were brought in by two saloon keepers. Dances at the community hall were sometimes rowdy. Trainmen's wives moved to Arrow to look after their wayward husbands.

A Sunday School was started. Just who was going to dominate the town? It would take a year to settle the argument. But the mothers would win out just as they did that wintry night they went over to the community hall and froze the girls out, sending them back to the saloons.

Such a town was Arrow: lively with the song of hammers in a race against the next storm. The days were balmy as the snow melted between the storms. Optimism was high. Business was good in the evening as lumberjacks and sawyers came in for their mail, a drink, and provisions. They talked over all kinds of stories about this great new railroad. At the bar, sawmill men grumbled how the boss had gone to Denver to get the pay and had not showed up for a week. The bartender felt sorry for he knew that some sawmills had three crews: the one that had left several weeks ago, the one that was thinking of leaving, and the one the boss was recruiting in Denver to replace those who would wait no longer for their pay.

Each noon Number 1 slipped down the hill from Corona with the combination car, and a boxcar of hardware, flour, and beef. The passengers were two or three tourists who would eat lunch and return

D. N W and Pac Ry

FORM 19 — C. & S. FORM 2399 — FORM 19

~~THE COLORADO & SOUTHERN RY. CO.~~

Train Order No. 1 — June 23 1904

To C & E Eng 300 101 and Work E, 20

At Utah Junct (STATION.) — X .... Opr.; .... M.

Eng 300 and 101 Will run as 1st and
2d No 1 Utah Junct to Mammoth.
1st No 1 Will run 20 Mins late
and 2d No 1 Will run 1 hour
and 20 Mins late Utah Junct
to Mammoth

WMC

CONDUCTOR AND ENGINEMAN MUST EACH HAVE A COPY OF THIS ORDER.

Made Complete Time 7 30 aM. Edgar Opr.

Passenger Train at Tunnel 29. The first passengers were in for thrills of tunnels, trestles, and awe-inspiring scenery which they could enjoy if they had not gotten soot in their eyes going through the first twenty-nine tunnels. Each cloud of smoke represents here smoke pouring out of a little tunnel. The people who rode the Moffat never were sorry to see the steam engine go. Tunnels and steam engines were just horrible. *McClure photo.*

Engineers had a multitude of duties after the line was located. They ran the grade lines and drove the grading stakes and were on hand to see that the work was thoroughly completed. They were diplomats handling hostile pioneers who did not want their hay meadows invaded and above all needled the contractors to lose no time in the race against winter. This scene is between Tolland and Ladora on the two per cent grade. *W. I. Hoklos Collection.*

Passengers on the first train were awed by the depth of South Boulder Canyon. They asked what the trestle was on the other side of the canyon and were told that hydraulic mining had been supplied by water by help of this trestle. Later, logs were floated to a sawmill. This can be seen from the California Zephyr today. *Mc-Clure photo.*

Yankee Doodle Lake photograph as produced by the matchless McClure made him famous. He enlarged this picture, tinted it, and produced such awe-inspiring beauty that it became the best piece of advertising of the railroad. Incidentally, McClure retouched in the locomotive that has climbed the weary grade which is one thousand feet above the lowest level as it leaves Needles Eye Tunnel. Because the snow slipped down the mountainside over the middle track, one civil engineer proposed and secured the snowshed over the middle level. *McClure photo.*

YANKEE DOODLE LAKE FROM ROCK, MOFFAT ROAD

McClure photo.

Looking east from Rollins Pass. One beholds thirty miles of mountains, canyons, and hills the engineers had conquered. These rails are less than two miles from Corona. To the right, timber is on hand to build the snowshed above Tunnel 32 or Needles Eye. The Rollins Pass wagon road crossed here and Yankee Doodle Lake is just 700 feet over the brow of the hill. *McClure photo.*

on the same train renumbered Train 2. There were a half dozen residents of Middle Park hitching rides on wagons hauling freight or being met by friends in a buggy. Of course, there was the ever going and coming of surveyors. They were scouting the route west where Steamboat Springs longed for a railroad, and the ranchers of Craig wondered if it could get through this time. Twice before they had been disappointed.

The field engineer brought to lonely workers the stories of the goings on of Arrow. The story was told that one evening the men in one saloon which sported girls had dared them to step outside. As dusk settled they stepped outside without a stitch of clothing. "I guess that will show the wives a thing or two." Then there was the wheelbarrow with which the town marshal hauled the drunks out of the mud hole from the bottom of the hill. He locked them up and was supposed to have rifled their pockets of most of the money. The next morning the J. P. heard the charge, "Drunkenness." A fine was paid, a fine for getting booted out of a saloon and slipping the rest of the way into the mud hole. Next morning one bartender would be shoveling out the sawdust that was kept in his saloon to catch the vomit of the sick men.

Then there was Indian Tom, a likeable fellow who was good with horses and shooting the balls off

...ast from Phantom Bridge. Only two wires on
...he telegraph pole place the date of this picture
...rior to the fall of 1905. *McClure photo.*

...de bridges east of Corona. For a moment we imagine our
...nstruction train is crawling into Rollins Pass. We will step off
...ie way car and take this picture looking back. It would have
...een a devil of a slide off this trestle, so we will call it Devil's
...ide. The weary track layers have no time to comment on the
...ouds which some days hang below this 11,550 foot elevation
...ke some great sea. But what are those barrels sunk in the
...round doing at each end of the trestle? Well, the next day in
...iswer to a passenger on the first train the fireman replied, "Oh,
...r. Moffat is hiring all Swedes, and they have to have a place
... shoot their snuff! Moffat is mighty particular you know."
...cClure photo.

First train to Corona. *Bob Bishop photo.*

Construction train on loop trestle. Engine 20 shoving a string of flats climbs the Loop above Tunnel 33 on her way to Corona to exchange the empties for loaded rail and tie cars. A few more trips and rails will be down to Arrowhead. Bridge and building carpenters have a ladder up as they prepare to build a short snowshed on the south end of Tunnel 33 where the snow drifted forty feet deep the winter before. One is looking through Rifle Sight Notch. *Billy Rush collection.*

Postcard of loop. "The Rotograph Co., N. Y. City (Germany)" had provisions for a two-cent stamp on this card.

Loop snowshed construction. The south side of the Loop is flanked with building materials for the snowshed on that end of the little tunnel, which was unfortunately timbered with native trees which rotted and caused the tunnel to collapse after the line was abandoned. Of course, this by-pass was supposed to be in use just long enough to get the main range tunnel built. Moffat Tunnel lies under the left part of this picture. This road bed is part of the fishing road over Rollins Pass today. *McClure photo.*

Page 50

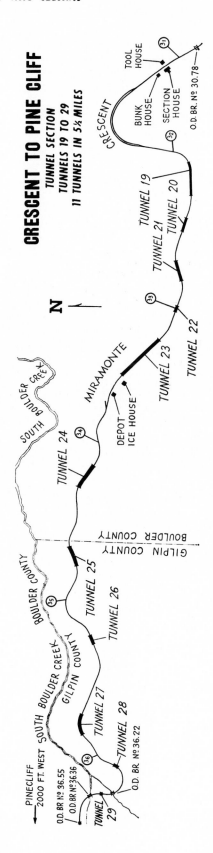

CRESCENT TO PINE CLIFF
TUNNEL SECTION
TUNNELS 19 TO 29
11 TUNNELS IN 5½ MILES

Station at Arrowhead. Rails were laid into Arrow September 18, 1904. The first agent, C. L. Robinson, found this station unchinked, so that when he awakened the next morning snow had drifted into most of the station. Everyone was living in tents. The watchful eye of forest rangers knew that against the law liquor was being sold from some of the tents. The bartenders always answered, "Oh, this keg is my private stock." However, they did not want to risk being caught, so they hired an attorney and filed to incorporate the town. The incorporation was completed by December 29, so that Arrow was the first incorporated town in Grand County. *Photo courtesy Mrs. Clarence Smith.*

the roulette wheel. He had gotten into a fight with Neil Ragland, a sawmill operator. This had happened one fall day at an impromptu rodeo held at the only flat place around, between the tracks of the railroad wye. There had been all the good old sports, even a potato race. One potato race was in question as to who won. The two men disagreed and hurled potatoes with baseball-pitching vigor at one another. So the fun of the day was spoiled, and the rodeo was over with bitter feelings, but without gun play. There was talk that this feud would end in a killing. Indian Tom was liked, for he was a gentleman with ladies, the hero of kids, easy game for girls, and a respected foreman in furnishing teams for contractors.

There was also the merchant that sold almost anything that was needed. He knew where his Bible was kept on that shelf up there where he could get it to read when he had a moment. So when the prodigal son died and no relative would more than admit the fact she knew him, this merchant took the Bible down and walked with the people to the

Aspen Street, Arrow and Middle Park. Aspen street of Arrow afforded a view of Fraser, a tie camp in 1905, in Middle Park. The passenger who strolled over to behold this view might have seen the supply train crews who disliked its feeble-minded schedule. In front of the Graham saloon a stump was carved like a beer bottle and across the street was one of the two gasoline boulevard lights that this enterprising community sported. By fall Fraser became the terminal and Arrow was on its speedy decline that nothing could stop. The rougher element had given way to solid citizens who supported a Sunday School rather than the two sporting houses that the saloons had offered. *McClure photo.*

hill north of Arrow and read the Twenty-third Psalm and the fourteenth chapter of John. The town had a heart.

The bridge carpenters finished the engine shed where several engines could be nursed. However, a freight only made occasional trips now that winter approached and the need for the helper engine was for snow fighting.

This was not the rottenest town in the world: mothers later said it was on a beautiful hill and a good place to live.

The stranger from the Old World might labor

three months in a cut some miles below in Fraser River Canyon and blow his pay in one poker game. More likely he took aim at home for the gal for whom he had bought a ticket to come over from Sweden. She was cooking on a ranch and fighting tuberculosis.

What impressed every one was the zest with which men moved. They were working in the greatest adventure of Colorado. Even the rancher who was starting to put locks on his doors felt the

Second No. 1 and Arrow. Arrow's businessmen fought a hectic winter in moving out of tents. Seven saloons were built to satisfy the thirst of two thousand people who were getting their mail in Arrow. Lumber and tie camps together with construction laborers boomed the community the summer of 1905, as the rails were pushed west. The track dropping to the left is the four per cent grade which continued down to Irving's, where the descent was cut to two per cent. This summer Number 1 arrived in Arrow, which was its terminus. Tourists crowded this train, spent the noon hour eating a fifty-cent deluxe dinner at this dining hall or in one of the restaurants where chicken dinners were served for forty cents. There was a roulette wheel in the back room of one bar. The hundreds of passengers would swarm back to the train and return on the train which was Number 2. Men called her the Arrow Turn. When rails reached farther west, Arrow struggled to stay alive by catering to tourists. Some summer days over a thousand people would be handled on the Arrow turn, which ran in several sections. *McClure photo.*

The fiftieth anniversary of Arrow. Author Ed Bollinger returned to Arrow fifty years later to re-elect the mayor of the ghost town with several of the young men of his parish. In the blinding sun it was twenty below zero. He is reading from the diary of General Manager Ridgway's comments regarding the weather fifty years before. Today this spot is unmarked thanks to vandals who stole the signs his boys club erected. This is Aspen street of Arrow. *Clifford Miller photo.*

Form 1304—3-12-5m.

THE DENVER, NORTHWESTERN & PACIFIC RAILWAY CO.

SLIP BILL FOR

~~EMPTY~~ LOADED } CAR

Made at OAK CREEK Station 10/10 1912

Initial Sys   Car No. 31072

From _Oak Hill_

Fraser Co

If Loaded Consignee _____

Empty for _____

Order of _____

Train	Date	Cond'r
"	"	"
"	"	"
"	"	"
"	"	"

Agents will bill empty foreign cars. If picked up at non-reporting stations, conductor will ask first agent or operator to procure destination from Chief Dispatcher, making slip bill for same.

tingle of the excitement of this great battle. David Moffat was the state's mining king. If he won this battle, he would be the state's railroad king by virtue of his daring insight.

There was one letdown for the eastern greenhorn and the foreigner: there just were no Indians on the warpath taking scalps. One evening a Swedish lass was left at the 4-4 ranch alone to clean up the kitchen. She stepped out to get some water. At that moment she heard the jingle of spurs, for a tall handsome half breed Indian had caused his horse to jump the fence. "I scared you, didn't I?" Instead of scalping the newcomer he helped her wipe the dishes at this lonely horse changing stop for the stage. Indian Tom was a gentleman among men and ladies. He was liked for his winsome ways and his ability to handle teams on the construction work. There was the other side of him (Tom Reynolds) which ended in a feud with Neil Ragland over some imported girls that two competing saloons had. Both men were expert shots but Indian Tom was the better. On this evening Arrow residents knew that there would be a shooting. Neil Ragland's only chance was to get Indian Tom at dusk when he would come for him at the Graham saloon. The lights were not lit. The spurs of the Indian were heard. He opened the door. A shot flashed and Tom stood dead, then fell to the floor with a thud.

This was rails-end, Arrow.

Hill Hell

The story of the Moffat is a story of snow. The story of snow on the Moffat is the story of the rotary. But even these plows found the hill above ten thousand feet hell. On the top was the land of eternal cold, where the wind swept fiercely almost the whole year round. The snowfall on the Rockies near Corona was not unusually great, but any efforts at snow removal only resulted in a great trough cut through the snow fields. Then, blowing snow sweeping along the ground soon sought out the channel of the tracks and filled it within minutes.

This chapter deals with the fight for survival to remove the snow and keep the line open. When a top-name passenger train became snowbound a few years ago near Donner Pass, newspaper headlines blazoned the fact. Unfortunately, such a situation was commonplace on the Moffat. To a large extent, this was due to Nature's adversity; sometimes poor equipment would fail at critical moments; and sometimes plain human failure, poor judgment, or cussedness would tie up the railroad.

Winter did not usually set in in earnest until after Christmas. Then the road needed the biggest rotary ever built. Such an order was placed. Every crew member had been trained on the toughest passes of Colorado. General Manager Ridgway had grown up battling blizzards on the Rio Grande under his father, "Old Tige." Conductor Barnes had been his trusted man. These fellows nicknamed this 11,660 foot pass "The Hill," as they portrayed their daredevil determination.

The blizzards of time have a kind way of treating the weary minds of men who have suffered. This chapter is lost in the blizzards of time, just as Number 1 was lost in the howling snows that whistled over the coaches from the low flying clouds on Rollins Pass. As we shovel the snow out of men's memories, we are not certain which was the first actual blockade.

One day, with Norbury as engineer, Number 2 got stuck as she came out of Tunnel 32 just below Rollins Pass on the east side. It seems silly for a

Alco photo, F. Bauer collection.

Tender to tender. According to the calendar the rotary plow would not be needed until late in December. But the first fall the storms came early when the great rotary was on the drafting boards back East. Moffat's men were veterans from other roads. So they took the precautions of coupling two engines, tender to tender, so if the butterfly plow was unable to open the drift, they had a chance to back out. But if the pony truck jumped the rail on the rear engine when it went to back out, an ugly tie up could occur before the gandy dancers could shovel out the blizzard that was blowing in. This method was still used in later days when the line had two rotaries on the hill, one in the shops, and trouble everywhere. The low headlight tells that the photo of these grimy engines was taken just prior to the opening of Moffat Tunnel. *Denver Public Library Western Collection.*

Engines stalled above Tolland. *Denver Public Library Western Collection.*

little train with no more than two cars to get stuck going *down* the much-feared four per cent grade. If Norbury had known how deep the snow was on the other side of Tunnel 32, he might have risked opening up his engine as he went in and knocked his way out of the drift. But who with the throttle wide open would want to enter a tunnel that curves sharply to the right and comes out high up on the almost perpendicular wall of a mountain hundreds of feet above the country below? Who would want to be feeding much steam at all on a grade on which it was almost impossible to control a train after it had gained a little speed? Hence, Number 2 was stalled here twenty-four hours before she was dug out.

With blizzards breaking through Indian summer, the road was ill prepared to battle a winter on the temporary branch line. A butterfly plow was winter equipment of Number 21 and a home-made flanger was built onto a flat car which was weighted down with rocks.

There is only one explanation for this lack of preparation. Dave Moffat was taking a long chance on a mild winter in hope that he could conserve every dollar for construction work the next summer. He could always lease engines for a trip or two in a pinch, but you could not get a rotary until the other roads were through cleaning out their own lines.

According to Joe Culbertson's memory, the first tie up occurred four miles down on the western side of Rollins Pass around the Loop. As we visualize it, Joe's office in Denver reminds us of a small town station agent's layout, except for the table with the great train sheet on it. Two telegraph tickers are quietly ticking away. One is from the Burlington and Missouri River dispatcher's office with the report of an occasional car of materials that will be shuttled over to the Utah Junction yards. The ticker from the Hill is turned on loud. The agent at Arrow is reporting Extra 179 east out of Arrow with the home-made flat car flanger. Possibly from a Blue Lunch Box tin popular in that day, George takes a sandwich and says, "We borrowed the 179 from the B and M. We've got to keep snow flanged out so it doesn't drift too deep or we will never handle it. Since Frank Campbell is at the throttle, expect no trouble. But after January sets in, the winter is likely to get rugged."

It is eleven miles from Arrowhead to Rollins Pass. We figure that at the worst, Extra 179 East should be reported in the snow shed at the pass in two hours. After a short chat with Joe, we take care of our business elsewhere.

Two hours later our curiosity gets the better of us. We see clouds boiling over the Divide and decide to annoy the young dispatcher by a second visit.

Extra 179 East has not been heard from. We pass away the next hour discussing the probable route the Moffat will adopt through eastern Utah and discussing the Gore Canyon injunction, which is denying the Moffat a right of way through western Grand County.

Meanwhile, Joe has talked with Arrow and Rollins Pass, learning nothing of the flanger. Then we see Joe intently listening to his key. He deftly taps back an answer, which makes us regret never learning the language of the telegraph key.

Between the calling of A. C. Ridgway and the calling of additional crews, we learn that the 179 had made the first six miles with little delay. Then came an engine failure because of the falling of the grates into the ash pan.

Campbell had no difficulty in dropping the 179 down to Loop Siding. Since his fire was in his ash pan, he dumped the fire under the engine to lessen the heat and eliminate the smoke and gas. Engines are equipped with slash bars and clinker hooks, so that Frank prepared to fish up the grates with one bar, while his fireman would work from the outside up under the ash pan with the clinker hook. Using old gunny sacks soaked in water for a kind of asbestos overshoe, Frank crawled backward through the fire door. The head brakeman handed him his bar, while the fireman was already trying to shove up the first grate. Fire boxes are lined with fire brick holding tremendous heat for hours. It would be as hot as blazes in there. Since it was a cold night, the hot flues would form a natural suction to pull the gas up from under the engine into the fire box. Frank worked skillfully getting the grates up. Unfortunately, with the shifting of the wind, Frank inhaled considerable gas into his lungs. It was a terrible experience, but the grates were finally put in. Soaking the gunny sacks, which were now dry as tinder, with engine oil and borrowing kindling from the caboose, Frank built a new fire in the engine. No doubt two hours or more were lost by this maneuver, which about wrecked Frank Campbell's breathing apparatus.

This delay made it impossible for the 179 to handle the fast drifting snow. The line was blocked.

Section house on Loop. *A. Clarke photo.*

One could have felt the chilled-steel attitude of Joe Culbertson. There was no raving or bellowing or loud cursing. Joe was too busy to waste his effort in that way. He just moved around from phone to telegraph, calling men, listening to Ridgway, and giving orders as unobtrusively as the 303 would later quietly pull a light train with limited cut off. Joe's pipe left a trail of smoke around the office like the one the 303 would leave when she had been built and was in operation. The story ends with the poor lungs Frank Campbell had for the rest of his shortened years. Frank had to give up making runs over the hill and went to work as a hostler in the Utah Junction round house. Later, he had to give that up. This was the price of devotion beyond one's duty.

Soon after the above incidents, Joe was handed weather reports off the hill that made him immediately light his pipe and call for more power and men to operate Number 1's 8:10 run out of Denver. On short call all they could do was to pick up someone around the shops working at something else. George Clarke had come to work that morning, had put his street clothes in the locker, and was wearing just his overalls.

Bob Bishop led the parade out of the Moffat station with engine 21 and no fireman, as he was to pick up George Clarke at Utah Junction.

The residents around Arvada raked leaves that morning and beheld Number 1 pulled by four engines with the butterfly plow built over the front end of little Number 21. The crew should have no trouble the first forty-seven miles unless some of the engineers eased the throttle to let someone else do the work. The passengers might well have been

Rotary at Jenny Lake. Pictured here at Jenny Lake siding in later years, the rotary was described as "all steel, thirty-six feet long, scoop wheel type, and able to take a twelve foot cut." The machine was actually the largest of its kind built to that time and exceeded only recently by more modern diesel types. It was built at the Cooke works of Alco for $22,476 delivered. The main wheel consisted of ten scoops fitted with knives which adjusted themselves automatically to the cutting position. *McClure photo.*

comforted by the thought that there was sufficient motive power to knock any drift off the right of way. As to what was in the Adams express that day or as to what was in the mail bags, we do not know. But Arrowhead and her lumber camps likely had items that were very important to their operations and life that early winter's day.

Number 1 should have arrived a little off schedule at Tolland from her delay in leaving Denver; if not, the time consumed by four engines taking on water at Tolland would surely have been more than the allowed ten minutes.

When the last engine had taken water and Barnes had given the high ball, Bob Bishop blew his two long blasts, followed by Billy Rush with the more important notes of the 100, and then the whistle of the last two engines echoed and re-echoed across the little valley. Number 1's four engines raced the one car, the combination baggage-express-mail and coach, up the two per cent and later the four per cent grade.

Here, at the head of South Boulder Creek, the rails gained altitude by circling the end of the valley and climbing skyward by means of giant switchbacks. Four levels of track were visible from Tolland. These were called the Ladder.

It was a long trip above the Ladder. The air was filled with expectancy.

The section men working along the right of way or huddling close to a fire to warm would have seen a grim portent in the passing of this four-engine train with one car. Its passing surely mocked the aspen leaf or willow leaf that persisted in hanging to its tree.

When this show of motive power hit the horseshoe curve around Yankee Doodle Lake, all firemen had their fires perfect and their safety valves throwing a feather of steam. They were ready for the usual big drive about a thousand feet under Tunnel 32. The snow always slid down from above so badly here that a snowshed was later built.

Bob Bishop's butterfly plow on his engine Number 21 handled the drift all right with the aid of his three helpers. The snow must have really burst out of that cut with the impact of those engines.

Everyone breathed easier now. All engineers could hook up their Johnson bar nearer the center. The wind would be howling over the trains, for they were on the high grade at Jenny Lake where they stopped to fill their tanks with water.

If any passenger had been crabbing about the time he had lost, this would be as good an opportunity as any to take out his watch and compare with the card. He would tell the trainmen what they already knew, "We are twenty-five minutes late."

Perhaps George Barnes, with his wit that could meet almost any situation, would answer, "If you wanted to get there on time, you should have started yesterday."

There was plenty of time to talk about the weather as the train moved an engine's length at a time

Page 58

permitting each engine to take on water. Here at Jenny Lake the wind dropped 1,500 feet off the Divide like a car on a roller coaster, sweeping across the lake over the railroad right of way with nothing to break its gleeful sweep.

When the last tender was filled to overflowing, the train whistled off. There remained only four and a half miles for the stub train to be pulled.

Number 1 plowed through everything that morning as she gaily took all the sharp curves in the next mile and turned herself around a time or two heading in all the drunken directions the surveys had taken up to Tunnel 32. If there was much snow at the entrance or exit, it mattered little. Number 1 was rolling on the home stretch, now a thousand feet above Yankee Doodle Lake and far enough away from the edge to have no fear of plunging over the side.

Bob Bishop was triumphantly leading the parade when they came to the old Rollins Pass-Boulder wagon road crossing, which is on a curve to the left. A hard crust of snow and ice had formed across this place so that Bob Bishop's proud little engine, Number 21, which had no pony truck, just bolted off the track and tried to follow the wagon road to the right.

Again there was a tie up which was not from lack of motive power.

Someone went to Corona to get the bridge carpenters, who were feverishly working to get part of a snowshed built before the pass snowed in. Twenty-five men walked down to help shovel out around the 21 so she could be pulled back on the track by setting frogs to re-rail her. The mail must get through to Arrow. One of these men stopped to rest on a boulder, as he was out of breath. A man does not work easily at 11,660 feet. One works by resting and getting one's breath. The rest of the men found that the storm set in now with fury, rejoicing in the victory won in sticking Number 1 so near her victory. The more the men shoveled, the harder the snow fell until the men realized they were making no headway. At last, the fight was abandoned as it was getting colder and the wind stronger.

The fires were knocked out of the 21; and George Clarke, who was shivering in his one pair of overalls, climbed in the empty fire box to get warm before bucking the blast of below zero gale from over the top. The other engines backed their one car down the hill while Bishop disconnected the

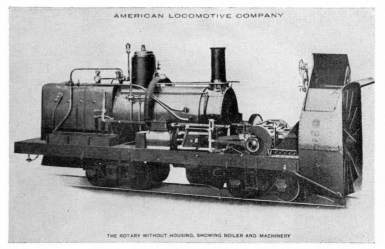

Rotary without housing. A steam engine with two cylinders was mounted within the cab to power the wheel, which was encased in a drum. In turn, the drum was provided with a reversible hood operated by an air cylinder, so that the hood could be turned to either side to suit the direction in which the wheel turned. Snow could thus be thrown to either side of the track. *Alco photo, F. Bauer collection.*

Rotary blades. Although the main wheel measured twelve feet, the hood extended to fifteen, and was set about fifteen inches in advance of the wheels, so that snow down to track level was cut off and forced into the spinning grinder. Typical of all rotaries, the machine was not self propelled but depended on other motive power to push it. *Alco photo, F. Bauer collection.*

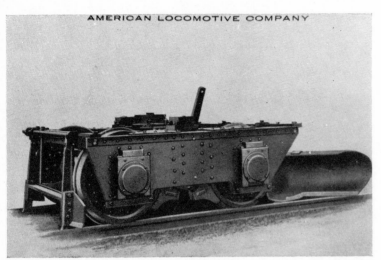

Rotary truck with flanger. The ice picks in front of the truck were fitted with shear pins which would "give" if a solid obstruction was encountered. It was the job of these picks to clear a path through the ice and keep the rotary on the rails.

main drive rods with wooden blocks carried on the rear of her tender for that purpose. For a moment Bishop looked back from this thousand-foot perch and could see clear to Spruce. Then he too crawled into Number 21's fire box to get warm. The men then headed against the wind for the Rollins Pass snowshed.

As they fought the biting wind they held shovels in front of their faces. They came upon the short bridge carpenter who was still sitting on his boulder. Bishop swung him up on his back and, thanks to his strong physique, was able to carry him to the pump house at Rollins Pass. The man was frozen from his neck up. Some of his fingers were lost and had not Bishop been rugged, the carpenter would have frozen to death.

This is the memory of Bishop, Billy Rush, and Barnes of what may have been the first blockade of that fall. There were not many days that fall and winter that Number 1 arrived in Arrow on the time card schedule—12:20 noon.

(One thought helped to compensate the Moffat "Rails" for their hard work, the Old Man was a democratic soul. On December 18 when his business associates presented him with an elaborate loving cup with a capacity of thirty pints, made out of silver dollars, a policeman took his turn among the great dignitaries in shaking Uncle Dave's hand. The leading banker turned to his associates saying, "That fellow is Mike Horkons. He used to be night watchman at the bank. He is as true as steel.")

The men found this hill was hell. "If we only had the rotary!" But when the rotary was being delivered, something went wrong. The boys had read in the daily papers that this monster plow was missing. "Biggest Snow Plow Ever Built Lost in Transit." Another day the story had read that the roads west of Chicago had feared to accept the shipment of the giant, as it was too heavy for their rails. Whether Harriman and Gould were annoyed, simply trying to wear down the ambitious "Short Line," we do not know. Hill's Burlington and Missouri River must have brought her west. Anyway, when she was needed on Rollins Pass, she was lost, but eventually got to Denver.

General Manager Ridgway, in an interview with reporters on the occasion of the rotary's arrival, said she had been named the "Red Devil," explaining, "We had it painted that way so it could melt any particularly obstinate snow bank it might encounter if it should not buck it out of the way."

The builder's photograph published in *Railway and Locomotive Engineering* of March, 1907, shows that the Moffat had the proper public relations attitude. On the side of the plow was painted, "The Rotary." Unlike the Monon, which years later renumbered all its box cars for simplicity beginning with "1," the rotary was numbered "10200."

The management lost twice in the gamble to have her delivered late in December. First, above 10,000 feet Rollins Pass proved an inferno of snow early in the fall. Second, her delivery came a month late, thanks to the hand of enemy roads refusing to accept shipment of the heaviest plow ever built. Rocks immediately proved her blades too light. When replaced, there came the human failure of a minor official who would not listen to veteran men.

Rotary at Fawn Creek water tank. *Photo by J. B. Culbertson.*

Page 60

Famous McClure photo of rotary. Early practice was to use a six-wheeled engine and an eight-wheeled Consolidation or two of the latter. The mallets were to replace both engines. In this photo the plow is shoved by a mallet, and the freight is pulled by a Consolidation. What is at the rear is anyone's guess.

McClure took this picture of the Moffat's first rotary. There was no more magnificent sight to be seen than one of these machines working its way through a large snow drift on a four per cent while climbing the mountains pushed by two or three Consolidations. Actually three rotaries were needed to keep the Hill open. One plow was always in the shops having her blades repaired, for boulders were the great hazard of snow fighting.

The Loop in winter. The first Hill Hell drama to occur at the Loop came early the first fall, when the D.N.W.&P. ran out of motive power and borrowed from the Burlington and Missouri River Railroad engine 179 to clean the line out with their homemade flat car flanger. On the return trip, the engine entered the photograph on the lower level of track at the right, cleaning out both ends of Tunnel 33 under the Loop Trestle shown in the center of the picture where snow had drifted badly (snow piled forty-five feet deep on top of the west end snowshed that winter in one bad storm).

Frank Campbell had gone the length of the Loop siding and had re-entered the picture on the upper level of track at the right, gaining speed for a drift a hundred feet past the trestle—the spot can be seen easily. He managed to get through the drift, but a little farther on, the grates fell out of the fire box down into the ash pan. Shutting off his steam, he made a quick decision to back down to the Loop behind the hill. at the right of the photo and there try to put the grates back in. If he failed, the engine would have to be drained, a very difficult proposition in severe weather at 11,092 feet. To better understand Rollins Pass snow fighting, J. W. Berry searched the records of the Environmental Science Service Administration in 1966. The first winter of operation through Rollins Pass was a mild one, both in temperatures and snow-fall in Denver and just fifty miles east. The only weather station operating that winter that could give any

Temperatures were consistently mild and snow fall below normal. October had .10 inches of snow; November less than an inch; December, eleven inches; January, fifteen inches; February, sixteen inches; March, nineteen inches. Then came April with seventy-six inches. *McClure photo.*

Hill Hell

She ran out of water and was helpless. Last of all, she derailed on ice just west of the Corona shed and was engulfed in a blizzard for days, helpless. These incidents should have proved the folly of putting off the building of the Main Range tunnel which was under such storms at 9,990 feet.

Now, let's get a look at the machine in action. February 10, 1905. "The Monster Termite" was coming slowly out of Tolland, shoved by engines 20 and 21, pulling at least two cars of merchandise, a tool car and two cabooses. Billy Woodlief was the pilot of the snowplow, and Mike Broderick was in charge of the train with Engineers Fuller and Sterling Way.

Number 1's engine, the 300 with her combination baggage-express-mail and passenger car, overtook the plow train at Jenny Lake, where orders had been given for the two trains to be coupled together. Experience had proved that above this point the track could drift so quickly that a second train would have only a slight chance of getting through.

A tie up that would prevent a plow getting over the line after eight hours meant that the Hill would have to be shoveled out.

The Rotary was provided with a crew of three men—an engineer, a pilot, and a fireman. It was the pilot's job to ride in the front part of the machine on a platform immediately behind the wheel where there were peep holes for him to see ahead.

Passenger approaches Tunnel 32. February 10, 1905, Train 1 with the 300 passenger engine, one car of merchandise, and the combination car was given the new rotary and the two six wheelers at Tolland. Thus began the greatest of all dramas, "Nine Extras East Light."

There was only a little over four miles for this train to climb after taking water and practically every foot of it is to be seen in this unusual photo. Jenny Lake is at the extreme right edge, marked by the box cars on the siding. All the track one sees here is on the four per cent, and the train in the photo is about to enter Tunnel 32. Edgar's train battled up the four per cent and encountered considerable second struggle about the tunnel. The rotary was "tops," as the boys said, but she took plenty of steam cutting the ten and twelve foot drifts.

The third struggle came the last two hundred feet getting into the abbreviated snowshed at Rollins Pass. Inside, the engines soon filled the shed with smoke and gas. Barnes got his face smoked like a smoke-cured ham consulting with the men, as they measured the water in their tenders. *McClure photo.*

Triple header below Loop. *Bob Bishop photo.*

Snow at cross arms of poles. Barnes telegraphed in and the nine men started walking out. George had taken the bell rope out of his snow-drifted coach. Each man held onto this bell rope, so that the strong could help the less robust. The only way Barnes knew where the track lay was by walking with his arm over the telegraph wire. Yes, the snow was that deep. Photo taken of wires after the storm. *Van Buskirk photo.*

Men felt their ways by wires. *Van Buskirk photo.*

He signalled the locomotive and plow engineers by blasts of the whistle when he approached snow banks or obstructions on the track. Should foreign material such as trees or rock be seen by the pilot, the train was stopped at once and the ever-faithful gandy dancers given a chance to earn their livelihood at 20° to 30° below by probing for the obstruction and removing it before the rotary attacked the drift. In reality, clearing the track at 10,000 to 11,000 feet with a 45-50 mile wind was about all that human endurance could stand.

Trainmaster Edgar was on Number 1 with George Barnes as conductor. A. C. Ridgway had made it very clear to Edgar, before they left Denver that morning, that he was to consult George Barnes when they got to Rollins Pass as to the advisability of going down the other side. Barnes had fought snow for thirteen years as trainmaster under Ridgway's father on the Rio Grande. Edgar was an experienced man in the drifting snows of the cuts and prairie lands east of Denver on the Burlington. Though the plains suffer fully as badly from storms as the mountains, different factors are involved in battling mountain storms.

At Jenny Lake, the wind blew as wild as any of them had ever seen it sweep off the Divide. The track was blown clear, as that is the nature of the spot. Engine 300 filled her water tank. The air was tested after the two trains had been coupled together. The plow train had already taken on water, so when the air test came through satisfactorily, they whistled off.

They began to lose time immediately for they ran into deep drifts within a quarter of a mile, and they had to let the rotary slowly chew her way through them. Every one was apprehensive at this loss of time because this struggle meant using water that would be needed to fight their way out of the western side of the Pass. No water had been provided at Rollins Pass that winter, because of the late date the line arrived there. Plans were made to pump water out of a lake below, but such a line could not be completed under winter conditions. The nearest water on the west side was Sunnyside, two and a half miles down, where it could be secured slowly from a siphon hose.

Billy Woodruff, the snowplow pilot, said, "We can't make it."

Engineer Fuller shook his head emphatically, "No."

Barnes, hearing the other men report the amount

of water, said to Edgar, "No use going any farther. Haven't enough water."

Perhaps Edgar was insulted when the general manager had told him to consult a conductor working under him. If so, it would not be the first time men have given vent to such a jealous impulse. Edgar made his decision and ordered the train to proceed, saying, "We can shovel snow into the tanks, if we run out of water."

With eyes smarting from the smoke and gas in the snowshed, Barnes went back to his combination coach, shutting the door behind him quickly to keep the smoke out. Edgar came in. The blasts of the engines whistling off split the ears of everyone in the shed. The train felt her way to the west end. The plow had been through this drift of snow yesterday. Although every engineer was blinded by the smoke of the shed, he did not need eyes to see the drift the rotary hit. They felt it and opened up on their throttles, shaking their heads and muttering, "There goes our water and hope of getting down to Arrowhead today."

With the snow way over the top of the outfit cars parked on the siding, the cut opened up the day before by the plow was probably ten or twelve feet deep with new snow.

We can hear Mike Broderick and Frank Spaulding cussing out Edgar, as they sat in their caboose cupola. The brakemen were on top bundled in all the clothes they could get on with scarfs over their faces to shelter them from the blizzard sweeping over the Pass. They were carrying out regulations, which demanded they be ready to twist the brakes down, if the air failed. They would be so cumbered with clothing that it is doubtful if they could have twisted on the brake clubs.

Going down the west side of the Pass, the train crawled for a mile, gradually picking up speed to about nine miles an hour as the drifts lessened. How the wind howled over the cars!

Within the coach, a passenger moved away from the right to the left side as the snow was sifting in the apparently tightly closed window. Barnes was very happy that Edgar had not sat down beside him. The minutes dragged on like hours. The blast coming out of Fraser Valley seemed enough to blow the train back up the Pass. Midst the howl of the wind, a whistle blew. One of the engines had whistled to stop.

Edgar's heart sank. He started buttoning his coats, just as George Barnes was doing, only Barnes was muttering something in his mustache.

The train was stopped. When Barnes and Edgar got ahead, they found one engine out of water. Edgar ordered the men to shovel snow into the tanks. They climbed up the tenders and started shoveling, but Edgar had not reckoned with the wind, which blew the snow off the shovels as fast as it was scooped off the snow bank. The snow was tender high at Ptarmigan Point. The engines died right there

No sooner had the engines gone dead than George Barnes warned his seven passengers that they should "hit the cinders" and make a run for their destination before the storm drifted shut their road.

The tragedy of the situation was that the train had gone dead after it had gotten through the worst of the snow, one mile and a half out of Corona shed. The right of way was not so badly drifted but that the train could have proceeded from this point even without a plow if the engines had not been low on water. But with the velocity of the wind and the increasing storm, their rescue was very unlikely.

Barnes sent the seven passengers ahead down the mountain, knowing that every foot of the way they would be dropping below the worst part of the storm. It was less than two miles to the Loop where there were parked outfit cars in which they could get warm.

Below the Loop there may have been a sawmill cabin. At Ranch Creek there were a sawmill and loggers camp, where two of the men were headed. The other five passengers could warm here and continue on their way to Arrowhead, which was 2,000 feet lower than the stalled train. No one traveled that train in such weather except lumberjacks and ranchers that had walked over the passes in winter on snowshoes or fought to save the lives of their cattle so Barnes knew what he was doing when he sent such men ahead.

Meanwhile, Trainmaster Edgar started back to Rollins Pass in the fast-filling cut. He must call for the two light engines at Tolland to come up and immediately pull the train back into the snowshed. We wonder if his ears rang with Billy Woodlief's words, "We can't make it." We wonder what he thought would be the humor of Mr. Ridgway, who had warned him to consult with Barnes. Ridgway was in the East inspecting the Mallet-Articulated engine of the Baltimore and Ohio at Rockwood, Pennsylvania. But what was the most powerful engine with no water? The pipeline to Corona should have been finished.

Edgar struggled into the wind. The altitude of 11,600 feet made him stop to pant many a time. He finally staggered into the snowshed. He asked the operator to call Tolland and order up two engines, Numbers 100 and 101. One engine may have had the butterfly plow on it.

What chance would those two engines have of ever making Rollins Pass from the foot of the mountain on the eastern side?

It must have been almost two hours since the plow had been over the line from Tolland. Would the crews for those two engines be able to get underway in less than a half hour? The crews would likely be sleeping, the steam would be low. Those engines might have to be coaled and watered. If those engines could buck the drifts without a plow, how would they be on water when they made that final climb from the last water tank at Jenny Lake?

Before Edgar reached the warmth of the operator's office at Rollins Pass and listened to the hurricane sweep over the sheds, George Barnes succeeded in making contact with Denver. He had climbed a telegraph pole, tied on the wires of his telegraph instrument, and from the chilly shelter of his combination coach, telegraphed in the news of their plight. "Engines gone dead because of low water and inability to shovel snow in the terrible gale." Barnes had learned telegraphy as a boy. Even though there were no women operators on the line, the story got out, and it made headlines.

Evening soon engulfed the stranded train crews. Barnes knew the sandwiches left over from their noon lunch were not sufficient for his men. He turned to Conductor Broderick, who had skippered the plow train which had included two cars of merchandise for Arrowhead, to find out what was in those cars. The waybills said, "Provisions for Bill Wood's Commissary." There were canned goods, potatoes that had frozen en route, and several quarters of beef. Their lanterns shed light on a box of axes. Out came an axe and they cut up the beef. (After that winter the road stocked every train with emergency provisions for just such predicaments as this.)

The combination coach was abandoned as the snow was sifting through the smallest cracks around the windows in an unbelievable manner. The men cooked their meals, first thawing their confiscated potatoes, on the caboose stoves.

The two cabooses were terribly crowded with the enginemen from three locomotives and the rotary plow, plus the two conductors, and at least three brakemen and perhaps three or four other men who had been brought along to assist in battling the snow. The men recognized that there was not bunk space enough in the two cabooses for so many men. The usual card games started, while they took their turns carrying coal from the engines to keep themselves warm. The usual story-telling and beefing continued. It would have been a miracle if they had not roasted Trainmaster Edgar for his stupidity. Undoubtedly, he was made to feel like the lowest worm on the face of the earth.

In such a storm, David Moffat paced the floor all night in his Equitable Building office, waiting for reports of his men on top of the world.

Although the blizzard was still howling, with morning came the discovery that the two light engines had reached Rollins Pass. After a great struggle with the snow in the last mile, they too were left so low on water that they were abandoned in the snow shed. Billy Rush had brought up one of those engines. Edgar left Charlie Peterson to keep those engines warm enough to keep them from freezing solid, while he and the other enginemen started immediately walking down the other side.

Their best bet was to find a rotary plow that some line could lend, and, with borrowed power, they could open up the line. These men could operate this power. Of course, there were section men at Rollins Pass and some men from a bridge carpenters' gang who might be able to shovel enough snow into the tanks of the two engines so that the crews of Barnes' train could attempt their own rescue. But the fury of the storm left little hope of getting water in these engines and of getting the engines, without a plow, down to the helpless train on the west side.

The only other engine the D.N.W.&P. had in service at that time was the wheezy old 390. This small passenger engine was no match for a four per cent grade in a blizzard. It seems her sister engine, the 391, had not been rebuilt for mountain railroading at this date.

At the stalled trains, morning revealed the blizzard still raging with no sun at all, so George Barnes again contacted the outside world over his telegraph wire to learn that the newspaper said that they were all starving and that Bob Bishop had been lost. Barnes told the dispatcher to let his wife know immediately that they had plenty of food. Bob Bishop had been called to run one of the engines that fateful February morning when they had left Denver, but inasmuch as his wife was ill, he had been allowed to stay home.

The card games continued and the stories went on, one after another. The second night, as the wind blew a gust of snow down the caboose-stack into the caboose, the men heard a noise on the roof. When an investigation was made, they found that the men in the other caboose were swiping some of the stove pipe to make their chimney higher.

By the third day, the little train was almost completely buried by this February blizzard and Barnes concluded, since no relief was immediately in sight and since there were too many of them to sleep in the cramped quarters, that they would walk out. The temperature had been below zero, but no one knew how low.

When the men arrived at the west end of Rollins Pass snowshed, they came on the outfit cars buried under the blizzard. These cars were occupied by John Daly's bridge carpenters. Seven pieces of stove pipe had been added to the cook car, so that the stack was above the snow. The men got down into the cook car through the skylight. The Italian cook baked the men some cannonball biscuits. With this fortification, the men went on through the shed and found Charlie Peterson starting to chop the snow shed down in his effort to keep the two light engines from freezing.

The storm abated somewhat, so they followed the track over to Tunnel 32. As they looked six hundred feet down to the frozen-over lake, Sterling Way, who had been one of the engineers, jumped on his scoop shovel and rode to the bottom like a bullet. They say he warmed up the seat of his pants. In fact, he burned the seat of his pants off on that ride and, hitting the lake, rolled over a dozen times like a ball. The rest of the men were more timid (if men are timid who brave such a storm), and they walked around the right of way, while Sterling nursed his "hot box," which was now subject to frostbite. The other eight men were able to take a short cut or two along the telegraph line.

Arriving at Jenny Lake boxcar office, George Barnes telegraphed in his famous message, "NINE EXTRAS EAST, LIGHT."

Number 1 and the Moffat plow were still at Ptarmigan Point. Among the men Bob Bishop brought back to Denver with his 390 that day, were Billy Rush, Sterling Way, Sam Henry, and Ernest Anthony. Those men welcomed their own beds and a good night of rest! How well General Manager

Rotary at Sunnyside. Days later the Colorado Midland plow A reached Corona late in the evening with an exhausted crew.

In the morning, the Colorado Midland plow pulled out of Corona again, headed down the four per cent. We look after the train as it passes Sunnyside. It was 7:45 A.M. when the plow reached Arrowhead, just four days and nights after she started from Denver, seventy miles away.

Ridgway slept as he approached Denver that night is not known.

Next day, Ridgway took over the relief of the blockade. It was apparent that engines 100 and 101 were useless; so the idea of using them was given up and the tired men struggled back home. But to secure the needed rotary plow and power was not easy, for the same storm engulfed the entire Rocky Mountain region and all lines needed every piece of snow fighting equipment they had.

Their only hope was to borrow some power from the Burlington and Missouri River line and see if they could find some road whose rotary plow was not needed for a few days. Edgar was wise in taking the men with him so he would have someone to run the engines when they were secured. Of course, there was a slight chance that the men in the bridge carpenters gang at Corona might be able to shovel enough snow in the water tanks to steam up the two consolidation engines in the shed. But the extent of the storm and its fury left small hope that engines 100 and 101 could reach the stalled train without a snow plow. Altogether, this was a tremendous undertaking.

The Colorado Midland's powerful small rotary was finally secured. Two engines numbered 250 and 251 from the Colorado and Southern furnished the power. It looked now as if the road could be opened.

The Moffat Road

How far the relief train with its plow got the first day is not remembered. The general manager's diary does record that Ridgway went up the next day on Number One which caught up to the plow train at Antelope which is midway between Tolland and the mountain pass. Ridgway was on hand now to see for himself why the progress was slow. The snow was above the rotary. This powerful little plow could hurl it over the highest cut but the snow had to be shoveled and dynamited down into the cuts. When the drift was lowered enough for its snout to be above the snow, she could then move through the cut. Another day of frost bites, exhausted bodies, and tired minds passed and the approach of sunset on the twenty-third was near when the borrowed engines and plow reached the pass, 3:00 P.M., February 23, 1905.

Opening of the blockade by the Colorado Midland rotary could only be photographed while the snowflakes were still falling, for seldom did nature cooperate for even a moment and give the much-needed light. Clay Blough shot the picture as the rotary prepared to head back to the Corona shed after having battled its way down to Arrow, which had been without train service for days.

Chief Engineer H. A. Sumner was on this plow train making observations of where snowsheds would need to be extended. The Hill Hell was fought in the biting cold of a gale with men groping to see through the blizzards. The camera can only produce clearly moments when the battle had subsided.

Two blades of the plow have been injured by rock that slipped onto the right of way. The train has stopped to let the engineers ascertain if more rock was in the cut from which this picture was taken.

Water for steam power remained the acute problem. The plow train must back down four miles to Jenny Lake for more water. How many times this happened that night and next morning, no one recalls.

The task was far greater than simply opening up the mile and a half of the track down the western side. The plow train would have to back up to the pass and uncouple the plow. Colorado and Southern engines 250 and 251 would drop down and attempt to drag back up the slippery four per cent grade, Number 1's combination baggage-coach, whose journals were frozen and whose wheels acted like sleds for a little way. When the coach had been dragged to the top, the 300 passenger engine was bumped and jerked until it was loose from the fifteen-day freeze to the rails.

After the 300 had been pulled back to the snowshed and put on the siding beside the Midland's rotary, the cabooses and outfit cars and two freight cars were taken back, perhaps two at a time. It was a tedious job to get the two engines loose, and lastly the rotary would be dragged back.

Now the two Colorado and Southern engines ran back down to Jenny Lake for some water. Having water, they hooked into the Midland rotary and cut on down from Ptarmigan Point to Sunnyside, a mile below, where there was water which could be secured by a hose. Then the Denver Northwestern and Pacific engines were brought down for water, or perhaps they were taken down to Jenny Lake for water, and coaled from some gondola standing by. Finally, the two boxcars and the baggage from the combination car were hooked onto the relief train and taken down to Arrowhead fifteen days late.

There was another blockade in April that year!

Springtime with sixty-eight above in Denver! But on the hills snow and rocks . . . there were tons of it that held the Moffat's rotary tight in a blockade east of Tunnel 32. The men shoveled snow, dynamited, fell asleep, dried out their clothes, and blew their noses from spring colds. Sunday evening, the rotary left Denver about the time the sinners were going to the theater and the saints were listening to the evening sermon. It had been a beautiful day in Denver, but not on the Hill.

This plow managed to open the blockade to Rollins Pass. Passengers were hauled to Arrowhead from Rollins Pass on the plow train in a mixed combination car. Everyone was breathing more easily

First Corona station. This was Corona in the early fall of 1904 when tourists began to realize the pleasures of snow-time above timberline. There were a lunchroom and a small waiting room.

The most vital adjunct was the ever-faithful telegrapher located in a nook reached by a passageway from the platform. Life here had its thrills. In the spring the shed caught fire and the station burned, too. In fighting the flames, the men were soaked. Fire out, they froze. The agent was bundled in a mattress and in this condition telegraphed out for help, so that they would not all freeze to death.

Snow would drift in through the smallest nail hole in the shed during the gales. Note the snow on both sides of the portal. *W. I. Hoklas collection.*

now that the line was open. There should be rest for everyone. And there would have been, but Engineer Fuller discovered a fire (Tuesday, April 11) in Tunnel 20. The only consolation the general manager had was that the equipment was nicely divided on both sides of the tunnel with ten days coal supply on the isolated western end.

This, the first, set the pattern for several disastrous tunnel fires. The flames, fed by a slow steady draft, roared out of the west end a hundred feet in the air. The tunnel timbering gave its turpentine willingly for the gigantic display of fire, smoke, and sparks while officials stood back wondering how long it would take to burn itself out and then cool enough to let men hole the tunnel through again.

Meanwhile, Engine 21 with a flat car picked up passengers who walked around the tunnel and

freight that was carried around, for most of the South Boulder Canyon tunnels were through the ugly protruding ribs of the canyon and not through a pass or divide.

The flat car trip from Tunnel 20 ended at Tolland where passengers and freight were protected farther west to Rollins Pass and Arrowhead by the plow train. So the flat car ride became that of a caboose or a combination passenger, baggage, and mail car.

After six days of such service west and with the coal supply dwindling, a circular was issued reducing service on the plow train to tri-weekly.

To add variety to the nightmare of springtime, slides began slipping into cuts, first in the cut west of

Coal Creek, then in cuts both east and west of Plainview. But hopes were rising, for on the fourteenth day after the tunnel had caught fire, it looked as though in another day they would be able to hole through and get the badly needed coal west.

However, the storm that was sweeping the pass that day was a mean one. The plow train had left Tolland at 7:00 A.M. and had taken until 4:15 P.M. to reach Rollins Pass, a distance of twenty-eight miles up to the top of the Hill. An hour later, after the men had eaten and the engines had been inspected, an attempt was made to continue to Arrowhead. But, after going a short distance, the effort was given up on account of the severity of the storm. So the train backed into the shed and tied up for the night.

The following morning another effort was made to go down the western side but Chester Foltz's engine found too much ice in the west switch to the liking of her pony truck, which derailed. The laborers went out to shovel the knife-like cut of the snow plow wide enough to rerail Engine 100. Billy Rush, hogger on the second engine, was concerned about low water, so he started his fireman shoveling snow into the tank. The blizzard was continuing severely with no signs of abating, and the snow was being blown back in as fast as it was shoveled out around the derailed wheels. Likewise, the men were freezing; with the men going back to the shed to thaw out, little could be accomplished. The coal was getting mighty low. Tunnel 20 just had to be holed through and some coal secured.

Tunnel 20 was holed through at 1:50 P.M. and three cars of coal were sent through ten minutes later. The line was open at the tunnel but the spring rains had caused the fill to settle so badly between Tunnel 1 and Coal Creek trestle that all trains were annulled. It looked as if it would take several days to stabilize the fill with carloads of cinders and slag.

Back on the pass things were not going well. The gandy dancers made another try in the storm. They continued digging around the front of the engine throwing the snow out of the razor thin cut between engine and snow bank. It was too crowded for many to work and in the rare air of 11,600 feet, they had to stop frequently to get their breath.

Blocks were carried on all engines. Great blocks of wood that looked like ties, had been sawed into rectangular pieces two feet long. These were placed beside the rails so that the wheels could be raised up on a wood block paving and could be directed

to run over the rail by the aid of a frog placed at the proper place.

The frog had to be spiked to the ties. The king snipe, or section boss, likely got down on his hands and knees under the engine to spike this in himself. Or in those days of real gandy dancers, the king snipe put his best man down there to do the work.

Did you ever try to hit a spike on the head? Did you ever get down on your hands and knees under an engine with the hiss of steam in your face and a mountain of steel above your frail little body, with perhaps only six inches to swing the spike maul to drive spikes in ties and your hands freezing in the cold and your body perspiring inside three pairs of overalls?

If you have done that, you are a full-fledged first class gandy dancer, who probably had plenty of advice to follow from the conductor, the king snipe, and the engineer.

The next day the clouds swooped low over the crust of snow and bumped against the cars, causing little whirlwinds to blow the snow and smoke under the engine, where the gandy dancer was on his knees praying for relief to all the gods he feared, the gods of wind, snow, and brass hats.

Lanterns were lit as evening approached and darkness engulfed the Divide. The frogs were set. Everyone got out of the knife-like cut around the front of the engine. The brakeman went back of the train to flag anyone who might get in the way.

The signal was given and the first engine whistled three blasts, which were answered by the engine's hogger, Billy Rush. It was hard to back up, the wheels spun from the snow that the men had kicked on the rails.

The attempt was given up and an effort was made to sand the rails by hand after the snow had been swept off. The train moved a few feet, sufficient to rerail the pony truck. But as so often happens when conditions are much easier for work, the pony truck refused to climb the frog, tearing it loose from the ties.

The king snipe swore the venerable streak of oaths according to the rich tradition of the Moffat at so early a date. He spat his tobacco cud against the snow bank as he crawled into the narrow snow gorge and ordered his men to start shoveling out another spot.

They worked in the darkness by flares, torches, and lanterns until the blizzard drove them back into Rollins Pass shed. It was midnight with a blizzard howling over the pass. In Denver, Joe Culbertson shook his head, and other officials shuddered at the thought of what would happen if this kept up.

And it did happen, for it was springtime in the Rockies. Even as the spirit of revolt shakes schools with new disciplinary problems, Old Man Winter revolted and hurled his deepest snow over the Pass. He made the snow wet. And when he gave men a breathing space of a few hours or so a day, he teased men toiling on top of the world, as a cat teases a mouse he has caught. He sent night when the thermometer saw the mercury try to curl up and sleep in the bulb. Or he would send beautiful days with the sun shining and everyone saying, "It is spring." But night again would freeze the melting snow water into ice over the rails.

Suffice it to say that rotary plow Number 10200, the pride of the Moffat and as powerful a plow as had ever been built, was snowed in with no power to push her on down to Arrowhead. The mail had been carried on by section men, who used a horse and sled part of the way.

But day after day and week after week, every effort to get the plow loose was in vain. Men carried coal in gunnysacks from the Pass down to the engines on improvised sleds made of boards. Hour after hour they shoveled snow into the engine tanks. Men's beards were long, their faces grimy and their spirits failing with fatigue.

The management could not lease a plow, for both the Colorado and Southern and Colorado Midland were continually busy with their plows, struggling to open up the blockades that engulfed their Rockies in springtime.

The last of April approached. All efforts to clear the trail had been given up until the weather improved. The entire Hill was drifted deep with snow. Here and there little avalanches had occurred. On warm days, as small rocks uprooted by frost and loosened by the heat of the sun started to roll, they brought great rocks and trees down with them.

Help arrived in Denver April 29. The Colorado Midland Railway running west from Colorado Springs sent her small rotary. The last day of April, this rotary chewed her way up the Ladder out of Tolland. Above the lake country the snow was drifted above her little snout that heaved out tons of snow. Unable to move ahead any farther, she whistled to back up. Her three blasts were answered, and she was pulled back a hundred feet by the two engines behind her. Men with dynamite crawled on the snow she had been unable to swallow, and blasted it into the cut she had opened. Then the snow plow pilot whistled two long blasts and the engines behind moved ahead, until she was stalled again by the depths of the snow that plugged her rotary blades and snout.

The plow pilot whistled "stop" with a long blast. This was followed by the back up signal. Back they would go to wait for the dynamiters to repeat their blasting of the deep snow into the cleaned-out track. After hours spent in this fashion, the deepest cuts were cleared. But the last day of April the famous little Midland plow was not half way to the pass. She tied up at Antelope.

It was May Day in Denver; children were all excited about May baskets and parties. On the Hill, Moffat Engine 101 was still off the track and the relief plow was chewing her way to the rescue. Mr. W. A. Deuel had taken over as general manager. He could rejoice that the line was opened to the pass by 3:40 P.M. "We will run Number 1 to Jenny Lake or perhaps to the pass tomorrow," he said. Meanwhile, cheers were going up as the Colorado Midland plow came out of the shed on the top of the world and moved toward the stranded train.

We hope that by now some of the frustration, numbness and desperate futility of the Moffat men can be understood. Undeniably, the Hill was the most important single obstacle on the Moffat.

No snowshed could keep the wind-driven snow from sifting through the cracks and nail holes. Plenty of snow had to be removed by the section men and the rotary. The shed was so big and the storms so frequent that the western half mile of the single track shed was cleaned only wide enough for the trains, with no clearance on the sides of the track in the shed, leaving a shelf or ledge on top of it, which on the day of this spring storm was seven feet above the track.

Section men were warned and ordered not to walk through the sheds even during storms, for fear they would get caught in the meat-grinder blades of a rotary plow coming through. But who wants to walk outside in a howling blizzard? Men would gamble, take chances, and sometimes lose. They have been known to be caught by the cylinder of some engine as they crouched on the side of a wall. The remains would be picked up in apple boxes. Ventilators (smoke stacks) had been built every few feet to carry out the smoke, but when a half dozen engines got in there belching forth gas and smoke the shed was an inferno. Men passed out in the gas, and it became a dreaded place.

George Barnes, as conductor of Number 2, was bringing his passenger train up the west side of the Pass about 1910. The train had been coupled in behind a three-engine freight which had a rotary plow. They lost so much time in the snow that Barnes was worried because of a second freight train which followed them by fifteen minutes. As they entered the Corona shed, Barnes prayed that the head engine would pull them through to the east end of the shed before stopping, lest the second train plow into his frail wooden passenger cars in the blinding smoke of the shed.

But the rotary crew signalled a stop at the first water plug and coaling station, though provisions were made for water and coal farther ahead. The flagman was Jim Baker, a new man, who Barnes immediately realized was unfamiliar with this shed and its terrors. So Barnes dashed out with a lantern and fusee. As he raced down the snowshed, the gas was so bad that his lantern went out. He passed the brakeman standing on the track without seeing him.

Barnes could hear the second freight coming in the rear of the shed. He lit a fusee and stopped under a ventilator. There the air was better, and there he was able to see the snow bank on the sides above him on which he could stand, if he could get up there. He made a jump for the place and fell back. He spied a bridge spike on the wall of the shed. If he could somehow make a lunge for the spike and grab it, he would not be ground up. He could hold on and brace himself on the snow and attempt to throw the fusee into the cab of the freight engine as it passed.

Panting in the high altitude air and coughing from the gas, Barnes made a second desperate lunge, grabbed the bridge spike, and pulled himself up on the ledge of snow, just as the engine came upon him. The smoke from the passing engine caused him to cough violently, so that he could not throw the fusee, but he did yell, as only a desperate man can yell. He heard the engine stop puffing, for Ernest Anthony, the engineer, had closed the throttle. As the cab passed, he could hear the fireman ask, "What's the matter?"

Anthony replied, "I thought I heard a man yell."

Barnes was now opposite the first freight car. He

May Day on the Moffat ends another drama. Some railroaders shot pictures that would carry the cheers of the men to the front pages of the papers and to this book. This was May Day on the Moffat, 1905, with the Colorado Midland rotary approaching from the left. Ice had derailed a pony truck on the first engine, leaving Number 1 helpless in a blizzard. But the rescue of the train took the best part of another day. After the rotary had opened the line down to the train, she was pulled back and uncoupled so that the two engines could slip down. Taking one car at a time and then one engine at a time, the Moffat's plowtrain was finally brought back to the snowshed. Frozen journals make some wheels slide like sleds. Meanwhile, another blizzard had overtaken this hard-fought-over spot. In fact, when May the second was over, all that could be said was that the CM plow had gotten one mile west. Back in Denver, topcoats were forgotten, the temperature read sixty-four degrees.

May third came and the new general manager still had no word by midnight that the plow train had reached Arrowhead. *Billy Rush photo.* **Page 72**

Plow train with flats. McClure photographed this westbound plow train at Corona and created a problem for the present authors. What was the purpose of the flats? They must have been used to haul snow out from the sheds. The snow depth here is eighteen feet, and constant drifting gradually caused a great deal to sift into the sheds. This had to be removed periodically. Apparently the plow train will proceed the short distance to the shed where work will soon commence for the gandy dancers. *McClure photo.*

climbed from the snow to the top of the car, crawled over the top to the front, and felt his way down the car's ladder. Coughing in the gas of Anthony's engine, he climbed up the ladder of the tender, crawled over the tank, up the coal pile, and slid down the coal to the floor of the cab. He yelled, "For God's sake, don't move. I think you have run over my flagman." Still coughing and gasping for breath, he told Ernest Anthony of the new flagman standing out there protecting his train.

"Now, don't move, no matter who tells you to move, until I come back."

Barnes crawled out the forward window of the cab of the 115 and walked ahead on the runway to the front of the engine. What this gas must have been, we can only guess, for down on the track it had been heavy enough to put out his lantern. He

climbed down the front of the engine and fumbled his way back. He literally bumped into his flagman, who was faithfully standing on the track, as Barnes had ordered. Jim Baker could not have been seen or heard by the engineer and he would have had no escape from the meat grinder.

Barnes and Jim Baker walked back to the pay car which was the last car of the passenger. They sat down and rested. Barnes knew that between the train of coal ahead with the brakes set and a three-engine train behind, the wooden coaches of his train would have collapsed and a fire would have burned alive the passengers that had not been killed in the rear-end collision. The passenger train could not have been bumped ahead by the crash, for the coal train would have held it immovable.

Both of the men were black from smoke and soot, their lanterns out, when they passed through the coaches. The passengers were innocent of the danger from which they had miraculously been saved.

Barnes was so done up, when he reached the baggage car, he had to rest again. Opening the door in the far end of the baggage car he crawled over the tender of his engine to tell his crew what had happened. From there, he crawled out the cab window along the side of the boiler on the running board of the engine, which is above the drive wheels. Then he went in the caboose ahead and blew up about what had happened. He proceeded out the far door of the caboose and crawled over the coal and freight

Extension of Corona shed. The Corona shed as lengthened in the fall of 1905; after the first winter, the short shed had grown to cover the wye, the long passing track, and the main line. In fact, the shed had been extended a half mile farther west of the passing track. The picture shows a clear view of the cross section of the shed. Another roof brace is being raised. Note the bridge-work on the top of the shed to carry the snow load.

John Daly's bridge carpenters spent most of the winter at Rollins Pass trying to complete more of the shed. Their outfit cars were parked just outside. The men had no trouble in keeping warm as the cars were completely drifted over in the deep sea of snow which inundated the Pass in this storm. John Daly knew that a half mile more of snowshed would be a great necessity even if the line were to be operated only three years, the length of time it would take to construct the Main Range Tunnel. But the tunnel had yet to be started. *Ocy Nelson collection, E. J. Francis photo.*

cars to the center mallet. He finally reached the snowplow mallet, where he exploded to the snowplow conductor. There were no words left in all of Hell, when Barnes got through, and God Almighty must have wished there had been more such words.

He looked up the conductor of the freight, whom he had trained as a brakeman. The man said the snowplow needed coal. Barnes replied, "You could have pulled ahead as usual, cut off, and got your coal from the dock on the passing track ahead. Or you could have pulled on the passing track and let our train run around you. You could have come to a stop right at the coal dock and water plug in that case."

Barnes said he would go to the Big Boss with this. The plow conductor mumbled that he just wanted enough coal and water so that they could get down the other side and back. There is no question that by this time everyone was scared. For who had ever heard Barnes pour out all Hell before?

Barnes had to repeat his performance of getting back to Ernest Anthony's engine. He wanted Anthony to back his train up enough so that it could go in on the siding. But Anthony said the blizzard was so bad that they would be helplessly stuck, if that were attempted.

The mess was untangled, but Barnes did not recover easily from his narrow escape from the meat grinder wheels of the 115. It was weeks until he was calmed down. After this, Barnes would never take his train over the pass between two freight trains. He no longer cared if he lost hours; he was not going through that experience again.

"This," Barnes said, "was my most miraculous escape from death." This was devotion, clear mindedness, quick action, and all out dash that kept the Moffat record intact, with "no passengers killed, no passengers seriously injured." Brakemen broken in under Barnes, as Chas. Clark, Lynn Holladay, and J. A. Pierson, inherited the fear of blockades and snowsheds and they, too, were trained to take all precautions.

Let us consider two stories of Chriss Lomax. The place is Corona. We do not think of the beautiful little lakes or the water falls across Middle Boulder Canyon. We think of gassed men in the Rollins Pass snowshed, the endless poker game that went on and on, and the rule that no wives were allowed to be brought to the top of the world. But there was a woman there, the wife of an operator. It was her

Hill Hell

first day. Her husband had been given special permission to have her come up.

Chriss Lomax was the operator on duty when the daily occurrence of a gassed man being carried into the office happened. It was the custom to lay such men on the floor until they came to.

This man was a strapping big fireman named Bill Gallagher. As he lay moaning and groaning on the floor, the operator's wife came into the room. She knew nothing about this being a daily occurrence and cried out, "Do something. This is terrible." But no one paid any attention. After they had attempted to make the explanation that this was the usual thing and that he was surely all right or he would not have been groaning so terribly, no one paid any attention to the woman.

But she was not so easily pacified. She went back to her room to get some ammonia. She hurried back to the operator's shanty, turned the fireman over on his back, and with trembling hands attempted to give him a whiff of the ammonia. But instead of a whiff, he got some of the genuine liquid down his nose. Gallagher came to life like three madmen. The woman fled as the train crew found themselves unable to hold him to the floor. The maddened man smashed furniture, tore the phones from the walls, and wrecked the office and instruments. Lomax and the train crew fled out of the office, down the little hall into the smoky train shed. As the liquid ammonia all turned to vapor, the fireman calmed down, becoming a normal man. The work of restoring the wrecked office became the emergency task.

As humorous as this story may be, it tells the terrible conditions that the men worked under and explains why so many Moffat men have such high doctor bills today.

Nels Johnson confirms the preceding story about the terrible conditions of gas with the story of several helper engines waiting on a siding in the shed. Johnson discovered that all the men were gassed except Conway and himself. Jack Hussell and Bill Miller were found in their engines. Miller was lying against an engine pipe with his face burned to the bone.

Engine men and firemen tried all kinds of smoke masks, and often presented a very ugly picture wearing their smoke snout and hog snout.

George Schryer recalls the time five helper engines were coupled together on the Corona siding waiting for a freight that was coming up the hill.

Corona shed in late fall. Note ventilators and bridge work to prevent weight of snow from breaking roof. On ground to right are extension stacks to go on the ventilators. A stairway leads up from the snowshed on the far side to the weather station. It was blown off the divide one night when the wind hit 105 mph. The water tank received water from the pump house lake one-half mile down the mountain. The crumbling brick foundation for the tank can be seen yet. *McClure photo.*

Corona in August. Even Nature has a conscience. As May came each year, the snowbanks receded a little. June brought forth minute purple flowers and the moss brightened to full color. Spring came late on the Continental Divide, but it did come. What a constrast to the winter! We see the main line in the foreground, the stub of the wye in the upper left, the stacks of the station, and far beyond the snug little hotel for the tourists. This was 1911, with snow remaining until August. *Denver Public Library Western Collection.*

Corona snowsheds in the middle of winter. Note extension stacks and bridge work as the snow has drifted from twenty-two to thirty feet deep in Rollins Pass. Under this protection men lived, operated engines, repaired track, cooked, and slept. Here, helper engines waited for orders to drop down to either Tabernash or Tolland. Under this snow, the poker game went on, the game never over—just new hands.

The terrible winters had borne out the prediction of a man by the name of Marsh who had said that it was against God Almighty to build a road over Rollins Pass. *A. L. Johnson collection.*

George was in the cab of his engine, which was near the middle of the line-up. Since the snow was high over the snowshed, the gas from the engines was slow in getting out of the few ventilators that were not buried under the snow.

Suddenly, George was aware that the engines were running wild down the canyon cut by the rotary through the twenty-foot snow west of the shed. He immediately guessed that he and all the other men had been gassed. His fireman was out, but now in the semi-dazed condition, was coming to in the bitter cold air, which had aroused Schryer.

George cut his engine's air into the brake line, which had been under the first engineer's control. Working his brake valve, cycling it back and forth to build up the pressure, George began restoring the braking power of the heavy engines on the four per cent.

He held onto his whistle cord warning the freight, which would be coming around Ptarmigan Point any moment. His fireman by now was recovering enough that, when he beheld the freight coming round the bend, he attempted to jump. George caught him, knowing he would be ground into hamburger under the wheels of the engine, for the cut in the snow was a hopeless wall over which no one could jump.

It seemed impossible to stop the five mallets, but the freight ahead could be easily stopped, for it was coming up the four per cent. Schryer kept working his brake valve back and forth building up the line pressure, so that the engines slowly came to a stop—thirty feet from the freight train.

The next problem was to render first aid to the men, several of whom were burned from collapsing against steam pipes.

Chriss Lomax tells what he calls a humorous story:

A five-engine train had pulled in from the west and was waiting on the siding for a two-engine train from the east. This siding was long enough to accommodate another train, which pulled into the snowshed and crept up behind the first train.

Rotary 10201. *Alco photo, F. Bauer collection.*

Hill Hell

But the head engineer could not see in the smoke and gas. Apparently no one was flagging behind the first train. The second train crept up behind and coupled into the caboose, which was behind the last engine on the first train. The second train's engineer, feeling his way in the darkness, did not realize that he had coupled into the caboose. It so happened that the roadmaster was sleeping in this caboose. Roadmasters and trackmen had to grab a ride any way they could, to get over the line. The roadmaster awakened with the shock of a second train coupling in and beheld the caboose folding up. He dashed ahead, jerked open the door, attempted to climb the ladder on the rear of the helper engine's tender. But the caboose caught up with him and reached up with a board and nail, which snagged him in the pants and lifted him high over the engine tender.

The roadmaster hoped against hope that the nail would hold, and that the engineers on the second train would close their throttles. But the hoggers thought the rail was just a little slippery, when they met the resistance of folding up the caboose, so they just opened their throttles a little more.

The roadmaster's pants gave way, and he tumbled over the side of the engine, sliding down the icy side of the packed snow in the snowshed, landing on his back under the engine. Here he was unable to turn over or crawl out. He dared not move lest he be mauled by the engine.

Well, anyway, the air was better where he lay. The man wondered how long it would be until he was discovered, for the noise of the crash and the hissing of steam from the engine drowned out his voice.

As he looked up, a red hot coal from the fire box dropped on his chest. The helpless roadmaster could not even get his hand free to shove the clinker away. It burned through the man's clothes, burning a space on his chest the size of his fist, until the man's blood cooled the clinker.

This is a humorous story, because the man lived and was able to go to work again after hospital treatment. But there were stories that were not humorous.

Corona living quarters. August revealed, too, a strange little town, buried all winter, a town of rambling buildings interconnected with passageways. Old box cars, camp cars, and sheds branched one off the other. This was a town of two seasons—winter and August. It was a town of constant struggle against the elements, one of the worst of which was snowshed gas, which necessitated the building of sleeping quarters and lunchroom far from the engines. *Denver Public Library Western Collection.*

And what did these men fight for? Here it is—their aim, a clear track—a thin lifeline to northwestern Colorado, a vital lifeline to Middle Park, a line upon which their own destiny and those of the Moffat Road depended.

Our story in this chapter has been of Nature's brute force, raw, unkind, unforgiving of mistakes, but open and honest nonetheless. Nature was a force to be reckoned with and fought with respect, but a force without intrigue. We turn now in the next chapter to man's crafty efforts to hinder Moffat by means of cunning, trickery, treachery, and even foul play. *L. J. Daly photo.*

Gore Canyon Conspiracy

Moffat and the chief engineer knew plenty about the absolute ruthlessness of the giants that controlled the nation's railroads. By proposing another line, Moffat had declared war on Harriman's and Gould's territories. This new short line was vulnerable to attack at every pass and gateway. H. A. Sumner had been pressed to put almost every survey crew to work securing the best line to the base of the mountains, although he needed crews securing routes through defiles farther west.

Reconnaissance crews were picking up the filings of the Colorado Railway which Moffat owned. Fortunately the competition had been taken unawares by Moffat's quick decision to build. Harriman would have to find men who were acquainted with this projected route to know where to block Moffat.

By December of 1902 crews in South Boulder

"CHECKMATE? WELL I GUESS NOT!"

Canyon were released and sent farther west to begin work that an early winter could cut very short. Some crews were disbanded for the winter. At this time they discovered engineers in Gore Canyon working for a hydroelectric company. There were only several hundred people in all of Grand County. Electricity was in its infancy. H. A. Sumner was alarmed!

Now where and what was Gore Canyon?

No railroad had been built before without long detours, between Denver and Salt Lake City, because of a series of barriers and walls. We have watched the railroad being ushered through the tunnel section. We have seen the hell winter made of the Rollins Pass route and cannot understand why Moffat continued to think he could do without a Main Range tunnel. His words were," Rollins Pass is just a matter of power."

Through the next mountain range there was an easy gateway—Byers Canyon just below Hot Sulphur Springs. This two mile gem of beauty had a natural pathway just above the Colorado River at the base of the north wall. Possessing the grade work of the Colorado Railway made Byers Canyon no problem had it not been for the fact that the Grand County pioneers had driven over this day after day. A dozen years had passed. This wagon road had even been improved by Grand County, which had taken a chance that no railroad was coming through. Sumner had been aware of the need for tact in getting Grand County to find another route for her wagon road. The commissioners had just a few taxpayers. It would be a great financial hardship to tax these people for the relocation of the road.

The fourth barrier was the Gore Range, which once had held a great lake. Some prehistoric upheaval had opened a crevice in this natural dam— Gore Canyon. The Colorado River had then begun cutting a knife-like wedge leaving her old spillway about a thousand feet above.

It was at the mouth of this crevice that surveyors

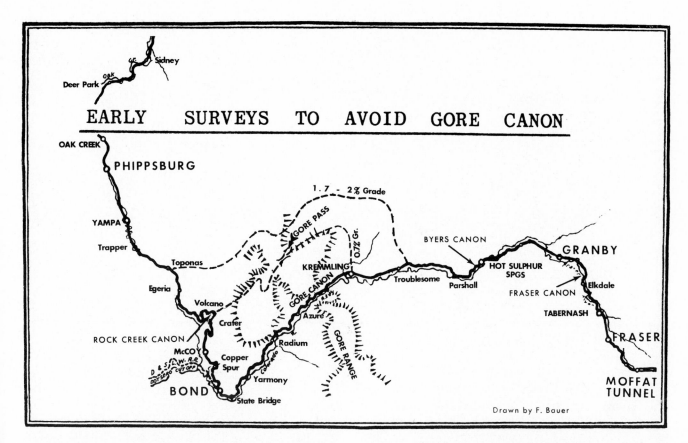

EARLY SURVEYS TO AVOID GORE CANON

Drawn by F. Bauer

were locating a pipeline to carry water to a hydro-electric plant. H. A. Sumner sent men to find out what their filings were for. The men were not secretive at all. They said they had no intentions of building a high dam. Nevertheless, the Chief was uneasy.

Let us look into the history of this crevice in the mountains. The Denver Utah and Pacific—in which Moffat had cooperated in the first effort to get west—had run a preliminary survey through Gore Canyon using boats. A grand scramble followed for this slim gateway. The narrow-gauge Rio Grande had raced to Leadville to battle for the new market there. Having caught its breath, it looked west with renewed courage but so ugly was the country west of Tennessee Pass that plans were dropped. She considered going west by extending her branch that climbed east to Climax and down to Dillon; an easy grade was possible for this extension by dropping down from the Blue River to Kremmling and Gore Canyon—the idea being to build through Gore Canyon and climb out of the Colorado River valley by way of Egeria Canyon. To hold her route, the Rio Grande invested $50,000 in construction work at the latter place.

But who was going to have Gore Canyon? Was

there to be another Royal Gorge war?

A third railroad, the Union Pacific, had considered a branch from Wyoming through Walden over Muddy Pass to Kremmling. Gore Canyon would enable the Union Pacific to tap the Grand Junction area and minerally-rich western Colorado.

A fourth line, a blue-print railroad, argued for this crevice.

But the slowness of Colorado's western slope to develop, and a panic, delayed the financing of any of these projects. So all the lines involved worked out a joint trackage agreement. Then the Rio Grande gave up and determined to go over Tennessee Pass west of Leadville.

With this history we see that Gore Canyon was indeed a much wanted gate through this range. No wonder Mr. Sumner was alarmed and not satisfied by the explanation given regarding the hydroelectric company.

Some time in the winter of 1902-03 T. J. Milner ran a preliminary survey line down the ice. The route was filed in the name of the Denver Northwestern & Pacific. Milner had been chief engineer of the Interurban effort west. Even though he had

McClure's Gore Canyon. Gore Canyon is the crevice formed in a dam of a prehistoric lake. The waters scrubbing away at the granite for thousands of years slowly widened this gateway through Gore Range. McClure took this magnificent picture of the rails that were laid on the right of way blasted from the walls of this canyon. Time of year is late fall when the last aspen leaf is gone and the Grand River (today's Colorado) is very low. But even this picture of victory for the right to use the canyon and victory over nature hints at what wet snows could do in rolling great slides over the track.

been excluded from the coveted new post as chief he seems to have continued his friendship with Moffat. In fact, he later spoke of begging Moffat to build the Main Range Tunnel.

Chief Engineer Sumner became a general whose strategy had to be planned skillfully to head off all moves of the enemy. Although there were plenty of natural reservoir sites farther west, the chief had to prove good faith in filing for this right of way through the canyon or else he would be vulnerable in court to the charge that this was just another blue paper promotion. For this reason courts had always insisted on construction work as the proof that a corporation was financially able and not just a scheme to block some legitimate effort and exact an exorbitant price for relinquishing the right of way.

With patience Sumner continued to extend the olive branch to Grand County residents regarding the legal right to use Byers Canyon. One of the railroad land agents, a native of the county, suggested to Mr. Sumner that one of the commissioners might change his mind if he were salted down.

In the answer that Sumner wrote we see the stature of this Christian gentleman, "Mr. Moffat does not do business that way." His enemies would stop at nothing, but Moffat desired to bully or crush no one.

How could the issue be settled out of court? The engineering department investigated what it would cost to build a wagon road over the mountain north of Byers Canyon. The estimate does not seem much to us today. But its price was almost equal to the price of their two new locomotives the railroad purchased—$24,000. This switchback road was offered to the County Commissioners who really wanted to see the Denver Northwestern & Pacific cattle trains roll into the county and longed to have a standard-gauge passenger train bringing in tourists. Of course, people could gripe about the Switzerland trail. It would blow shut in winter. Reasonable people understood they had no legal right to the canyon.

Grand County people always stood by David Moffat. He had gone the other mile with them when they were hard pressed. They gave the right of way his enterprise needed. Their future was tied up with the necessity of his victory. For without a railroad, transportation was very costly. They began to feel that the Moffat was their hope.

There was an exception. It was expressed by several ranchers around Kremmling, who were offered from ten to twenty times the value for their land if they would sell out for a new reservoir corporation. This proved to be another company rather than the hydroelectric. A three-way struggle followed for the mouth of Gore Canyon.

The railroad hired men, shovels, and wheelbarrows to begin construction. The promoters of the reservoir fought back with a court injunction to stop the railroad, then they bought out the hydroelectric company for $60,000.

Who was behind this?

In the courts the battle was fought. The reservoir firm tried to prove that the canyon was not necessary for the railroad. T. J. Milner released a statement to the press that he had been fired by the Moffat Board of Directors for recommending the canyon route! This was very damaging. What other route could a railroad take?

H. A. Sumner had crews running two lines over Gore Pass. Two grades were established. All the rise in elevation was not lost as one line dropped down a short distance in elevation to Toponas. This saved the heavy two per cent grade up out of Gore Canyon. The Gore pass route was practical in reaching northwestern Colorado. H. A. Sumner did not recommend this route because it excluded any connection with the Rio Grande.

Into the court case came a new enemy! The Interior Department filed to build its own reservoir. It proposed to set aside the canyon country for a wild life reserve. The intrigue now burst out clearly, for the Interior Department claimed that the railroad had never filed its right of way.

David Moffat had reasons to believe that the enemy owned the Interior Department of the United States. For his men had filed the survey. Detectives were hired to get the truth about the reservoir company. But how had a skunk gotten in the Interior Department?

Into this fantastic battle of American enterprise came a protest from the Los Angeles Chamber of Commerce in favor of the Interior Department's reservoir. Los Angeles said that the reservoir was needed to insure the future storage of water for the growing city!

It did not take long to find out what member of the Los Angeles Chamber of Commerce had promoted this. It was the Southern Pacific Railroad. And who owned the Southern Pacific? The same man that owned the Illinois Central, the Union Pacific and several other railroads—Harriman.

Locating party in Gore. J. J. Argo was unable to get his "squirrels" into Gore Canyon until spring flood season because of the long fight in the courts for this right of way. These men—dressed in all kinds of clothing including bib overalls—surely do not look like men of steel nerve and great physical stamina, but they were. These foot-walks were floated to location, shoved out over the swirling waters by the "squirrels," and held to the walls by rope hung over horns of the wall. Special machined pegs twenty inches long were driven into crevices to hold the rope. And when no crevice could be found, diamond drills were put into the hands of the boys who slowly dug the holes in blue granite.

The man to the right holding survey stakes, W. I. Hoklas, slipped into the flood. He caught himself way down stream on a boulder. The boys were so unnerved that they knocked off work for the day. *W. I. Hoklas collection.*

Meanwhile, the court case with the reservoir company revealed some startling facts. Blue prints showed that the reservoir engineers had made no provision for a connection with the hydroelectric plant. A dam with no opening for water to reach the turbines!! This discovery by the venerable chief engineer caused the railroad to hire detectives to find out just what kind of a man this promoter was. They found that he was wanted in a confidence game!

The railroad still had to contend with the Interior Department's plans. At this time Carl Ewald came west. He was Teddy Roosevelt's right-hand trouble shooter.

All parties were called to Washington by Teddy himself, who presided at an investigation of the Interior Department. Teddy was out to get the trusts. His eyes snapped. His teeth gleamed under his mustache as he barked, "Oh, so you represent the opposition railroads!"

Mysteriously the filings for the right of way for the railroad were found. Explanation was that a clerk had misfiled them!

Teddy Roosevelt shook the devil out of his Interior Department. The courts considered the reservoir company a fake. Gore Canyon was open to the severely and badly beaten Moffat. On his desk in his Denver First National Bank office, David H. Moffat placed a statuette of Teddy Roosevelt.

Now H. A. Sumner could send his men into the crevice to make the survey prior to advertising for bids.

The winter snows had by now caused the Colorado River to overflow her banks. How could the men get down? The locating engineer, whose name was J. J. Argo, had twenty-inch machined steel pegs turned in a Denver machine shop. He was going to build a cat walk on the wall of the canyon and survey it from this catwalk. Most places these pegs could be driven in crevices. Other places star drills would have to cut holes.

Three thousand feet of rope were packed to the site. Slim lodgepole pines were trimmed of branches and made into ladders at this remote location far away from civilization. Logs were floated down to the spot for foot logs for this engineer's walk.

Daring lads drove the pegs as they were held by ropes to the wall of the canyon. The logs were likewise held by hundreds of feet of rope hung over some horn of the canyon wall. In this way the catwalk was built. The men went out to set up their transits and make the ten foot contour survey. One day W. I. Hoklas slipped into the raging icy torrent. Luckily he had sneaked away from home as a boy and had learned to swim. After a struggle he was washed up on a boulder. So shaken was the crew that surveying was called off for the remainder of the day. These men had become a team dependent on each other. No one had dared take one step without thinking what would happen if a rock were let loose on someone else.

One shaky fellow had been frozen out of the group. The men felt he was too nervous. But he built up his courage by climbing out on a dangerous rock where he spent the entire day taking his watch apart and putting it back together again. Thus he showed the men his skill and courage. He was revived back. This team surveyed the canyon without loss of life!

The team was now ready for easy work and a holiday ball game with the young cowboys of nearby Yampa. One game was lost from too much liquid spirits and one won by dried out spirits.

Word came that another enemy appeared west of Steamboat. Another reservoir site was filed, and still another. Moffat would be licked by costly delaying tactics and rumors on Wall Street that he was going bankrupt. Who would invest in a mortally wounded company?

This was not a white glove job. But no hand could take the work without tough gloves. More rope is needed just around the corner to extend the foot bridge (picture above). This magnificent June day is invigorating in the year 1905. The fellows are getting hungry. So might as well take the lunch bucket up and not have to wear oneself out a half hour later.

Surveyors in Gore Canyon. Just plain luck to find a ledge like this for setting up the transit. Note snow in upper right. *H. Eno photos.*

Rio Grande survey through Gore Canyon, 1878. Second from left, S. P. Sunergren, father of Ed Sunergren. *Ed Sunergren photo.*

Moffat's Last Stand

In the midst of the Gore Canyon battle, Uncle Dave was faced with making a terrible decision regarding the Main Range Tunnel. He was all set to construct it. The temporary line over the hill was finished, so that the tunnel could be reached from both sides. The site had been selected for a 2.6 miles bore at 9,960 feet which was safely below the most furious assaults of winter storms. Tragically, Uncle Dave was forced to proceed now almost entirely on his own. Men in the East who had promised to support him were either afraid of Harriman or worried that Harriman had mortally wounded the short line to Salt Lake. No longer did Uncle Dave have the support of the one other great man of Colorado, Walter Cheesman, with whom he had made so many ventures. Moffat's total assets were still enough to build this tunnel, but only enough more to lay rail a few miles down into Fraser Valley.

What could the Denver Northwestern & Pacific count on for traffic with a line ending somewhere in Fraser River Valley? Heavy summer tourist business, a trickle of lumber and seasonal cattle which could have been handled by a mixed train tri-weekly in the winter. Operating expenses would have been met, for with the tunnel there would have been no costly snow removal. But those who had invested would have found no dividends. Moffat would be reduced to that income of a hundred thousand dollars which he had carefully set aside to protect his wife, just in case.

The opposition railroads would have won unless in the late years of his life David H. Moffat had been able to sell his idea to some fearless fools fed up with Harriman domination.

General Manager Ridgway said, "The hill is just a matter of power." Ridgway had seen the power of the B. & O.'s Old Maude. This was the mallet power on the drawing boards later known as the 200's.

So Moffat made his great gamble. He temporarily gave up the big tunnel in hope that his money would stretch the line into the coal fields of Oak Creek.

Early in the fall of 1903, H. A. Sumner had been instructed to proceed the following spring to build west avoiding any costly construction that could be postponed. Because Mr. Moffat had thoroughly investigated the quality of the semi-anthracite coal in Routt and Moffat counties, he was certain that the public would accept this clean hot coal for heating and for industrial use.

But the winter of 1903-04 disillusioned Amos Caryl Ridgway's belief that Rollins Pass could be operated with new power. He left, saying, "The Moffat is going to be a graveyard for railroaders."

In May of 1905, Uncle Dave began his last stand which was to be fought until his heart gave out six years later.

Economical construction which would involve many line improvements in the years that followed became the policy. Below Arrow the sharp curves and four per cent grade were continued as far as Irvings (today's Winter Park). From here to Hot Sulphur Springs no money could be saved; so original plans were followed as to curves and grade.

It was a beautiful summer after the terrible winter. The Swedish lumberjacks enjoyed it so much that they stacked the ties too close to the right of way at Irvings. The Irish track-layers stopped their singing for a while and cursed the Swedes. But what is more beautiful than summer time in the Rockies? The Roberts track-laying machine laid ties and rails down into Fraser, which was a sea of ties. No one dreamed that a President of the United States would some day fish there. After all, the fish were almost all gone then. Magnificent stands of timber for miles back in the mountains justified the building of first-class sawmills. Enterprising merchants tried to lure the railroad to make its new subdivision for helper engines at Fraser by offering labor, ties, and some money to put in a wye. Hard up for money and stymied by a rancher who wanted a fortune for his meadows at what became known

Moffat at his desk. Moffat slumped in his chair as this photo was taken, just after a bank robber had threatened him with a vial of nitreglycerine. Photos of Marcia grace the wall. *McClure photo.*

Thirty pint loving cup. This enormous loving cup was presented to David H. Moffat, Jr. by his friends in Denver. It is now on display at the Denver Museum where its beautiful silver etching tells the story of the Moffat Road. *State Historical Society of Colordao.*

Wood's sawmill at Irving (Winter Park) shipped the first car of lumber out of Grand County by rail. Such mills at Fraser and Tabernash and many other places were heavy shippers on the new road. *Columbine Pictures photo.*

as Tabernash, Fraser became for a few months the division point.

But train service was not offered to the public below Arrow except by the supply train for the construction gang. This train was dubbed "the Feeble

Minded" by the disgusted pioneers who did not hesitate to deflate the proud trainmen who prided in the plush seats on the recently acquired luxury equipment from the Chesapeake Beach. Sold on Uncle Dave, these trainmen were expecting, in another three years, to be shepherding limiteds to the Pacific Coast. They knew their trains, they knew the magnificent thoroughness of the road up to Tolland. To them this was the great line of the century.

To the rank and file operator the line was a certain success. On the Fourth of July 1905 more than 1200 passengers were carried to Arrow and back to Denver. The Denver Northwestern and Pacific was always having to borrow power and coaches. The equipment roster included only three consolidation engines that weighed 170 tons, two 150 ton passenger ten-wheelers, the two former Chesapeake Beach passenger engines weighing only ninety-eight tons. There were the two six wheeled switch engines weighing 117 tons bought for the construction company. There was the famous "Red Devil Rotary" which had been the pride of Mr. Ridgway. It weighed 103 tons. There was one steam shovel which had been useful in widening the right of way, fifty flat cars for ties and steel, three way cars for the crews to camp in, forty second-hand bunk cars for the men to live in, and the ten beautiful coach

Fraser furnished ties, lumber, and cold nights for the Moffat. Early in the summer of 1905 rails were laid nine miles below Arrow to Fraser, which was a sea of ties. As they disappeared, houses, saloons, and stores were built. Helper engine crews froze at night in the paper thin shacks. Fishing was not very good, because construction men had fished it out. Years later President Ike enjoyed stocked stream fishing just beyond the great meadow, and the station was filled with telegraph instruments even to the freight rooms, since Fraser was the capital of the U. S. But if the enginemen thought Fraser was cold, they discovered Tabernash five degrees colder when the division point was moved there. Trains froze to the rails on some occasions and required much patience to be knocked loose. *Out West Photo Shop, Denver.*

and parlor cars from the Chesapeake Beach road that had gone electric.

The management was not investing in one piece of equipment that was not needed every day of the year. There were always engines and cars to be rented. But the need for equipment was, to the men, just a sign of the overwhelming success of the line that all summer long carried special after special of picnickers to Tolland and Arrow.

The specials ran as far as Hot Sulphur Springs with from 600 to 900 people a day in September, since the rails had been completed and a station built. On September fifth there were 1503 people who bought tickets to Hot Sulphur. Rail Road Day, 1905, came on September fifteenth with most people back home from their vacations. Yet, 900 Denverites bought tickets for Hot Sulphur's glorious day of history.

But the new men coming from the Northern Pacific and elsewhere did not find even the foundation of a railroad hotel being dug at Hot Sulphur Springs, which was the end of the line for 1905. They were offered a tent for the frosty nights. David H. Moffat was hard pressed for money. Enemy agents warned investors in the East, "Just hold off another year and see if the second winter does not prove that Moffat is crazy! No line has ever been put through the Rockies."

Soon service was reduced to a tri-weekly mixed train for the winter. This adequately took care of Middle Park business. Restless stockholders in Denver demanded rails be laid. So the section crew was instructed to lay a rail.

During the summer Mr. Moffat had not been

The Swedes were tired of shoveling carts full of rock so they decided to blow the cut into the river . . . some landed on the engineers' tents clear across the Fraser River. *Art Weston photo.*

A pile driver with literal horse power works in Fraser Canyon summer of 1905. *Clay C. Blough photo.*

successful in getting powerful J. P. Morgan and Company to float a loan to complete the Denver Northwestern and Pacific. In the fall Uncle Dave sailed for England. He took his sister, Mrs. Strong, along because he had found her a tower of strength to him.

After two weeks of staying at the Hotel Cecil, Moffat returned home. The English investors respected the judgment of J. P. Morgan and Company on American investments.

The second winter proved rugged on Rollins Pass. The drains had been built of twelve-inch-wide planks. During the daytime they were adequate for melting snow water. But when they froze solid

The tri-weekly mixed is ready to leave Hot Sulphur in snowy May, 1906. *Denver Public Library Western Collection.*

with ice, the water ran down the track and froze later to derail even the mighty Red Devil Rotary. Hours were spent with frost bitten fingers trying to rerail the plow. Sometimes storms swept in and men gave up for the night to return in the daylight hours to find engines and plow buried except for their stacks. Coal had to be carried in the thin air of 11,000 feet on the backs of gandy dancers to the engine that threatened to freeze up. Snow had to be shoveled into the tanks of tenders where the radiators thawed the snow into needed water to keep them hot. Dozens of men slaved and were willing to go to hell for Deuel, the new general manager, who was a little David Moffat. What wages were adequate for the terrible conditions of rerailing power on the hill?

Then with the power rerailed and backed off, the ice was picked. Exhausted men were happy to retreat to watch the monster chew into the drift and open the line.

These stories were quickly spread wherever Moffat went seeking investors. The truth did not have to be exaggerated. The conspirators only needed to say, "Just ask Mr. Moffat what the cost of snow fighting is this winter. Write and ask the Post Office department how many times the mail does not get through. I hear that it always got through on the stage even if the man had to walk in on snow shoes."

But any stories to the contrary, rails were being laid through Byers Canyon the next summer, through the beauty of the Canyon and on down eighteen miles to Kremmling by running around hills and avoiding gulches. By the first of July, 1906, the supply train had reached Kremmling, which for three years had been the saloon town for Gore Canyon construction workers. A three-day celebration began on the Fourth with the nine saloon keepers pitching a tent to feed every one "for free."

Rail Road Day was similar to the one celebrated in Hot Sulphur the fall before. There were games for every man, woman, and child. A dance was held each night in the big tent. A medal was struck and given to the people. It was heart shaped with a burro and pack, shovel, pick, and gun in the center. Above were the words "Moffat Road Celebration, July 4-6, 1906." The cowboys livened up the days as they raced around town shooting, raising dust, and setting a pattern for Hollywood to copy for all their Western pictures. And those free meals included rainbow trout, venison, and mutton cooked by a famed fisherman of that day. Eighteen little

girls, all starched and ironed to perfection, went through a flag drill. Speeches were made by secondary railroad officials while the "big boys" were East raising money.

Moffat returned from the east to ride the first train through Gore Canyon. It was a moment of triumph even though he knew that the remarkable genius H. A. Sumner could have had the rails into Oakland Bay if the Wall Street men had kept their promises. Several miles on down the very narrow confines of Grand River Valley the train stopped to have the engine turned on the wye. This was rails end. Forty-nine miles from the nearest coal mine and sixty-nine miles from the profitable railhead of

Steamboat Springs, center of Routt County's coal resources.

Moffat had exhausted his fortune of $7,000,000 in this enterprise. He was hurt because men whom he had saved from being swept away in panics did not come to his help. True, only one man had a sizeable fortune. But thousands were being invested out of the state. This was for the good of Denver and northwestern Colorado.

As to how much it hurt to send out an S.O.S., no one knows today. Walter Cheesman did not answer. But Colonel Dodge, who distinguished himself in building the Rio Grande, came to his help with a heavy subscription although he was seventy

Engine 301, polished for her official Schenectady photograph. This faded print came from Alco files and represents the classic railroad photo. *Both photos Schenectady History Center.*

Passengers found that Byers Canyon had a beauty all its own. A wagon road had been built here without rights which the Moffat had bought up from the still born D.U.&P. Highway 40 scars the south wall today. Here is the first passenger train east out of Kremmling with men riding the pilot. *McClure photo.*

The Greatest One=Day Scenic Trip in the World

After passing Tolland (see page 2), the road by intricate windings rises by a uniform grade until the backbone of the American Continent is reached at an elevation of 11,660 feet (the highest point reached by any standard-gauge railroad). Here the tourist may gather wild flowers while standing on huge banks of perpetual snow. Then, by a gradual descent for 11 miles, Arrow, the western terminus of the one-day round trip, is reached. The round trip from Denver to Arrow can be made in a day and offers the greatest scenic attractions imaginable.

From sultry heat to Colorado's NORTH POLE.

TIME TABLE

WESTWARD		Elevation	STATIONS		Miles from Denver	EASTWARD	
No. 3 Pass. Daily P.M.	No. 1 Mail & Ex. Daily A.M.					No. 2 Mail & Ex. Daily P.M.	No. 4 Pass. Daily A.M.
5.00	8.30	5170	**DENVER**	Lv. / Ar.	0	6.10	8.55
f 5.12	f 8.43	5213	**UTAH JCT.**	"	3	5.56	8.43
f 5.20	f 8.52	5248	Ralston	"	7	f 5.46	f 8.32
f 5.33	9.03	5687	Leyden Jct.	"	13	f 5.33	f 8.19
f 5.45	9.13	6162	Arena	"	18	f 5.22	8.09
f	f	6602	Coal Creek	"	22	f	
6.01	f	6783	Plainview	"	24	5.05	7.54
f 6.09	9.28	7040	Crags	"	27	f 4.57	f 7.46
f 6.22	9.36	7457	Crescent	"	32	f 4.43	f 7.33
f 6.28	9.50	7650	Miramonte	"	34	f 4.36	f 7.27
f 6.39	9.57	7958	Gato	"	37	f 4.25	f 7.16
6.49	10.09	8367	**ROLLINSVILLE**	"	42	4.13	f 7.06
7.00	10.22	8889	**TOLLAND**	"	47	4.00	6.55
Arrive Daily P.M.	10.45	9155	Newcombs	"	50	f 3.32	Leave Daily A.M.
	10.58	9380	Ladora	"	52	f 3.16	
	11.15	9905	Antelope	"	56	f 2.55	
	f	10270	Frantz	"	58	f 2.35	
	f	10860	Jenny Lake	"	61	f 2.14	
	11.37	11660	**CORONA**	"	65	1.55	
	12.00	10980	Loop	"	69	f 1.40	
	12.17	10158	Fawn Creek	"	73	1.20	
	12.36	9583	**ARROW**	Ar.	76	1.15	
	12.50	9583	**ARROW**	Lv.	76	12.58	
	1.10	9510	Pacific	"	77	12.48	
	1.15	8935	Vasquez	"	81	f 12.39	
	f 1.32	8560	Fraser	"	85	12.28	
	1.42	8310	Tabernash	"	89	12.15	
	f 1.51	8150	Elk	"	93	f 12.02	
	f 2.02	7935	**GRANBY**	"	99	12.15	
	f 2.15	7760	Willows	"	104	f 11.28	
	2.27	7665	**SULPHUR SPRINGS**	"	109	11.13	
	f 2.45	7595	Parshall	"	114	f 11.00	
	f 3.02	7345	Troublesome	"	121	11.50	
	3.30 P.M.	7322	**KREMMLING** (Present Terminus)	Lv.	126	A. M.	

f Train stops on signal.

TRAINS LEAVE "MOFFAT DEPOT," 15TH AND BASSETT STS. Through tickets sold to all points in Routt County.

The Greatest Short Scenic Trip in the World

Is over the "Moffat Road" from Denver to Tolland, a distance of 47 miles. Tolland is situated in Boulder Park, at the foot of the Continental Divide, surrounded by snow-capped mountains, and affords excellent picnic and camping grounds.

New and elegant equipment, huge engines and vestibuled coaches combined with a perfect roadbed, make the trip one of exceptional enjoyment.

Wild flowers grow luxuriantly among the mountains, and South Boulder Creek affords good fishing.

Excellent lunches and hotel accommodations can be obtained at Tolland, lunches at Corona and Arrow.

years old. Sufficient capital was gathered by Dodge to get rails laid into the coal field and Steamboat Springs.

General Palmer was even more interested in helping, but when he sold his great block of stock in the Rio Grande, he signed an agreement not to venture into any Colorado railroad project.

During the construction of these sixty-nine miles H. A. Sumner ran into the most costly mile of railroad construction on the entire route. The Rock Creek crevice was far too costly to bridge, at that time, so the line was run up the canyon to a convenient place where the creek was crossed by a high trestle and the line brought back on the west wall by the expediency of trestles and tunnels so that the line could be hung to the canyon wall. The price

Moffat placed his hope in pushing the Denver Northwestern and Pacific into the coal fields of Oak Creek. Since this coal was so much superior to that used in Denver and to the east, it was concluded that immediately the demand would be so great that a profitable freight business would develop. Then investors would not be afraid to subscribe to the completing of the road to Salt Lake and to boring the Main Range Tunnel. However the coal business developed very slowly, for Denver was stagnated industrially with no direct West Coast outlet. The road's slim profits were immediately eaten up in the cost of fighting snow on the detour over Rollins Pass.

This photo taken by McClure shows the Hayden Brothers mine at Haybro years later when World War I demands for soft coal gave the mines an opportunity to take over the heating market and prove the superiority of this semi-anthracite for industrial power. *Denver Public Library Western Collection.*

tag was $250,000 for one of these miles which compared to $60,000 a mile for the costly tunnel section and $20,000 a mile for the line over Rollins Pass.

By the time the line had reached Steamboat Springs, the entire cost of the road was $9,861,829.59, which was below H. A. Sumner's estimate for that distance. However, this had been possible because of the economical construction policy adopted west of Arrow. Figures are no longer available as to how much of this money was the personal fortune of Mr. Moffat, but it was reported that he was worth $7,000,000. It is known that he converted every mining equity and investment to complete the road into Steamboat Springs early in the winter of 1909.

David H. Moffat was no longer the mining king of the state. He had lost the support of the second wealthiest capitalist out of blue blood jealousy for fear Moffat would be known as the Railroad King. His kingdom was ruled by a kindly hand that had come to discover that the only men not to fail him were his own employees. The men that handled his locomotives had come to love him. Had he not signed a blank piece of paper and told his enginemen to write their own contract? "I know that you will not cheat me." They also recalled how he had left orders to cash his hogger's checks, and if the check bounced to take it out of his personal account. To these men the name Moffat was a great cause for which they had given their strength far beyond devotion, remaining at the throttle without relief or crawling under engines at thirty and fifty below zero to re-rail them.

Moffat was a weary man but not too tired to continue to make efforts to sell the cause of a line that could build Denver and northwestern Colorado.

The terrible conditions above 10,000 feet bled the road to bankruptcy. The temporary line over Rollins Pass continued to suffer from its little culverts, its sharp curves, and its terrific grades. It was not adapted to be a practical main line of a railroad.

With the little profits from the slowly developing coal business being eaten up by snow removal that a tunnel could have avoided, Mr. Moffat renewed his efforts to get to Salt Lake and to build the tunnel. It is legitimate to ask why the coal business was so slow in developing. Even Colonel Dodge wondered. Both he and Moffat were practical business men. As to the answer, we can only conjecture that if the enemy's hand was not in this, then this was the first time the enemy had failed to lift its hands against the Denver Northwestern and Pacific Railroad.

The 300 engines were designed to handle the regular passenger business without help over the Divide. When tourists flocked in great numbers, the 100 hogs and the 200 mallets doubleheaded these ladies up the Hill. Specials were handled with freight engines. *Alco photo.*

Early in 1911, David Moffat asked his favorite engineer to haul his private car *Marcia* into Steamboat Springs. The young, slim, athletic hogger was Bob Bishop. At the end of the run the chef was asked to call Bob to have steak with Moffat in the *Marcia.* Thus the last trip of David Moffat brought out his democratic feelings for men who had proved true. The next day Bob Bishop hauled his boss over the line to Denver. Moffat went east for the last time. Harriman offered to complete the line for fifty-one per cent of the stock. Moffat saw the trap and refused his plot.

Bob Bishop, guest of Dave Moffat. *W. Stedman drawing.*

Engine 112. Note "Moffat Road." *Alco photo.*

The Moffat Road

What would have happened if Moffat had built his main range tunnel and thereby been financially unable to go beyond Fraser? Would Colonel Dodge have thrown his efforts to have raised the money to Steamboat, when the distance would have been 129 miles instead of sixty-eight? Would eastern men have helped him because the line constructed was below the winter's storm? These questions are legitimate. Moffat may have made a wrong decision. The reader must be the judge.

The name David H. Moffat was now a cause. He had returned to the state every dollar he had earned in his beloved Colorado. The cause was honest. Each day the need grew greater.

Tourists had no trouble around Tolland finding such a fishing stream. They could watch Number 10 heading over the hill and perhaps get the latest gossip about the main range tunnel that was so badly needed in winter. *F. Bauer collection.*

Brick station at Tolland. This beautiful little station of brick and tile was the original Moffat station in Denver. But when the great crowds of tourists could not be handled, it was torn down and rebuilt brick by brick at Tolland to take care of the hundreds of picnickers that the specials brought through the tunnel district. *Denver Public Library Western Collection.*

This picnic shelter was erected at Tolland to protect families against the showers that dripped out of the feather-like clouds. While delicious picnic baskets were opened, others tried the lunchrooms and souvenir shops. The original name of Tolland was Mammoth. *McClure photo.*

517 PICNICKERS ARRIVING AT TOLLAND BOULDER PARK.
Ω MOFFAT ROAD Photo BY L. C. McCLURE, DENVER.

Picnic special at Tolland. The picnic specials handled crowds of more than a thousand people so that more and more facilities were added at Tolland. On several occasions the crowds ran over two thousand people, who tried to pick flowers, to fish, to hike, and to litter the countryside in good old American fashion. The Toll family became greatly displeased, so that the railroad had a clean-up problem if they did not want "Keep Out" signs over the valley. *McClure photo.*

Rock trouble for No. 1 below Loop. Road foreman of engines, Billy Rush, climbs over boulder that caught Train 1 a mile below the Loop. To see how far the 302 could have rolled, see photo on page 100. *Billy Rush collection.*

Tourists were hungry for dinner at Arrow, others thirsty for a drink at the wide open town. Lumberjacks could follow Billy Rush and hit the cinders. *W. Stedman drawing.*

Engines were buried for hours in bad storms. These men have uncovered the bell on one of the powerful mallets. *Bert Smith photo.*

Engine 302 and rock below Loop. *Billy Rush collection.*

Passenger service ended at Hot Sulphur, but construction proceeded west in Gore Canyon. Here no surveyor lost his life in his most dangerous mission. But contractors lost several of their men between the continual blasting and the carelessness of the laborers. Several of the carts used to haul rock can be seen. *McClure photo.*

Sugar Loaf from west of Gore Canyon. *McClure photo, Denver Public Library Western Collection.*

Trestle west end of Gore. Temporary water plug for work train engines is on the hillside. *McClure photo, Denver Public Library Western Collection.*

Unloading fill near Piney Ridge. The work train was loaded in Gore Canyon by shovel 10100. By such methods the work was put to a double purpose. *Denver Public Library Western Collection.*

Page **102**

Steam shovel 10100 was put to use in widening the right of way, even though it rarely could be used up ahead. *Denver Public Library Western Collection.*

Col. D. C. Dodge answered Moffat's SOS when Moffat's enemies froze out Eastern capital that had agreed to finance him. *State Historical Society of Colorado collection.*

Number 1 double headed by Engine 200. The Arrow turn needed a helper this summer day in 1909. On the wye at Tolland stood the world's largest freight engine, Number 200, which was at hand to help freights over the hill. To the thrill of the passengers she was coupled ahead of the tourist extra. A passenger, Mrs. Clarence Smith, took this picture as both firemen were swinging heavy on their scoop shovels as the 200 proudly pulled them up the four per cent grade. *Mrs. Clarence Smith photo.*

Mallet 200 arrives in Denver. Joe Culbertson says, "It was a great day when the 200 was delivered to us at Utah Junction." Faithful to his self-appointed trust, McClure was on hand to record the delivery of the original 200. The fashionably dressed figures at either end of the locomotive, and the moppets in the cab, betray the open house that must have taken place. *Denver Public Library Western collection.*

Mallet 200—left side. Note outside steam line from chest to cylinder, which was later changed. This engine was copied from Baltimore and Ohio's "Old Maude." This engine was built without a pony-truck from a design which Alco touted highly. Shortly thereafter a photo of this engine graced the cover of an Alco advertising book on their mallets. *Alco photo, Schenectady History Center.*

Train 1 has left the box car station of Orestod on the bank of the Colorado River and is now climbing the two per cent grade toward Congre Mesa. The curve in the foreground took the line a mile up Yarmony Creek Canyon, where an easier crossing could be made. A bridge could be considered at this spot as a future refinement when business to Salt Lake would pay for it. Though Number 1 never reached Salt Lake, the California Zephyr does today by running down the Dotsero Cutoff from Orestod (Bond) along the Colorado River to the Royal Gorge line from Pueblo. *McClure photo.*

Train 1 in Yarmony Creek Canyon. Several trestles were needed to hang the line to the walls of the canyon. After the trains went through the tunnel, they began swinging left to cross the creek on a high trestle. A flag stop was established here and called Copper Spur, but the copper ore proved to be of such low grade that it would not pay its own transportation bill to Denver. *McClure photo.*

Entering Rock Creek Canyon. Bridges on far side are visible. *Photo by Paul Snyder.*

How they built Tunnel 48. Most tunnels had sections timbered because of the fractured condition of the granite. This picture is of Tunnel 48 during construction days. Early engineers begged management to replace timber with reinforced concrete to reduce maintenance and the fire hazard. See also picture on page 127. *W. I. Hoklas photo.*

Rock Creek Canyon was a deep gash in the mountains confronting the engineers in the most direct path through this rugged terrain. To bridge the crevice might be too expensive even when refinements of the line could be considered. The line entered the canyon high up on the east wall and clung to this wall on a ledge blasted out of hard rock. Several tunnels were necessary to get the line up the canyon and across a high trestle and back down the west wall. The water flume that irrigated Congre Mesa was unfortunately above the east right of way and on several occasions brought slides down in front of trains which were almost rolled off the precarious ledge. H. A. Sumner is reported to have asked himself if this line was not a mistake. *McClure photo.*

Depths of Rock Creek Canyon. This picture was taken from the water ditch and shows the depths of Rock Creek Canyon. Trestle enabled the road to cross the creek and return on the west wall. *D.&S.L. Engineering Department.*

Rock Creek trestle. This was the largest timber structure on the Moffat and was flanked by two tunnels, one at either end. The depths of Rock Creek Canyon were later tamed by a fill which completely engulfed the trestle, which today is no longer visible. *A. Clarke photo.*

Another view of Rock Creek trestle. Every effort was made to bring business. A travelogue over the line was made in this fashion. *Denver Public Library Western Collection.*

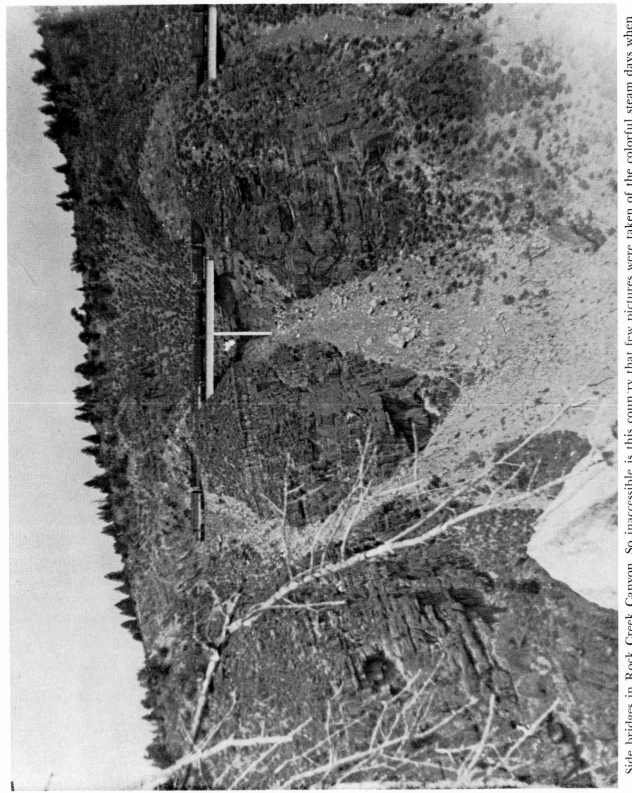

Side bridges in Rock Creek Canyon. So inaccessible is this country that few pictures were taken of the colorful steam days when many coal drags clung to this wall and crossed the side bridges. A D.&S.L. conductor, protecting his train, stepped off here in a blinding snowstorm and fell to his death. *George M. Bollinger photo.*

Henry Swan knew the Moffat intimately when he was asked to be a co-trustee during the Rio Grande receivership, for he had been a sub-contractor. Left to right: Allen Weston and Henry Swan. This was their office near Oak Creek. Henry Swan has been instrumental in preserving Colorado history through many years of service as a director of the Board of the State Historical Society of Colorado. The fine railroad collections at the Society are a special monument to Mr. Swan's historical interest. *Henry Swan collection.*

Denver Station. Horse-drawn vehicles have brought the mail and express. One transfer driver is passing the time of the morning with the engineer, perhaps asking him why Number 1 has engine 109 instead of one of the 300 class ten wheelers? The two coaches of the morning commuter Number 4 from Tolland and Miramonte are on track two. The passengers for second Number 1 are strung out from the ticket window to the cars. Is this a picnic special to Tolland? Or is it the Arrow turn? A Fifteenth Street electric has lost half her passengers. Someone has come down in a mule-drawn cart. And who rated the one and only gas buggy? From Sixteenth Street viaduct little of the spacious beauty of Moffat Terminal is seen. Up till the last it was kept well painted and clean. *McClure photo.*

Straw hat time finds great drifts west of Corona on Rollins Pass. Photographers set up their cameras carefully on tripods as Extra 100 East lets her safety valves roar. Note the steerhorns Billy Rush put on his engine. Note also the location of the flags. This photograph was the favorite of the late Wilson McCarthy, president of the Rio Grande. *McClure photo.*

"Moonlight Scene on the Moffat" McClure named this beautiful picture which he took just south of Needle's Eye tunnel. This picture was a three-and-a-half hour exposure. The stars were painted in. Such sights caboose crews saw from the original vista domes as they shepherded the freights over the Hill.

The Arrow Turn pauses east of the Corona snowshed for a picture of the neat swath the rotary had recently cut. Old-timers were unable to recognize a newsbutcher or crew member of this extra section which must have picked up some boomers for a crew. *McClure photo.*

Five engine freight with rotary near Sunnyside. This train has crawled just above timberline on the western side thanks to the help of a rotary plow and five locomotives. They should be in Corona in fifteen minutes or less, unless this beautiful day is turned into a howling storm without notice. A mile ahead is Sunnyside with emergency water and coal, plus, more important, an operator, to announce to the world that a blizzard has snagged the top of the world, or that all is still clear the next several miles. *Photo by Allen Gillet, Moffat fireman*

Rotary in deep snow. The snow has stopped blowing, so that the crew can see what they are doing and even pause for a picture. Thanks to those crewmen who carried cameras, most of these pictures are possible. *Bert Smith photo.*

Rotary crew probes for rock. *McClure photo*

West end of shed on blustery day. Clarke took this picture of the west end of the Corona sheds in 1920. One should feel the moisture of the blowing snow on his cheek. The shed has been braced to withstand the next assault. *A. Clarke photo.*

Freight and passenger stalled by ice. Since snow could drift seriously in even fifteen minutes, and every train could not be given a rotary in bad storms, it became the practice to tie the passenger on behind a freight with rotary and five engines. This double headed passenger train was coupled behind the caboose, but the rotary hit ice and derailed and now all is lost as another storm sweeps up out of the valley. *A. Clarke photo.*

Rotary and engine almost buried. This rotary and engine were almost buried but were kept hot by these men who paused a moment to record their battle with the ice that derailed them. The afternoon before, the sun had sent streams of water down the rails until the chill after sunset turned the cuts in the snow into ice-paved roads. Then came the new storm and the call for the rotary which derailed and was swallowed up in a howling blizzard. *A. Clarke photo.*

Shoveling snow in tender. L. H. Myers is shoveling, not coal, but snow. His engine is very low on water and cannot get to the nearest water tank. Tenders had steam pipes to keep the water from freezing. These also melted the snow. If an engine ran out of water and the fires had to be dumped, she would soon have a dozen frozen pipes. Some tie-ups occurred when enginemen did not stop to fill their tenders when all was going well; then, overtaken by a storm, they soon emptied their tenders. The cylindrical object on the tender top is a coal pusher to move the coal down within reach of the fireman. *A. Clarke photo.*

Rotary walking. Three rotary plows kept the hill open. One was almost always in the shop having her blades rebuilt from chewing rocks or trees. Other times the repairs were even more serious. If a derailment blocked the hill so that no rotary could operate for eight hours, the line would have to be dug out, for the cuts would be deeper than the hood of the rotary. *McClure photo.*

Ranch Creek Wye and Water Tower. Rotarys worked above this spot continually in bad weather. *A. L. Johnson collection.*

Almost in the shed. The tragedy of ice on the rail is pictured here. Number 2, protected by rotary plow and four engines, including mallets, goes on the ground a hundred yards from the Corona snowshed. Since the Rollins Pass line had been constructed as a temporary line, it was drained with small plank culverts which quickly froze solid. *A. Clarke photo.*

Rotary out of coal. The ice on the rail has been picked off by gandy dancers who now have trudged back to Corona for sacks of coal to replenish the empty tender of the plow that has business ahead. *A. Clarke photo.*

Snow blockade, 1915! During the delay caused by a derailment, this cut drifted so deep the rotary could not exhaust the snow through its chute. Gandy dancers warmed shovel handles until the roadmaster brought up dynamite to blast snow low enough for rotary to plow it open. Note snow churned by blasting as rotary moves in. *Van Buskirk photo.*

Plow on Devil's Slide trestle east of Corona. This side bridge spanned a slide that dropped hundreds of feet below and made men shudder to think what a derailment would mean here. *Neal R. Miller collection.*

Extra 100. Head Brakeman Barringer was blown off the Moffat and landed a job on the Southern Pacific. Boiler of Engine 100 skyrocketed ahead, leaving the frame and wheels on the track. Explosion occurred on a wintry day above timberline near Dixie Lake. *A. Clarke photo.*

Wreck of 390. The 390 collided with her sister, the 391. The bankers commuter was her work below Tolland in summer. Her last regular job was pulling the Miner's Special from Phippsburg to Oak Creek. *A. Clarke photo.*

Timbering at Tunnel 48, Rock Creek Canyon. The sub-contractor finds himself in rotten granite and is timbering the entrance to the tunnel. Farther in the rock proved hard, but frequently the rock air-slaked, causing rock falls and more timbering. The Rockies breathed day and night and did not like to have their sides tickled by men. Nature fought back so successfully by exerting pressures one way and another that two tunnels in the "tunnel district" were abandoned. *Art Weston photo.*

David Moffat's wife, Frances, in the library of their mansion at 808 Grant Street, Denver. Here she withdrew from public life after his death, for there was heartache caused by those who had failed to help her husband in his hour of crisis even though he had rescued them from panics. The Moffats had not been in the mansion very long. David was away from home desperately trying to save the road. Most of their years were spent in a neat frame home, to which she retreated some years later when the trust fund was unable to keep up the mansion. It was impossible to get to see her and learn the inside story of his betrayal. *State Historical Society of Colorado.*

The two pages on the left are from a D.N.W.&P. folder of the early teens. The D.&S.L. a year later used the identical artwork as shown at the right. *F. Bauer collection.*

David H. Moffat, Jr.—later years. Bronze engraving in State Museum.
State Historical Society of Colorado.

Medicine, Men, and Mallets

Truly, David H. Moffat was the beloved man of northwestern Colorado. He had championed its cause for the need for transportation. The only transportation that could develop the country at that time was a railroad. This Moffat supplied. Their cause had become his cause. His enemies became their enemies.

The railroader was in constant touch with the people along the line in a way that is no longer true today. Moffat had won the respect and esteem of his men, so that they sang his praises all the more.

One person who heard the stories of the personal interest he had in his men was a woman doctor who

Doc Susie Anderson of Fraser, beloved Moffat Railroad doctor. A commercial photographer happened in Cripple Creek, Colorado, the day Susan Anderson was leaving her father and brother to study medicine. She was graduated from the University of Michigan in 1897, but found Denver too conservative to accept her as a doctor. Years later she was accepted in the twelve-house community of Fraser, which was very raw around the edges. She gave her life to the lumberjacks, ranchers, and railroaders of Fraser River Valley as the only doctor living there continuously for fifty years. At the age of ninety her body was worn completely out and was returned, according to her request, to Cripple Creek. She left her never-completed log house at Fraser with its art glass windows, her medical records, and her furniture.

had come to be known as Doc Susie. She had visited Fraser in 1907 for a two-week vacation. She loved the wooded country just as President Ike did fifty years later. That year she returned to Fraser thinking that she had T.B. This was a good place to die. She had been worn out from nursing, since women were readily accepted as nurses but not so easily as doctors. Her first patient was a horse that had been caught in a barbed wire fence. Doc Susie loved all living things except wolves. Though there was a railroad doctor in Fraser, she had the touch of gentleness that mothers are known for. The lumberjacks loved her. The railroaders preferred her.

She carried a loaded six shooter and slept with it under her pillow. She was realistic in the rough country. She never had to use it, even though her graduation picture from college reveals a most beautiful woman. The lumberjacks almost always "threw" a dance for her when she visited their backwoods camps to set a broken leg.

She was a plucky woman—as much at home in the cab of an engine as in her front room office. In this country the only road open in the winter was the path of the railroad. So time and again she was helped into the cab of the lone helper engine that she had hailed down on her errands of mercy. On horseback or on foot in summertime, on skis and snowshoes or sled in the winter, she brought the memory of home back into the hearts of men far removed from their families.

One of the authors had Doc Susie take care of his family time and again and heard from her lips the praise the men gave of David Moffat. He was referred to her by men who had personal contacts as union committeemen working out contracts for the enginemen. George Schryer told how he had asked for a new contract. Mr. Moffat astonished him by pulling out and signing a blank sheet of paper, saying, "Write your own contract. You fellows will not cheat me."

These railroaders had moved to Tabernash about the time David Moffat had died because the division point was established five miles north from Fraser at Tabernash. The wives of these men found Doc Susie a woman after their own hearts, as she brought a taste of better things and even culture to the roughness of this ice-box. There were not the number of wild shots fired in Tabernash that there were in the saloons of Fraser. Young brides did not miss that when their hubbies were up on the Hill and they were in the lonely rooms of a boarding house.

Indeed, Tabernash was and is always from five to ten degrees colder than Fraser. The railroad's first and last Chief Dispatcher, J. B. Culbertson, tells that extreme temperatures of 65° and 70° below zero were reported to him. Not only did the cold slip down, but a haze rose over Tabernash from the steam of nearby sawmills, the many engines and the streams. This haze became the wet blanket that wrapped itself around the journals of standing cars. Wheels froze to the rails in the short time that mallets were cut into the trains. The six-track Tabernash yard had its unbelievable problems, such as how to knock loose a train frozen to the rails.

Eastbound freights came in with one engine called the road engine. At Tabernash a mallet was doubled-headed and two more cut into the train. This was power enough to get a heavy train easily up the two per cent through Fraser to Irving Spur (Winter Park), where two mallets would be waiting to couple in a short distance ahead of the caboose. These engines had dropped down the four per cent from Arrow and stayed there until they were needed at the foot of the four per cent for a freight going up the Hill.

Tabernash was cold because the Fraser River dropped down north from Fraser with the cold that slipped into the Fraser Valley from the peaks around her and from St. Louis Creek. At Tabernash more cold quietly slipped down Crooked Creek and Ranch Creek, which had their confluence there. By this time there was not much chance for anything to have any heat left in it.

So cold was Tabernash that during World War II when the University of Colorado wanted to test an aeroplane engine for the armed services, they set up a testing lab at Tabernash and let the motor drone on for hours, days, and months to see if it could take the cold.

In this arctic-like community regular train crews waited for their run back the next day, helper crews boarded, and machinists made extensive repairs on power. Here man proved that he could take it. All of them lived in hope that Uncle Dave would win out, and they could be rewarded with the best runs on the varnish that would run to the coast.

Doc Susie followed her patients here by sled or helper engine, whichever was most convenient. Here she saw her first 200 engine and was proud to climb into its cab.

Doc Susie once said, "Mr. Bollinger, you should have Mrs. Schryer tell you about the first church service in Tabernash." Number 2 had been held two days in Tabernash while the railroaders were trying to open a blockade. A prominent eastern clergyman was on the train. When Sunday evening came, he suggested that they hold a church service in the coach. As the railroad had only very feeble oil lights, the word was passed around Tabernash to bring hymn books and hay-burners (lanterns). With a rancher or two, railroaders and passengers crowded in that coach with lanterns hung from the baggage racks. The people thumbed the indexes of their different hymnals finding the hymns common to most of the song books. A quartette, composed of Conductor Charlie Clarke, Bob Parrott, the Negro porter from the Pullman car, and one other man whose name is forgotten, led the singing. After the clergyman had preached the sermon and the lanterns had burned dim from the lengthy singing, a Negro spiritual was begun by the Negro: "Some folks say that a preacher don't steal, but I found one in my corn field." The eastern clergyman held his sides as he laughed. The benediction was sung. The first religious service had been held in Tabernash in a railroad coach.

The coach was warm that night. They rarely had a long train in the winter. It would have been tough to keep the steam line from freezing in a tie-up at Tabernash, if the train had many coaches.

It is part of our American ballyhoo and way of doing things to have the longest bridges, the tallest buildings, and the most powerful engines. Nothing is more characteristic of the Moffat than the two-engines-in-one, 200 class mallets (or "Malleys" as they were nicknamed) built by the American Locomotive Company after the style of "Old Maude" of the Baltimore and Ohio.

The first 200 engine was ordered in November of 1908, as the rails were being pushed by Colonel

Dodge into Steamboat. Enthusiasm was running high among the railroad men, so that these engines were greeted royally as the most powerful in Colorado.

A mallet has two sets of drive wheels; the first can swing under the boiler to enable the engines to go around curves. You'll recall the Moffat had plenty of sharp, sixteen-degree curves on the branch line over the Hill, with plenty of four per cent grades. When these engines were delivered, they were of the 0-6-6-0 type having 55 inch drivers, weighed 181 tons, and had a tractive power of 76,400 pounds. They cost $33,045.

Engine 200 immediately replaced a six-wheel switch engine and a consolidation which had been used to push the rotary. The 200 was a preeminently successful locomotive, except that it needed a pony truck placed ahead of the front engine. This was added. Two more mallets were acquired the next year, the sisters being made from the same plans and

patterns with a consequent reduction in cost to $29,805.

But with the increased size of engines came the increased difficulty in re-railing them. The Moffat had hesitated to buy a wrecking crane because of financial difficulties. The much-feared jam came on a February day, when Engine 201 got out of control above Antelope (on the east side of the Continental Divide) and turned over on her side with the tender and three freight cars shooting through the air like sky rockets, trimming the tops off the trees.

For several days freight was carried around the wrecked 201, and passengers had to walk around the monster that lay helplessly on its side. Officials wanted to save the expense of renting a wrecker. A method used on small railroads and on the narrow-gauge lines to right an engine was the use of block and tackle tied to anchors buried in the ground. But could this monster be re-railed this way?

George Barnes, trainmaster at this time, had used the method on many occasions; so the job was hand-

Mallet 201. Note headlamp protection prior to shipment from Schenectady. *Alco photo, Schenectady History Center.*

ed to him. He arrived to find the anchors poorly located. The section men growled when they were asked to dig new holes in the frozen ground. It was a bitter cold morning. Other officials added to the usual confusion. George Barnes, however, had complete authority. He used it. The heavy engine was slowly lifted to its feet.

The impossible was accomplished without a wrecker. Superintendent Deuel said, "Barnes, you have re-railed the largest locomotive in the state." Barnes thought he might have done the job better if he had cut a rail. There was a tradition, long before established by an earlier roadmaster, that no rail would be cut before they got to Salt Lake City. Barnes accomplished the feat of re-railing the giant

without breaking the tradition. The frame of this engine was broken in nine places.

Indeed those old 200 mallets could tell many a story about George Barnes and all the things they had to do under his orders out on the line.

The mallets caused a great deal of trouble when they got off the track. Engine 207, for example, derailed going down the four per cent after having gone through Needle's Eye Tunnel (Number 32) on the east side. It would have been simple pulling her back on the rails, if she could have been pulled down hill.

Unfortunately, she had taken off at too severe an angle on the shelf road to do this. The only thing that could be done was to set rail-high blocks on the ties and then drag the 200 mallet up the four per cent across the frogs that were spiked down.

Cab of the 201. What a Herculean task faced the fireboy who had to shovel fifteen tons of coal a night through these hand-operated firedoors. *Alco photo, Schenectady History Center.*

Cab of the 212. The later "Malleys" incorporated much additional piping, and the firedoors were air operated. *Alco photo, Schenectady History Center.*

Several mallets were brought down from Corona to pull the 207 back on the rails. But since the 207 was on the ballast and ties, she seemed permanently anchored. The mallets could only spin their wheels.

More engines were called out of Tabernash and run up to Corona and on down to the derailment. When eight engines had finally been coupled behind the 207 she gave up her stubborn fight to stay off the rails and block the line.

On another occasion Engine 208 derailed in a wrestling match with a snowslide at the sharp curve below the Loop. Sid Kane was at the throttle with fireman Tom Conway. As they were running low on water, the only thing that could be done was to shovel snow into her tank. Roadmaster Paul Paulson ordered his section men to go into the tank and shovel the snow back in the tender away from the manhole. It got stifling hot in there from the heating pipes that were provided to keep the tank from freezing solid. The section boys claimed Sid Kane and his fireman, Tom Conway, were having it entirely too easy shoveling the snow in the manhole, so the crew traded places and got into the tank.

It was about midnight. Nels Johnson came off the Loop with another 200 engine and pulled in behind the 208. Nels and his fireman, Pinky Lewis of Phippsburg, started setting frogs under the derailed engine. The safety valves of Nels' engine were popping on and off so that when Pinky and Nels turned around the side of their engine to pick up another frog, they did not hear any unusual noise. When they returned with the frog, the 208 was gone. She was seven hundred feet down the mountainside, having been swept by a second slide of treacherous wet March snow that had piled up in the form of a cone on the cliffs above.

Nels and Pinky, together with George Schryer and his fireman, started hollering down, just in case a miracle had happened and someone would be alive.

Tom Conway and Sid Kane climbed out of the engine tank, which had fortunately landed right side up. Risking their lives in the spot where two slides had occurred that night, Nels Johnson and Pinky Lewis slid down the steep mountainside to help the two men climb up the very slippery wall.

Ten Wheeler 303. This trim beauty was the road's only custom-built engine, and was designed by George Thompson, Moffat's Master Mechanic. Built by Alco in 1910, she was caught in the Moffat Denver station yard by Dick Kindig in 1939. Her 34,150 pounds tractive effort was just a little less than half that of the 200's, and for that reason the 303 saw mainly passenger service. This engine was scrapped in 1948 after the Rio Grande integration. *Dick Kindig photo.*

Mallet 208 in snow at bottom. Only by extreme good fortune is this hurried snapshot of the derailed 208 available. Taken early the morning after the wreck, it shows the debris seven hundred feet below the rails. The boiler, rear engine, and cab are at the left, the tender in the center, and the front engine at the right. Fellow trainmen risked their lives climbing down the near vertical wall to render assistance. The ramp built down the mountainside to recover the engine is clearly visible to this day. *A. Clarke photo.*

Nels acknowledged that if it had not been for the fact that the boys had suffered only slight scratches, as they slushed around in the two feet of snow and water inside the tank, they would never have gotten the men up, a difficult task even in the summer time.

Roadmaster Paul Paulson and the section men could not be found. They were apparently buried under the snow at the bottom of the slide. One man was found dead two hours later. Nels Johnson went back to the Loop telephone to call in the news of the disaster. The rescued engine crew, meanwhile, had been put in the caboose of the freight train that had come down off the Hill. Here they thawed out and rested.

That night the men attempted to shove slim poles down through the snow to locate the bodies. By morning the search for the men was taken up in earnest, with reinforcements arriving. The men on hand were exhausted from exposure and the altitude. Charlie Johnson was among those who had arrived. He had been caught in a similar slide and rescued only by shoving a long two-man wood-saw through the snow, for the saw's teeth would catch on the clothing of the men.

A telephone call was sent to Fraser for all the saws that could be found. An engine rushed these saws up to the spot, while valuable time passed. When the engine arrived one handle of each saw was taken off. That end was shoved through the deep snow

and the men carefully sawed through the snow. Several bodies were revealed. It was, however, a week later before the last body was secured. The pet dog of one of the men had been brought out of Denver, in hope that it could smell his master.

With this story in the papers of the nation, the following story understandably got started. A Middle Park woman had taken Number 2 out of Grand County for Denver. The train was running on a night schedule at that time. The lights within the Pullman were out. This good woman awakened just as the train crawled by the spot where the disaster had occurred. The spring moonlight of Easter season illuminated the scene, and she beheld coffins lined along the right of way for the bodies they hoped to find. The combination of moonlight, fresh snow, and a sudden awakening produced the story, but the coffins were only railroad ties.

Engine 208 was left for many months where she had fallen. As the engine and tender had landed right side up, she appeared to have just run to her resting place. A ramp was therefore built down to her on a thirty-degree grade. Rails were spiked down the ramp and piles driven at the top with anchors placed. An engine came up. George Schryer was at the throttle of the mallet that pulled her up by the aid of block-and-tackle arrangements. George simply had to pinch off the air and let the weight of his mallet raise the 208 inch by inch. When she had reached the top, she was blocked and a switch spiked in. The job was over. Those who

Plow down the mountain. There is no more useless piece of equipment in the world than a rotary hundreds of feet down a slope from the track. Extreme caution was required of the crews to prevent such occurrences. A ramp was built to retrieve this runaway. See appendix travel guide for location. *A. Clarke collection.*

drive up the west side of the old right of way to Corona today can still see the rotting ramp by walking down the old right of way from the Loop.

It seemed that the 200 engines tried to outdo one another in the pranks that they pulled. On December 5, 1924, the 210 had helped a freight up the hill and was sent back to Tabernash following ten minutes behind two other mallets, the 206 with George Schryer at the throttle and the 204 with Bert Clarke at the throttle. When Schryer looked back as he dropped over the Loop Trestle and saw the 210 gaining on them, he opened up his throttle and came off the Hill a little faster. He was running quite fast when he passed Loop siding. He dashed into the Loop tunnel and sped on down to Ranch Creek, where he had a wait order for another train. As the 210 was included in the wait order, the line was tied up until the 210 showed up. They waited and waited.

Finally, they went to the telephone to talk to the dispatcher. About this time Tom Carr, who was the engineer of the 210, came on the phone. His story was that near Sunnyside, the 210 had stripped herself as a drive rod broke and cleaned off all the air pipes, so that there were no air brakes or air reverse gear to control the monster. He and his fireman immediately unloaded while she was still moving slowly at about ten miles an hour. The 210 soon ran wild; George Schryer knew immediately that was why he had observed her gaining on him.

Tom Carr said he ran on down beyond Sunnyside until he could see both tracks of the Loop, and there below both of them lay the 210, which had hurled itself from the upper level, bounced on the right of way at the lower level, and then gone on over the cliff to her final resting place.

George Schryer fully believes that the 210 must have almost jumped on top of his engine. He figured that the noise of their driving rods had prevented him from hearing the 210 jump. George and Bert could not have been more than two minutes away from disaster.

Some say the boiler blew up when the 210 did this marvelous broad jump. Others violently disagree. In any event, a mass of wreckage lay below track level near the Rifle Sight Notch tunnel. A ramp was built down and the boiler and engines were run up the ramp and taken to the shops to become parts of other engines. The rest of the locomotive was not salvaged and was simply left to rust where she lay.

The 200's are a legend of slow-moving bull-dog type power that rarely slipped their drive wheels. The Moffat mallets were built to run twenty miles per hour and could do thirty-five. According to Master Mechanic Fisher they were not excessive in repair work. The Moffat Railroad originally ordered twelve mallets (200-211) and five more (212-216) were delivered just before World War I. The opening of Moffat Tunnel found the D.&S.L. with more than sufficient motive power.

Cab of Mallet 210. When this photograph of the 210 was taken, the numerals were still on the cab side. One of the writers has the steam dome of this engine at his home; someone else beat him to the idea of cutting off the numerals. Souvenirs can be picked up today, for some of her junk is still there—even to the cab curtains. The ramp can also be seen. *A. Clarke photo.*

The Road Ends at Craig

With the death of Moffat, who would champion the line? There was business at Craig that needed the line extended. W. G. Evans had been the vice president of the road from the beginning. As the new president, he hoped that some of the men Moffat had been talking with would come through. A railroad promoter by the name of Newman Erb stepped forward saying that he was sure he could interest Dr. George S. Pearson of London, England, to come to Colorado to see for himself. Erb assured the Denver Northwestern and Pacific investors that he would furnish half the money to build the Craig extension.

Upon his promise to secure half the funds required to extend the road from Steamboat Springs to Craig in Moffat County, Erb was elected president. The fact that he had no money of his own must have worried the Moffat investors, but their

Mallet 210 before she took her famous nose-dive. New and shiny, she rests on the grounds of the American Locomotitve Company in 1913. *Alco photo, Schenectady History Center.*

hour was at hand and they could not be choosey. Two million dollars were required to reach Craig, and Denver investors (principally Phipps, Dodge, Porter, and Hughes) promptly raised their quota. Erb, however, failed to come through so that when construction did start, Colorado money was responsible. The rails inched toward Mt. Harris, seventeen miles from Steamboat, to tap new coal mines there. The coal business, however, was developing too slowly. With unfailing optimism the promoters expected the deficit to be overcome, but they found time is required to develop a raw country.

The Craig extension of the line passed by the famous Cary Ranch in October, 1913. This ranch had 2,700 acres of irrigated land and 11,300 acres of pasture. At one time there were supposed to have been three hundred registered standard bred Percheron and Oldenberg coach horses, 4,000 registered Shorthorn and Hereford cattle, as well as Berkshire hogs from the best blood in England. The ranch had a complete waterworks system and an acetylene gas lighting system.

John S. Cary and Robert Cary of the Mine and Smelter Supply Company used this place as a dude ranch to entertain their guests and prospective customers for mining supplies.

The railroad was still trying to get financial aid to extend the line beyond Craig, where it stopped in November, 1913. Mr. Weston's prospectus, a sixty-two page booklet, had gone into another edition in 1914, telling in particular about the tremendous values of coal.

When it was seen that the first train into Craig would arrive late in the 1913 football season, the two coaches of the rival high schools of Craig and Hayden were delighted to arrange a game. So a new feature was added to Moffat Railroad Days. But an unwanted visitor arrived—SNOW. This very wet snow made the countryside a sea of ugly mud. The local newspapers carried a fine account of that November day.

In the weeks that followed, stories were printed about the new sources of financing. But the road ended at Craig. Events were transpiring now which would threaten to end the road.

In 1915 the great London banker Pearson did come to Colorado. He rode in Moffat's private car to Craig. He was impressed. He said he would go back to London and dispose of his Mexican Central interest and complete the line to Salt Lake.

Hopes were high again.

The ship Dr. Pearson sailed on was the *Lusitania*. The German U-boat sank the hopes of the line.

Newman Erb was not able to secure any other financial interest. World War I had the Allies in a death struggle. Erb had to resign September 16, 1917.

Charles Boettcher became the new president. He and the men who had reorganized the road were Senator Lawrence C. Phipps, Sr., and his son Lawrence C. Phipps, Jr., and Gerald Hughes. These men were determined to make something out of their investment.

But the same U boat that triggered off the war also developed the coal fields as the American economy stretched itself to accomplish a gigantic battle. The war caused an unprecedented demand for coal that was in part met by the Yampa coal fields. This gave the Moffat a tremendous increase in traffic. The continued drain on finances from snow fighting over Rollins Pass had taken forty per cent of the entire income of the railroad, so that bond holders were becoming more and more restless.

With the demand for coal, no one dared think of scrapping the line during the war except the regional U. S. director of railroads. Thus the Yampa

Mallet 200—later years, with a pony truck. As the years went by, changes came to the Moffat and to the Moffat engines. Dick Kindig took this picture of the original 200 at Utah Junction in November, 1947. Comparing it with the photograph of the same engine as it was being delivered in Denver exactly thirty-nine years earlier, we notice that the pilot has been lengthened and wheels added, the headlight lowered, generator and whistle relocated, and the tender completely renovated with sideboards, doghouse, and improved trucks. *R. H. Kindig photo.*

Here's what it was like, decorating the tops on the Hill. "Cut in two" is the signal being passed as the mallets grind to a halt approaching Corona. The sixteen-hour law was not observed on the Moffat until a much later date. Men have worked without relief as long as ninety hours at a time under conditions like these, and worse. The high altitude caused a man to be in agony for his breath if he ran a hundred feet. He had to walk these icy planks to set hand brakes as regulations required on every train. The severe

Slide in west end of Gore, 1915. The "canyon of eternal troubles" might well be the name given this place after fifty-five years of struggle. Moffat operating men wished the Road had been built over Gore Pass, but this would have denied the Moffat the Dotsero Cutoff. *Allin Gillett photo.*

coal fields were expanded after the fashion that Moffat and Dodge had hoped for eight years previously. But without a Main Range Tunnel, the road continued to go in the red. The men went on strike tying up the line. They had $180,000 coming in back wages. The cost of living had skyrocketed. The terrible privations that the men suffered over the Hill in winter did not leave them in a good mood to receive only part pay for their work. Bondholders resented that their money was hopelessly tied up in the road, for men with money were making the enormous profits of war time speculation.

July 13, 1918, the Denver papers carried headlines announcing—"U. S. Comes to Aid of Moffat Road With $1,300,000." Sub headlines read, "Rail Administration to Take First Line Receivers Certificates to Advance Cash, to Wipe Out Bills, and Leave Million for Betterments."

Denver was awakening to the danger of the Moffat being torn up immediately following the war emergency, when the roads were expected to be returned to the owners.

Businessmen and civic leaders formed a committee headed by W. G. Evans, that reported to the Federal Rail Board in Washington. Again the papers carried such headlines as "Report Filed Shows Great Rail Need in Northwest Colorado." The later development of Rangely oil field is delayed proof of this truth.

The war ended. The Moffat had business that she never had had before. But the deficit in 1918 had been $1,067,057.11. Bill Freeman, co-receiver, had "hung the road together with baling wire," as the boys said, so that this deficit was cut to $956,-282.96 in 1919, and to $670,519.19 the following year. During those three years, the deficit incurred through Rollins Pass alone could almost have paid

First train to Hayden. The railroad has come! The residents of Hayden turned out to see the first train just after a midsummer rain in 1913. The celebration was made all the more successful when the train backed out of town and reentered, whistle screaming, for this lyrical shot of early twentieth-century railroading. Behind the engine were three flats loaded with ties, a caboose, and two coaches. Folks nodded and agreed a new era was coming to Colorado. *F. R. Carpenter collection.*

Cowmen meet first train. A close-up of the first train to enter Hayden, Colorado. The engine is off the picture to the left. Hayden was in cattle country and the early-time cowmen were much in evidence. Note the signal light on the top of the caboose, used by the Moffat until about 1915. Farrington R. Carpenter as a college lad came out to spend his summers working on the neighboring Cary Ranch. He worked his way up to ownership of his own ranch and leadership in the life of the state. Hayden, which had originally been laid out with the promise of the half-way division point between Denver and Salt Lake, ended up as the post office for Carpenter. *F. R. Carpenter collection.*

for the originally planned Main Range Tunnel. The coal bill during the war to pull trains over Rollins Pass was $2,000 a day.

All kinds of rumors got into the press as the Bankers Trust Company of New York got restless.

January 1, 1920, Denver citizens read this headline—"Consolidation of Line Makes Nation Cross Roads Center. Burlington Main Factor With Tunnel Either Under James Peak or Berthoud." The Berthoud Pass route was considered the shortest. It necessitated either the rebuilding of the Colorado and Southern narrow gauge through Idaho Springs, or a complete relocation to the 3.5 mile tunnel site under Berthoud.

Anyone with an idea was able to find some newspaper reporter who could make copy out of it. One story that made headlines was a far fetched tale about how the Georgetown Loop line was to be extended beyond Silver Plume connecting with the Breckenridge and Dillon line. A new line was to be built down the Blue to Kremmling. This most outlandish line would have necessitated the straightening out of a most crooked narrow gauge, rebuilding every bridge, and laying all new ties and heavy rails in making it standard gauge.

Craig layout. With its last gasp, the Moffat Road reached Craig, the final burial ground for David Moffat's hopes to reach Salt Lake. A trim brick depot was constructed. About 9:30 on a summer morning No. 2 waits in front of the station to go east, a 200 mallet stands beside the gilsonite shed, and No. 11, the Hog-and-Human, rests on the wye after its all-night run from Denver. Sheep wool is stacked in right center. The Hog-and-Human incorporated the country's only combination Pullman-coach car. *L. J. Daly photo.*

The Road Ends at Craig

Moffat men and counties supported by the Moffat had their hopes kept up, but most of it was only newspaper talk. The last serious attempt to complete the Moffat had been by the Rock Island which in 1910 had caused extensive estimates to be made.

Moffat men were beginning to wonder if A. C. Ridgway had not been right when he said, in leaving the road, that "it is going to be a graveyard for railroad men." Many men left the line, seeking jobs elsewhere. Such headlines as came out October 26, 1921, encouraged this. "Moffat Road Again Menaced in New Move to Junk Line." November 4, the men were made restless by this announcement in headlines—"System Faces $2,500,000 Deficit. High Wages Responsible—According to Freeman and Others Involved in Suit."

But high wages were not responsible. It was the money that should have gone into a 2.6 mile Main Range Tunnel that was putting the line in the red.

October 26, 1921, the *Denver Post* carried an article announcing that "The Bankers Trust Company of New York, trustee for the bondholders, petitioned District Judge Samuel W. Johnson of Brighton to shut down the road at once, unless wage scales and operating costs are reduced to 'a basis adequately remunerative for the proper conservation and upbuilding of property.'" The story was continued that "the line was losing about a million a year."

The court answered that it "is not going to say

Moffat's private car, *Marcia,* at Craig. President Wilson McCarthy felt that David Moffat's car should be restored and turned over to the City of Craig if they would accept it and take care of it. This Craig did, making it the permanent headquarters for their Chamber of Commerce. *Denver and Rio Grande photo.*

Interior of the *Marcia*. Prospective investors were time and again shown the unfinished line and told of its potential in this very room. Likewise the loneliness of defeat was borne here by a man who had saved others who would not lift their fingers to help him. *Denver & Rio Grande photo.*

the wages paid are unreasonable, until evidence has been introduced. . . . The Moffat Road ought to pay as good wages as any other road similarly situated."

November 25, 1921, the morning papers announced that the Moffat road was to close her shops in an effort to reduce expenses.

The court case went on and news came that the receiver might ask for the right to cut wages twenty per cent, as the receiver had only a few days to make a showing to the court that the line could be operated without a loss. Freeman further asked the right to reduce passenger service to tri-weekly.

The fall was mild, so that little coal was ordered by Moffat company patrons, cutting down the amount mined and shipped out of the Routt County fields over the Moffat. It seemed the very gods were against the Moffat continuing any longer.

One did not have to be a high-salaried man to figure out that, though the road was saving $2,000 a day with the shops closed, a payoff was coming when the line would be crippled from run-down equipment. As evidence of where the road would soon be, Friday morning's paper told that three engines were smashed in a collision in Corona snowsheds between a freight train and helper engine. How long could the line operate with closed shops?

The *Denver News* carried a challenging article on December 18, 1921, by the editor of the *Steamboat Pilot* of Steamboat Springs. Charles Leckenby wrote that "the matter that has worried the northwest part of the state is the evident fact that there is something on foot, apparently something agreed upon affecting our interests, of which we are not informed and can obtain no information.

"Wages were reduced approximately twenty percent, time and a half for overtime was abrogated, as likewise the double time service for operation over the twenty-seven miles of excessive grade on the Hill.

Plow train overtaken at Jenny Lake. The D.N.W.& P. operated weeks of sunny days when the deep snow melted. This plow was called out to remove a slide. The overturned Chicago and Alton gondola is typical of the troubles that came to the Hill. Rather than tie the line up in rerailing, this car was just shoved off until there was time to pick it up on a sunny day. The plow crew were specialists in general trouble shooting. *F. A. Van Vrankin photo.*

"Arbitrary closing of coal mines of the Moffat road territory amounting practically to a lockout has prevented the receiver from showing during the limitation of time allowed him for showing a balance on the right side of the ledger. This may be taken advantage of to show the court that the Moffat road is an insolvent and impossible utility."

In these statements are held the fears and thinking and pondering of the rancher, coal miner, and merchant of northwest Colorado.

December 21 the *Post* carried the headline "Moffat Railway Granted a New Lease on Life at Brighton Court Hearing. Freeman and Boettcher Given Another Chance to Operate as Conditions Better."

Eight days later Charles H. Leckenby sent out a striking call. "If Colorado and especially Denver permit the junking or the passing of the Moffat road, this catastrophe will mark the rise and fall of the great city and the greatest state. . . .

"Is not there one real unselfish, courageous hero left among us?

"If there be, let him step forward and we will follow. And we will not desert, and we will not run away. Who is the man of the hour?"

The Moffat road may have been a bottomless pit to financiers for only one reason: sacrifices of those who began a line were not backed up by adequate capital, which existed within the state. If the three or four million needed to construct the Main Range Tunnel had been provided in the days of Colonel Dodge, when Moffat had a heavy heart because of business acquaintances who refused to back him in Denver, we would have seen in the Moffat a financially sound road, even though it might never have been completed to Salt Lake.

Coal business saved the D.&S.L. This trains climbs the one per cent grade through Gore Canyon. Note that the second engine is cut in the string of gondolas. Old box cars were used to haul coal. The road's color was black for all equipment except passenger cars. The first cabooses were red but were repainted black. *L. J. Daly photo.*

The originally surveyed Main Range Tunnel was reached by a continuation of the two per cent grade to an elevation of 9,930 feet. There were no curves over ten degrees except possibly one or two twelve-degree curves. This 2.6-mile tunnel was below the elevation where terrible winds and drifting snows tied up the line.

The twenty years' fight against the grades, curves, and blizzards of Rollins Pass proved that the blockades occurred higher than this tunnel. The Ranch Creek wye (10,200 feet) and the Spruce wye (10,-990 feet) were well above 10,000 feet and it was between these two wyes that the rotaries chewed their way continuously in bad storms. It must also be remembered that the temporary branch line was not provided with ample drainage to handle water freezing in culverts and running over the tracks, as would have been provided by the line to the proposed tunnel.

H. A. Sumner himself recommended that this tunnel be built, considering the density of traffic expected. Had such a tunnel been in operation as late as 1910, the Moffat would have weathered the financial storms without the loss of the average fifty days a winter. With the road paying dividends, it is entirely conceivable that capital might have been interested in completing the line. Modern power would have handled that elevation through the tunnel just as satisfactorily as Soldier Summit is fought and Tennessee Pass (10,240 feet) is operated on the Rio Grande today. The money to accomplish all of this went out in useless snow fighting.

The Moffat was saved by the wage cuts. Freeman was given a chance to hold the road together. Leckenby came back from the court case to tell the inside story that no railroad was seriously considering buying the Moffat and that every one should back Freeman, as there had been entirely too little cooperation by everyone in any way involved with the Moffat.

Under David Moffat as president and under W.

Pump station at Coal Creek. The water tank at Coal Creek trestle was supplied by this steam pump station. Note the chute that brought coal down from a way freight. *McClure photo.*

A. Deuel as general manager from 1910 to 1913, a devotion was built up by the men for the road. Joe Culbertson said the feeling of the men was that they would go to hell for Colonel Deuel. No wages ever paid a gandy dancer could get them out in the storms, but W. A. Deuel could, for he was just one of his men. Now with Bill Freeman as president and general manager, the men were driven and their devotion began to ebb. It is a wonder that they had any devotion left at all. But the Moffat was in their blood, as steel cars and engines rarely were, for the road was Dave Moffat and Colonel Deuel and northwest Colorado.

The board of directors never seriously questioned Freeman's ability and held him in high esteem. So did the press picture him when he retired. The un-

fortunate fact is that the Moffat boys took a loss that they never gained back.

Many men sought other railroads. Their places were taken by "boomers," most of whom had been fired for inefficiency on other lines and could no longer secure a job on a decent line.

The Moffat was saved but at a terrible price paid by the men who operated the line. Coal and oil saved the Moffat. Freeman juggled the repairs and improvements to paper thinness to keep the road going. The men paid for the snow fighting out of their low wages. Thus, when we say that the road was saved from scrap by the increase in the coal business and the discovery of oil, we add the ability of President Freeman "to take food out of the bellies of the men by the low wages he paid." These

The photo shows the combination of freight power used most frequently—a five engine train with rotary plow, consolidation engine and mallet in the lead, two mallets in the center, and one cut in several cars ahead of the caboose. The photo was taken in 1911 of a freight 300 feet from the Corona shed and is from the collection of Neal Miller.

Texaco oil over Corona. There was coal to haul, and there was oil. Oil had long been known to exist in northwestern Colorado. It was brought into production in 1918 and shipped over the line in solid trainloads until the completion of a pipeline years later. This photograph served as the inspiration of a Texaco calendar of the Twenties. The scene would appear to be near Sunnyside with Corona in the distance. Later the Rangely oil field and extensive deposits of oil shale proved the vision of Moffat to be correct. In more recent years, the authors have witnessed the dismantling of oil shipping facilities at Craig as business was diverted from the railroad to the pipeline. *L. J. Daly photo.*

men gave up twenty per cent of their wages, time and a half for overtime, and double time for working on the Hill. Thus their pay dropped far below the money other mountain railroads paid.

The hope to get the Moffat to Salt Lake was dead. The road had ended at Craig, together with Moffat's magnificent way of dealing with men.

Boilers of 208 and 214 (?). Remember, man, that "thou art dust, and into dust thou shalt return." Gen. 3:19. To this ignominious end as a stationery boiler at Oriental Refinery Company, Denver, Colorado, came two of the proud 200's. (208 & 214?) *Photo May, 1952, by Gordon Rogers.*

A plow train rounding Ptarmigan Point, ascending the home stretch to Corona in 1920. James R. Harvey, later Assistant Colorado State Historian, writes of his experiences: "How well do I remember firing one of the five big engines that were pushing a snow plow all night at far below zero and on up and up to Corona and of many and many another time after shoveling my fifteen tons of coal in a matter of five hours and then to have to jerk the fires (and fast) because of running out of water with the expectation of the boiler blowing up any minute. And I remember that winter back in 1914; the elements (snow, cold, grade, snow-slides, altitude) beat us more times than we overcame them." *A. Clarke photo.*

Improved Operations

As the Twenties wore on, financial conditions on the Moffat improved but little. If they did improve, it was only because maintenance was neglected and every expense cut to the bone. Nevertheless, the picture brightened because the men learned to bring the Hill under control.

Even in the earlier days of the Moffat, shortcuts had been found to overcome some of the obstacles. Here is an example. When the road first began operation and for many years thereafter, sidings were too short even for the short trains operated. Now, a meet on a single track line with sidings shorter than the trains is, at best, inconvenient and, at worst, potentially dangerous. When you add the physical environment and realize that such meets were a common occurrence, the beauty of the simple solution will be evident.

A signal light was rigged on top of each caboose and operated from the cupola. These box-like structures can be seen on most of the early photographs. When a meet was planned, the engineer would pull into a siding as far as he could. The conductor might then discover that several cars and his caboose were not in the clear. He would—hurriedly, no doubt—set the signal box indication to red. His engineer would understand, and leave the engine headlight on full.

The opposing train would have knowledge of the meet by train orders, of course. Upon seeing the lighted engine waiting in the siding, the approaching train would know that the main was still fouled and the second engineer would stop his train before getting to the end of the siding. The train in the siding could then pull around, or saw by if both were long.

On the other hand, if the caboose got in the clear on the siding, the conductor would arrange his caboose signal light to show green through the box. His engineer would then turn out his headlight, and the train they were to meet could charge on down the line knowing that the main was clear.

This is a system that must have made hearts skip a beat more than once. It was fraught with peril. Nevertheless, it did enable the struggling little line to save its resources for further extension, even though a peril was put upon the men. We cannot say when this system dropped out of use, but photographs of the late 1910's and early 1920's no longer show the signal boxes; so the obvious safety hazards must have convinced the Operating Department that longer sidings were a must. The caboose on the frontispiece painting is equipped with this device.

In the days of Vice President and General Manager W. E. Morse, a method had been found to untangle the blockades that developed when the Hill got snowed under. The "method" was Barnes—who was made aware of it when he was in a caboose card game at Arrow. The operator brought in a bulletin proclaiming that Barnes was "dispatcher extraordinary" in charge of everything west of Tolland. George said to his friends, "Just hand over everything you have. I am your new boss."

Barnes' success came from the fact that he, himself, had operated over, and knew, every foot of track on the Hill and on the line. He realized that one of the primary problems on the Hill was that of personnel. Crews out of Tabernash would be held up by slides or blockades and be exhausted by the time they reached Denver. Very often the line would be blocked when the crews were in Denver, or on their way back. Tabernash would thus have the need for men when the men were elsewhere.

Barnes immediately began sending the crews east out of Tabernash over the worst part of the Hill to Ladora or some other siding. Here the engine and caboose were uncoupled and quickly run back over the hill and down to Tabernash. In this manner the sidings beyond the worst part of the Hill were filled with trains, which could be picked up by crews originating out of Denver.

It was during one of these battles with snow that a boomer brakeman in disgust at the Moffat said,

Engine 300. Note the crew signal light on the caboose cupola and the wooden end sills. Engine 300 rests at Phippsburg before being called to pull Number 2 back to Denver. The hostler crew has filled her tender with Oak Creek coal, but has not taken the time to wipe the soot off. The tunnels of Egeria Canyon will soon have her smeared again, just as the men who serviced her remained wedded to waste, dirty gloves, and ugly overalls. To understand the Moffat tunnels one needs to spend a day working in a tunnel dodging trains, side-stepping holes in the gutter, and ending up with a cinder in an inflamed eye and hands that seven wash basins of water will not clean. *A. Clarke photo.*

"The only reason they made the line standard gauge was to enable them to borrow cars from other roads." The Moffat was short on cars, but under Freeman and his master mechanic, Charlie Peterson, she became the best equipped road in the world to fight snow. The severity of the storms and the length of the blockades necessitated the best snow-fighting equipment. The Moffat's entire security was tied up in its ability to battle snow.

Any delay that would tie up the line so that the rotaries could not make their rounds for eight hours during a storm was almost certain to precipitate a blockade. If the snow got over twelve feet deep, the rotary was unable to handle a drift until it had been lowered to that depth by dynamiting and shoveling.

The sudden changes in temperature between a sunny spring afternoon, when the sun blistered through the thin high-altitude air, and the low temperature to which the thermometer plummeted a degree a minute after sunset, caused rails to snap. The rails would be surrounded by ice, leaving only a groove for the flange of the wheels. The ball (top of the rail) would break off when the warm morning sun struck the exposed part of the rail, while the lower part was buried in twenty-to-forty-below-

zero ice. The fact that trains moved only ten miles an hour saved many a serious wreck. When a new rail had to go in, the rail would be tied behind an engine and dragged to the place. The section crew walked in the light of the rear headlight, which was left on. Oh, what a life the section men put in on the Hill! Shoveling snow, crawling under derailed cars, picking ice out to put in a new rail, freezing as they worked, huddling by a fire made of kindling and kerosene. Yes, Bill Freeman's gandy dancers led a terrible life on a twenty-per-cent cut in wages.

The most serious problem was ice forming on the rails. By the time the winter was half over the ice had formed solid between the rails leaving a groove next to the rail, which the section men kept picked open. The track looked like city paving around a street car line. Then a warm spring day would come and the water would run. The culverts were plank affairs not more than eight inches square because they had been built only as a temporary measure. These soon froze full of ice. Thus with the poor drainage provided for the line and the enormous quantities of water that would run, the ice filled

Page 150

Crawling into Corona shed. Corona operator Ben Stone took this monumental photograph of a plow train, with the rotary and four engines visible, nearing Corona from the west. This single epic picture is a composite of this entire book. To get any coherent story of these great blockades, which cut off Middle Park and the northwestern part of Colorado entirely from the rest of the world, is not easy. The battles were so hard on the men that, in the words of F. A. VanVranken, the oldest conductor, "I don't want to remember it. I want to forget it."

Two trains above Sunnyside. This picture was taken from the caboose of a descending freight train by conductor L. J. Daly.

From Fraser to Tabernash field glasses and telescopes were turned toward the Hill when the clouds lifted. Wives, mothers, and sweethearts watched the smoke of plow trains trying to break through. Prayers were offered for the safety of the men, who were exposed to rock slides, privations, and sickness. Although these two pictures were not taken from Fraser, they do show the vista of distant smoke against the white landscape. The upper picture was taken from the caboose of a freight descending the Loop and shows one freight rounding Ptarmigan Point with another five-engine drag following. The lower view includes the Loop, two engines on the Loop trestle, and Tunnel 33 directly below them, as seen from Ptarmigan Point. *Upper—L. J. Daly; lower Neal Miller collection.*

the groove for the flanger, and the engine derailed.

When we behold the enormous culverts Berthoud highway has built in the years since then, we see the problem. Even these culverts freeze solid.

During a blockade, while men were hand picking the rails clean around the Loop, the track nearer the pass drifted deep with ten feet or more of snow and the ice would form under the snow over the rails as high as ten inches, as it built up day after day. All the men that could be coaxed off Larimer Street in Denver would be put on the Hill to pick snow in great extra gangs.

A rotary plow was helpless on ice. There was simply a derailment to handle besides the ice to pick. The worst thing that could happen would be for the rotary to derail. If the derailment required the big hook, it would be hours before it arrived. How could the wrecker get over a snow-choked line unless another rotary was on the right side of the derailed rotary?

The derailment of a car necessitating a wrecker was certain to cause a long delay that would turn into a blockade if heavy snow continued to fall. If we are to picture the Divide, we picture continuous snow, not just one storm, but continuous winds that kept the track full.

Tri-weekly train service with the west end was established whenever blockades developed. The mail would be dropped off at State Bridge and carried over on sleds or wagons to Wolcott, thirteen miles south on the Rio Grande. This was the only contact with the outside world except by telegraph and telephone.

During a two-week-long blockade one March, Tabernash was about out of food. Medicine could be brought in by first class mail. Some men walked out from State Bridge to Wolcott and took the Rio Grande back to Denver.

During a one-week blockade not only was Corona isolated, but so was the Sunnyside weather report station and block office two miles below the pass. At that time two men kept the road informed about the weather. One man was an Irishman by the name of Chancey McCrow. His partner was Albert Lee. They worked twelve hour shifts. During this blockade the Irishman died. Albert Lee phoned off the Hill, "What shall I do? We have only one bed and Chancey is dead in it." The dispatcher told him that they would have been up before, had it been possible. Lee was advised to dig a hole in the snow outside and place the body in it, then secure it against coyotes with ties and rocks until the line was opened.

The coroner lived in Tabernash. Naturally he had to go up to Sunnyside on the first engine that reached there to make his investigation. But no sooner did he get up there than the line was plugged with snow again. The county commissioners almost went crazy, for each day cost the county six dollars. The story went around Sulphur that the county would go broke paying the coroner. Finally the plows got through to Sunnyside and rescued the body. The coroner rode in the cab of an engine dispatched down the Hill, while the body was left to ride on the engine tank. Chancey was buried in the Fraser cemetery.

In 1917 a forty-one day blockade of the line began on the west side, when a train ran into deeper snow than expected and floundered for lack of power. The train was brought back off the hill in pieces. This

The railroad was blocked in 1920; this highway plow had to open Berthoud Pass. The spring snows of April and May in 1920 found ranchers without hay. The blockaded railroad was of no help, so an effort was made to open Berthoud Pass, which had been closed for the winter. This plow made history with the help of men with shovels and dynamite. Train crews even walked over Berthoud on homemade skis after weeks of loneliness in Tabernash. Ice on the rail had the railroad licked. *Lambert Howel collection.*

process took several days. In such trying moments with the rotary unable to back out, engine after engine that was sent to clear up the blockade went dead.

In northwestern Colorado the railroad was not held in too high esteem at such times. A passenger might have gone to Denver on business and been stranded there, while the ranch and family needed him in Middle Park. The railroad could not help leaving a feeling of exasperation in the minds of people who suffered so many inconveniences from the delays. Business life was jeopardized and bottlenecks in crucial items developed.

The normal running time of freights from Tabernash to Tolland was five hours, but one time it was

Food for hungry Tabernash. The families of terminal employees at the division point of Tabernash began to run out of food because of the six week blockade of the spring of 1915. L. Van Buskirk and A. A. Gillett went out in this manner to get fish and wild life. *L. Van Buskirk photo.*

George Schryer poses with his fireman, A. A. Gillett, in all the grime and soot that went into the glorious steam engines. *A. Gillett collection.*

six weeks before a freight got through. The men at Corona lived in fearful memory of the March 10th wind of 1916, which unroofed the snowsheds by its one hundred-mile-an-hour hand and completely paralyzed the Moffat.

When engines were caught between places in blizzards, the men used to fry their steaks on their scoop shovels. Billy Rush conceived an idea of cooking meat in a pail under the petcock of the water gauge, with just a little thin spray of steam over the meat. Another method used to cook meat was under the ashpan of the engine.

The most disastrous of the blockades was somewhere from twenty-three to forty-three days long in April and May of 1920. Late spring snows had inundated Middle Park and the northwest with tre-

Improved Operations

mendous drifts of snow. Ranchers ran out of hay to feed their cattle as each day brought more snow. Then the snow stopped and the sun melted it in the daytime and the nights froze the water.

Cattle began to starve as the road was tied up with new blizzards sweeping in. The coal mines in Routt County were closed down. One mining superintendent sent up a carload of miners, who began chopping their way over the Hill. But since Bill Freeman and this superintendent clashed, the miners went home.

Since Berthoud Pass highway had never been opened in the spring, tractors were fitted with plows and volunteer crews of men from Middle Park began a desperate effort to open the highway. Dynamite

and shovels were used. Each town sent up food, quarters of beef. Men fried their steaks on their snow shovels. It was an epic battle.

Freeman gave this statement to the press regarding the railroad's battle to open its clogged line. "It has settled down to be a dogged fight. The men report tough progress. Ice six to ten inches on the rails threaten to derail the plows. Snow is generally ten feet deep. The plow can drive ahead only for its length and then the ice must be picked out. No one can even guess just when we will get through, but with continued good weather we will have the track open in a few days."

The battle of the Moffat went on. Cattle thinned out; ranchers went broke. Then the line was opened up.

The first train was a solid train of hay. The

Rotary shoved downhill by mallet at Sunnyside. *L. J. Daly photo.*

Mallet 210, April 1913. Only engine scrapped after 1924 wreck. *Alco photo, courtesy Schenectady History Center.*

second train, so they say, was snuff for the Swedes. And the third train was the long overdue Number 1 with mail, express, and passengers.

Perhaps no one thing did more to raise a cry for the Main Range Tunnel than this terrible experience. For five years Master Mechanic Charlie Peterson kept the motive power in such perfect shape that Interstate Commerce Commission inspectors gave the Moffat a one hundred per cent record at Utah Junction. Can a road in the country beat that record? To the lasting credit of Freeman is the fact he kept Charlie Peterson as master mechanic.

Thus equipment for snow and ice fighting was developed that was second to none. Every efficient mallet was kept in the best of shape so that during the years while Moffat Tunnel was being built the blockades were reduced to a minimum. It could be said that "the Hill was well nigh licked" mechanically speaking, but the financial drain mounted in maintaining this superb snow fighting equipment.

After one disastrous tie-up, a five-engine coal train was started east out of Tabernash to climb the pass. George Schryer, one of the engineers who had helped open the pass, had warned an official that a snow cone overhanging the track below the Loop ought to be shot. This process of inducing a harmless avalanche was common; no doubt the officials were afraid Freeman would fire them for wasting time and powder.

The coal train was composed of a rotary plow, two mallets, twenty cars of coal. Then came George Schryer's mallet followed by the fourth mallet and fifteen cars of coal, the caboose, and the fifth mallet.

Their orders were to wait at Ranch Creek for the passenger out of Denver. It was to have pulled into the wye. But when the freight went through Arrow, it received new orders changing the meeting place to the Loop.

When the coal drag got to Ranch Creek, the five engines and the rotary took on water one after another. When all were ready, the plow whistled its two long blasts, which rang shrill through the cold night air. The mountains echoed the call, which was answered by the locomotives. The first engines lunged ahead, the rumble of cars running down the line. Soon the other engines pushed the slack ahead, and the train was moving with the slack shifting back and forth between the engines.

They moved around the hill on up past the old log-loading benches and headed east and then south, ever upward. Schryer had a hunch about the snow cone. When he was under it, he turned on his headlight, which reflected against the coal car ahead. His fireman asked, "What did you turn the headlight on for?"

George replied that he had a hunch the slide was going to let loose on them from the snow cone. He said he wanted to see it hit.

Hardly five seconds followed when the slide hit and Schryer cried, "Prepare yourself!"

The fireman said, "Prepare yourself for what?"

George did not need to answer. Boulders, tons and tons of snow, came with tree trunks, and still more snow and boulders ringing against the bell and

Page 156

steam domes with terrible thuds. The windows of the cab on George's side were crushed in, as the snow piled in the gangway and windows, filling the cab. Coal cars could be heard rolling hundreds of feet down the steep mountainside. They sounded to the ears of the men like dynamite explosions.

More of the slide struck, the engine started to turn over. It settled back down on the rails again, as more snow came in the cab from the back curtain. Gas and smoke belched out the fire door. The snow was over the stack. George and his fireman tried wildly to stamp the snow down to keep above it.

The engine started tipping over again. A boulder cracked on the bell making a sound like the toll of death. Another car rattled on down hundreds and hundreds of feet below. But the engine settled back to the rails. The men still frantically jumped up and down to keep above the snow. Their heads were against the cab roof, the gas was terrible, the engine was buried under the slide.

While the Irish fireman thought of his little ones at home, and the Canadian engineer thought of his wife, a third onslaught of the slide struck with terrible force, and it seemed an eternity before the engine settled back for the third time buried under snow, the gas and smoke choking the men. The fireman used the entire Moffat vocabulary of curses and foul language on the disaster. The men were spared being hurled seven hundred feet to their death.

Schryer handed the Irishman his extra handkerchief. An explosion of gas occurred in the engine. The men dug with their fingernails to crawl out of the lower side of the cab to get to air. Finally the snow must have melted at the engine stack, as the gas was relieved. The men were out in the air. The ledge the engines stood on was so filled with snow that they almost slipped over the embankment.

They saw the second mallet was on the track. Its crew crawled out. Seven cars were over the cliff behind that mallet and eight ahead of George's mallet.

Both firemen refused to stick to their engines. The Irishman said, "You can. You don't have a family of kids." There was imminent danger of

Ice pick that licked ice conditions. To Master Mechanic Charlie Peterson goes the credit for having invented the world's largest ice picks. Engine 211 (shown here outside the Corona shed) and two others, all mallets, were equipped with hydraulic cylinders which can be seen on either side of the boiler above the pilot. The "picks" were connected to the cylinders so that they could be raised going over switches, and were actually thirty-inch chisels, six inches wide, and two inches thick. These mallets would start at the top of the pass and shove the ice picks down inside the rails, ripping out the ice as the mallets snorted and spun their wheels.

Then the mallet would back up and the rotary would slip down and pick up the ice and hurl it out of the cuts. The ice pick engine would return and root up more ice, while the rotary waited its turn to come down, pick up the ice, and hurl out the ten feet of snow drifted over the ice. Often these big chisels were broken off digging out heavy ice. *Ben Stone photo.*

Train caught in slide. The slide almost rolled two mallets down the mountain. Coal cars ahead and behind George Schryer's engine were carried down the mountainside at the right, while the engines were buried. *George Schryer collection.*

more snow slipping any moment. So George and the other engineer took over shoveling their way back into the cabs.

The passenger train, which had fallen down somewhere in its run from Denver, was saved by the delay. Otherwise it would have been caught in the slide and the Moffat would have lost its record of no casualties to passengers.

After the slide, Blaine Markle, the conductor in charge of the train, telephoned the report to Freeman, who asked with great worry, "Did any of the mallets go over?" "No. And neither did any of the men!" came the burning sarcastic answer of indignation.

During these grueling battles a close fraternity was established among the men. Management highly respected the moves the men on the top of the world resorted to in fighting these epic battles. There was

no rigid rule-book play for every move as has grown up on many railroads. If the men devised some idea or felt that they by common consent had a better idea, management kept hands off the men who fought the battles. Perhaps this liberty in part appeased their scalping from low wages.

Not only was a fraternity formed among the railroad men but also with many non-railmen who had interests in the line. Frank Carlson was most gracious and accommodating to men who lost mittens, or wore out shoes and galoshes, or needed warmer caps. Notes were sent down on engines for the needed supplies. The men never forgot these friendships even after the Hill was abandoned for the Moffat Tunnel.

Would that it were possible to give a day by day

Page 158

Improved Operations

Two more views of the slide below the Loop. It came through the trees from the left, and perched one tree trunk atop the second mallet. This is another spot reached easily today; one can look down upon the Routt County coal lying where it was spilled three decades ago. These pictures were taken the next morning after rescue operations were under way. *George Schryer photos.*

George Schryer beside his engine. Fourteen hours after the wreck the remainder of the train was backed down to Tabernash and Schryer began to remove the snow from the engine with a pick. It was piled six feet higher than the cab roof, as can be seen in the photo. *George Schryer photo.*

Plow train thunders over Loop. Opening up the last blockade on the Moffat, just before service began through the Moffat Tunnel. The rotary is followed by two mallets on the Loop Trestle, then a caboose filled with section men, a tool car with picks and shovels, and consolidation in reverse. This last engine had an important function. When the plow train became stalled, its only hope to break free lay in the butterfly plow bolted on the pilot of the last engine. *A. Clarke photo.*

picture of a blockade! But the minds of men tried to blot out the memory of those battles. It was like the war. It was best forgotten. But what has been presented is representative of the piercing cold, the panting for air in working above timberline, the curses that seemed to help warm the air and cut the ice, and the loyalty of men who were good and not so good, as all men are.

As has been seen, the Twenties saw the Denver and Salt Lake surmounting most physical problems which beset it in the crossing of the Continental Divide. Realization and resignation had set in; the Hill was no longer considered a branch line. Although the Main Range Tunnel was still hoped for, all officials realized that it was the main line of the Moffat which passed through Corona and that line had to be kept open.

Gradually, with the improvement in operating methods and the reduced frequency of blockades, came an increased acceptance on the part of shippers and the public. Many special trains were run. Elsewhere we have described some of them. The Moffat Road became a Colorado tourist attraction in its own right. The authors have in their possession a pictorial folder, dated 1904, which modestly admits "Words have no power to adequately picture the

wonders of the trip beyond Tolland. It has no equal in the world." The round trip fare from Denver for a full day's outing from May 15 to October 31 was $5. Apparently, this fare was continued until 1915, because the February folder of that year shows the round-trip fare to Corona as $4.50. Tourist business flourished, aided by a surprising output of tourist literature from the Denver and Salt Lake offices. The achievements of the operating personnel were matched word for word by the platitudes of passenger traffic and public relations experts. In 1925 the road operated Numbers 1 and 2, the overnight trains to and from Craig, and in addition the "Scenic Special" ran during the summer months as Numbers 3 and 4 carrying the vacation bound tourists on flower-picking specials to Boulder Park in the leisurely days before the great automobile era.

Many a time it seemed as if the winter were so elastic as never to end. When summer did come, it arrived with a beauty of snowcapped mountains set against a background of blue sky and fleecy clouds. A profusion of wildflowers sprang up in a kaleidoscopic changing pattern against the green mountainsides. At Corona enthralled tourists picked flowers

Two views of Yankee Doodle. These two pictures taken years apart reveal interesting differences in the features around Yankee Doodle Lake. The upper was taken by McClure just after the opening of the road. Clearly visible, jutting into the lake, is the Denver, Utah & Pacific's dump for their ill-fated tunnel. At the far end of the lake in the upper picture, the season's first chill blast has left a collection of snow under Tunnel 32, visible at the top. The lower shot, by L.J. Daly, looking almost straight down from Tunnel 32, is of a 200-series mallet easing thirty-six cars downhill with the crummy concealed in the shed. The shed was erected to circumvent the slides caused by the snow mentioned above. Note that the snow in the lower photo is higher than the cars at some points. *L. Van Buskirk collection.*

Cooling wheels. Another view of Yankee Doodle Lake in winter. The same scene can be seen today (with the railroad sadly lacking) from the location selected by the early-day photographer. In the shed in the upper distance the railroad made a 180 degree turn and headed back up to the right toward the tunnel. *L. J. Daly photo.*

A life was sacrificed to obtain this scene. It is a shot from the "Trail of '98," a Hollywood production made on location along the Moffat in February, 1927. Fayette Bishop, son of Bob Bishop (the Moffat's third oldest engineer), stepped out on a snow bank and disappeared under the snow as he shot down the bank. Thus ended the life of a fine lad, and the motion picture world never produced the true tragedy of that setting, although actors played such parts. "White Desert" was also filmed in part on the Moffat by Metro Goldwyn on February 12, 1925. *L. J. Daly photo.*

from the snowbanks left from winter and little realized the struggle the D.&S.L. had gone through to keep its lines open through the long winter. Above the timberline, dwarf oak, reindeer berries, and waxlike flowers grew out of patches of snow. Colorado's state flower, the columbine, grew in luxurious profusion on the mountainsides intermingled with Indian paint brush and delicate blue flowers. Dan Cunningham, an outstanding D.&S.L. Master Mechanic, said, "This natural bouquet was as if God wanted to compensate the people of this land for the awful hardships they had to endure during the cold months of the winter."

But with the coming of each September, tourists on the Moffat dwindled to a trickle and then stopped. After all, freight was king on the Moffat line as it is on railroads universally.

Little by little techniques had been developed for the Hill, so that traffic could be maintained. One of these, intimately related to moving heavy trains down these grades, was brakes.

Students of the Moffat ordinarily think of "heavy" trains as those operated in the winter with four or five engines and a rotary . . . and they were heavy, too. But one Moffat special train topped them all, for the tonnage record and collection of motive power used to handle it were never reached again. This took place during the air brake tests of 1921.

Here is the story:

The Moffat was a "modern" road. In those areas

where large outlays of cash were not required and where ingenuity could be brought to bear, few roads were better equipped. Second only to devotion, Moffat men possessed resourcefulness. They had to.

By 1921, the year of the brake tests, the original two and a half mile Main Range Tunnel had been given up, and in its place was projected a bore 6.04 miles in length almost on the exact site of the present Moffat Tunnel. It would be more correct to say that the bore was little more than a dream, there were so many frustrations.

It is difficult to imagine the privations attendant to chaining up a car at 40° *below*, at the bottom of a snow trench near Ptarmigan Point. Yet this was the result of poor train handling. Absolute finesse was required to coordinate the power from four or five mallets to prevent dangerous slack action. And if one lost footing for a moment. . . break-in-two!

The first Westinghouse air brake patents were drawn up in 1869, but the design included a fatal weakness—all the air was pumped back to the cars from the locomotive. The "automatic air brake" introduced on the D.&R.G. in 1872 was unique in that it utilized an air pump and reservoir on the engine to charge a train line leading to reservoirs on all the cars. Each car also contained a "triple valve" which continually tested the air in the train line and applied the brakes if pressure dropped. The type K

Advertising folders. The Moffat was aggressive in pushing excursion and passenger business. Advertising folders throughout the years invariably carried cover pictures of Corona and Yankee Doodle Lake. The D.N.W.&P. folder at lower left is the earliest shown, dating from April, 1905, when the line had reached Arrowhead. Efforts to conserve funds resulted in two brochures being identical throughout with the single exception of a change from D.N.W.&P. on the cover to D.&S.L. *F. Bauer collection.*

A vacation spot on the Moffat was Hotel Crags near Tunnel 9, reached only by the railroad. This was popular in the early days, and the path leading down from the train is easily seen. Fire consumed the hotel, so that today only the foundation can be seen from the California Zephyr; this is the last view of the plains as the climbing train turns directly into the mountains. Eldorado Springs in South Boulder Canyon is beyond the hotel in this picture, with the right of way of the Denver, Utah & Pacific nearby. *McClure photo.*

brake was developed about the turn of the century and was used on all Moffat equipment purchased in the early days of the road.

Attempts to improve efficiency by increasing the train lengths made it obvious that more than 1250 tons could be handled up the Hill if there existed brakes adequate for the downhill trip. The search for a solution to this problem led D.&S.L. management to conduct a series of brake tests to determine the comparative capabilities of the then-available Westinghouse equipment against the newly-developed "Automatic Straight Air" brake which

was under consideration. Forty of the Moffat's fifty-ton coal cars were equipped with the new brake, so that the action of trains equipped with this type could be studied and compared with a train having a mixture of Westinghouse and ASA brakes.

August 10, 1921, was the day picked for the test, and the train was notable because it moved intact up to Corona from the bottom of the four per cent on the west side. This also required the greatest collection of motive power assembled at one time on a

Summer objective for many picnickers and tourists was South Boulder Park, situated at the foot of the Giants Ladder, as shown in this early spring scene. *Denver Public Library Western Collection.*

Touching in a train. The white lies told by Moffat publicity agents are aptly illustrated here. McClure took the top picture shortly after the opening of the road past Tolland. Note the freshly laid track with open ties. The lower picture is a reproduction of one of many in a 1905 pictorial folder "The Trail of the Iron Horse." The artist apparently had little conception of a Moffat engine. McClure's copyright was also "fogged" out. *F. Bauer collection.*

CLIMBING THE CONTINENTAL DIVIDE.

Improved Operations

The girls at Corona in 1915. That early-day writers waxed poetic is shown by the caption to this photograph contained in a 1915 pictorial booklet. These young ladies are portrayed as being "Just under the turquoise sky —the utmost rocks of the summit of the majestic Rockies near Corona twelve thousand feet above the level of the sea. Bravely and long these charming maidens climbed on a summer's day. Further they could not go without the attachment of wings triumphant, which one radiant day may surely follow their terrestrial attachments." *F. Bauer collection.*

DENVER & SALT LAKE RAILROAD

Moffat train. Railroad and brake officials had arrived at Tabernash the previous day, and interest was extremely high in the train parked on the siding next to the eating house at Tabernash that morning. It consisted of thirty-four fifty-ton coal cars equipped with the ASA brake, and a Westinghouse caboose, the total weight behind the road locomotive being 2431 tons. Movement of this train out of the Tabernash yards and up the broad valley of Middle Park required three mallets, each with a tractive effort of 78,000 pounds, and two consolidations of 44,000 pounds each. (Today many five-unit diesel trains sail past Tabernash without a helper at all. Yet, there's seldom a thrill like riding on the helper kept at Tabernash as it boosts its train up to the Moffat Tunnel where it cuts off on the fly and returns to the valley.)

The five-engine train must have made an impressive sight puffing toward Berthoud Pass through Fraser to Irving at the foot of the four percent. There, two more mallets were added to make a total of seven locomotives with a combined tractive effort

The Moffat Loop is located close to the summit of the Divide. This loop is of surpassing interest, as its construction was very difficult.

Another example of touching in trains on a touched-in road-bed which results in a very artificial picture. The remark about difficult construction probably irked locating engineers, who had found this temporary hill line easy to locate and build in comparison with the South Boulder Canyon section. *F. Bauer collection.*

Page 167

Copyright 1905 by W. Weston

Yankee Doodle Lake and up. One of the scenic highpoints was the view straight up from Yankee Doodle Lake. This is one of few illustrations available showing a train leaving Tunnel 32 headed for Corona. It was taken by W. Weston sometime before 1905 and was used in an institutional brochure showing the industrial and commercial potential of northwestern Colorado. Snowslides frequently traversed the 900 foot drop between track levels and resulted in the construction of a snowshed on the far side of the lake. A few venturesome souls undertook to slide down the snow on the seat of their pants, with more or less disastrous results. *F. Bauer collection.*

Improved Operations

At Corona was constructed a neat little hotel. To withstand winter's storms, cables visible in the picture attached it to the Continental Divide. The hotel was later razed by the U. S. Forest Service. Today only a few crumbling bricks mark the spot near the precipitous eastern side of the summit. Refer to layout map of Corona on page 179. *McClure photo.*

Naturally, any excursion would stop at some convenient snowbank along the way. A strategically placed sign reads, "Telegraph your friends from CORONA, THE TOP OF THE WORLD." *Photo by passenger, Mrs. Clarence Smith.*

Page 169

of 478,000 pounds. The train left Tabernash at 9:10 A.M. and required nearly five hours to climb the twenty-three miles to Corona. Each water stop required considerable time to spot so many engines. Of course, there was the usual delay in meeting Number 1 on the Hill. Just think of the number of flimsies each operator had to make for the meet! Think, too, of the sight such a train would be—seven columns of smoke from laboring engines blasting up through the pines and floating away on the late summer breeze.

The actual running time up the four percent was three hours, and the sight was a moving one for even the hard-bitten Moffat men used to heavy power. Movies were taken of the train from the Loop trestle as the train approached and entered the Loop tunnel and again as it appeared on the upper level of the Loop. More pictures were taken as it approached and entered the Corona snowsheds. No trace of any of these pictures can be found at present. This is certainly a pity, since it is doubtful if any other railroad before or since could furnish a portrait better typifying the pinnacle of steam. Many words will yet be written eulogizing the glory of steam locomotives. Men will remember them and try to describe the thrill of the sight to generations who will never smell the smoke or hear the hiss of oil-laden steam. On the Moffat that Indian summer afternoon, steam railroading reached its high water mark. Like Pickett's Charge, the effort almost succeeded.

Here we see the plight of the Moffat expressed in the most simple terms. It was summer. There was no snow to fight nor howling wind to force privations upon the personnel. Seven locomotives with a total

No. 1 out of Plainview. It's 10:54 A.M. August 23, 1937, and Number 1 with Engine 303 has just made the flag stop at Plainview. Just west of the station it blasted into Tunnel 2 and emerged into the sunlight again on this trestle. Here is the epitome of American short line railroading—rugged landscape, thundering drivers, hogger in the cab window, and a slick engine trailing a short string of varnish topped off with an open observation car. Classic railroading, classic road, classic picture by Dick Kindig. Tunnel 3 lies just ahead, then 51 tunnels more before Number 1 comes to a stop at Craig at 6:40 P.M. that summer evening. The trestle has since given way to a fill, but at this writing one can still ride Number 9 and 10, the diesel-descendant of Number 1, through this magnificent evergreen scenery. *R. H. Kindig photo.*

Eastbound lettuce train in Gore Canyon, before the days of CTC or slide fences. This train of fifty cars handled by one engine to Tabernash would have to be split into three trains going over the Hill. Such inefficient operation led to the brake tests of 1921 during which the heaviest train ever operated tried out the new ASA brake system. *L. J. Daly photo.*

Test train out of Tabernash on two per cent with five engines, consolidation 108 on the point. *D.&S.L. Engineering Department photo made by Mile High Photo Co.*

Seven engines lifted test train on four per cent above Irvings. Train is moving ahead at Ranch Creek water tank so that seventh engine can take water. Note dirty snow near last engine, James Peak in background, engine and cars on wye, low rail joints ahead of first engine. *Mile High photo.*

President Freeman, in straw hat, stands in front of the Model T inspection car with justifiable pride; the test train has dropped safely down the mountain and stopped at Dixie Lake. Left to right: Ainsworth, Freeman, Phelps, three unidentified, Master Mechanic Peterson, and Ferguson next to engine, Bishop in cab. *Mile High photo.*

Page 172

of seventeen men in train and engine crews were required. The geography, the grades, the Main Range Tunnel that wasn't built and was so sorely needed served to eat up the substance of the Moffat. On the other hand, Rio Grande Employees Timetable No. 15 shows the rating of a four unit F-9 or GP-9 diesel to be 3675 tons and a four unit F-3, 2530 tons on the two percent from Denver to East Portal. One can easily speculate on what might have been, had diesel locomotives been available in the early 20's. With a three or four unit diesel and a crew of five men such a test train of 2431 tons could have been handled up the two per cent and through the proposed tunnel. If only such equipment had been available, the engine failures, the difficulty of procuring water, the slow handling and time consuming process of melting snow, the running for water while cuts were again filled with snow, might all have been eliminated—but this must be relegated to the realms of fancy.

What might have been ... The Moffat might have been saved by electrification. It might have been saved by the Main Range Tunnel. It might have been saved by a helping hand from Gould. It might have been saved by a little more financing at critical moments. What might have been ...

But let us return to the train now, the crews and officials have had lunch and there is a nip in the air at Corona at 4:35 P.M., foretelling winter soon to come. While the long train was stopped at Corona, the retainers were set up.* After the highball, it crawled through Needle's Eye Tunnel and along the shelf road overlooking Yankee Doodle Lake. This scenery can be seen from one's car on the old grade.

The trip up the four percent had been uneventful, and the descent began that way. Soon, however, the train ground to a shuddering halt and no doubt more than one Moffat man or brake specialist had a moment of anxiety. It proved to be due simply to a too heavy brake reduction in rounding a sixteen degree reverse curve at MP 62.5 in the rock cut just west of Dixie Lake. Happily for all, the train was on its way in three minutes after pumping up the air.

A count of brake cycles showed that only half as many were required with this train, *double the normal tonnage,* as would have been needed with the normal 1250 ton train.

At Dixie Lake, four and a half miles from the summit, the usual brake inspection was made and it was found that wheel temperatures were very uniform and every wheel in the train could be touched with the fingers without discomfort. The train left Dixie at 5:41 and reached Antelope, the next inspection point, at 6:08 P.M. Uniform temperatures had continued with the heat radiating more toward the hub. It was possible to feel the wheels without discomfort three inches in from the tread. At Antelope, the brakes on two cars were cut out, leaving thirty-two brakes to handle thirty-five cars since the brakes on the caboose were not working. The remaining two and a half miles down the four percent was made and the caboose occupants reported the slack action to be nil. Once, on the two percent, an intentional emergency brake application was made to spot the train for a picture and to see if it was possible to shake up the rear end. Even here, however, the observers reported a stop as smooth as the usual service application, with no slack action.

The train arrived at Tolland at 7:30 P.M. There

---

*Retainers are devices to assure that the brakes on a car will not release entirely. The retainer valve is located near the brake wheel and has a "ten pound" and "twenty pound" position. Retainers are used primarily on long grades, and the line from Corona east is a striking example of their application. Before the train left Corona, the retainers were "set up" on all cars, a process which required the brakeman to traverse the entire train. When the engine whistled off, there was no air in the brakes and so the train was able to get a rolling start. A five pound reduction was then made and quickly released, followed by another five pound reduction and release. Any such applications throughout the train provided a minimum of at least ten pounds in each brake cylinder and thus charged the retainers.

When the brakes were then released from the locomotive, they did not release on those cars with retainers set up and so prevented the train from gaining momentum until there was enough newly-stored air in the locomotive for another application. This process of applying the brakes and then allowing the train line to recharge is called "cycling" and requires considerable skill. On the four percent it was a fine art.

Because the retainer valve itself is so important in this operation, and because it is seldom used in ordinary service on flat lands, it was the habit of the Moffat to put known good retainers on all foreign cars arriving at interchange points. The Moffat shop-tested valves were connected with a short nipple underneath the car after the retainer pipe had been disconnected. Upon departure from the Moffat, the tested valve was removed and the car restored to its original condition. This bit of extra work demonstrates one of the many fringe hazards sapping the strength of the road, while at the same time helping to explain the unparalleled safety record enjoyed by the D.&S.L.

Engine 118 had a new paint job for test run. This engine handled the test train down the Hill. Note emblem did not get painted. *Mile High photo.*

crews were changed, but only one engine continued on to Utah Junction at 7:50. Two additional regular cooling and inspection stops were made in the tunnel district and the condition of the wheels found the same as on the four per cent. The train proceeded without incident to Denver, arriving at Utah Junction at 12:15 A.M. to complete an interesting day in air brake and Moffat history.

We wish this story had a happy ending. But it does not. The frustration which weaves its way through so much of the Moffat history is present here too. Exhaustive search of Westinghouse records, Purdue Air Brake Test Laboratory, and Association of American Railroad files reveals that the D.&S.L. tests were part of a Power Brake Investigation lasting from 1925 to 1931. What records did exist, were later destroyed by water in the basement of the AAR, when a fire broke out in an adjacent building.

Engine 216. The drawbar lying beside the track speaks of the woes of big power. The last engines built for the Moffat were engines 212-216 in September, 1916. *McClure photo, Denver Public Library Western Collection.*

John Brisbane Walker's castle became the Moffat Road's general office. This relic of the defunct Riverside Amusement Park was handy to the Moffat station one block west and became the operating headquarters of the railroad. The walkway reached to the Sixteenth Street viaduct. President Freeman saved pennies by refusing to repair the roof; office employees worked under umbrellas when it rained. *Denver Public Library Western Collection.*

We do know, however, that very few cars were so equipped, probably no more than those on the Moffat. The ASA equipment was set up for rack tests at Purdue and tested by AAR and ICC representatives who rejected the system.

No further road tests were made, and the system was never used commercially.

But one very important point needs to be made: even before work on the Moffat Tunnel began, there were evidences that the Road had passed its greatest difficulties. Improved methods of operation, a steady increase in the production of coal mines, oil wells, and agricultural products gave investors a ray of hope. In his book, *The Moffat Tunnel of Colorado,* Edgar McMechen gives his opinion with which we fully agree, "Although the road never could have been other than a local line without the tunnel there was reason to believe that it would have survived in any event."

But soon to come was the Moffat Tunnel, a turning point for Colorado and its railroads.

Foxholes dug ahead of rotary. *Drawing by Don Johnson.*

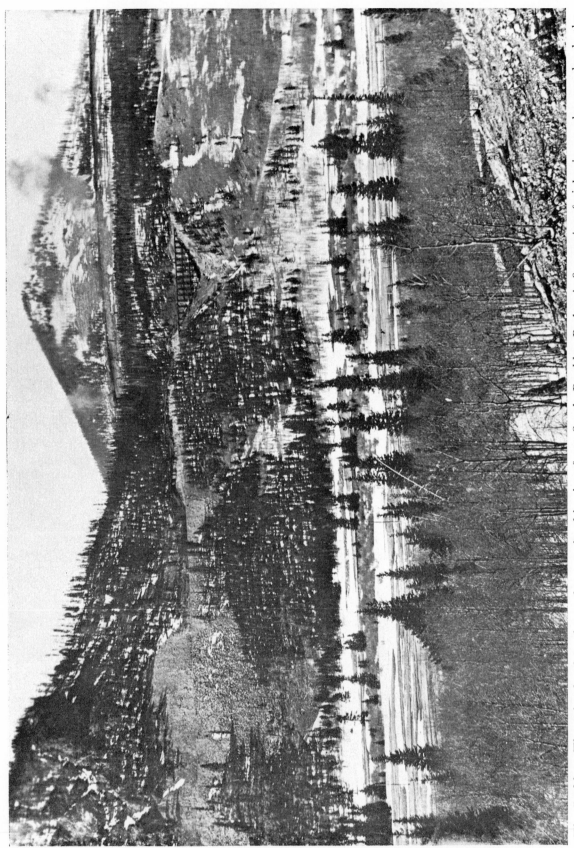

The Ladder. Three levels of track can be seen in this view from South Boulder Park. A five-engine freight is on the top level, the second is partly obscured by trees, and the trestle is on the lowest. This picture clearly illustrates the ascending grade on the two per cent. The reader can easily visualize what the four per cent would be like. Not all the expense on the Moffat was due to snow. There was also to be considered the "lift," that is, an extra resistance of twenty pounds for each ton for each one per cent of grade. On the four per cent this added eighty pounds per ton to which must again be added the resistance effect of the sharp curves on the Hill line. Furthermore, these curves were so sharp that steam 'had to be worked on the downgrade. As a consequence, a freight on the few stretches of straight track would be out of control in three minutes unless an experienced hogger handled the air. One does not have to be a practical railroad man to grasp the combined effect of these physical factors. *Denver Public Library Western Collection.*

This train is laboring up the second level of the Ladder, having just emerged from Tunnel 31. It has just passed the great trestle and unique square water tower on the far side of the hill, and will momentarily send a shower of cinders down upon the photographer. The hogger widens out on his throttle, for he is on the last stretch of two per cent before the grade is doubled, where the grade change indicates the point of departure for the approach to the

proposed 2.6-mile Main Range Tunnel. A short stretch of the approach right of way was graded, and can be found today in the trees at the left of the picture. *Denver Public Library Western Collection.*

The men who located the Ladder and ran the line down from the 2.6 mile tunnel site prepare to leave Idlewild in 1902. *Art Weston photo.*

One way the Passenger Department attracted tourists on a hot July Fourth in Denver! Loaded near Corona by gandy dancers, snow was hauled to Denver in a gondola and transferred to wagons for this parade forming downtown near City Auditorium. God's snow-conditioned climate was less than four hours away via the Moffat. *Denver Public Library Western Collection.*

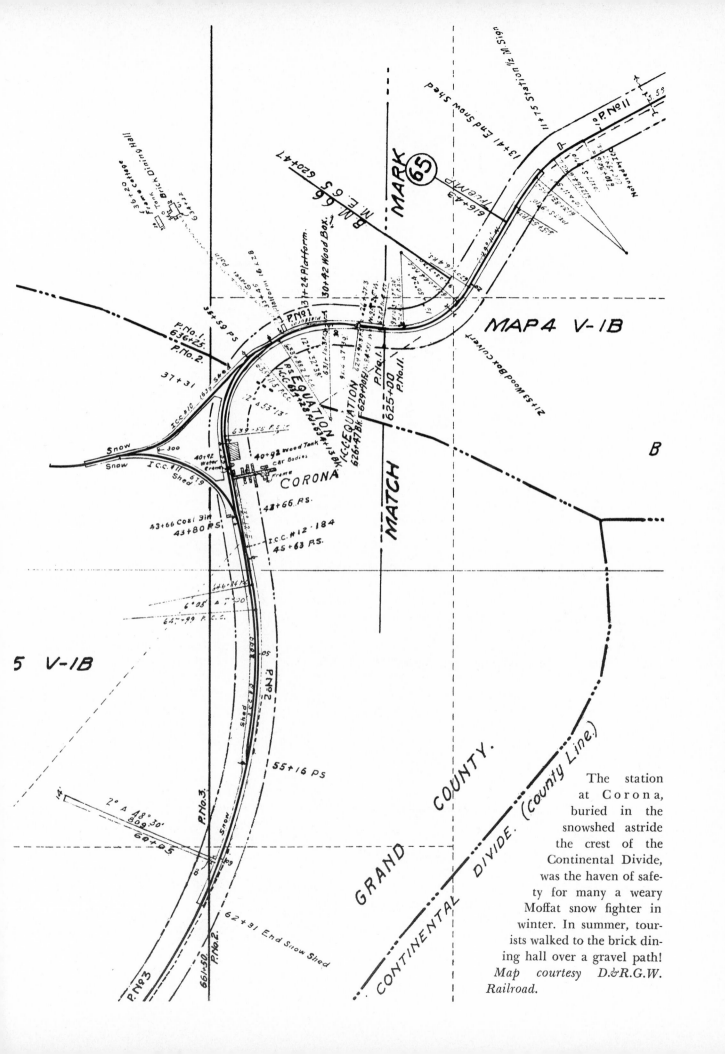

The station at Corona, buried in the snowshed astride the crest of the Continental Divide, was the haven of safety for many a weary Moffat snow fighter in winter. In summer, tourists walked to the brick dining hall over a gravel path! *Map courtesy D.&R.G.W. Railroad.*

The Moffat Tunnel

Dusk at West Portal the evening of July 30, 1926. . . . A few vacationers in Model T's pass the construction buildings, chugging their way up Berthoud Pass, brave souls. The lights of the construction shacks are just beginning to be discerned against the waning daylight. In the tunnel, murky and damp, a timber crew of six men is working. Their shadowy shapes dance upon the walls from the naked bulbs used for illumination. Here ages ago some gigantic upheaval has sheared and twisted the rock into a confused mass of seams and faults running in every direction. Erecting timbering . . . big, heavy 12 x 12's . . . is no easy job in these slippery rock formations. The men are sweaty in spite of the constant 50 degree temperature. "One more push fellows!" and six grimy shapes strain against the plumb post.

The rock of the ceiling is permeated with water. Suddenly, without a sound, and without hope of human intervention, one hundred twenty-five tons of rock separates from the tunnel ceiling. The mass meets the tunnel floor with a terrific crash. The lethal seam, previously hidden and against which precautions could not be taken, now showed in the dim light as the new face of a twenty-five foot hole in the roof.

There was no need to pass word of the accident. The concussion was felt in nearby passages and cross cuts. Soon moving lights betokened helmeted figures working their way across the broken pile of rock, the monument to six men. There was no need to call for volunteers. Rock men live hard and die hard, but they also work in ever-present danger and wear courage on their sleeves.

Knowing that a second deadfall might occur momentarily, and knowing that there was not the slightest hope of survival for the timber crew, they toiled constantly for seventy-two hours. First a false ceiling must be erected to support the weakened roof. A loud shout, a big timber roughly handled scraping against the wall, might precipitate another cavein. Only the most imperative orders were even spoken, and then in low tones. Men with no sense of theatrics

had to be dragged away from the work when they bordered on sheer collapse. Finally, as the rock was lifted bit by bit, the huddled figures were revealed—one with a shovel still in hand, one with a pick—struck down without warning or opportunity to acquit themselves with their Maker.

This wasn't typical of the Moffat, perhaps, but the difficulties brought about by man's attempt to circumvent the mountain were in every way characteristic of the troubles and frustrations which hung over the Road since its inception. Today these things are forgotten or unknown to passengers on the California Zephyr as they roll through the six-mile artery in the heart of the mountain.

We think of the passengers on the California Zephyr threading their way from Rollinsville through Tolland. The mountain stream on the left is water that has come through the Moffat pioneer bore Water Tunnel and is merely the crowning glory of a perfect mountain scene. The CTC relay house boldly marked "East Portal" comes into view along with a "high green" signal beckoning the train down the tangent track and into the tunnel. Just before the Vistadome slides into the darkness, we might consider what kind of men toiled *over* the mountain instead of *through* the mountain before it was pierced by the tunnel.

Early hunters and trappers knew of Rollins (then Boulder) Pass as the narrowest crossing of the Rockies. Later a wagon road company was organized to construct across Berthoud Pass from Denver to Salt Lake City. In September, 1865, a group of surveyors together with an escort of California Volunteers totaling one hundred fifty men and two wagons crossed Rollins Pass on their way to Denver from Salt Lake. Thus was made the first transit of Boulder, or Rollins, Pass by wheeled vehicles.

John Quincy Adams Rollins, for whom the pass was named, arrived in Denver in 1860 with a nineteen-team ox train. Some time in 1865 he guided a party of one hundred Mormons to Utah over the pass, enduring in the process heartbreaking hardships. Men, women, and children were forced to carry the contents of their wagons in order to lighten the load. Rollins saw the potential that the route afforded, however, and by 1873 had completed a wagon road over it forty miles long. After he had obtained a territorial grant, the route became known as the Rollins Pass Road.

In the early sixties, when railroads were advancing west, it was assumed that the Union Pacific would build through Denver. There were many reasons: first, Denver was a booming city, equal to any to the north or west; second, new minerals being found almost daily promised considerable traffic; and lastly, General Grenville M. Dodge, Chief Engineer of the Union Pacific, openly favored a route through Denver and west to Salt Lake via the Yampa Valley—this being the route the D.N.W.&P. later adopted. General Dodge's men surveyed all passes from Wyoming south to the Royal Gorge in an attempt to break through. Indeed, he was present personally when the route over Boulder (Rollins) Pass was rejected in November, 1866. To cap the climax, his party barely escaped with their lives in a roaring mountain blizzard near what is now the East Portal of the Moffat Tunnel.

Despite the fact that Colorado was first among the states in bituminous coal with reserves lying at less than three-thousand feet elevations, the Union Pacific detoured far to the north. Rapid construction was imperative requiring the Union Pacific to avoid the three-hundred-mile length of the high range of the Rockies. After operation had begun over their lines both the Union Pacific, and the Santa Fe to the south opposed any new competitor who was rash enough to attempt the more direct mountain crossing fifty miles straight west of Denver.

The first definite suggestion of a tunnel under the Continental Divide was made by Andrew N. Rogers in the form of a pamphlet addressed to the President and Directors of the Union Pacific Railroad in a last desperate attempt to dissuade them from the route through Cheyenne. Rogers was a distinguished engineer, having already located many rail lines in the Blue Ridge and Cumberland Mountains. He invented several important mining innovations while superintendent of the Bob Tail Mine at Central City. He was later destined to be on the board of three commissioners to settle the dispute between

the Rio Grande and Santa Fe in the Royal Gorge War. His proposed tunnel pierced the Continental Divide at Hog Back, a narrow portion of the spine of the mountains two miles south of the present Moffat Tunnel. This location is still known as Rogers Pass and lies roughly midway between Rollins Pass and James Peak. Later there was a survey for the Jefferson and Boulder County Railroad and Wagon Road in 1867, followed by a survey of the Kansas Pacific Railroad Company in 1869.

The uncompleted tunnel at Yankee Doodle Lake represents perhaps the high water mark of effort by the Denver, Utah & Pacific. The intent was to come up South Boulder Canyon through a series of switchbacks from the site of present-day Eldorado Springs, ultimately reaching the hogback bordering the north side of Yankee Doodle Lake. After passing through the tunnel the route was meant to proceed generally along the course subsequently taken by the D.N.W. &.P. Dave Moffat contemplated this route when projecting his narrow-gauge interurban at the turn of the century. In 1908 the Colorado & Southern, through its Denver & Interurban, actually built an electrified standard-gauge line into Eldorado Springs —some say with the intention of building farther west, possibly over the projected D.U.&P. route. The latter, however, was doomed to failure. In 1882 construction was halted and contractor Streeter took over part of the route for debt, with a good portion later being acquired by the Burlington.

Although the D. U. & P. had failed, attempts to penetrate the mountains did not cease. Rather they were intensified. The Denver & California Short Line Railroad began business in 1882, attempting to cross the Continental Divide near Argentine Pass. The road was unique in projecting a water tunnel with the railroad tunnel—this being the first proposal to bring Western Slope water through the mountains to Denver. The line was actually surveyed in 1883-4, but construction was not started. By this time the pattern was becoming more clear; first a probe here, then there, by different railroads, all seeking a direct route west to California and the Pacific Northwest.

To the Burlington, however, went the dubious glory of the most ambitious unsuccessful effort, the narrow gauge Colorado Railway. That road had purchased the surveys and completed right of way of the D. U. & P. Four survey parties were placed in the field in 1884 and spent three years making very extensive surveys over Rollins Pass,

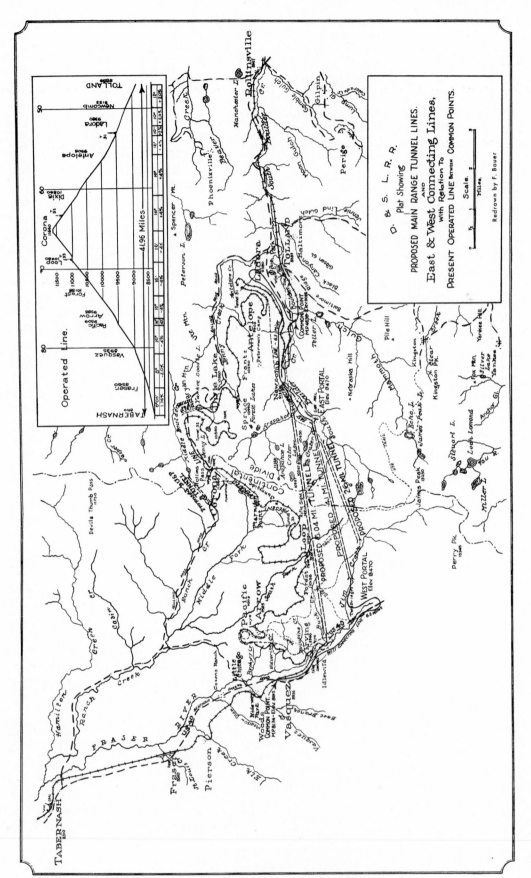

and westerly through Gore Canyon as far as Glenwood Springs. Indeed, H. A. Sumner, the famous locator of the Moffat Road and its first Chief Engineer, was in charge of the crew on the west side of the Divide near James Peak. The Burlington proposed a three-mile tunnel through Rogers Pass at approximately the location suggested by Rogers in 1867. A five-mile tunnel was also surveyed, together with a highline over the Divide which reached a maximum elevation of 12,220 feet. The latter, however, was never considered seriously despite the fact that the three-mile tunnel was expected to cost only $3,292,000—but a terrific sum then. Work continued until 1887 and a considerable amount of grading had been accomplished when the locomotive engineers' strike of 1887 stopped the operations.

Now David Moffat entered the picture a second time. He was, at that time, President of the Rio Grande. In that capacity, he was instrumental in purchasing the Colorado Railway right of way near Glenwood Springs for the D.&R.G., and this portion is still operated as part of the Main Line through the Rockies.

The construction of the Colorado Midland Railroad in the mid-eighties, beginning at Colorado Springs and crossing the Divide westerly therefrom, placed an entirely "new look" on Colorado transportation. Ultimate existence of the narrow-gauge Rio Grande was indeed threatened because of the lower costs made possible by the Midland's standard gauge. In order to meet this competition, Moffat at once began plans for a standard-gauge crossing of the Rockies on a new route. His proposed competitive new line ran from Denver to Buena Vista, roughly paralleled the South Park, and successfully reduced distance and rise and fall. Grading was begun in the South Fork of the South Platte southwesterly out of Denver and continued until it was obvious that construction costs were exceeding the estimates by wide margins. In disgust, Moffat ordered cessation of the work and then began a direct assault of the Front Range west of Denver. Surveys were run over five passes to the south of Argentine. The cost of any one of these high routes would have been over $16 million and a decision was reached to abandon all such attempts and concentrate attention on improvements and standard gauging of existing narrow-gauge lines. This was done rapidly under Moffat's direction. This episode had one unfortunate repercussion. Although worth much more, Moffat's surveys had cost in the aggregate of $100,000 and he was

severely criticized for this expenditure. Some feel that his departure from the Rio Grande was thus hastened.

Something new. Something hard. Something worthwhile. All were combined in Moffat's greatest dream. Yet his dream had been shared by others and all had lost their gamble. In the thirty years prior to 1900 twelve to fourteen passes had been surveyed, eighteen to twenty railroad projects undertaken, about half of which incorporated tunnels. While some had never passed the promotion stage, many had involved actual grading. Nevertheless, rails did not cross the Divide directly west of Denver, and only skeleton evidences of unsuccessful attempts remained. Those crossings that were successful, such as the South Park, were narrow gauge with sharp curvature and steep grades and were not of the type that could be worthy long-range competition to the Union Pacific's low-level, standard-gauge crossing in Wyoming. By this time over $4 million had been spent in surveys and unsuccessful grading, not including the Colorado Central or South Park. This amount would have been ample to have drilled many of the proposed tunnels. Yet all was dissipated.

Surveys were begun again to find the best point of crossing. Best from a standpoint of the tunnel—a tunnel was never questioned for a moment.

This background is necessary to understand the location of the Moffat Tunnel, to understand the many men and many attempts which it represents. Moffat's men ran ten distinct lines: five over the hogback just south of the present tunnel, three over Rollins Pass (in places above the present tunnel), and one each over Devil's Thumb and Caribou (Arapahoe) Passes, both north of Rollins. Ten tunnels were surveyed by hard-working parties high on the Divide. These men covered literally every foot of ground for miles up and down the Range. Their contribution was not only to the Moffat Road, but also in the information gained which permitted location of the long-planned Moffat Tunnel.

We have seen that the construction of the Moffat was frustrated at every turn—as was its operation. The spring of 1911 saw the deaths of Senator Hughes and Moffat himself. Gore Canyon—60 miles west— had broken David Moffat financially and physically. At this critical hour construction funds were not to be had. William G. Evans, vice president of the Denver, Northwestern and Pacific and president of the Denver Tramway, had succeeded Moffat as president of the railroad. Meanwhile, almost without knowledge of the railroad, a bill had been introduced in the State Legislature in 1911 for issuance of bonds to construct a tunnel under James Peak. This was the first attempt to use public funds. The tunnel mentioned in the bill was to extend from Tolland to Arrow and was not to exceed five miles in length.

The location and projected length were self contradictory. A glance at a topographic map today will show that the contemplated length was seriously in error since the actual distance would have been closer to seven miles if the portal was actually planned near Tolland. On the other hand, this would have given a 1.9% grade descending to the east favoring the direction of maximum tonnage and would have avoided an apex in the tunnel, an important consideration which later events were to prove. Incidentally, the bill also proposed the Dotsero Cutoff, the first such proposal of record. The inconsistency in the figures was acknowledged by the D.&S.L. in 1915. The advertising folder of that date reproduced in this book shows the "Panoramic View of Beautiful Boulder Park and Tunnel Site" with the portal retouched in slightly west of Tolland. It is interesting to note that the previous advertising folder alike in every other respect shows no mention of the tunnel. The caption gives the intent at that time—a 6.4 mile tunnel costing a mere $4.5 million.

These attempts for construction by the entire state of a Moffat Tunnel directly west of Denver were rejected by a popular majority of the people in the southerly portions of the state. They felt rightly that they would receive no benefit and should not assume any such costs. In order to appease the objectors, the next attempt was made in the Tri-Tunnel Project of 1920. The latter envisioned three Trans-Divide Tunnels, a Monarch Pass Tunnel to by-pass Marshall Pass, a Cumbres Pass Tunnel on the D.&R.G. narrow-gauge line to Durango, and the Moffat

East Portal as construction started. The need to get underground was imperative because any delay would mean construction of the necessary buildings and portal equipment in the massive snows of Winter Park and Tolland. This might mean cessation of construction until spring. Should such misfortunes come about, interest would pile up quickly. Therefore in July, 1923—even before the tunnel contract was let—the Commission got busy. At East Portal, here shown in the winter of 1923-1924, living quarters were constructed, together with baths where the men could shower after work. Experience in European tunnels had shown this latter point to be of extreme importance since illness soon overtook men who passed quickly from the winter warmth of the tunnel into the biting cold outside. Recreation halls and eating houses clustered about the tunnel mouth and formed the nucleus of a little city whose citizens obviously preferred Model T's to competitive makes. Private business enterprises pulled strings, and sought political influence to secure their concessions. But to the great credit of the Tunnel Commission, they were not granted. The entire income from this venture was $600,000 clear which was applied to the cost of the tunnel construction. Indeed, an engineer like H. A. Sumner would have been pleased with the wholesome atmosphere for the men and the use put to these profits. In addition, a high voltage transmission line was brought over the mountains to supply energy at both portals. *Denver Public Library Western Collection.*

West Portal, Moffat Tunnel. These skiers high above modern-day Winter Park can look out across the Main Range, little realizing the drama inherent in hot-shot freight SPD entering the tunnel. The original site of the West Portal was behind the lodgepole pine at the right. Several small lakes were noted during the preliminary survey on the east side over the summit visible in this picture; although soundings had not been taken, it was felt that they would not in any way affect the rock underneath, or the amount of water in the tunnel 1,000 feet below them. At West Portal a number of pits had been sunk in the moraine lying across the tunnel entrance to test the material overlaying the rock. An influx of water prevented sinking them to bed rock, but enough information was obtained to show that it was very improbable the old glacial channel was deep enough to reach into the tunnel. Just before dirt began to fly, a change in alignment became necessary. Acting upon the counsel of geologists, the West Portal was moved 400 feet farther north to secure better solid rock cover. As it turned out, this action was no help at all. We know now what the geologists then did not—that the entire hill just back of the tunnel entrance was a moraine pushed there by an ancient glacier which descended into the valley at the right. There was no solid rock in the moraine. *D. & R. G. W. R. R. photo.*

The tunneling plan. The Pioneer system of tunneling illustrated here was to be used. This highly stylized drawing was created for the original publicity and shows the Pioneer concept. Although minor changes were made as construction advanced, the overall system was not changed. In this plan two tunnels are driven side-by-side. The smaller, or Pioneer, functions as a service tunnel and cross-cuts are made into the route of the main tunnel. The latter is drilled undersized at first, and then enlarged. The Pioneer system was advocated because it was old and established, having been used on the twelve-mile Simplon Tunnel and five-mile Rogers Pass (Connaught) Tunnel in British Columbia. The advantages claimed for it were: (1) a high rate of progress would be possible in the Pioneer because work is not impeded by construction in the main tunnel, (2) each cross-cut to the main tunnel could be worked on two headings doubling the rate of progress possible, (3) advance information would be available relative to unusual conditions to be encountered in the main tunnel since the Pioneer tunnel is always ahead, (4) the Pioneer could be used as a drain in wet ground, (5) operations could be carried on in any number of locations in the main tunnel, (6) drilling and blasting could be carried on more easily, (7) better access could be had to all parts of the tunnel, (8) all piping and electrical circuits could be located in the Pioneer and so protected from enlargement operations, (9) the Pioneer could itself be used as an air conduit to supply the main tunnel and save five miles of pipe, (10) progress on the Pioneer could be pushed to the limit without interference from the enlarging operation, while at the same time sufficient cross-cuts could be provided to permit progress on the main tunnel to keep pace, and (11) since the interest charges would amount to $1,000 a day, days saved by the Pioneer would mean a significant saving. *Denver Public Library Western Collection.*

Tunnel extending from Tolland to Vasquez. In this proposal the Moffat Tunnel was shortened to 6.2 miles in length and the statement was made by L. D. Blauvelt, a very famous Colorado engineer, that the savings on the Moffat Tunnel alone would pay for all three. This plea for three tunnels was again de-

feated by the people's vote. Hence, the outcome was the proposed creation of a Moffat Tunnel Improvement District to finance the projected Divide penetration. The District included only the City of

The Moffat Road

Denver and an area adjacent to the constructed Moffat line. This was approved by a vote of those included in the District.

Since the details of the tunnel financial battle and the efforts to secure public assistance are covered elsewhere, we will not repeat them here in further detail. Suffice to say that upon passage of the Moffat Tunnel Improvement District bill, the 1920 location for the tunnel was adopted. This was conceded by all to be the best location possible since it was below timberline and deep snow conditions, and did not require excessive length. It culminated fifty years of search for a passage.

Upon formation of the Moffat Tunnel Commission, D. W. Brunton, Colorado's famous mining engineer, was appointed Chairman of the Board of Consulting Engineers. He summarized the Tunnel plan in an after-dinner speech to the Colorado Scientific Society in October, 1923; he stated that the State Geologist had examined rock conditions at both portals and reported no structural features evident which would interfere with construction.

But there is another side to this story. From the first the pioneer bore was envisioned by far-sighted men of Denver as a water tunnel to bring water from the Western Slope to the city. The Improvement District Tunnel bill was passed, however, solely for the specific purpose of placing Denver on a transcontinental railroad route. Some engineers contended that every foot of rock removed created added expense which would have to be paid for in taxes. Art Weston, a pioneer railroad locating engineer, wrote an article in the December, 1922, *Colorado Engineers' Bulletin* titled "Why Two Tunnels?" Weston summarized his purpose in writing that article, "I knew that this 'pioneer' tunnel was intended to be used to bring water from the Western Slope to Denver. But 'they' did not come out in the open and say so."

Why was a six-mile tunnel needed at all? Moffat's first and most famous Chief Engineer had recommended a 2.6 mile tunnel unless the traffic became very heavy. D.&S.L. President Freeman was satisfied with a short tunnel at this location. Colorado's Senator Phipps was not particular as to which location was used, for his main determination was to get

The first railroad to leave a permanent mark upon the Rollins Pass Country was the Denver, Utah & Pacific Company. From a train about to enter Tunnel 8 one can see the construction work of this earlier effort. The grade is in use today as an access road by the Denver Water Board. Historic Eldorado Springs shows clearly in the valley to the left of the grade. The D.U.&P. was formed December, 1880, and included David Moffat with H. A. W. Tabor and others on the board of directors. It can be said with no fear of contradiction that this was Moffat's first direct, forthright attempt to build a railroad over Rollins Pass. The line started in Denver and was surveyed up South Boul-

der Canyon on 4% grades. Streeter & Lusk, who later built the Moffat, undertook the construction in separated segments. Although this view shows the section of the old route which is most evident today, other portions can still be found at Rollinsville and Tolland. Clear traces exist still at Tunnel 30 where the old D. U. & P. grade crosses the present main line. *McClure photo.*

Survey lines over the Main Range. Surveyors were busy in the summer of 1923 setting the final stakes. This magnificent view of East Portal, taken years later of a Rio Grande time freight leaving the tunnel, clearly shows the two survey swaths cut over the mountain in line with the tunnel. They are visible to this day. The Continental Divide at the tunnel is located on a plateau where a view of each portal can be had from the top. Because of heat refraction errors during the daytime, which threw lines off three feet, all accurate surveying was done at night. The crews would leave the base camp each afternoon and climb slowly to the top, where they would work all night. This procedure was fine for summer evenings, although even at that season high altitude temperatures were near freezing. Note the old Moffat grade at the right. *D. & R. G. W. R. R. photo.*

Denver on a transcontinental line. Gerald Hughes, however, saw Denver's need for water. He had been with the Denver Union Water Company when there was a growing deficiency in the water needs of the city. Hughes, a man of great vision for Denver's future, felt that a transcontinental railroad line could not build a city alone without an adequate water supply. But he knew the taxpayers of Denver would not hear of, and would not vote bonds for, the boring of a water tunnel through the Divide to bring Western Slope snow water to the city.

With the popularity of the railroad tunnel, Gerald Hughes saw an opportunity to get a water tunnel if the railroad tunnel was located at the 9000 foot level and constructed with the aid of a pioneer bore. It was his philosophy that the people might be fooled, but it would be for their own good.

Use of a pioneer bore was not an open-or-shut affair. Worst of all, the tunnel was public property and judgments could not be made on a strictly engineering basis. As we shall see, some of the advantages claimed for the pioneer were proved in practice. Others fell cruelly short. Yet today the water tunnel is undoubtedly as important as the railroad bore.

So sure of rock conditions was the Tunnel Commission, that they assumed all risks of construction. This decision developed when the first set of bids was found to be high because of the charges made by the bonding companies for the performance bonds, and because of the contingencies which the bidders had included to cover emergencies. The Tunnel Commission decided to assume the cost of contingencies because they considered there was not more than one chance in a hundred of the worst materializing. So, for about $1 million saving, the Commission took the risk of striking excess water or poor rock.

The decision was made on the best information available, but was wrong in the extreme. Because interest charges on the bonds were accruing at the rate of $1000 a day, the final contract was hurried through and allowed a fixed fee for the tunnel construction, plus a share of any cost saving made, plus a time bonus or penalty.

From the outset, excavation at the west side ran into trouble. In fact, the fanfare surrounding the start of construction had hardly died away when it became apparent that construction was proceeding much more slowly than projected. Hearts sank, for this meant increased cost. Geologists had believed that the west slope consisted of a solid core covered by glacial drift. Instead, the opening of the portal revealed shattered, fractured ground. "This won't last long," men said. But it did. Shift after shift passed. In all, nearly three and a half miles were encountered. Water seeping between the seams made the whole mass unstable. Then later, talc seams were found which were slippery in the extreme. At best, timbering was required, and at worst the pressure inside the mountain caused the earth to flow like a live creature bent on encircling and crushing the intruder gnawing at its vitals. Progress at the west end was limited by the speed of timbering. It was found necessary to place timbers tempor-

Mechanical equipment had been ordered; but procurement and transportation took time, with the result that opening the portals was done by hand, much as in the old Moffat days in the "tunnel district." As a matter of fact, heavy machinery was still arriving well into the winter, and sleds were used to bring in mine locomotives and other supplies from Irving Spur nearby. These two-foot gauge locomotives, incidentally, were no small machines; five ton mining locomotives powered by batteries were used close to the working faces, and four ton engines with overhead trolley worked long hauls. *Denver Public Library Western Collection.*

ily to support the roof and sides of the heading and later replace these during the enlarging operation when the tunnel was driven full size. The vertical plumb posts to support the ceiling arch were made from 12"x12" Oregon fir.

How could such a thing happen? Several test pits had been sunk at West Portal before construction began. They were abandoned before reaching down to Tunnel elevations, however, when water was encountered and funds ran short. When solid rock was found, later investigation revealed it to be only boulders. Today in any work of large magnitude, diamond drilling would be undertaken as a routine measure to determine precisely the underground conditions. Yet in the Moffat Tunnel, no funds were available before the bond issue was sold and the Tunnel Act authorized no preliminary investigation. After the bonds were sold, interest charges piled up so fast that the Commission felt impelled to begin construction. Certainly no work of equal magnitude was ever begun based upon such fragmentary information. It is no wonder that the final cost was over twice the estimate—and the taxpayers in the Improvement District were called upon to assume the bill.

At Crosscut 9 West, 12,600 feet from the portal, the Tunnel crossed the Ranch Creek Fault. This sheer zone, born of some prehistoric upheaval, was so badly shattered that it amazed men of life-long tunnel and mining experience. It is said that this rock was the worst ever encountered in the world. Although semi-dry, the ground flowed like a viscous liquid. No dynamite, or very small charges were required. Sometimes the material flowed into the working face requiring breastworks to be erected to prevent it from moving into the tunnel proper. By this time, steel side posts with arches and invert steel floor sections were being utilized.

Strangely, however, this ground was not dangerous, so long as movement or flow was prevented. Baled hay was even used. There were no sudden deadfalls. Ample warning was given by the mountain in the form of small rock fragments which dribbled down from the face or ceiling.

The use of steel lining encased in concrete again contained the earth pressure. As though engaged in a gigantic chessgame, the mountain then brought up its Queen. With the ceiling and sides firmly supported, the earth pressure came to bear upon the floor of the tunnel which began to rise, just a little at first, then *swelling and buckling upward.* This threatened to undermine the footings for the sides and threatened collapse of the entire steel tube. This "swelling ground" is the most dreaded because it is the hardest to control; to do so required an inverse arch to be constructed—a depressed steel floor, if you will, completing encirclement of the tunnel periphery.

It was at this point that the efficacy of the pioneer tunnel was most truly demonstrated. Instead of a crosscut every fifteen hundred feet as originally planned, connections were bored every few hundred in order to provide more working faces. At one time in June, 1927, fifteen faces were being worked on the west side alone utilizing four Lewis Cantilever Bars.

Excavation at the West side ran into trouble. In fact, the fanfare surrounding the start of construction had hardly died away when it became apparent that construction was proceeding much more slowly than projected. Geologists had believed that the west slope consisted of a solid core covered by glacial drift. Instead, the opening of the portal revealed shattered, fractured ground. "This won't last long," men said. But it did; shift after shift passed; in all nearly three and a half miles were encountered. Water seeping between the seams made the whole mass unstable. Talc seams were slippery in the extreme. At best, timbering was required, and at worst the pressure inside the mountain caused the earth to flow like a live creature bent on encircling and crushing the intruder gnawing at its vitals. Progress at the west end was limited by the speed of timbering. It was found necessary to place timbers temporarily to support the roof and sides of the heading and later replace them during the enlarging operation when the tunnel was driven full size. The vertical plumb posts to support the ceiling arch were made from 12″ to 12″ Oregon fir. *Denver Public Library Western Collection.*

Very little timbering was needed on the east, and then only for a few feet at a time. There were a few cases where the rock showed a tendency to disintegrate and spall upon exposure to the air, but this was overcome easily by applying a coating of gunite—liquid concrete, shot out by air—to the roof and walls as required.

Conditions became steadily worse. Sometimes the roof segments were driven into the wall plates, crushing them. The faulting was so irregular that conditions in the two tunnels only seventy-five feet apart were invariably quite different. After the timbering had been set, the grinding, crushing earth pressure caused the plumb posts to rotate, or to bend inward until they splintered and cracked. It became necessary to use 12″x18″ timbers—and they failed, too. Spacing between them was decreased until they were being set side by side continuously in the tunnel wall. Then 14″x18″ posts were tried and, finally, in desperation, double timber sets were used, 12″x12″ on the inner ring and 14″x18″ skin tight on the outer. Progress was extremely slow. The timbers were very heavy and hard to handle. Morale was low. Experienced workers were quitting, discouraged by lack of progress. Competent engineers agreed that the decision to hold this heavy ground permanently with timber was a bold one. There was no record in engineering literature of anyone having seriously considered such a thing practical, nor is it considered likely that it will ever be attempted again. As a matter of fact, one crew at West Portal was kept busy continuously replacing bent, twisted, and failed timbering. *Denver Public Library Western Collection.*

George Lewis, general manager of the Tunnel and inventor of the Lewis Cantilever Bar, is here shown about to leave for Denver. He was a man of extensive mining experience at Cripple Creek, and in addition had an inventive bent. One evening he and his companions discussed the problem which was eating up the substance of the Improvement District. Various plans had been suggested, but, as usual, nothing tangible had developed. Mr Lewis retired and while awaiting sleep in his restless state, an image struck his brain. He recalled a house being moved on dollies to make way for the then-new Denver Civic Center. From this he conceived an idea for a traveling "needle bar" to hold up the roof of the tunnel, so that excavating could proceed underneath. He awakened some of his companions to discuss the idea. All night long they worked. First thing in the morning, he dashed by automobile into Denver to present the idea to Cliff Betts, Office Engineer. After refining it still further, he presented the idea for his expensive machine to the Commission. Those to whom he talked were dubious. Finally, to demonstrate his faith, Lewis offered to pay for the machine himself, if it failed. *Denver Public Library Western Collection.*

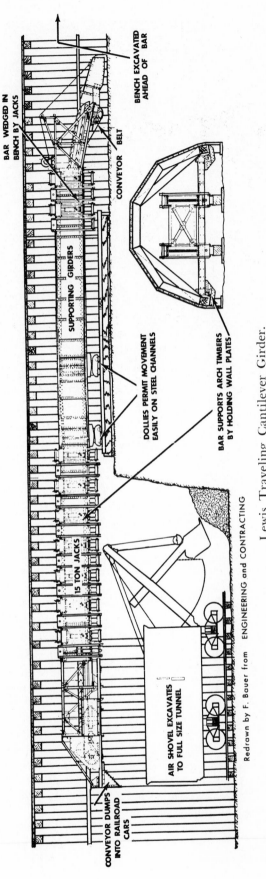

BAR WEDGED IN
BENCH BY JACKS

BENCH EXCAVATED
AHEAD OF BAR

CONVEYOR
BELT

SUPPORTING GIRDERS

DOLLIES PERMIT MOVEMENT
EASILY ON STEEL CHANNELS

BAR SUPPORTS ARCH TIMBERS
BY HOLDING WALL PLATES

15 TON JACKS

AIR SHOVEL EXCAVATES
TO FULL SIZE TUNNEL

CONVEYOR DUMPS
INTO RAILROAD
CARS

Lewis Traveling Cantilever Girder.

Redrawn by F. Bauer from ENGINEERING and CONTRACTING

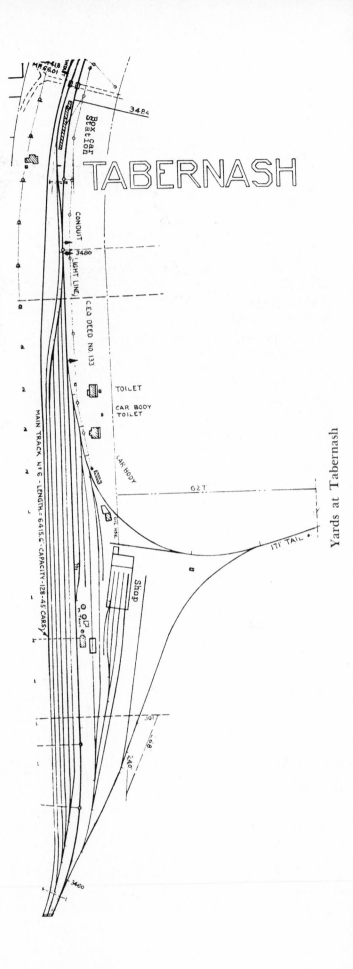

TABERNASH

Box car
Station

CONDUIT

LIGHT LINE

CE2 DEED NO. 133

TOILET

CAR BODY
TOILET

MAIN TRACK N°6 - LENGTH=6415.6 - CAPACITY=128.45 CARS

CAR BODY

OIL HSE.

Shop

3484

3480

62T

ITI TAIL

Yards at Tabernash

The Lewis Bar at work. The Traveling Bar is felt by many to have saved the Moffat Tunnel. This shows its general construction. Basically, two massive steel girders 65 feet long and 3½ feet high are tied together with struts into a structure resembling a bridge. One end is held firmly by the advancing top excavation using jacks as a wedge. The other end then becomes a cantilever, very much like an arrow embedded in a target. The rear end of the cantilever supports the tunnel roof, permitting excavation and timbering to be carried out. The shovels have moved back from the face for a moment, and we have a clear  view of the top excavation in which the bar is mounted to support the three-segment arch being constructed. Meanwhile, benching goes on simultaneously below. *Denver Public Library Western Collection.*

Lewis Bar with conveyer. The conveyor system shown here was placed between the two girders. This permitted much easier excavation ahead of the machine with rapid dumping of muck into railroad cars placed at the rear. After timbering was complete, the bar could be advanced to a new position. By this means progress was doubled and costs cut. Note the five-segment arch here which was mixed with sections of three-segment. This intermixture was years later to give trouble during concreting operations. *Denver Public Library Western Collection.*

Page 193

Number 1 behind 301 at Newcomb. The buckboard is down to meet the train, together with several local residents and their dog. Up the track lies the Hill which the doughty little engine will soon tackle. The passengers idly gazing out the windows at the bright summer scenery are due for a rougher ride than usual because the D. & S. L. sees little sense in maintaining the Hill when the Tunnel is planned to be in operation the next year. The short spur to East Portal heads directly toward the photographer. This is now the location of the wye at East Portal. *Denver Public Library Western Collection.*

On St. Valentine's Day, 1925—before the East Portal pioneer tunnel reached the Apex—a serious flow of water was encountered. Driven by some extreme pressure, over 1800 gallons of water per minute sprayed into the small confines of the pioneer. The hip-deep water was, however, handled easily with no discomfort other than the temporary cessation of work. Within a month the flow dropped to 150 gallons per minute. Nevertheless, the amount of water found demanded an explanation, and this was soon forthcoming.

The course of the tunnel led directly under one

Work at the east side settled down. A "jumbo set" has been erected acting as a scaffold for placing the permanent three-segment arch. Later the plumb posts will be set if required. The mining process begins when a train brings the drill crew to the working face in the pioneer tunnel. There, compressed air drills produce holes varying from four to ten feet long, spaced in a pattern which outlines the shape of the tunnel; the charges of dynamite are then gingerly set. The firing of a round becomes perfunctory to the miners—the explosion at first is a sullen boom. Then quickly follows a shock wave, described as a curious, low, beating sound that seems to shake the walls and ceiling. Another and another! as the delay fuses act in sequence. *Denver Public Library Western Collection.*

Muckers converge on the debris to clear the railroad tunnel. With the aid of rugged Conway mucking machines and compressed air shovels like this one, the job is done rapidly. Pushing up to the muck pile created by the blast, the machines begin to digest it. With a rattling and clanking of the conveyor belt and powerful scoops, a railroad car is filled every two minutes until at last the pile is gone. The cycles repeats as often as three times in an eight hour shift if conditions are right, with work on the pioneer and railroad tunnels being done alternately. *Denver Public Library Western Collection.*

of four beautiful little glacial lakes formed in the bottom of a cirque near the Continental Divide. In the investigation following a large inflow of water, a fissure was suspected connecting the lakes with the tunnel 1400 feet below. Although it was the middle of winter, a small party of men on snowshoes was sent up to investigate. There they found ice two feet thick. Although local gossip had reported the lakes to be bottomless, they were actually only ten feet deep. On a chance, copper sulphate was placed in the water and mixed with an explosion of dynamite. Twenty minutes later tests of water in the tunnel showed traces of this same chemical. The flow subsequently decreased as the seam silted up from sediment on the lake bottom. Similar tests made later, however, showed that chemical detection was possible after two hours time. Many sacks of manure dumped into the lake possibly helped the sedimentation.

Because of the fortunate conditions encountered, progress on the East side was much more rapid than on the West. Summer came and went with no extraordinary events, culminated with a minor triumph when in November, 1925, the pioneer passed the midpoint and started down. This was called the Apex of the tunnel because it was higher than either end to facilitate drainage. Immediately a new problem arose. From this point westward a

An aerial view, looking west through the clouds, of the Crater Lakes with the crest of the Continent in the background. At the bottom of the picture may be seen one of the survey lines over the Divide. On St. Valentine's Day, 1925—before the East Portal pioneer tunnel reached the Apex—a serious flow of water was encountered. Driven by some extreme pressure, over 1800 gallons of water per minute sprayed into the small confines of the pioneer. The hip-deep water was, however, handled easily with no discomforture other than the temporary cessation of work. Within a month the flow dropped to 150 gallons per minute. Nevertheless, the amount of

water found demanded an explanation, and this was soon forthcoming. The course of the tunnel led directly under one of four beautiful little glacial lakes formed in the bottom of a cirque near the Continental Divide. *Denver Public Library Western Collection.*

descending grade would be followed in the digging of the tunnel. Drainage water would have to be pumped up to the Apex until the tunnel was holed through. The comparative tranquility was soon to come to an end.

On February 28, 1926, the attack came in the main railroad heading. A round had just been fired and the mucking machine was preparing to move in to clean it up when the muck pile suddenly became alive.

Shouts went up, drillers and muckers fled as streams of water seemingly came from everywhere. Soon they were in full retreat as three thousand gallons of water per minute flooded the heading. Tools and equipment were completely covered as the water filled 381 feet of the railroad tunnel, then moved over through a cross cut and filled another 1054 feet of the pioneer tunnel to the Apex. The railroad tunnel had run into an underground lake. This type of below surface water collection is known to exist throughout the Rocky Mountains in Colorado.

Once over the hump, of course, the flow was by gravity, but all operations west of the Apex were completely under water. The mountain's second line of defense then took up the cudgel. Fine running silt of gelatinous character was discovered flowing with the water. This was deposited out along the bottom, covering everything, and packing as hard as rock. It later had to be chiseled and blasted out at monstrous cost.

The flow continued unabated at 3000 gallons per minute for about six days and then dropped to 1500. Two large electric pumps were ordered from Denver, brought up to the tunnel quickly, placed on narrow-gauge flatcars, and installed near the Apex. These pumps worked well and by April 21 the workings were unwatered and ready for operation again—the first in nearly seven weeks. The mountain, however, was possessed of motivation and intelligence. Every creation of mechanical ingenuity was soon matched by the malignant forces of nature. Just when success seemed in grasp a severe mountain storm began high on the Hill and roared down into South Boulder Canyon with a fury of snow and wind that broke the power lines. The water again began to rise. Working in the semi-darkness of the tunnel with oil and carbide gas lamps, workmen scrambled to save the pumps, for by this time they had been permanently mounted in sumps and would soon be

This is the scene in the pioneer tunnel February 28, 1926. It seemed that the mountain was only marshalling its forces for a greater attack on the insignificants tormenting it. The attack came in the main railroad heading. A round had just been fired and the mucking machine was preparing to move in to clean it up when the muck pile suddenly became alive. Shouts went up, drillers and muckers fled as streams of water seemingly came from everywhere. Soon the men were in full retreat as three thousand gallons of water per minute flooded the heading. Tools and equipment were completely covered as the water filled 381 feet of the railroad tunnel, then moved over through a cross cut and filled another 1054 feet of water tunnel to the Apex. This photograph shows the condition in the latter. Once over the hump, of course, the flow was by gravity, but all operations west of the Apex were completely under water. The mountain's second line of defense then took up the cudgel. Fine running silt was discovered flowing with the water. This was deposited out along the bottom, covering everything, and packing as hard as rock. It later had to be chiseled and blasted out at monstrous cost. *Denver Public Library Western Collection.*

covered. They were saved, but in the ten hours that were required for line crews to locate and correct the break in the electric power line, the tunnel was again filled to the Apex.

And a new start had to be made. Once more the pumps were mounted on flat cars, moved over the Apex and down the tunnel to suck up the water and force it back over the hump. Again the flood was bested and the headings made ready for drilling, when power failed again. This time the water rose so rapidly that one pump was covered before it could be moved. Again the tunnel was flooded to the Apex.

This time air pumps were put to work, relaying water to the single remaining electric pump, and finally on May 25 work was successfully resumed. Water was a constant nuisance, nevertheless, and required the construction of concrete gutters to carry it off. All told, there can be little question that the underground crevasse lake and river increased costs well over a million dollars in all. The hum of pumps as they were forced to operate twenty-four hours a day was tangible proof of the curious parallel between the difficulties of the Moffat Road and the Moffat Tunnel.

To the great credit of the Tunnel Commission, this complex undertaking was carried out when it looked repeatedly as if the impossible was ahead.

Among the tunnel workers were some men who liked Middle Park well enough to adopt it as their home. To this day they will tell you stories of how tools were wasted by the contractor because he was paid on a cost plus basis. This makes interesting talk, but is not true. A little of it is possibly fact, for in any business the same thing occurs; the disease of waste is not a government disease alone, it is sadly part of the American way. But to understand what happened, we must remember that the unexpected broke loose time and time again, flooding machinery with silt and fractured granite or water and that in such emergencies the loss of tools was secondary to the job of getting the pumps going and the crisis met.

Slowly - steadily - painfully the two pioneer tunnels being driven from the east and from the west approached each other. At 1100 feet apart the sounds of blasting could be heard between headings. At 150 feet the battering of air drills carried over. When the headings were thirty feet apart, pilot drills, twenty-three feet long, were used every round to test for daylight. Tension became terrific, because this is the most dramatic moment in the history of any tunnel, the moment when the first zephyr of clear air would venture from one portal to the other. Denver newspapers had been keeping the Colorado public steeped in news, and, although engineers were confident, there was ever a question in the public mind as to whether the headings would actually join. With twenty minutes of their time still remaining, the graveyard shift of West portal on February 12 tried a pilot drill without success. Assistant Superintendent C. M. Paul was prepared that night. Bringing up a forty-foot bar of reinforcing steel, his West crew jammed it into the hole with their bare hands and jabbed until finally opposition gave way. The Moffat was holed through!

Tunnel men are superstitious; they believe that a curse falls upon the losing crew in a race like this. Knowing from the sounds that the West crew was up to something, the East Portal men grabbed the emerging bar in a last minute attempt to gain victory. There, in the heart of the mountain an impromptu tug-of-war took place; muckers and drillers on both sides, oblivious of cut and bleeding hands, fought stubbornly as the bar alternately gave each side a fragrance of victory. But Paul, wise in the ways of tunnel men, had prepared well. Before

The winning tunnel crew shivering outside West Portal, as they made ready to dash over Berthoud Pass to Denver for the celebration. *Denver Public Library Western Collection.*

trying the bar, his men had put a kink in their end to make sure it would not be stolen from them!

The Denver papers had a field-day of excitement bringing the news to the public. The winning crew was treated like the royal house of England at a celebration given in Denver. No doubt these men deserved the honor more than many kings. A ceremony, of course, had to be provided for the next day. Distinguished guests from Utah and Colorado were taken by President Freeman of the railroad over the Hill to West Portal, but this special train battled the wrath of Old Man Winter, who forced the Moffat to use two rotaries to keep the Hill open.

Arrangements had been made so that President Calvin Coolidge could explode the final charge by telegraph the evening of February 18, 1927, but great vigilance was required to prevent a fiasco. The miners who had drilled the final round were disdainful of ceremony other than that provided by a raw blast of dynamite, and they were restrained only with difficulty from taking over the President's prerogative! Outside the tunnel another storm raged. The Commission's teams were kept busy on the roads, clearing them and helping stalled automobiles.

Telegraph apparatus, and a radio receiving set, had been installed at Crosscut 13 East, 14940 feet from West Portal. Promptly at 8:10 P.M. the electric command sped from Washington. Twenty-four dull booms followed in sequence. When the

Unheralded, Engine 120 was actually the first through the tunnel. The mine locomotive tracks had been removed, as a mere handful of workers witnessed the historic event. *H. F. Eno collection.*

Four trains of ten cars each merrily followed the proud 200 mallets up the two per cent to East Portal. The 203 heading Special Number 2 is on the way up, near Tolland. Regular Number 1 was in the rear of the parade, with engine 303 and Chester Foltz at the throttle. Dave Moffat would have been proud of his men that day. They handled the motive power well. No oversight occurred to embarrass the little road. Old Man Winter's stronghold was conquered on a typical blustery day high over the tunnel. *Otto Perry photo.*

Mallet 205, with a U.P. baggage for a buffer, handled the first official train through the Moffat Tunnel. Newsreel cameras grind and cheers ring out while Louis A. Larsen, engineer, and T. F. Carr, fireman, wave to the crowd. Frank Spaulding was the conductor and F. A. VanVranken brakeman, with R. E. Dunlap flagman on the special. The veteran conductor, George Barnes, failed to be the first through the tunnel. He claimed Bill Freeman, the president, was angered by the probable line-up of trains the newpapers had printed, and side-tracked his train out of spite. Joe Culbertson, chief dispatcher and very loyal friend of George, differs, thinking that the engine pulling Barnes' train fell down, causing the delay. *Denver Public Library Western Collection.*

blue-grey smoke had cleared, miners dashed for the opening without testing the overhanging rock, and crawled over the rock pile to join their brethren. Governor W. H. Adams of Colorado and Mayor C. C. Neslen of Salt Lake City were there to shake hands and perform the more official opening.

Standing to one side, no doubt, were the engineers who had supervised the drilling of this bore. Upon investigation, it was found that the two tunnels met within $3\frac{1}{2}$ feet vertically and $1\frac{1}{2}$ feet horizontally, and that the actual length varied from the computed length by only twenty-one inches.

To the public the holing-through meant a completed tunnel. This was far from the case. The needle-thin pioneer tunnels had met. The railroad heading was far behind, and the completed full-size railroad tunnel was behind that. The railroad tunnel was holed through without much fanfare in July, 1927, while timber crews in the completed portions of the tunnel were hammering home

California redwood ceiling planks as protection against locomotive sparks, and concrete crews were pouring the portal at the west end. Drilling continued at a more rapid pace as ventilation conditions improved greatly through the free passage of air. Rails and ties were laid through the tunnel and the first week of February, 1928, the first pilot train went through.

Canny President Bill Freeman initiated full freight service through the tunnel February 14, 1928, but was careful to do so unofficially, and all passenger trains ran over the Hill. In a lawsuit ending in 1930, the United States Circuit Court of Appeals held that the D.&S.L. did not take possession until they were served by the Commission with a written notice of completion on February 26. This maneuver saved the railroad just about $13,000!

Now, having weighed most of the factors which influenced the building of the tunnel, we continue with the story of the official opening of the tunnel on February 26, 1928. Both Denver papers seized the opportunity presented, and magificently told the story, letting the entire nation know that faith had moved the mountains. We smile today when we remember that bombs exploded on the *Rocky Mountain News* roof at the opening. Each paper tried to out-do the other paper in bringing this Big Story to its readers as their own exclusive story. It is all part of the romance of the way Denver does things. It was a privilege to live in Colorado and read the Denver papers!

History cannot record whether the parsons said prayers for the lost souls who cut out church-going that Sunday; we do know that four trains sold out their tickets and Rocky Mountain statesmen and railroaders from all lines accepted the invitation of President Bill Freeman of the D.&S.L. The Sunday program for the celebration as printed in the *News* of February 24 was as follows:

12:15 PM   Invocation by the Rev. Charles Marshall
12:16 PM   Driving the Gold Spike by ex-Governor Oliver H. Shoup and Governor William H. Adams

12:17 PM   Formal delivery of possession of railroad tunnel to the Denver and Salt Lake Railway Company by William P. Robinson, President of the Moffat Tunnel Commission.
12:20 PM   Acceptance of the tunnel on behalf of Denver and Salt Lake Railway Company by William R. Freeman, President.
12:21 PM   Address by Oliver H. Shoup, ex-Governor of Colorado.
12:24 PM   Address by William H. Adams, Governor of Colorado.
12:27 PM   Address by Benjamin F. Stapleton, Mayor of Denver
12:30 PM   Address by John F. Bowman, Mayor of Salt Lake City
1:20 PM   First train enters tunnel.

The *Rocky Mountain News* fired six bombs on the top of its building to mark the passage of the first train through, just as they had fired the same number to mark the completion of the Golden Spike ceremony.

Stubs of each ticket sold to passengers and signed by the passengers were saved, together with newspaper accounts, and placed in a steel box to be opened by the governors of the two states, Utah and Colorado, fifty years after the opening of the Tunnel. The authors of the present volume prayerfully hope they may be present in 1978 to witness the Golden Anniversary Party.

The most humorous incident of the day occurred when the first train quietly drifted out of the West Portal of the tunnel. At Winter Park stood a sign with these words: "WE BUILT THE TUNNEL. THE POST DIDN'T." Superintendent A. L. Johnson ordered the sign torn down by the section men, but he never knew whose idea it was until twenty years later. The residents of Middle Park had been denied the right to walk through the Moffat Tunnel, even though it was not in use, before the celebration. Among these people were the construction workers, who with Doc Susie Anderson of Fraser would have had to take the night train

over the pass and spend nine cold hours at East Portal waiting for the celebration. The soft-spoken, kindly Doc Susie blew up, and with the help of bystanders took an old broom and dipped it in some tar and painted the sign with the same hands she had used to care for the injured. Her venom was taken out on the *Denver Post*, which had ballyhooed the celebration to such an extent that these hard-working people wanted it to be known who built the tunnel. The sun blistered the eyes of those who gathered at West Portal to see the 205 come through with her twenty-car train. Yes, Dave Moffat's victory was headline news in New York, where men had said "No" to his idea twenty years before. History would certainly have been changed if the scene had taken place in 1907 instead of 1927! *Doc Susie Anderson collection.*

After turning at Tabernash, the 205 again dives into the blackness on the way back to Denver, arriving at East Portal just in time to meet some adventurers who had attempted to drive up the narrow county road. The snow was too deep, cars stalled, and men became a fraternity of brothers chaining car to car and pushing and shoveling. The Tunnel Commission sent down teams to extract the helpless cars, and though the worshippers of the gas buggy arrived too late for the best of the celebration, coffee and sandwiches were waiting for them while they pondered the bare statistics of the tunnel:

Length: 32,800 feet, 6.21 miles, sixth longest in the world.

Excavation: 750,000 cubic yards of rock, equivalent to sixteen hundred freight trains of forty cars each, or a shaft 100 feet square rising three and a half times as high as the Eiffel Tower to 3600 feet.

Blasting: 2,500,000 pounds of dynamite fired.

Drilling: 700 miles of holes were bored to set the dynamite, requiring 800,000 pounds of drill steel and 1500 drills a day to be sharpened.

Timbering: 11,000,000 board feet, equivalent to two thousand miles of 1″x12″ plank road. *Denver Public Libary Western Collection.*

But there occurred one of those unbelievable "goofs" that make the role of a historian so fascinating. Twenty years later, in 1947, this same steel box was found by Rio Grande officials in the Moffat Station—not in the Tunnel at all! It was then temporarily placed for safekeeping in the office of Public Relations Director George Dodge until a hole could be drilled in the East Portal face of the Moffat Tunnel and the box belatedly placed therein. Why President Freeman had slipped up on this will never be known.

During the building of the tunnel, a dispute arose between the Tunnel Commission engineers and those of the railroad. The consulting and construction men unanimously recommended that all trains be handled through the tunnel electrically, either by electric road locomotives, or electric engines hauling steam trains. They felt this system was a necessity to obviate the need for a ventilating plant, and to reduce the possibility of fire, which in the case of a long timber-lined tunnel would be unusually great. Unfortunately, all connection of the Commission engineers ceased upon tunnel completion, and the "D. & S. L. would not consent to electrification, but insisted on operating through the tunnel with steam locomotives and attempt to clear out gases by artificial ventilation." This is a quotation from *Mechanical Engineering Magazine* and constitutes an uncommon criticism in the technical press. Most engineers felt that any proposal which did not include electrification would be strictly a temporary expedient until traffic increased to the point where it was required. H. A. Sumner was known to have favored electric operation, and we come now to the story of its rejection.

The decision of D. & S. L. management and operating personnel which so miffed the Tunnel Commission and its engineers was based upon a number of factors. First, there was no water power located near the tunnel, and what power was available could only be purchased at premium rates. With a maximum daily load of only five freights, five helpers, and two passenger trains a very high daily power demand and excessive plant cost would be required considering the small daily total power consumption. Second, pulling steam locomotives through with banked fires would not result in the elimination of ventilation since tests had shown that the amount of poisonous gases increased enormously under drifting or light working of the steam locomotives. Means would have to be developed to get these gases out. Third, electrification would introduce delays in changing motive power and require separate man-power at the tunnel. Lastly, the cost of ventilation would be considerably under the cheapest estimates of electrification and require only a fraction of the power.

It would be improper here not to recognize that there also existed—and still exists—a controversy over the choice of the Apex. Railroad engineers and operating men feel the tunnel should have been de-signed without the Apex. The only argument for it was the matter of drainage during construction, and experience proved that sadly in error when East crews passed over the center and had to pump water back over the Apex. If the tunnel had been built with a steady descending grade from West to East, it would have favored the direction of heavy traffic, and made unnecessary the use of helper engines up

to the Apex in the days of steam and even occasion-ally now in diesel times. Sumner himself recom-mended a symmetrical tunnel with the elevation the same at both ends and a minimum 0.3% grade both ways from center. Even this would not have worked steam locomotives very hard.

Once ventilation was decided upon, a further de-cision was then made to blow the smoke back over the train. To do otherwise would have meant that train speed would be limited by the speed with which the smoke could be blown ahead of the train through the tunnel; hence the size of the blowers would need to be much larger. Blowing the smoke back over the train also provided a clear view ahead for the en-ginemen. Therefore, two large fans (one for reserve and for a booster if required) were installed at East Portal together with a system of dampers. It was necessary to close the east end of the tunnel when the blowers were operated. The canvas door to do this operates vertically just inside the portal.

When a westbound train cleared the east entrance,

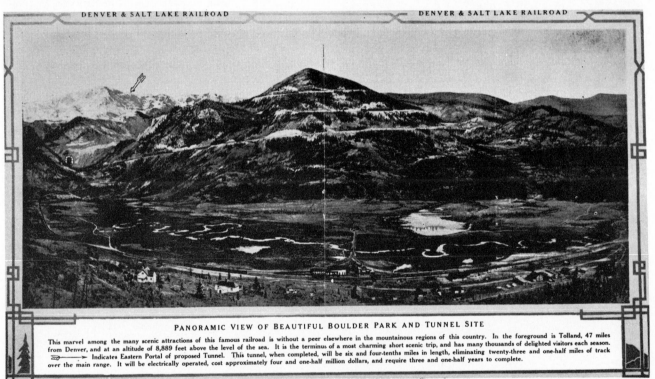

DENVER & SALT LAKE RAILROAD — DENVER & SALT LAKE RAILROAD

PANORAMIC VIEW OF BEAUTIFUL BOULDER PARK AND TUNNEL SITE

This marvel among the many scenic attractions of this famous railroad is without a peer elsewhere in the mountainous regions of this country. In the foreground is Tolland, 47 miles from Denver, and at an altitude of 8,889 feet above the level of the sea. It is the terminus of a most charming short scenic trip, and has many thousands of delighted visitors each season. ➡ Indicates Eastern Portal of proposed Tunnel. This tunnel, when completed, will be six and four-tenths miles in length, eliminating twenty-three and one-half miles of track over the main range. It will be electrically operated, cost approximately four and one-half million dollars, and require three and one-half years to complete.

The unbounded optimism of the Moffat Road was portrayed eloquently in the caption to this center spread of an advertising booklet. There is no doubt that when the tunnel was being talked up seriously, electrification was an integral part of the plan. D. W. Brunton, chairman of the board of consulting engineers, stated at the outset of construction that a ventilation shaft could not possibly be constructed at the Apex due to the mountain overhead. He felt that electric haulage was a necessity with the fires of road engines being banked while the trains were being pulled through. The cost of electric traction was estimated as $450,000 and the design of the tunnel proceeded with the assumption that it would be used. *Fred Bauer collection.*

the curtain over the door was lowered, and the dampers rigged so as to suck air through the tunnel from the west end, exhausting it out the east. For eastbound movements, the dampers were rearranged to blow air in at the East Portal, through the tunnel, and out at the west. The latter meant bucking the natural draft and required some extra electrical energy. The magnitude of the task can be gauged when we consider that the 350,000 cubic feet of air blown each minute is equivalent to 10½ *tons* of air in that time.

Unofficially, the decision to install the fans at East Portal blowing against the natural draft was an error. The D.&R.G.W. *Green Light* comments, "Had circumstances been different, the fans would have been installed on the west end of the tunnel. According to reports, barometers were located at each end of the tunnel during construction. One day a young engineer allegedly adjusted the West Portal barometer.

"The adjustment gave all indications that a slight two-mile-per-hour wind moved from east to west. The error was not discovered until after the fan facilities were installed."

The canvas door has steel members along the sides, but none at the bottom. There is a means to replace the canvas quickly if engines run through it—which has happened twice despite the fact that track circuits provide for opening the door when a train is 1800 feet away. The first such inglorious incident occurred the day before the tunnel was dedicated in 1928 when the curtain didn't completely raise. A similar circumstance took place several years later. In both instances steam locomotives were involved. The 4½ ton door opens in eight seconds and closes again when the train is 100 feet past the door.

When the door was first placed in commission, and for years thereafter, the dispatcher notified the tunnel operator of each train movement. Setting the door and damper controls, and starting a generator to drive the fans required 2½ minutes, after which

PROFILE
OF
═ MOFFAT TUNNEL ═

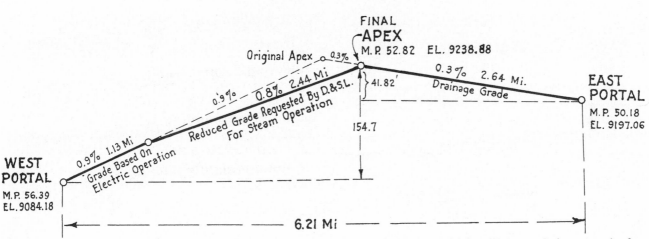

The decision against electrification resulted in basic changes to the tunnel which will leave their earmarks forever. This diagram shows the tunnel as it climbs from each Portal to the Apex. The tunnel originally was intended to have a 0.9% grade on the west, and a 0.3% on the east, the latter being the minimum for proper drainage. When the D. & S. L. decided upon ventilation vis-a-vis electrification, they objected strenuously to the 0.9% grade because it would result in far too much smoke and fumes from multi-engine trains. As a result, the grade was lowered to 0.8% after construction was partially complete. This had the effect of throwing the Apex farther east. Using ventilation was a bold step here, because the great length of the tunnel impeded air flow, and because the Apex was higher than the West Portal by 155 feet and the East by 42. In addition, penetration of the Continental Divide would mean wide barometric fluctuations between the ends. *Courtesy D.&R.G.W. Railroad.*

This fine photograph by McClure shows the ventilation plant at East Portal. The left side was occupied originally by the control equipment alone. Soon a diesel-driven generator was added to reduce power costs after ventilation had proved itself. The canvas door to close the mouth of the tunnel operates vertically just within the portal. The exhaust ports for tunnel smoke can be seen on the second story at the right side just back of the portal. James Peak, 13,250 feet, appears just behind the flagpole. When a westbound train cleared the entrance, the curtain over the door was lowered, and the dampers rigged so as to suck air into the west end, exhausting it out the east. For eastbound movements, the dampers were rearranged to blow air in the East Portal, through the tunnel, and out at the west. The latter meant bucking the natural draft and wasted some electrical energy. The magnitude of the task can be gauged when we consider that the 350,000 cubic feet of air blown each minute is equivalent to 10½ tons of air. The canvas door has steel members along the sides, but none at the bottom. There is a means to replace the canvas quickly if engines run through it—which has happened a number of times in spite of the fact that track circuits provide for opening the door when a train is 1800 feet away. The 4½ ton door operates in eight seconds and closes again when the train is 100 feet past the door. *McClure photo.*

the operator notified the dispatcher and the train was given the right to enter the tunnel. In the two year interval after the opening of the tunnel, total train waiting time for the tunnel to clear of fumes was less than twenty hours.

According to the technical press, there was never any trouble during the several years of early operations with smoke or gas, although many trains operated with as many as three mallets through the tunnel; likewise there was never any report of damage to livestock. At one time a passenger train was held three hours in the tunnel due to an engine failure without the slightest discomfort. On several occasions freight trains stopped for considerable periods with no concern.

So, at the outset, at least, the ventilation system worked properly. During the Depression Years, the curtain was left open for a natural west-to-east flow of air to clean out the tunnel while saving the cost of electrical operation of the fans. The self-cleaning wind required six hours for completion of ventilation.

That was when traffic was light. But as it picked up, conditions became bad. Prior to and during World War II the train-operating men invented all kinds of nose masks and even tried oxygen masks to breathe the air on rear helper engines. The tunnel became at times almost the hell the snowsheds at Corona had been. In later years it was sometimes worse; once when two 3600 D. & R. G. W. engines were doubleheaded together, the temperature in the second cab was measured at 130 degrees F. During the war years at times twenty-eight trains, most with helper engines, passed through the tunnel during a twenty-four hour interval.

As part of the planning for concreting, a minute foot-by-foot inspection was made of the tunnel. Here we see the special, consisting of an engine and flat with shielded lamps, passing through a section on the east end which illustrates the ideal tunnel condition through solid rock. This condition existed only a little more than a mile, and it was recognized at once that almost all of the tunnel required extensive reworking before any concreting could begin. *Denver Public Library Western Collection.*

World War II changed many things, and among them was the ventilation system. As tonnage and train movements increased, the method of blowing air counter to the train caused a plug of smoke to be blown back and forth in the center of the tunnel—sometimes for hours—until a long interval between trains permitted it to clear. Severe corrosion was found in the blower fans and tower vanes and on the west end rail particularly. Three inches of cinders were deposited yearly on the west, and half as much on the east; humidity in the middle four miles was always 100%. Tie deterioration was excessive and signal failures frequent because of the bridging effect the wet cinders had across the two rails. To overcome this situation new larger fans of 420,000 cubic foot capacity per minute were installed and arranged to blow west only, except in cases of emergencies when the flow could be reversed. The westward direction was decided upon so that clean air was always brought in through the tower vanes and fed through the blowers despite the adverse natural draft.

For westward movement, the curtain is now dropped after the train clears the East Portal and ventilation continued for thirty minutes after the train leaves the west end. Ventilation is not used against eastbound diesel trains. Instead the curtain only is closed so that pressure gauges in the ventilation plant will show if the train stops. Ventilation is applied later when the train has left the tunnel. The tunnel equipment was automated in 1959 to eliminate the need for three shift operators.

After the ventilation system was revised, considerable fog and ice were encountered in the east half during winter because of the cold air entering the tunnel, but the overall conditions improved. We should hasten to add, however, that the authors of this book have ridden diesel trains through the tunnel following a five unit freight drag and have been literally lost inside the mountain. It is not possible to see more than a few feet ahead through the brown murk under such severe conditions. In fact, visibility is sometimes so reduced that the numbered trackside location signs cannot be read from the cab; these signs indicate twenty-one refuge stations built into portions of the plugged crosscuts to the pioneer bore, eleven of which are equipped with telephones.

It is further true that with modern diesel power, all present traffic could have been handled through the 2.6 mile proposed tunnel. With a financially sound road and low cost power it is likely that the line would have been electrified at an early date from Tabernash to Denver. This would have been a most desirable mode of operation when used in conjunction with regenerative braking, cutting power costs up to forty per cent. Electricity might have been the final answer to the present Pueblo Division, Subdivision 1-A, up to the advent of diesels. Power produced by the Big Thompson project became available at a price at which electrification might have been preferable to steam power. Engineering departments of two major electric companies have worked on plans for this division. Arthur Ridgway as Chief Engineer of the Rio Grande urged his company to begin setting aside money for the electrification of this division soon after the D.&R.G.W. began operating over it in 1935. With the coming of dieselization, however, all talk of electric operation has stopped and further work may never be done. It should be noted, however, that even as this is written some other railroads contemplate replacement of the individually-powered diesels by central-station-powered electrics. Nevertheless, diesels now operate through the Saint Clair River tunnel of the Grand Trunk at Port Huron, Michigan, and the 7.8 mile Cascade Tunnel (G.N.Ry.), all previously electrified.

Before proceeding to the more recent history of the tunnel, it is only fair to cast an eye back over its first famous twenty years and ask how such a major engineering work could get so far afield cost-wise. There is no one answer. The original costs were very roughly done. The late Erskine R. Myer, a Denver attorney, wrote how he personally drew up the tunnel bill at the suggestion of W. G. Evans, one of the originators of the old Tri-Tunnel plan, in the library of Mr. Evans' home. When asked how much the tunnel would cost, Evans stated a million dollars a mile and two years in time. They therefore figured six miles, six million; plus six percent on six million, $360,000 a year for two years interest; total $6,720,-000. That figure went into the bill. This rough figuring indicates a lack of concrete information upon which to base sound financing. But no dollar figure by any man could have been predicted without some X-ray sight—seeing through into the interior of the Continental Divide at that time.

The greatest increase in cost over the estimate certainly came from unforeseen rock conditions. H. A. Sumner in October, 1909, had advised the management of the railroad "there is always an un-

Welded rail being pulled into East Portal. Outside the portal a timber structure was built for rail storage. The rail was first joined into 1000 foot lengths and work progressed on four lengths side by side. Welds also were made in groups of four—one being poured, two more preheating, and the mold being applied to the last. When a number of long lengths were ready, as shown here, they were spiked in pairs to ties placed crosswise on the track leading to the tunnel and a small diesel pulled them into position. During a break in traffic they were hurriedly spiked down and held temporarily with heavy clamps between sections. Then, when six or more thousand foot lengths were ready, the tunnel was closed and the crew went inside to make the closure welds. *W. C. Jones photo.*

Page 206

certainty as to conditions to be found in a long tunnel; the material changes in character, the water conditions are unknown, the amount of lining cannot be determined, and there are a number of doubtful questions which only actual construction can determine."

Very possibly the railroad's Chief Engineer, L. D. Blauvelt, if ever consulted about the Moffat Tunnel, made little leeway in any estimate for conditions that might be expected because he lacked the aforesaid X-ray sight required. The fractured condition of the rock encountered in almost all of the short tunnels that the Road had previously constructed, the terrible pressures found in two tunnels which resulted in their abandonment, are well established in the letters of H. A. Sumner. All of the first thirty tunnels were in Blauvelt's district as field engineer during construction of the Road, and were well known to him.

Sumner had estimated the cost of the Road, including fifty-four tunnels, and had built it for less than estimated. Sumner estimated his costs exceptionally well and did not overshoot his estimate.

Certainly much was learned by this first piercing of the Continental Divide; this benefited those engineers who have followed with trans-mountain water diversion tunnels through the Divide.

There were other reasons for not foreseeing possible costs and conditions. Geological information was limited; general thinking was that the mountain would be solid rock. Just prior to tunnel construction, the state geologist did recommend moving the west portal about four hundred feet southward to obtain more solid rock. There was no defined doubt expressed about the type of rock condition which was later found to be very poor. Had better information been available concerning adverse water conditions, it is an open question whether there would have been an Apex and possibly any tunnel at all, a fearful loss to the growth of Denver. No doubt was countenanced relative to rock conditions, and so no diamond borings were taken. Test pits sunk were abandoned prematurely. In short, those concerned with the geology were so lacking in funds that they could not conclude that there was need for proper precautions against surprise. Although only a few hundred feet were thought to require support, the actual fact was that most of the western half needed both temporary and permanent timbering.

The tunnel bill was framed partly on pre-World War I conditions and estimates of cost; these estimates did not even include a pioneer bore or a water tunnel, and no consideration was given to advances in cost post War. The Engineering Board and staff came to the construction of this new project with their hands tied—on a definite location and elevation with the estimated cost written in the law. There was no provision for any preliminary work to verify or disqualify important assumptions. The limitations upon the engineering caused by legislative action and legal contracts illustrates well the interdependence of the two.

The 1000' lengths of welded rail have been pulled into Moffat Tunnel. Now sheer manpower is required to pry them into approximate position for later use. *Rio Grande photo.*

Credit should go to the engineers, the contractors, Hitchcock and Tinkler, and the workmen for a job well done. Where the work was under conditions that had been envisioned, it was constructed below the cost estimates. Until unforeseen ground was encountered, the cost of headings was running $10.36 per cubic yard against a bid of $17.00. Again, the Commission felt sure there were only minimum risks ahead and therefore bids were requested without built-in contingency funds.

The real complaint returns to the citizens, who as small investors prior to World War I saw the green grass outside Colorado to the tune of many times the cost of the originally proposed 2.6 mile tunnel. There were few men of great wealth in Denver, but millions were being invested outside the state by the rank and file. More than enough money was lost in useless investments and in wildcat oil schemes to have built the tunnel through the main range as H. A. Sumner recommended in the early days.

Enough of this theorizing! Let's get back to the tunnel; it's built now and the celebrations have subsided. No longer does Number One battle snow. Men whose feet touched only snow for nine months of the year could begin to lead more normal lives. Then what happened?

The Moffat Tunnel began to deteriorate. It deteriorated fast.

Again, and again, and again the curse of the Moffat was cash. Here once more is a case in point. There were delays in obtaining authority for enough money for a first-class concrete-lined tunnel and a wood lining had to suffice. But wood just couldn't stand up in the dark, damp recess. Not that this came as a surprise. The Tunnel Commission had recommended a concrete lining program be carried out as maintenance wherever the timber needed replacing. This would do three things: it would get the most out of the investment in timber, it would defer interest charges on the concrete, and it would provide an opportunity to study the unusually severe ground pressures before concreting. Moreover, from the time the tunnel was turned over to traffic in February, 1928, it was recognized that the wood lining would require complete replacement or reconstruction in a few years. At the time the railroad took over the tunnel from the Commission, there were 16,577 feet of timber, 9078 feet of gunite, and 5400 feet of solid rock which required no lining. Concrete was confined to the two portals and 920 feet of "tubing" encasing the entire tunnel where it crossed the Ranch Creek Fault and another lesser fault of 160 feet. Excessive pressure caused a 65 foot extension of concrete in 1932.

As anticipated, the timber lining soon became a major cause for concern. The timbering disintegrated under the pressures of the mountain, and the water seeped in large amounts through the tunnel from the lakes or crevasses above. The air, which was blown by the ventilating fans from East Portal to West Portal, combined with the humidity to decrease the life of the timbering. Furthermore, the uniform 65° temperature assured optimum conditions for fungi growth, and the rate of decay was rapid. Timbering was replaced by more timbering at a cost of $133,000 yearly. Chief Engineer Jones estimated very accurately that the tunnel could be concreted for $875,000.

To change the policy of replacing timber with concrete was a job requiring the conversion of President Bill Freeman and the railroad owners. The original tunnel had just been bored when engineers and tunnel and bridge maintenance superintendents began crying for something more permanent than timber. But even in the days when money was at hand, that money was wanted for railroad bond interest payments by Freeman and the owners. This made it difficult for Jones to obtain approvals for concreting. Some short sections of failing timber had been replaced by concreting with timber forms. Jones proposed the purchase of movable steel forms, and the installation of a complete concrete mixing plant with equipment capable of efficient placement of the concrete. This met much resistance from the president and others associated in the management of the railroad and its income. There was very little precedent for such a large project and Jones literally sweated blood in obtaining permission to proceed. At times when it was discussed, Freeman said, "Jones, you're crazy, it can't be done."

Jones would not be defeated. He argued. He planned. He fought for every item in his estimate. He was a man who drove himself relentlessly—a competent executive.

At this time an engineer with mining experience and great mathematical ability to figure stresses and design forms was needed. Bill Jones was a brilliant man, but was unable to design the lining. Ed Sunergren was hired to do this. He proved to be the perfect partner for hot-tempered Jones. Sunergren was a quiet gentleman and deliberate thinker who won the affection and respect of all men. Jones found Sunergren to be invaluable and assigned to him solution of many hitherto unsolved problems.

Finally, after much discussion and considerable use of unprintable words, Jones' plan was accepted and the job started. Surprises began to manifest themselves at once. While the old timber lining was presumed to have been placed so that there would be clearance for a concrete lining inside it, pronounced variations were encountered. The width ranged from fifteen feet to twenty-one; the height from twenty-one to twenty-five. Moreover, the lining was not symmetrical about the tunnel centerline. It became necessary to make the track angle as much as ¾ foot off the supposed straight centerline in order to make it stay in the middle of the timbering. Thirteen angles (admittedly small) or changes in direction of the track through the tunnel were required. In addition, it was found that the tunnel roof was in many areas made of a three segment arch in contrast with the accepted standard of five segments. In places they were mixed indiscriminantly; the plumb posts were out of line. As a consequence of all this, the work of preparing the old timber lining (by adzing away or by removing and replacing with bent rail sets to receive the concrete) required a larger work force than the construction of the new lining. The three segment arches had to be removed entirely to get required clearance in the concrete lining. These were replaced by semi-circular arched rail sets.

Work in the tunnel was again extremely difficult. Construction men were constantly interrupted by traffic and the loss of work time averaged sixty per cent. Even with the ventilation, smoke and fumes were a problem. Men came out of the tunnel looking like coal miners. Work was started where the timber was most deteriorated, and it was planned to replace the timber faster than it failed. Work was carried on throughout the winter, and the entire concrete plant and tracks outside the tunnel had to be protected against the minus 40 degree cold. The concrete was applied right over the solid rock where possible. If sufficient clearance was available, it was also applied right over the timber, using forms which could be collapsed and moved along to a new location. Where timbering intruded on clearance limits, however, it was necessary to cut the timber back so that the concrete could be allowed room. The new lining provided a clear width of sixteen feet, and a height of twenty-two feet from rail to crown of arch.

The Salt Lake, however, was engaged in an argu-

ment with the Rio Grande over maintenance payments, and work on the tunnel relining was shut down for ten months, resuming again only after the flow of hard cash.

The Moffat always seemed forced to do things the hard way. The tunnel was located within the Arapahoe forest preserve and no tunnel timber could be burnt at the portals. All of the scrap timber had to be shipped to Utah Junction for possible salvage! There's where resourcefulness entered the picture because it was soon found that about a quarter of the timber was sound. A sawmill was set up and 6000 ties were cut from the old tunnel posts, together with fifty sets of switch ties and planks. Like the parable of loaves and fishes, the odd sizes created were then sawed into planks and sold to individuals.

By such methods costs were kept within bounds. The tunnel was concreted for the estimate, and $1,190,000 in timber maintenance was saved, as not one cent of repairs was made to the concrete until the line was absorbed by the Rio Grande in 1947. In 1937 this program was in full swing. Moffat Tunnel was completed and other tunnels were attacked so that 14,567 feet of guniting and 18,233 feet of reinforced concrete became the new lining replacing the rotting timber.

For years after the pioneer bore was drilled, Denver did not use it for water. Fortunately, W. P. Robinson, president of the Tunnel Commission and former president of the original Denver Union Water Company, kept up a relentless campaign to revive this interest.

Just about this time the water requirements of Denver rose to a point where it became necessary to put the pioneer tunnel into service for transportation of water. To do so required the west half to be concreted. This was because the west half was under water pressure, and the rock was leaky as a sieve. On the eastern half, the rock was sound generally, and the tunnel at this point operated as a syphon at a negative pressure, so concreting was not required.

It is fitting to add here the solutions of several problems in the use of the tunnel in more recent years. We've mentioned how the deposition of cinders amounted to over three inches a year in the steeper western end. The cinders acted as a wet sponge to soak up the sulphuric acid created in the exhaust of steam and smoke from steam locomotives. The coal used in Moffat engines came from Routt County and was excellent for efficient operation, but was high in sulphur. It was so evident that one could smell sulphur dioxide after a three-hundred series engine went through the tunnel. This was not quite so striking in the case of Rio Grande engines which burned bituminous coal from other fields. The short life of the rail occurred at the top or ball of the rail and at the tie plates. Various coatings painted on the rail were tried but could not cope with the problem—particularly since the top of rail could not be greased.

It was also found that passenger trains became quite soiled with soot and cinders while passing through the tunnel. Automatic pressure water jets were installed at the west portal to give the train a quick washing as it passed. Welded 112 pound rail was first installed in the tunnel in 1938. Simply speaking, this is rail which is joined by a series of welds instead of bolted rail joiners. A Thermite mixture was used made of iron oxide, aluminum and magnesium; when ignited this fused at 5000°, running down into a mold placed around the joint. The result is a weld which after grinding and finishing provides a smooth, jointless surface.

By 1943 it was found that this rail was worn out again despite the chemicals and cathodic protection used. An interesting phenomenon was observed when examining the rail; the creep of the 1938 rail was 1/4″-5/16″ downgrade at the two portals, but was 1½″ upgrade at several points in the central portion of the tunnel! The rail replacement program of 1943 consisted of 66,000 feet of 130 pound rail. The old rail had lasted only five years, and to secure longer life a special rail section was chosen having the same base and webb, but a much heavier head. Experience later showed that this rail resulted in a fifty percent increase in life. When one considers that about one-half the cost of track maintenance is due to wear on the joints, the saving in the tunnel by using welded rail can be appreciated.

Three men whose futures were to be curiously related worked laying that 130 pound rail. The first was a young man not long out of college who was Roadmaster of the Moffat—Gus Aydelott. G. B. Aydelott is now president of the Rio Grande. The second was the lumberjack preacher of Fraser, E. T. Bollinger. Al Perlman was then on hand as Chief Engineer of the Rio Grande. The penny-wise policy of the deceased Bill Freeman (and the like unreorganized Rio Grande) completed the job in a pathetic slip-shod manner with little regard for effi-

ciency of modern tools and machinery. The officials were tops in doing the job limited by making bricks without straw. Gus Aydelott was thinking how he would like to do it with better but unavailable means. Perlman was chafing because he thought there should be greater latitude for efficiency. The preacher and every gandy dancer could have commanded better equipment by invention or guesswork, but there were time and financial restrictions everywhere. Again, we have the contrast of a shortsighted interest versus good long range planning.

But with the scrapping of steam power, the life of the rail has now been extended from its best record of eight years previously to the present rail which has been in service over ten years with every indication it may even be good for another fifteen years. There is still some rusting of the rail because of diesel exhaust gases and wet spots in the tunnel. To take care of this problem, umbrellas have been built in one-hundred foot sections at several locations. These umbrellas are built of corrugated iron which has been treated to reduce oxidation and are hung at the spring line of the tunnel on frames. The water is drained in gutters and downspouts. The later are made of plastic tubing so that if they should break loose little harm will result. The entire cost is $100 per foot.

A rubber apron has been installed where moisture seeps through cracks in the tunnel. Near the East end a great deal of water leaked through for twenty-eight years. Some men felt this was from a faulty water tank serving East Portal. The idea was not explored, however, until an icicle removed a mirror from a business car. So now the last wintertime chopping of ice has ended thanks, first, to a new leakproof tank and water line, and, later, to the elimination of both. There is still some moisture that gets between the base of the rail and the tie-plate in spots. The Research Department has developed a rubber shoe which seems to reduce wear and corrosion.

Ed Sunergren, Office Engineer for fifteen years on the D.&S.L., derived for the railroad the strengths of the various timber types of lining both by graphic statics and mathematics. He prepared the general type of plan for concrete lining and initiated a study of the electric precipitator during the days of steam operation. This is a particle ionizing device widely used in cement plants to remove ash from stack gases and is one of the most efficient air purifiers known. Los Angeles also used the same principle in dealing with the elimination of sewer gases. So Ed designed, obtained bids, and worked until he had several ideas for its use in smoke boxes of engines or in the refuge places in the Tunnel. The idea was never tested or approved, primarily because the $25,000 outlay did not appeal to management for a previously untried system in a railroad tunnel. It was characteristic, however, of the type of engineering that went on within the little line that had problems which did not confront some of the world's largest railroads.

This has been the story of the Moffat Tunnel from the construction standpoint. The story which follows constitutes one of the greatest prestidigitations ever carried off in public financing.

MOFFAT TUNNEL COMPARED WITH OTHER MAJOR RAILROAD TUNNELS OF THE WORLD

Name	Construction Period	Length, miles	Boring, months	Average daily progress of headings, feet	Cost millions	Cost per lin. foot	Location	Remarks
Mt. Cenis	1857-1870	7.97	157	4.4	$15	$356	Cottic Alps France-Italy	First use of compressed air.
Hoosac	1858-1874	4.75	241	3.0	10	398	Massachusetts	Later electrified & then removed.
St. Gothard	1872-1882	9.26	88	6.2	11.3	231	Alps, Switzerland	800 lives lost in construction.
Arlberg	1880-1883	6.20	40	13.6	5.9	162	Alps, Switzerland, Austria	Favorable rock conditions.
Simplon	1898-1905	12.40	78	13.7	15.7	239	Switzerland, Bernese Alps	Longest in the world, swelling ground, hot springs. Pioneer tunnel used for second track. 2000 fatalities
Loetschberg	1906-1911	9.30	54	14.2	10.3	211	Bernese Alps	5,900 foot cavein
Roger's Pass (Connaught)	1913-1916	5.02	22	21.1	6	227	CPR, British Columbia	Center heading method, exceptionally favorable rock. Pioneer adapted from Simplon used for water.
Cascade	1926-1929	7.79	37	36.9	15+	340	GN Ry. Cascade Range Washington	Pioneer used for drainage, originally electrified, now has ventilating plant and diesels on trains.
MOFFAT	1923-1927	6.21	48	21.0	15,577,817	475	D & S L Continental Divide, Colorado, 50 miles westerly from Denver	Nineteen lives lost. Has ventilating plant and diesels on trains.

The Moffat Tunnel Steal

Drawing by W. Steadman.

No story of the West seems real unless Indians make a raid and take plenty of scalps. This chapter is the story of some very paleface men who scalped the residents of the Moffat Tunnel District for $25,-258,191. When they were brought to court, their action was found to be legal. For this reason, a Moffat Tunnel tax was necessary.

The amazing part of this story is that the Moffat Tunnel District almost slept through the raid. Perhaps this was possible because men were weary with the unsuccessful battles with the blizzards which isolated northwestern Colorado. They relaxed and went off to sleep, to be awakened only by the difficulties of construction which could be ascertained only when one dug the hole.

The Act providing for the Moffat Tunnel District was passed by the Colorado Legislature in 1922. It provided for the usual pattern of special improvement districts. A Tunnel Commission was created with the authority to build a small and a large tunnel, the former for water and the latter for railway use. The estimated cost was $6,720,000; and the Commission was authorized to issue bonds in that amount secured by the real estate of this district, which included the City and County of Denver, the Counties of Grand, Routt, and Moffat, parts of the Counties of Eagle, Gilpin, Jefferson, and Adams. Ninety-five per cent of the District's assessed valuation was in the City and County of Denver.

The Act further provided that the Commission should prorate the cost between the two tunnels, and this was found to be one-third for the water bore and two-thirds for the railroad tunnel. The Act went on to say that the Commission was empowered to make contracts for the use of the tunnels, but stated, "No such contract shall be made with any person or Corporation unless and until such person or Corporation shall bind himself or itself to pay as rental therefore an amount determined by the Board and specified in the contract, which shall be a fair and just proportion of the total amount to pay interest on the bonds provided for in this Act, plus a just proportion of the amount necessary for their retirement and plus the cost of maintenance of the Tunnel, its approaches and equipments."

The story of how private interests got control of the railroad tunnel for a fraction of its total cost and left the taxpayers of the District with a fifty-year burden of taxation to pay for the balance is reminiscent of the buccaneering days of the Nineteenth Century. The facts, chronologically arranged, are as follows: On June 21, 1923, the $6,720,000 bonds specifically authorized in the Act were sold. In September, 1923, work on the tunnel was begun. On January 1, 1925, a supplemental issue of $2,500,-000 bonds was sold. This supplemental issue and other later issues were not specifically authorized in the Act, but lawyers for the Commission and for the bonding houses were satisfied that there was enough of a mandate in the Act to complete the tunnel and enough general authority implied to make the supplemental bond issues legal.

At the time this first supplemental issue of bonds was made, the tunnel was only one-third completed. Rising costs and unexpected physical obstacles had now made it certain that the final cost would be more than twice the original estimate. On January 1, 1926, a third bond issue of $3,500,000 was sold. January 6, 1926, a contract was entered into between the Tunnel Commission and a newly formed Delaware Corporation known as the Denver and Salt Lake Railway Company, to distinguish it from the

The Moffat Tunnel Steal

Denver and Salt Lake Railroad Company, which was then operating over Rollins Pass. This Railroad Company was in receivership and its securities worth very little. The new Company was owned by F. H. Prince of Boston; Alex Berger of Martin, Virginia; and the following men from Denver, Colorado: Charles Boettcher, Gerald Hughes, Senator L. C. Phipps, and L. C. Phipps, Jr. Very little publicity attended the execution of this contract, and both its makings and its terms bear investigation.

Almost immediately after the creation of the Moffat Tunnel Commission, Norton Montgomery, an attorney at law, was employed as its counsel, and was continued as such by the Commission until 1929. Sometime in January, 1924, Mr. Montgomery was employed by the law firm of Hughes and Dorsey, of which Gerald Hughes, Chairman of the Board of Directors and substantial stockholder in the new Railway Company, was a member. He continued to be so employed until March of 1927.

Mr. Montgomery, who was at the time the Tunnel Commission's Attorney, prepared a contract for lease of the railroad tunnel. This contract was, in effect, an option to the new Railway Company for a 99-year use of the railway tunnel. The Railway Company, by the terms of the lease, had the right to terminate the lease at any time before July 1, 1943, the date on which the first payment of principal on the bonds was due, with no further liability than the payment of rentals "up to that time." Not only was it not bound to pay for "a fair and just proportion of the total amount required to pay interest on the bonds," nor "a just proportion of the amount necessary for their retirement" but also it was left optional with it to pay *any* amount for retirement of the bonds. The only rental which the Railway Company was obliged to pay if it decided to keep its lease, was for two-thirds of the first two bond issues only.

As the result of this deal, together with the nominal rent the City of Denver pays for the use of the water tunnel, the final picture of the payment for the tunnels is as follows:

No. 6 leaves Winter Park for Moffat Tunnel. Rio Grande No. 6 has more than nine cars today so that the 1200 series "Mike" road engine is given a 3400 series helper out of Tabernash. *Ed Bollinger photo.*

Winter Park nightmare. D.&S.L. No. 2 is holding the main line after slipping past a D.&R.G.W. freight (which cannot be seen) on the lower end of the passing track below the crossover. A D.&S.L. coal drag with a helper engine behind (not seen) has cut off her double header, a humble consolidation, to let passengers and mail reach No. 2. Now what about the 3410 which has crowded into the passing track? She has just returned through Moffat Tunnel after having helped No. 6 of the Rio Grande from Tabernash to East Portal. Winter Park was nerve wracking for all operators because of moments like this. Moffat Tunnel is too busy to be cleaned out of smoke and its terrible gas. Pity the crew of the rear helper of the coal drag. They will shove the train to the apex of the tunnel and cut off and hope to be alive in the gas and heat of all these engines. *Ed Bollinger photo.*

The total principal of the four bond issues $15,470,000
Total interest payment over 50 year period 28,765,901

Total cost of bonds $44,235,901

They will be paid from rentals and taxes as follows:

Rentals on Railroad Tunnel over 50 years $18,252,710
*Rentals on Water Tunnel over 50 years   700,000
Telegraph Rentals over 50 years   25,000

Total Rentals $18,977,710
Estimated tax requirements over 50 years $25,258,191

*The Water Tunnel rentals will be increased to 25c per acre foot for water brought through the Tunnel in excess of 56,000 acre feet in any one year.

On February 17, 1927, the first train went through the tunnel, and the tunnel went into continuous use for railroad travel. Although the Moffat Tunnel Commission was a public body and its books and records were open to inspection by any taxpayer, it is a curious thing that such an outrageous contract should have escaped all notice. Three years were to expire after the execution of this lease before it was challenged in court. The litigation that ensued is almost as incredible as the making of the lease.

On January 18, 1929, Farrington R. Carpenter, a young attorney at Hayden, Colorado, brought a taxpayer's suit in the District Court of Moffat County to set aside the lease as illegal and collusively ob-

The Moffat Tunnel Steal

tained. On January 28, 1929, the Tunnel Commission started a suit in the Federal Court in Denver to collect rentals due from the Railway.

The same day the Railway filed a suit in the same Federal Court, denying that it owed any rental and asking that its title to its leasehold of the Tunnel be quieted. The Railway then asked that the suit in the District Court of Moffat County be removed to the Federal Court in Denver on the ground of diversity of citizenship.

The issues raised by the Tunnel Commission and the Railway Company in their two suits in the Federal Court were then tried without any serious attempt to do more than modify a few of the minor provisions and no change was made in the rentals. The Federal District Court then refused to send Carpenter's suit back to the State Court on the ground that the same issues had already been tried in the Federal Court.

Meanwhile, the publicity given the contract aroused the people of Denver. The Denver Chamber of Commerce, represented by James Grafton Rogers and Harold Healy; the Denver Real Estate Exchange represented by Grant, Shafroth, Ellis and Toll; and the City and County of Denver, Thomas H. Gibson, City Attorney, all entered appearances as *Amicus Curiae* (Friends of the Court).

When the Federal District Court's decision was taken before the U. S. Circuit Court of Appeals in Denver, Gerald Hughes himself appeared for the Railway Company. When F. R. Carpenter attempted to argue the matter of fraud in the procurement of the lease, because one lawyer had represented the opposing parties, the Court refused to listen and ordered the argument stricken.

With all objectors now neatly disposed of, the Railway went on and let the U. S. Supreme Court affirm the Circuit Court's decisions and the lease

Colorado Pioneers who attended the Tunnel celebration had their picture taken before Engine 205 which pulled the first train through on February 26, 1928. *Denver Public Library Western Collection.*

L PROBE PAF

S NEARING DIS

NEW MOFFAT LINE TO ACCEPT TERMS OF TUNNEL COMMISSION

Denver & Salt Lake Railway Is Organized to Operate Old System Thru Bore.

The Denver & Salt Lake Railway company, which will take over the reorganized Moffat road, will accept immediately the terms of the tunnel commission for rental of the railroad bore at an annual rental sufficient to retire and pay two-thirds of the tunnel bonds under a contract involving payment of $16,736,310 in the next forty-six years.

This was reported for a certainty yesterday after the company made formal application for rental of the bore and after it had qualified to transact business in Colorado by filing copies of its articles of incorporation with the secretary of state. This corporation will succeed the present Moffat road, the Denver & Salt Lake Railroad company, under reorganization plans now nearing completion.

Reports that the railroad system has completed or is about to complete negotiations for rental of the tunnel were given out in financial circles following an executive meeting of the reorganization managers for the company here during the past two days.

Vesuvius Crater Erupting Ashes, Residents in Panic

Dangerous Disturbance Indicated by Activity of Volcano

LONDON, Jan. 6.—(By Associated Press.)—Brief dispatches received here from Italy report that Mount Vesuvius suddenly has become more active than in the past eight months, indicating a possible dangerous eruption.

The dispatches say that much smoke and hot ashes are ascending from the crater, but that there has as yet been no lava from it.

A new fissure, however, has opened on the western side of the crater and lava is pouring from it down the mountainside. Another crack has appeared on the northern side.

Dwellers on the mountain are greatly alarmed.

Sharp Earthquake Felt In San Francisco Region

SAN FRANCISCO, Jan. 6.—(By Associated Press)—A sharp earthquake was felt in the San Francisco bay region at 9:54 o'clock tonight. Two distinct shocks, lasting about five seconds, were felt in Oakland, while San Francisco and points south along the peninsula received a sharp shock.

The shock was sufficiently intense in some districts to rattle windows and sway pictures on the walls.

Along the water front the tem-

In this article the reporter did not realize that there was no money available to finish the tunnel until more bonds were floated. These bonds would have to be paid for by the tax district. *Denver Public Library Western Collection.*

SECTION 9. The Board shall have the power to enter into a contract or contracts for the use of said tunnel, its approaches and equipment, with persons and with private and public corporations, and by said contracts to give such persons or corporations the right to use said tunnel, its approaches and equipment for the transmission of power, for telephone and telegraph lines, for the transportation of water, for railroad and railway purposes, and for any other purpose to which the same may be adapted, no such contract to be for a longer period than ninety-nine (99) years, and the tunnel shall be put to the largest possible number of uses consistent with the purposes for which such improvements are constructed. In making such contract or contracts and providing for payments and rentals thereunder, the Board shall determine the value of the separate and different uses to which the tunnel is to be put, and shall apportion the annual rentals and charges as nearly as possible according to the respective values of such uses. No such contract shall be made with any person or corporation unless and until such person or corporation shall bind himself or itself to pay as rental therefor an amount determined by the Board and specified in the contract, which shall be a fair and just proportion of the total amount required to pay interest on the bonds provided for in this Act, plus a just proportion of the amount necessary for their retirement, and plus the cost of maintenance of the tunnel, its approaches and equipment. The Board may require any of such contracts to be entered into before beginning the construction of said tunnel or before the expenditure of funds under the provisions of this Act, if in its judgment it is deemed expedient.

There shall be no monopoly of the use of said tunnel and its approaches by any one use, or by any person or corporation, private or public, in respect to the several uses, and the Board may continue to make separate and additional and supplemental contracts for one or more uses until, in the judgment of said Board, the capacity of the tunnel and approaches for any such use has been reached. When such capacity has been reached contracts for the use of said tunnel shall be given preference in regard to such uses according to their priority, and subsequent contracts shall be subject to all existing and prior contracts. The Board shall have the power to prescribe regulations for the use of such tunnel by the parties to contracts for such use, or any of them, and to hear and determine all controversies which may arise between such parties, under such rules as the Board may from time to time promulgate; and all contracts shall expressly reserve such power to the Board. All contracts may be assigned or sub-leased, provided that the original contracting party shall not be thereby relieved of any obligations under said contract or lease. Subsequent leases or contracts for the same use must provide for the reimbursement to the prior users of an equitable proportionate amount theretofore paid for the retirement of bonds, including interest thereon, said amount to be determined by the Board, and the judgment and action of the Board on all matters referred to in this section shall be final except as specifically in this Act limited.

SECTION 10. (a). To pay for the construction of said tunnel, its approaches, equipment and expenses preliminary and incidental thereto, and to pay interest on bonds issued as hereinafter provided for during the period of construction, the Board is hereby authorized to issue the negotiable bonds, of said District in an amount not exceeding Six Million Seven Hundred Twenty Thousand Dollars ($6,720,000), to bear interest at a rate not exceeding Six per cent. (6%) per annum, payable semi-annually. Said bonds shall be due and payable not less than ten (10) nor more than fifty (50) years from their date, and shall be known as "Moffat Tunnel Bonds."

(b.) The form, terms and provisions of said bonds, provisions for their payment and conditions for their retirement and calling, not inconsistent with law, shall be fixed and

The Denver and Salt Lake Railway got a monopoly despite what the law read. (From Edgar C. McMechen's book *The Moffat Tunnel of Colorado*.) *Denver Public Library Western Collection.*

In the early years of advertising for passenger business via the new route, the Rio Grande avoided mention of the Moffat Tunnel, thinking that cosmopolitan easterners would consider it just another subway. Many Colorado people who pay no Moffat Tunnel tax benefit equally with those carrying the tax burden. *D.&R.G.W. Railroad photo.*

became forever *res adjudicata* and unassailable.

The story is not finished. Since everyone was re-writing the spirit of the Tunnel Act, Denver decided that since it had to pay taxes on the Tunnel, it did not matter much at all if it paid its third or just ten thousand a year. But it did matter that it was unfair to Grand, Routt and Moffat Counties, for these little counties were left holding the sack for what Denver did not pay in rent for the water tunnel which was made out of the pioneer bore. So a period of distrust between the Western Slope and the Eastern Slope was the end of what started out to be a tunnel to unite the two. Now, Pueblo can laugh and laugh at the people who got their tunnel, not for $6,720,000, but for $44,235,901 when the last interest and bonds are paid up. The taxpayers were just scalped for $25,258,191 while the railroad pays $18,252,710. Of course, Denver gets water through the tunnel, more water each year for her tax part.

But who benefits by this tunnel? Denver, of course, which has grown tremendously, thanks to Moffat Tunnel and other favorable conditions and opportunities. Who else? The Grand Junction area, which pays no tax; the Pacific Northwest that ships through the tunnel; Chicago, etc. Former Chief Engineer Arthur Ridgway of the Rio Grande did not hesitate to say that though it would be adverse to his company, a much fairer way of renting the tunnel would have been on a wheel basis, and it would have been of no great hurt to the Rio Grande.

Of course, the Rio Grande was not the culprit and had paid heavily for the Moffat, whose stock under the old company had been about worthless. But when the new corporation appeared with the lease, the Rio Grande had to pay $155 a share to buy the Denver and Salt Lake Railway Company. The *Denver Post* on November 24, 1930, said that this lease made the Rio Grande pay five million more than it would have the day before the lease was signed.

In buying the Denver and Salt Lake Railway, the Rio Grande bought the lease that left Grand, Routt, and Moffat Counties holding the bag for more than the Denver area. For this reason, despite a heavy loss, the Yampa Valley Mail must run for the convenience of the passengers from Denver to Steamboat and Craig. For these taxpayers deserve something for their money.

As the final victory that David H. Moffat fought for came close to realization, and the original tribe of scalp-takers was driven to a remote reservation by

West Portal. *Drawing by W. Steadman.*

the Interstate Commerce Commission, the successor of Moffat took up the fallen war clubs and knives to scalp the Tunnel District for better than $25,-258,191.00.

Twenty-five years after the Moffat Tunnel was opened those involved in the Moffat Tunnel Improvement District are unhappy. The Rio Grande Railroad is no longer controlled by the Van Sweringens of the Missouri Pacific. It is a reorganized company with new blood in the management, challenging the decline of railroad transportation with the most progressive thinking. It sees increased valuation of Grand, Moffat, and Routt Counties and asks if these counties have not received in the years past their investment in the Moffat Tunnel? It asks why should it always have to operate a two-car train to Craig? And the Rio Grande has given top service on this train. It has been advertised, the rates have been cut. But fewer people travel it, and the loss mounts. Highways have been improved. Rails are being forsaken for truck and private car.

The City of Denver looks at its growing suburbs which beg for Moffat Tunnel water and pay no tunnel tax. Denver may be at a greater disadvantage than the outlying counties in the Moffat Tunnel Improvement District.

Today the long-distance shippers get the benefit from a tunnel which suffered from all the disadvantages of public enterprise. Cascade Tunnel was built quickly, effectively by a railroad for a railroad. And that railroad took up the tab for the costs completely.

We may look ahead to a more unhappy future for everyone involved. The Tunnel began with a noble businessman, David Moffat. The Interstate Commerce Commission drove the white men who scalped

Page 219

him onto a reservation. But now we find the taxpayers of the district scalped by a new tribe of white men, and there are many who suffer the scalping.

Once a great teacher asked men to enter by the narrow gate to travel on a narrow road even though there be few who go that way. This chapter ends with the erosions of the best in men as they go to their destruction from the unfair advantages they took.

The hill line becomes a Forest Service recreation road. With the completion of Moffat Tunnel the Rollins Pass line was not needed. But so well were the trestles built, like this one at Devil's Slide, that the U.S. Forest Service could make it into a recreational road. Here we have history being recorded on September 2nd, 1964, on the sixtieth anniversary of the first train to Corona. Second from left is Ranger Wayne A. Parsons. It's a thousand feet down to Middle Boulder Creek. This is the side bridge that got caught in a late August snowstorm in 1904 so that the carpenters had to give up twice in one day. Rails were precariously dragged above the site so they could be laid. *Photo by Mel Schieltz,* Rocky Mountain News.

The Dotsero Cutoff

The story of the Cutoff does not really begin after the story of the Moffat Tunnel. The Dotsero route had been proposed years before. In fact, the earliest surveys for this route had been made by the Denver, Utah and Pacific engineers. Union Pacific and Rio Grande fathers had at least considered a route through Gore Canyon on down the Colorado River to Glenwood Springs. The Colorado Railway ran a survey and made filings. H. A. Sumner saw that a route survey was run down the river mainly to get the drop in elevation. Sumner had included in his arguments for the use of Gore Canyon the need for a connection with the Rio Grande at Dotsero to offer a western outlet for Routt County coal. The letters of Sumner indicate that the early construction of this thirty-eight mile line was considered. But he advised against it, because it was considered that cattle shipments from the Glenwood Springs area would go via Moffat without the branch being built, as the route and rate were so much cheaper—one hundred fifty miles less via Rollins Pass. So hostile was the Rio Grande under Gould that it was plain no interchange in traffic could be expected between the Rio Grande and the Moffat.

In 1913 Edward Cowden, a locating engineer of long standing in the State Highway Department, also made a survey.

During all this time, the railroad giants were maneuvering for position. Where such a vital development as the Moffat Tunnel was concerned, no one of the parties could afford to act disinterested, lest one of its rivals get the advantage. The muddy water of 1923 was made even more opaque when the Interstate Commerce Commission proposed to group the D.&R.G.W. and the Colorado and Southern with the Sante Fe. William G. Evans and his Colorado Committee on Consolidation of Railroads at once entered strenuous objections to the ICC proposals. The subtle effects of such a consolidation may not at first be apparent, so that it is important to look into Evans' criticisms. He said that Sante Fe control would leave Colorado without an independent railroad and deprive the entire area of the competition upon which good service and the commerce of the area had been built. Second, the proposed combination would remove the stimulus for needed railroad improvement, and consolidation would be likely to leave the state without the benefit of through east-west transcontinental service. In fact, the largest cities of Colorado—Denver, Pueblo, and Colorado Springs—might well be side-tracked completely.

Evans proposed, instead, that the D.&R.G.W. and the D.&S.L. be established as an independent system of bridge lines for through traffic to serve all the railroads that reached both ends of the "Bridge"—Denver and Salt Lake City. Such an arrangement would assure that Colorado would receive aggressive and competitive rail service without the disadvantages inherent under the ICC plan. Evans added that if the Commission felt the D.&R.G.W. must be integrated with one of the systems to the east, Colorado would be harmed the least if only the Burlington, Rock Island, and Missouri Pacific were to be considered, since all were rail routes reaching the base of the mountains and combination with any one of them would still result in transcontinental routes through Colorado.

Gerald Hughes, chairman of the Moffat directors, knew that the Rio Grande's Van Sweringen owners had no intention of building a cutoff or allowing one to be built. He did not trust the Rio Grande under its leadership at that time. Moffat men had conceived the idea of building the cutoff themselves and securing from the ICC a high portion of the total rate on the interchange business they would have with the Rio Grande. Arthur Ridgway, then chief engineer of the Rio Grande, said that the difficult country through which the Moffat operated would have given the D.&S.L. the major portion of the Denver-Salt Lake rate. This would have meant the ruin of the Rio Grande, which therefore heatedly opposed Moffat ownership of the cutoff.

The opposing forces joined in battle December 24, 1924, when the Denver and Salt Lake Western, a Moffat subsidiary at the time, petitioned the Interstate Commerce Commission for permission to extend their tracks 41.3 miles to Dotsero on the Rio Grande. This was a logical third step after, first, the

building of the Moffat Road, and, second, the beginning of construction on the tunnel. Nearly four years were to elapse, however, before a final decision. In the meantime, arguments were heard and the tunnel completed. D.&S.L. morale then soared because the ever present financial burden of snow removal was licked, schedules could be maintained, and tie-ups could be completely eliminated.

The D.&S.L. exuberance was well founded. Transcontinental traffic would no longer be forced to

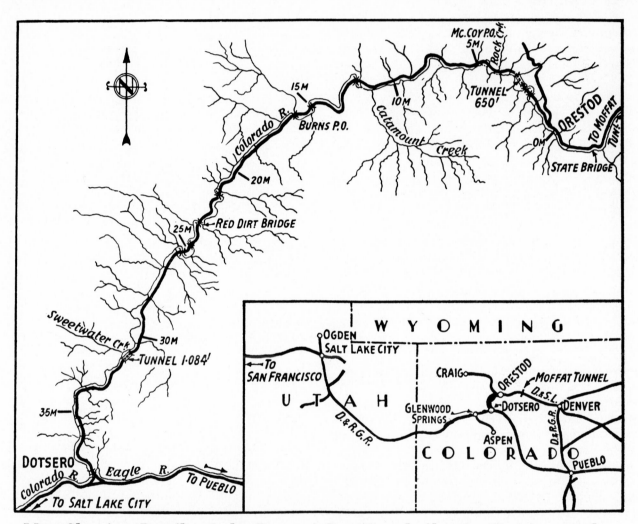

Map Showing Details of the Dotsero Cutoff and Also Its Position in the Denver and Rio Grande Western System

The distance on the Rio Grande between Denver and Salt Lake City via Pueblo and Tennessee Pass was 745 miles, or 69 miles longer than the route of its principal competitor, the Union Pacific via Ogden, between the same points. At one stroke the Dotsero Cutoff would reduce the distance to 572 miles via the joint D.&S.L.-D.&R.G.W. route. The 173 miles saved would give the latter roads a considerable advantage. Chicago-San Francisco and St. Louis-Salt Lake City distances could be reduced correspondingly. Although this was an important new link, it marked the death-knell of David Moffat's ambitious plan to reach Salt Lake City. His route was still the shortest. *Reprinted from Baldwin Locomotive Magazine, Vol. XIII No. 3.*

traverse Tennessee Pass, and the additional traffic would possibly finance a large portion (perhaps all) of the D.&S.L. tunnel rental.

There can always be two sets of opinions stemming from one set of facts. Two schools of thought quickly flared up on the cutoff issue. Towns and cities along the Rio Grande old main line, such as Pueblo, were frightened that loss of traffic would bring eventual decline. Allied were interests along the Moffat, such as Craig, which rightly surmised that construction of a short route would throttle construction on the original D.N.W.&P. route farther west.

Lining up on the other side of the fence were groups which would benefit. The Tunnel Commission jumped in right away on the side of the application because the increased tunnel rentals to be secured would place the tunnel on a more nearly economic base. Cities on the Main Line west of Dotsero could see more business coming, and Grand Junction civic leaders therefore touted the saving in time the new route would afford. Oddly enough, even the Rio Grande favored the petition, but only on a tongue-in-cheek basis so long as its interests were protected. The Rio Grande, in addition to losing a large portion of the rate on interchange business, knew that traffic would surely be transferred from its Royal Gorge route. The D.&S.L. had been negotiating with the D.&R.G.W. throughout the four-year delay on the manner of handling traffic, but had been unable to reach a mutually satisfactory solution.

In saying "so long as its interests were protected," the Rio Grande meant that it wanted to lease the Moffat-built cutoff. The Rio Grande would thus control transcontinental passenger and freight schedules and, through connections at Denver, provide a service attractive to shippers. The Colorado Public Utilities Commission entered the fray and recommended in favor of the application, if the D.&R.G.W. were permitted trackage rights Dotsero to Denver.

The ICC had an exceedingly complex issue to settle. If the D.&S.L. received the go-ahead, it would become a potentially powerful, vital link in a transcontinental system. Such favorable action must inevitably have a drastic negative reaction on the Rio Grande. The public interest would not be served by degeneration of the latter. Moreover, the competition given to the Union Pacific on the north and the Sante Fe on the south might be destroyed. Separate operation of the cutoff would result in three engine

districts between Denver and Grand Junction, whereas only two would be required through unified operation. It was pointed out that the Western Pacific, partial owner of the D.&R.G.W., delivered more than half of its perishable freight to the U.P. at Salt Lake City and this traffic would naturally go Rio Grande if schedules could be competitive. Some experts testified that eight hours would be cut from freight schedules, while other experts proved that only an hour could be cut.

The Van Sweringen interests showed calculated thinking. Acknowledging that a short route was vitally needed and was bound to be built, they proposed an all-Rio Grande cutoff roughly paralleling the Moffat Tunnel route starting at Minturn and crossing the Continental Divide with another long tunnel similar to the Moffat. They pointed out that their route would be a bit shorter—five miles—and would be under one management. Thus, the Rio Grande would not have to split rates and would not jeopardize its own Royal Gorge route. They did not mention how this would duplicate facilities or put more burden on the ratepayers. Thinking financiers considered this threat simply a lawyer's maneuver, for the owners of the Rio Grande were mostly bankrupt men.

The Commission had to weigh the competing interests in a tangled case. Upon it would most certainly hinge not only the fortunes of the two roads involved, but also the likely development of vast areas of Colorado and the destinies of untold numbers of men. Ultimately the Commission decided that the cutoff should be built by the Moffat. Obliquely, it gave control of the cutoff to the Rio Grande.

The decision changed the history of both roads. Once before, in the Royal Gorge War, the Rio Grande's destiny had been changed by legal action. If the decision had been in favor of the Moffat, it is conceivable that the Moffat would have taken over the Rio Grande in time.

In January, 1926, the Denver and Salt Lake Railway leased the yet-incomplete tunnel for fifty years and agreed to retire and pay interest on two-thirds of the tunnel bonds amounting to $9,220,000. Remember this box car-number, for it is important. The rental amounted to $346,000 each year for the first six years, and varied thereafter. In addition, the D.&S.L. Rail*way* was incorporated to take over the assets of the Rail*road* in receivership.

The members of the Tunnel Commission were to

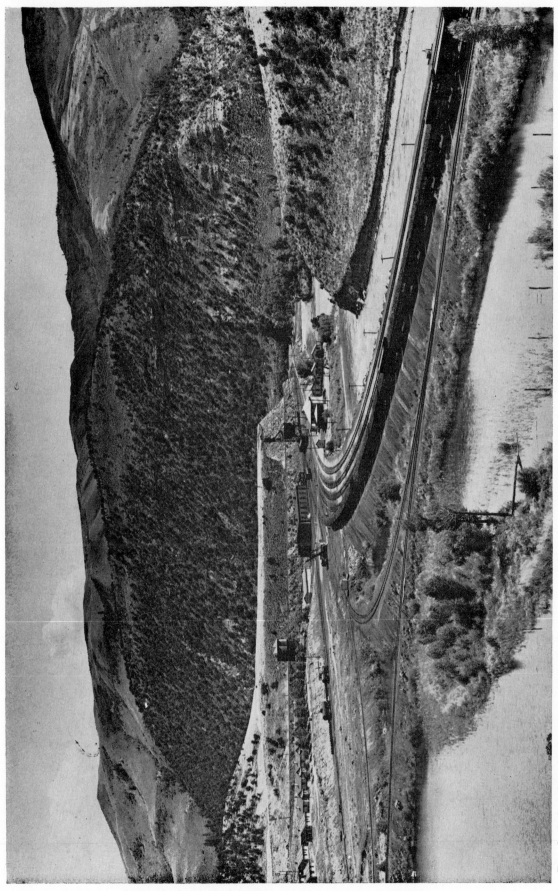

Bond, Colorado—the beginning of the Dotsero Cutoff. The original Moffat Road to Craig entered the photograph around the hill in the center of the picture, and climbed up the two per cent back of the water tanks to the left center. The new trackage follows the Colorado River in a sweeping curve in front of the Rio Grande employee hotel and leaves the right of the picture for Dotsero, thirty-eight miles distant. Bond is on the lower level, marked only by stairway and signal. The celebration at the opening of the Cutoff took place along the river, while President Freeman's private train was stopped at Orestod overlooking it. Since this picture was taken many changes have occurred. The coal tipple has come down, as has one of the water tanks. Trees have grown to considerable height inside the wye, and the cottages back of the hotel have been removed. The engine shed has been torn down and the steam locomotive waiting outside has been deposed by the diesel-electrics. One thing remains unchanged. To this day you can still get the state's biggest porterhouse steak in the basement railroad lunchroom for $1.95. *Rio Grande*

receive some cruel shocks from the Railway. The Commission expected that the D.&S.L. would raise funds for immediate construction of the Dotsero Cutoff, giving a through connection west. It was the intention of the Moffat owners to do this. They bought up the right of way and incorporated the Denver and Salt Lake Western Railroad Company to handle the construction. To the consternation of the Commission, construction on the cutoff did not begin even after completion of the tunnel. *Railway Age* asked, "Will Moffat's Dream Be Realized?" pointing out that changes in railroad geography would be forced as a consequence of the great expenditure financed by Denver taxes, that the cutoff was an easy piece of construction, and that the Craig extension must be dropped in favor of the route provided by the cutoff.

The Tunnel Commission's embarrassment was complete when the Salt Lake paid the first tunnel rent bill on July 1, 1928, and accompanied the check for the first four-and-one-half months usage with a statement that the rent was more than the savings in hauling costs over the abandoned Hill line, and unless more freight could be found the tunnel would be a liability. Through the minds of the Tunnel Commission must have passed the history of the Colorado Midland under similar circumstances. In that case, the railroad voluntarily gave up usage of the Busk-Ivanhoe tunnel, and began to run their trains over the top again in an abortive attempt to reduce costs.

The reader will recall that the tunnel was supposed to cost $6.72 million. The rent was set when the projected cost was $9.22 million. When total costs of $15.47 million were accumulated, the Commission found itself in a very hot political spot. The taxpayers felt they had been hoodwinked; resentment led to a suit against the Commission for issuing the last $8.75 million of bonds. That portion of the story is covered elsewhere: suffice to say that the members of the Commission must have slept a little easier when the bonds were ruled legal.

The Commission, however, realized that they must do something to recover the added cost and therefore attempted to raise the tunnel rent from $346,000 based on a $9.22 million tunnel cost to $550,000 based on the total amount of the outstanding bonds ($15.72 million).

Any honeymoon that might have existed between the Commission and the Railway was blasted when the D.&S.L. refused to pay, claiming its obligation was based solely on the tunnel lease, regardless of what the monster had cost. As indicated in the last chapter, a series of court tests left the Tunnel District with no way to recoup the cost of more than half the tunnel, except to place additional taxes on the District.

Yet who *was* to build the cutoff? The answer was the result of railroad strategy. It was obvious to the insiders that the D. & S.L. would not be the builder, even if financing were available, because the cost of the cutoff could not be justified by the volume of traffic commanded by an independent bridge line. On the other hand, no interest was manifested by the D.&R.G., because the cutoff would entail a diversion of traffic from its Royal Gorge route with resultant loss in revenues.

Imagine this complete turnabout in events from just a year or two before, when the two railroads were squabbling to see who would have the privilege of construction. We can find reason in the attitude of the D.&R.G.W., if we stop to think that it was a creature of its joint owners, the Western Pacific and Missouri Pacific. While the former would benefit by a through connection from Denver, the M.P. could not be expected to favor any new route which would detour traffic around its Pueblo gateway.

On the other hand, there was a community of interest between the W.P. and Burlington because of interlocking directorates. If the "Q" should obtain control of the D.&S.L. a new transcontinental route could be formed with the D.&R.G.W. placed in the position of a bridge carrier, earning a mere fraction of the revenue obtainable.

All through these maneuvers the Denver papers and Chamber of Commerce were diligent in seeing that the Rio Grande did not get some agreement by which it would bottle up the Moffat Road and refuse to use it as a transcontinental line.

The Rio Grande itself supplied the solution, aided by strategy errors of the D.&S.L. Rio Grande knew full well that if the cutoff were not built, the Moffat would become a stronger road in time because of the economies afforded by the new Moffat Tunnel. Eventually, the Moffat would be thwarted no longer and would certainly build the cutoff, or it would complete the Craig extension to Salt Lake City. Either would result in strong competition, with the odds favoring the Moffat because of its shorter line, reduced rise-and-fall, and more favorable maximum grade.

It has been more than thirty years since these events took place. In some cases this passage of time

The future location of Bond. This view was taken from a moving train on the D.&S.L. main track about one mile west of Orestod. Motorized equipment is building a diversion dam along the Colorado River. The stream bed is now occupied by yard tracks and the wye. *D.&S.L. photo.*

has served only to hamper the historian. Here, however, three decades enable us to look with fresh clarity upon the events of 1929 which irrevocably placed the future in the hands of the Rio Grande and put the handwriting on the wall for the assimilation of the Moffat. We believe the Moffat lost this battle because of shortsighted management bordering on the inept. The Moffat had long-term rights to the use of the tunnel which would end all its snow fighting; yet, it maintained that the rent was excessive. The Moffat had been granted authority by the ICC to build the Dotsero Cutoff; yet it did not. Moffat management apparently did not believe traffic statistics which suggested that trackage right payments by the Rio Grande only five years later would amount to $600,000-$700,000 yearly—a tidy profit without the need to turn a Moffat wheel.

At no time did President Freeman show more clearly how incapable he was of sound leadership than in allowing the Moffat owners not to seize this opportunity.

The Hughes-Phipps-Boettcher-Freeman control of

the D. & S.L. missed this shrewd maneuver. They were content with having scalped the taxpayers through the tunnel lease. However, these men protected Denver in not selling until the transcontinental link was assured.

At this moment Freeman considered himself a success and David Moffat a failure. Freeman thought he was a hero in resurrecting a little, bankrupt road. But he was only able to be a tough man and cow the rank and file. He had even played traitor to his bosses by selling his shares of Moffat stock.

It was 1932 that the Rio Grande secured a Reconstruction Finance Corporation loan to build the cutoff. The hearts of Moffat employees sank, for they longed to run the trancontinental trains. Little did anyone realize that seeds for future financial turmoil were planted when the RFC required the D.&R.G.W. to deposit D.&S.L. voting trust certificates as security for the loan.

In 1924 during the construction of the Moffat Tunnel a former Rio Grande engineer, Lee Furman, ran a survey for the Moffat from Dotsero to

Grading and blasting at Orestod during construction of the cutoff. Motor No. 1 is on the D.&S.L. main track, Colorado River at the left. *D.&S.L. photo.*

The Dotsero Cutoff

Orestod. The Rio Grande finally got around in 1931, three years after opening the tunnel, to run its own survey. With an eye to transcontinental business, it directed J. G. Gwyn and Lee Furman, who ran the line, to reduce curvature for high speed operation. How successfully they did it can be seen from this table:

	Maximum curvature	Total curvature	Miles Length	Tunnels
1924 Survey	10°	6758°	41.4	1— 400'
1931 Survey	6°	4200°	38.1	2—1734'

	Bridges	Bridge Steel
1924 Survey	2—340'	400 tons
1931 Survey	10—2390'	2000 tons

Obviously, the Rio Grande felt that the additional river crossings and tunnel length were worth the cost to achieve a shorter line and a high speed track.

The future was placed in the hands of the Rio Grande, because that road had the vision (or audacity) to propose to the ICC it obtain control of the D.&S.L. in order to build the cutoff. The ICC was disposed in favor of the Rio Grande because of lack of action by the Moffat.

In 1930, the Denver and Rio Grande Western formally accepted the conditions imposed by the ICC under which it might acquire control of the Moffat Road—to start construction of the cutoff in six months and finish the work in two years. The ICC took this step for only one reason, to force construction of the cutoff.

The time for building to begin passed without the promised construction. The Rio Grande's attempts to secure financing were launched in the midst of the Great Depression, and it is not surprising that the project was delayed, although there were some who blamed the may obstacles upon the Van Sweringen desire to find a way to hold the Moffat, yet without using it as a transcontinental link.

Yes, the depression was on, and the Rio Grande was launched on a new adventure. In this adventure President J. S. Pyeatt had been bitterly opposed by the Rio Grande chief owners. It was an unfortunate time to prove he was right. Anyway, the Van Sweringen empire crumbled.

Art Weston indicates that the route map was greatly complicated because the original land surveys in this area were so defective that a resurvey had to be made and that there were two sets of land lines in the territory.

The cutoff was in actual construction in November of 1932. Arthur Ridgway, chief engineer of the Rio Grande, had years of experience and was indeed the most able man to supervise this modern piece of construction. Gwyn was field engineer, with Furman his assistant. Art Weston was office engineer. The contract had been let to three companies who had been among the six firms building Hoover Dam. The winter was a severe one with low temperatures and little snow, with the frost line sinking deep.

The methods used were to set the pace of railroad construction for many years afterwards. No rail equipment was employed at any point during the building of the roadbed. All grading and hauling was motorized. In fact, some trucks were brought from the Hoover Dam job, along with 850 men. Since the existing roads were only winding country trails, access was difficult. The line runs through the broad valley of the Colorado at both ends, but its central twelve miles lie in the narrow cleft of Red Canyon. A drive along here on the modern county road is well worth the experience. At points there

Historic junction. Looking west from the west switch at Orestod, the Dotsero Cutoff track approaches from the west. The man in the center foreground is standing opposite the staked point of the switch for the Cutoff connection to the D.&S.L. main line. *D.&S.L. photo.*

Bond during the construction days. This view was taken from the D.&S.L. main line showing the yard under construction and one of two water tanks nearing completion. *D.&S.L. photo.*

Busy at Bond. The opening celebration was not far off as the yard at Bond neared completion. The engine house, coal dock, and hotel had yet to be started. *D.&S.L. photo.*

Bond after completion of the Cutoff. The 150 ton automatically-operated coal chute is astride the passing track. The elevated track to the right serves the coal-chute hopper. The buildings on the left are the pump house, taking water from the Colorado River, office, lunchroom, and sleeping quarters. *D.&S.L. photo.*

The Dotsero Cutoff

is barely room for the road and the track. The almost-gradeless line avoided high water stages of the Colorado, although ten bridges crossed it, and one was needed across the Eagle at Dotsero. It was June 15, 1934, before the track was completed.

It is a good story in itself how Bill Freeman needled the Rio Grande during the construction of the cutoff, for the old animosity in denying the Moffat the right to build this cutoff lingered.

The Moffat president kept himself informed on every move of the surveyors and construction workers, waiting for some opportunity to embarrass the Rio Grande. Naturally he relied on his chief engineer, W. C. Jones, to supply him with this information. The already overworked Jones was forced to check on the construction. About this time President Freeman left for New York, giving his chief engineer orders to keep him informed on the progress or lack of progress. Jones's first wire was a concise statement in a telegram. Bill Freeman fired back that he did not want any notes; he expected a complete report.

Bill Jones cussed out loud some mighty words and dragged his sick body over to the right of way by hitchhiking a ride on a construction truck. Jones had come out to Colorado a man condemned by ulcers. Johns Hopkins doctors had given him up. At first he had been so sick that he had to eat raw eggs and drink milk. How in the world he ever was able to stand up is beyond understanding. But his iron will enabled him to live, and his sick body should account for some of his temper. When Bill arrived at the construction train, which was working out of Dotsero toward Orestod, he saw no need to travel the last seven miles. How else could the train have gotten to this place if the rails had not been laid? So he conferred with the engineers, cracked

his good and corny jokes, winning the respect of the Rio Grande men. They readily supplied him with their records.

When he returned to Orestod, he had a full report. This he wired by Postal Telegraph. The cost? $125.00. This brings up the subject of Western Union. Freeman had fallen out with them and had broken their contract, bringing in the much smaller company.

But this was not the end of the incident. Some months later Freeman flew into his chief unmercifully for not having traversed the last seven miles. The Moffat president had an espionage system and technique that enabled him to get his trembling men to tell on one another unknowingly, so that he found out everything. He even had the railroad wires cut into his own home in Denver, so that in the middle of the night he could listen to what was going over the wire. Freeman knew the language of the dot and dash also.

But if Freeman worried his men, he scared the mighty men of the Rio Grande who were carrying out orders for the Van Sweringens. President J. S. Pyeatt was afraid of Freeman and would not deal directly with him or go to Freeman's office. Arthur Ridgway, chief engineer, was on occasions sent over to deal with Freeman.

As the cutoff was near completion, Freeman refused to cut in a switch to hook up the cutoff to his line at Orestod. George Berry, an engineer of the Rio Grande, finally cut the line and built the switch. The newspapers again buzzed, as a tie was chained across the cutoff by George, for fear that some Rio Grande car would mysteriously run onto the Moffat track and start a wreck, if not a war.

The Rio Grande was staggering under the bad weather of the depression, whereas the Moffat was

Bond, Colorado, the actual beginning of the Dotsero Cutoff, one-half mile west of Orestod on the D.&S.L. Having been completed in time for the opening day celebration, the enginehouse pits were used to cook the barbecue. The coal chute and enginehouse seen here have since been removed. *D.&R.G.W. R.R. photo.*

faring considerably better. As a result of the Rio Grande's distress, the RFC advanced $3,182,150 in 1934 to the Denver & Salt Lake Western, a Rio Grande subsidiary by that time, to complete the cutoff, because the D.&R.G.W. was unable to make financing arrangements independently.

The joint trackage agreement for the use of the Moffat track from Utah Junction to Orestod was signed October 15, 1928, and provided for the joint line to be upgraded to D.&R.G.W. standards with the Rio Grande to share the cost of the work through increased rental. The Moffat went ahead in 1928 with a heavy program of ballasting and rail replacement. But as the delay in starting the cutoff—without which the Rio Grande could not use the Moffat—became prolonged, the betterment program waned and stopped. Meanwhile unpaid Rio Grande bills piled up on Freeman's desk despite statement after statement sent out.

Bill Freeman surely helped the newspaper reporters with spicy news. As the day approached for the grand celebration for the opening of the transcontinental service over the cutoff and through the Moffat Tunnel, he found an opportunity to collect the outstanding bill which the Van Sweringen brothers had seen unwise to pay the Moffat until the line was opened.

It was June 13, 1934, and Bill Freeman was feeling very well. A Rio Grande official came over to Freeman's office to say something about the running of the first trains over to the celebration. Bill Freeman quietly asked how they expected to get over to the Moffat. The official answered that they had a contract allowing them to do so. Freeman roared back, "Yes, but you do not have a contract to get over the switch from the interchange track. Unless you have every cent of the $388,000 the Rio Grande owes us, I will not let you over the road. You will have to have it in the bank before closing time, so the bank has time to find out if the check is good."

The *Rocky Mountain News* came out with a headline "MOFFAT ROAD ASKS $320,000 OF RIO GRANDE." June 14 the headline read, "$388,-000 ASKED FOR," and carried the story that the debt amounted to a million for three years. When newspaper reporters asked Freeman about what would happen to the ceremony planned, Freeman replied, "The celebration is the Rio Grande's show."

The switch was spiked shut, and the Rio Grande officials knew they had overlooked in the contract a small item which Bill Freeman had gleefully dis-

RIO GRANDE RY. PAYS AND ENDS DOTSERO ROW

Sum Given Moffat Line Is Secret, but Celebration of Opening Assured

BY FRED D. FLEMING

The controversy over opening of the Dotsero Cut-off was settled yesterday when the Denver & Rio Grande Western Railroad made a cash payment to the Denver & Salt Lake (Moffat) Railroad.

The amount of the payment was not made public. The total amount involved in the controversy, railroad officials said, is more than $1,000,000.

W. R. Freeman, president of the Moffat Road, said the amount involved in the immediate dispute was $388,000. Asked if the Rio Grande paid the entire sum, Freeman refused to make a positive statement but said it was a "substantial figure."

"There is another very large sum involved, however," Freeman said, adding that all claims against the Rio Grande "are more than $1,000,000."

Moffat officials charged there had been defaults and breaches of contract by the Rio Grande and that certain claims dated back for a period of three years.

J. S. Pyeatt, president of the Rio Grande, would not comment on the settlement of the controversy other than to say that trains will operate

Freeman tweaks the nose of the Rio Grande. The *Rocky Mountain News* of June 15, 1934, tells of the D.&S.L.'s demand for more than $1,000,000.

covered. To the joy of the directors of the Moffat and the laughter of the Moffat men, Freeman announced that he had every cent on the barrelhead. Investigation proves the Rio Grande paid cash for most of the sum and the rest was held in escrow by the First National Bank, so that the evaluation committee could adjust any items over which there was a dispute. Some adjustment was later made.

The same evening that the cash was put on the

FIRST TRAINS RUN OVER DOTSERO CUTOFF, MARKING NEW ERA IN PROSPERITY OF WEST

The Post Telephone MAin 2121

HOME EDITION

Paid Circulation of THE DENVER POST Last Sunday Was 301,027

NRA WE DO OUR PART

THE BEST NEWSPAPER IN THE U. S. A.

PRICE TEN CENTS

THE DENVER POST

84 PAGES   DENVER, COLO., SUNDAY, MORNING, JUNE 17, 1934   VOL. 42—NO. 312

HIGH OFFICIALS OF TWO STATES DEDICATE LINE

Colorado Hails Regular Rail Traffic to Coast Via Direct Route

(By I. A. CHAPIN.)

(Denver Post Staff Correspondent.)

Bond, Colo., June 16.—The way is open and the track is clear. The Dotsero cutoff is in operation.

Denver—your Denver and mine, the capital of a region embracing one-fourth the area and one-sixth the population of the nation—is now off the side track for good and on the main line.

That means a greater city, a greater west, a more prosperous and a happier Rocky Mountain region generally.

It is a straight shoot now from Denver to the Great Salt Lake and on to the Pacific.

THE WEATHER

'Tis a Privilege to Live in Colorado.

Sunday—Sun rose in Denver at 4:30 a. m. Sun sets in Denver at 7:31 p. m. There are 15 hours and 1 minute of sunlight in Denver Sunday, the same amount as on Saturday.

Highest temperature in Denver on Saturday, 71; lowest temperature on Friday night, 51.

Denver and Vicinity (radius 20 miles)—Partly cloudy and somewhat warmer Sunday and Monday; generally fair.

Colorado—Partly cloudy Sunday; warmer in north and east; Monday generally fair.

Wyoming—Partly cloudy Sunday; warmer in east and south; Monday generally fair.

Nebraska—Partly cloudy and cooler; showers in east portion Sunday; Monday generally fair.

Kansas—Partly cloudy, scattered showers in east and central portions Sunday; probably fair; not much change in temperature.

New Mexico—Generally fair Sunday and Monday, except probably local thundershowers in north central portion.

South Dakota—Partly cloudy Sunday; Monday generally fair and slightly warmer.

Idaho—Generally fair Sunday and Monday, but widely scattered afternoon thunderstorms in mountains; little change in temperature Sunday and Monday; little change in temperature.

FULL WEATHER REPORTS FROM ALL OVER THE U. S. ON PAGE 8, SECTION 4, COLUMN 6.

Paid circulation of The Sunday Post over 190,000 greater than total paid circulation of all other 72 Sunday papers printed in Denver and Colorado, Wyoming and New Mexico combined.

Average Paid Sunday Circulation for May 301,202

CLOUDY

RUSH OF BILLS DELAYS CONGRESS ADJOURNMENT

KIPLING WAS WRONG—BROTHER!

JAM IN SENATE FORCES RECESS UNTIL MONDAY

Principal Legislative Pro.

The Denver Post was exuberant. "The way is open and the track is clear. The Dotsero Cutoff is in operation . . ." read the Sunday morning edition, June 17, 1934. F. Bauer collection.

Freeman's ace. The *Rocky Mountain News* of June 13, 1934, pictures the "Gateway" at Utah Junction through which Denver and Rio Grande Western trains must move to get on to the Moffat tracks. J. S. Pyeatt, president of the Rio Grande, left, and W. R. Freeman, president of the Moffat. *F. Bauer collection.*

barrelhead, as the hands of the clock yawned, the first freight of the Rio Grande crossed over the much disputed switch. Louie Larson climbed into the cab to pilot the first run of the now famous freight, the Flying Ute, which was to give the Union Pacific competition into San Francisco.

Everything was against the Rio Grande that day. Bill Freeman had raved and ranted, threatening to fire any operator who failed to hand up an order hoop or delayed the specials or the regular passenger service of Five and Six. So the men were shaking like aspen trees in Indian summer, thinking they might disappear in the frosty breath of Freeman.

June 16, 1934, dawned over Denver with officials still wondering what new invention or discovery of cussed contrariness Freeman might concoct. The first train to leave Denver Union Station for the celebration was the now-famous Pioneer Zephyr of the Burlington, which President Budd had brought

out to honor the occasion when the Burlington secured a direct west coast connection. Zephyr 9900 picked up two Moffat men at Utah Junction at 6:47 A.M. Conductor F. A. Van Vranken and Engineer W. L. Smith acted as pilots, and the Zephyr reached Orestod at 11:58 A.M. The three twelve-car trains followed on thirty minute intervals, but did not have uneventful runs. Veteran Rio Grande train crews handled these trains with Moffat engineers and conductors as pilots. Not having run a test train, the Rio Grande found that her consolidation engines lost time in dragging twelve Pullmans up the two percent. The consolidation engines, having worked hard and carrying no water car, ran out of water at Coal Creek water tank. When they attempted to start on the two per cent, a drawbar came out. Drawbars come out every once in a while, but why they had to on this day, no one knows. The most humorous version told about the incident is that

The Burlington's Pioneer Zephyr was the first train to leave the Union Station June 16, 1934, on the way to the opening of the Cutoff. Crowds turned out at intermediate stations to see the new-fangled styling. This is the scene at Hot Sulphur Springs as the dawn of a new diesel era passes through. *George Barnes collection.*

Freeman had insisted that Moffat men handle the throttles of the engines, and that since the Moffat boys were not used to big power, they yanked the train in two. The men who handled the throttles, however, were one hundred per cent Rio Grande men with plenty of experience going up to Palmer Lake. Most embarrassing of all incidents was the dumping into the lap of Governor Johnson's wife the entire contents of a dinner table when the coupler went out. This was in President Pyeatt's car.

The air was charged with trouble from the spiking of the switch, and the law of averages came to bat that day against the Rio Grande. At Plainview an operator, filled with the fear of Freeman, pulled a boner and delayed one train.

On ahead, the operator at Kremmling put out an order with the date 1914 instead of 1934, and Conductor Allen asked the officials what they should do. The officials cussed and said, "We might as well keep on running." They did.

Meanwhile, Bill Freeman's special ran to Orestod and on up around the curve, where Bill Freeman could look down upon the ceremonies at Bond.

The crews fumed and the officials cussed Freeman, who was blamed for everything, while the passengers sang "Sweet Adeline" and "How Dry I Am." One reporter said the passengers in his train cheered when they went across the switch on which Freeman had collected the back money. But very hard luck struck the third section, which had the president's private car on it. In Denver a drawhead was pulled. Time was lost as cars were switched around. This delay was serious, as the time set for the ceremonies was determined by the hour of the national radio hookup. The time was short now.

Harold Eno, then secretary to the executive in charge of passenger operations, tells how L. Warrington Baldwin, Chairman of the Board of Directors,* saw President Freeman's private train beyond Orestod looking down on the celebration scene at Bond. Mr. Baldwin, knowing that President Freeman was not on speaking terms with President Pyeatt of the Rio Grande, turned to Governor Blood of Utah and said, "I should see that Mr. Freeman gets an invitation. . . . Mr. Eno, would you go over to Orestod and in my name extend an invitation to President Freeman?" So Harold Eno trudged through the rain one mile to Freeman's private train standing at the boxcar office. Mr. Freeman could

*Also, President of Missouri Pacific Railroad and a D.&S.L. director at the time.

Box car office at Orestod. President Freeman of the Moffat backed his special down this track. He went into the box car office and bawled out the dispatcher for not getting the dedication day specials over the line. Mr. Eno, meanwhile, walked the mile from Bond entering this picture as he sloshed through the rain along the track to the right. Trembling as he heard the raving president, he entered the private car and invited Mr. Freeman to the celebration. He was well received. *Ed Bollinger photo.*

be heard yelling all kind of abuse over the phone to the dispatcher about the delays caused the Rio Grande specials.

"If you do not get the trains over the road, we will be sued for everything we have!"

"Yes, Mr. Freeman."

"Get the trains into Orestod!"

"Yes, Mr. Freeman."

Harold says he was afraid to walk into the private car with a man so angry, but getting up his courage, he did. Freeman glared at him as he was announced.

The Moffat Road

"Mr. Freeman, Mr. Baldwin sent me over to extend you his personal invitation to come to the celebration."

Freeman became a changed man. "Will you thank Mr. Baldwin for me!"

At Bond, Rio Grande dining car chefs had barbecued beef over the pits of the future engine house. Thousands of people could sit down to the fine food. But the trains were arriving late. The first section had been an hour late. Reports on the last section, which was short on time to begin with, showed that it was one hour and twenty-five minutes late. The president of the railroad was on this section and could not possibly make Bond in time to deliver his radio speech.

The vice president of the road said to G. F. Dodge, "What shall we do?" Mr. Dodge, in charge of public relations, had fought for years for a good advertising department, and he was not going to give up this national hook-up just because the brass hats were on a late train. This likeably courteous and yet determined man was prepared for this emergency. He pulled out of one pocket the speech Harold Eno had written for the president and gave that to the vice president. He pulled out of his other pocket the speech he had written for the governor of the state, Edwin C. Johnson, who was riding in President Pyeatt's private car. The newspaper reporters looked up into the heavens and saw the rain coming. Dodge had an umbrella to cover his head.

The clock said that it was time to begin. The governor of Utah, Henry H. Blood, had assured Dodge that he would keep on talking about anything to fill in the time if necessary. Dodge never forgot that. So the two carbon copy speeches were read and the world knew little about the trouble down in the out-of-the-way spot, where autos had gone crosswise of the trails leading in, and where the trains were late. The president of the railroad was relieved to hear from his private car the delivery of his speech. Governor Johnson later congratulated Dodge on making the best speech he had ever made. The speakers huddled under umbrellas. A shot rang out from a cowboy, who added his touch to the occasion. Someone, who was so lucky as to have ridden on the Zephyr, told how that train had scared a deer. In the midst of it all the third section of the train with the business men of Denver and the railroad presidents pulled in.

The special trains from the west had been on time. High school and veterans' bands were striking up their tunes. Western Colorado would now have a cheaper freight rate to Denver.

The Rio Grande, which had been unable to parade a magnificent million-pound mallet over the Moffat, was ready to parade her before the speakers' stand. The fine equipment had come in from the west. The Zephyr took her turn, and everyone cheered, as all the trains paraded by in review.

The honor of master of ceremonies had been shared by Chancellor Frederick M. Hunter of the University of Denver and Heber J. Grant of Salt

Rio Grande's 1100 series consolidations were the heaviest power permitted over the Moffat at the beginning of the trackage agreement. With 48,100 pounds tractive effort, they represented respectable main line freight power at the time of their construction in 1906-08, but could only be used on lesser trains over the Moffat. *Alco photo, Schenectady History Center.*

The Dotsero Cutoff

President Freeman handicapped the Rio Grande for a time by permitting no power heavier than the 3400 series mallets. His concern is easily seen in the view of the 3404 2-8-8-2 on one of the Moffat's wooden trestles. These sixteen engines were originally built by Alco in 1913 numbered in the 1075 series with a total weight of 458,000 pounds, considerably more than the 361,000 pound weight of the Moffat 200's. Large front cylinders identify the true mallet compound. *D.&S.L. photo.*

Lake City, who was president of the Mormon Church.

Gerald Hughes and the rest of the Moffat trustees relaxed, for the cause they had fought for was now secure. These men began to sell their stock and bonds at a good price. Hughes, who had invested with his father and Dave Moffat from the beginning, found that his investment had never borne any interest. But he was not sorry. Denver was on the main line, for which Uncle Dave had fought.

By December, 1934, the Rio Grande was in the poor financial condition of dozens of other railroads in the United States. The RFC then moved into the picture in order to protect its security (the Moffat) in loans made to the D.&R.G.W. and the D.&S.L.W. Uncle Sam took over the prosperous subsidiary of the D.&R.G.W. to prevent entanglement with its heavily mortgaged parent. It assumed physical control of the Denver and Salt Lake by voting the stock which had been pledged to it as security for the $3,182,000 loan to the D.&S.L.W. Wilson McCarthy, later to become a Rio Grande trustee, was elected president of the Moffat on December 21, 1934.

Headlines told how democracy was threatened by the RFC's owning the Moffat. Labor was likely to run wild. Would the United States government have to pay taxes to the state of Colorado and to the counties? If it did not, schools would close and Middle Park would be bankrupt, so men talked, like old gossipers.

Wilson McCarthy took a sane course. The Moffat paid taxes, though it was not required to. School districts continued to receive their forty-per-cent handouts to keep them going.

McCarthy was, as *Business Week* pointed out early

in 1935, in a good position to keep an eye on the D.&R.G.W. He could foreclose, if creditors other than the government made any trouble. Actually, the inter-relationships of the Missouri Pacific and Western Pacific (D.&R.G.W.'s owners), with other transcontinental systems staggering under heavy RFC loans, might easily have developed a condition from which Uncle Sam could have emerged with the railroads in his hip pocket. But that didn't happen.

So much for the cutoff itself. Its completion merely served to show how bad Moffat maintenance had been in the early twenties, for the rest of the Moffat was in no condition to accept the traffic which the tunnel forced upon it.

The grand scale of railroad construction, which Sumner had had to exchange for the most expedient way possible to get to the coal fields, now had a yellow light. West of Sulphur, line changes could soon be made. Neglected maintenance could be carried out—all because the building of Moffat Tunnel had ended the costly snow removal and disastrous blockades.

President Freeman had guided the road in a period when some men would have been happy to make a fortune junking the line. He, however, had discovered the way to make a fortune by hanging onto the road, buying its bonds cheaply, knowing that in the not too distant future there would be a good market for this little indispensable cutoff. So he determined to hold maintenance to nothing as long as that was possible.

A. L. Johnson, Joe Culbertson, and in fact the entire Moffat staff knew that the line had kept going on such slender repairs more by miracle than by

Trial run up to the Tunnel. A rare and unique photograph is this of the first 3600 series engine to pass over the Moffat. Attended by engineers who are busy checking bridge deflection, the 3607 slowly wends her way to East Portal to verify clearances and curvatures. While this class of engine was not quite so heavy as the 3700's which were to follow in a few years, these 2-8-8-2's had a longer rigid wheelbase. *L. J. Daly photo.*

wisdom. If the many trestles were not filled, the tunnels gunited or concrete lined, disaster would overcome the line.

The man to whom the fun of rebuilding the Moffat fell was W. C. Jones. As chief engineer, he had a chance to marshall his great drive behind his powerful imagination. But unruffled by this intense new flurry of exciting activity, Office Engineer Ed Sunergren, quiet and thoughtful as ever, continued as the principal support of his "Chief," solving intricate engineering problems and devising practical methods for accomplishing the work at hand. These two had become a great team.

To secure ballast, a pit on Congre Mesa was reopened. With unique strategy, trainloads of volcanic ballast were blown off the side of the mountain.

This ballast was porous, serving the road admirably. Jones had the old ties split in the winter into 12,000 fence posts, and later a great part of the right of way had its first fence.

So line changes were brought about that had been on the original survey line of H. A. Sumner. Naturally the sidings were too short for the increased tonnage the long trains hauled. Frequently these extensions involved some heavy grading in canyons. But perhaps worst of all was the condition of the 175 wooden bridges, which had a total length of two and five-tenths miles and were entirely eliminated by fills and line changes.

The next most serious problem was the condition of the timbering in the original fifty-one tunnels. For years "the Chief" had been conspiring to correct their defects. Tunnels, tunnels, surely they were the Moffat signature. Nowhere else in the Western

Typical of many line relocations made during the rebuilding of the Moffat under Bill Jones was two miles of tortuous track through the Colorado River badlands near Kremmling. Motor 17 rests on the new 60 m.p.h. track which crossed the old 20 m.p.h. alignment in six places between MP 94 and 96, reduced curvature by 421° and shortened the line 825 feet. Several abandoned timber trestles and much relocated line can be seen from the California Zephyr near Parshall. *D.&S.L. photo.*

Replacing Bridge 48.41. Upgrading an entire railroad which has been neglected for years is a job that takes time and money. The girders for bridge 48.41 between Tolland and East Portal had been fabricated in advance. Here the Salt Lake wrecker sets the entire assembly into position on April 24, 1941, with a minimum interruption to traffic. Just a short year later peak loads imposed by wartime traffic were to make this one of the most vital rail arteries in America. At the time the Moffat was completed to Craig there were 272 timber structures amounting to just over four miles in length. By 1937, 175 had been replaced by fills, and three more were abandoned. The 94 remaining were replaced entirely as in this instance or partially upgraded with concrete. At the present writing timber can be seen only on the west end. *L. J. Daly photo.*

Hemisphere exists such a concentration of tunnels and mountains as in the "tunnel district" of the D.&S.L. Casual visitors who make the acquaintance of the Moffat via travel folders or a ride on the California Zephyr are surprised to learn that the unpublicized western end beyond Orestod contains thirteen more tunnels, and more incomparable scenery.

The original tunnel construction utilized timber exclusively for tunnel support except in those few tunnels through sound rock. Tunnels on the transcontinental route have all been gunited or concrete lined, as is shown in the table. All tunnels are single track. The shortest is Number 40, only 63 feet, and the longest (exclusive of the Moffat Tunnel) is Number 17, 1,730 feet. Bill Jones in 1937 faced the problem of 12,514 feet of old timber—more than two and a half miles. To combat it, collapsible steel forms were designed which could be moved from one location to another in about an hour. Even with this speed, an hour of uninterrupted activity was an infrequent occurrence. By this time a heavy procession of time freights and transcontinental passenger trains had been added to the Moffat coal drags and cattle trains. Helper engines had to get back to terminals. It was not an easy job.

Pressure from the fractured conditions in the rock had to be met, and these pressures varied in the direction from which they came. Moisture, the many curves in the tunnels, plus the narrow confines of the sunless canyons, all added to the problems. Very rarely was a tunnel located where a man could drive

a car, or bring supplies in by truck. Shortcuts were adopted where practical, such as mixing concrete outside the portals and then pumping it under pressure through a six-inch pipe to the forms. This permitted continuous placement even during train movements. Sills and the lower ends of posts subjected to alternate wet and dry conditions were found to have the most serious deterioration. Very often the lower end crumbled and the entire tunnel settled a bit, reducing clearances. Where such conditions existed, the lower ends were cut off and a new concrete footing poured.

While we are on the subject of tunnels, mention should be made of the two which were abandoned during construction. These were Number 9, and "old 17." The former can still be seen by a trained eye by reason of a thin line of timbering in the gravel alongside the track where a recent line relocation has encroached upon the original structure. Both tunnels were by-passed by kinks in the track, that at "old 17" being most severe. Because of the trouble it caused Rio Grande engines, the latter tunnel was restored as a cut and can no longer be seen.

If one is to understand the man who rebuilt the Moffat, one must remember that he was away from home more than he was at home—a home he loved. Sleet, snow, cold winds, and the blasts of President Freeman he had fought. To understand Bill Jones was to have seen him arguing, battling with the other Bill. Those battles had been epics! Even in the days

The Dotsero Cutoff

when money had been at hand, that money had been wanted for bonds by the president.

When Wilson McCarthy became president in December, 1934, he retained Freeman on the board, thinking he would be valuable.

One day a board of directors meeting was in progress to discuss Jones's proposal to fill trestles with material that needed to be removed from the right of way. One of these trestles was the famous steel one at Coal Creek. "The Chief," having presented his material, was interrogated by the one-time president. His questions were carefully answered. Then a cross examination began with the same questions asked over and over again, until the temperature of the chief engineer flashed and he replied that he had answered those questions several times.

President McCarthy immediately excused Jones, who went down to his office to gather his personal

Storming up South Boulder Creek. The twilight of her years was approaching for 302 as she chuffed up the head of South Boulder Canyon near Tolland November 5, 1939, with Train Number 1. She had a pint-sized kitchen in this coach. Delicious pies were baked in the oven, soups were heated from cans, tasty sandwiches made, and pop dispensed. There was one table between two seats. And if one wanted special dishes, arrangements could be made, such as the time veteran conductor F. A. Van Vrankin brought deer steaks to feed Ed Bollinger after the train left Steamboat that late afternoon. Another time the steward bought ice cream for Mr. and Mrs. Bollinger, knowing that they were celebrating their wedding anniversary. This was Moffat service for the patrons who welcomed a safe ride when highways were just about impassable. Notice the fine roadbed which had been built of volcanic ash from Volcano near McCoy. Very little tie replacement had been accomplished since the original construction in 1903. Temporary replacement of the worst ties as needed for safe track was done when the Cutoff was finished. In 1936 replacement of every tie on the entire line was started, with 172,000 replaced the first year. Although the Hill line over Corona had been abandoned in 1929, it was only in 1936 that the last rail and ties were removed. Up to elevation 10,000, few ties were worth reclaiming. Above that most of the old ties were well preserved, and above 11,000 feet about eighty per cent were removed, recreosoted and placed in main line service. *Otto C. Perry photo.*

Replacing Coal Creek viaduct May, 1939, with fifteen-foot diameter corrugated steel pipe under forty-five foot fill. *Ed Sunergren photo.*

Removing old sixty-five-foot girders from Coal Creek fill at viaduct in 1939 between train operation, about three hours. *Ed Sunergren photo.*

Heavy power comes to the Moffat. On September 10, 1939, Dick Kindig was perched overlooking the Moffat near Scenic. He captured this truly great shot of the 3603 climbing the two per cent with 33 cars at 15 m.p.h. The Utah Junction-Bond segment of the D.&S.L. had been beefed up sufficiently to take this heavy power. *R. H. Kindig photo.*

West Portal before U.S. 40 was relocated. Number 6, the "Exposition Flyer," climbs the Divide entering the Moffat Tunnel at West Portal. Pioneer bore of the Moffat Tunnel is clearly seen with the tram track. This later became the water tunnel for the City of Denver. *Sanborn photo.*

effects. Some time later he was summoned, expecting to be fired.

"Sit down, Jones. That man Freeman made me so mad that I lost control of myself most shamefully. I closed the Board of Directors meeting and told Freeman he was fired. He started crying. I said, 'Cut out the tears. You don't have a heart. You never thought a kind thing. In fact, cracked ice pumps through your veins.' "

The Moffat staff breathed easier with Freeman gone. The light was green for the work of rebuilding the Moffat. A. L. Johnson and every old time Moffat official and man knew what was needed from the experience of the years. The only question now was which method would prove the best in making these changes. For example, should the big trestle in Rock Creek Canyon be replaced with a steel trestle? Or was a fill the proper move? Jones was in his glory and not as sympathetic to old ideas as A. L. Johnson, who was open to the suggestions of most men. The little Moffat family get-togethers, in which these

plans were discussed, found Johnson giving everyone a chance to speak his opinion and reasons. Then "A. L." weighed the problem and made his decision. In time these conferences were naturally held over at the Rio Grande office, for the Rio Grande was renting the right of way for its transcontinental business. Here the same pattern of conference was held. Even safety men and roadmasters were being called in to listen and make comments on plans. A vote would be taken in a very democratic fashion and a report made to the board.

So it came about that General Superintendent A. L. Johnson saw the Moffat become a first-class road. The Rio Grande in the last hours exerted more and more influence in Moffat affairs, which was natural and right, for it owned the Moffat.

Most prominent among the men was A. E. Perlman, assistant to President McCarthy and advisor to the engineering department. He brought with

The Exposition Flyer. Number 5, Engine 1704, a 4-8-4, hurrying seven cars through Tunnel 28 near Pinecliff. Today both tunnel and train are gone—both to their reward. The Exposition Flyer was superseded by the streamlined California Zephyr and Tunnel 28 was daylighted in 1951. *R. H. Kindig photo.*

him the idea of off track equipment. He questioned if the volcanic ballast was standing up under the pounding of the heavy Rio Grande power.

Jones did not take easily to this newcomer. The two constantly argued. And caught between them was the young graduate fresh from the University of Illinois. He was a transportation major (1936) who had first hired out on a Rio Grande extra gang as a laborer and later brought to the Moffat as a roadmaster. This lanky fellow was G. B. Aydelott. "Gus" would be told by Al Perlman to do it his way. "Gus" had risen from laborer to extra gang foreman, track inspector, and engineering assistant.

This new job was not pleasant, though G. B.

Track gang in Rock Creek. The original eighty-pound rails had been laid in 1903-09 as far west as Steamboat, and eighty-five pound rails in 1911 to Craig. In 1927 one-hundred-pound rail was laid for twenty-five miles. By 1930 the heavier rails reached MP 66 near Tabernash, and by 1935 they were in Orestod where the Rio Grande joined the Moffat. May 27, 1941, saw the mechanized track gang changing rail with an adzing machine in the foreground and Burro crane beyond. *L. J. Daly photo.*

Page 242

Work train dumps fill on new culverts. This fill was shoveled out of the cuts, thus improving drainage of the roadbed. This one was the old trestle over Vasquez Creek at Woods (today's Hideaway Park). *Ed Bollinger photos.*

Allin Gillett was a fireman on Engine 207 when he took this picture of the mallet under the Utah Junction water tank, November, 1939. Gillett later became a conductor.

Beginning and end of the line for Engine 301. May, 1905, saw this builder's photo of the trim 301 outside the American Locomotive Company plant. Thirty-seven years later the handwriting was on the wall—missing headlight and bell—as the once proud engine awaited scrapping at Utah Junction. *Alco, Schenectady History Center, and L. Van Buskirk photos.*

Aydelott's mind was sharpened by the battle of ideas between Parlman and Jones. Most of all his heart was made to grow toward all men caught in such circumstances. "Gus" determined to eliminate such friction, make pleasant as possible the work that men were to do and above all appreciate the best that lay within men.

Aydelott began to meet the wonderful veterans of the Moffat who had done such a remarkable work despite some of Bill Freeman's policies.

A. E. Perlman's work was a full time education on the Rio Grande. He had great problems, for we were at war. Where else could Perlman have received better experience to become president of the New York Central? And Aydelott? He is now president of the Rio Grande.

Page 244

No.	Mile post	Location or nearest siding		DNW&P Length	construction Timbering	New portal	Timber added (A) repaired (R)	Timber replaced by gunite (G) concrete (C)	D&RGW length	Remarks
						MAIN LINE				
1	23.43	Coal Creek viaduct	∧ —	330'	89'	West 1958		16' 1936 G 89' 1947 C 55' 1947 G	356'	
2	25.44	Plain		515'	29'			29' 1953 G	516'	
3	25.79	Plain	Frontal Escarpment	369'	None				369'	Exists today as built.
4	26.00	Plain		174'	None				174'	Exists today as built.
5	26.11	Plain		559'	111'	West 1942		107' 1942 C 65' 1954 C	585'	
6	26.35	Plain		536'	None				536'	Exists today as built.
7	26.63	Plain	| ∨	191'	62'	West 1951		84' 1951 C	208'	
8	26.91	Plain	∧	738'	190'	E 1951 W 1942	12' 1932 A east end	176' 1942 C 27' 1951 C	753'	
9	27.00	Plain		120' approx.	Most				0	Caved in when almost complete, pressure on timbering. Abandoned and by-passed 1903. Never operated. Line of timbers showing 1961, hardly visible.
10	27.42	Plain		1561'	1176'			12' 1937 C 815' 1944 C 213' 1950 C	1572'	Disastrous fire, Sept. 20, 1943.
11	27.81	Crescent		230'	All	1941		230' 1941 C	238'	
12	27.93	Crescent		400'	All	East 1941		52' 1938 C 235' 1941 C	429'	
13	28.14	Crescent		312'	46'			58' 1940 C	312'	
14	28.28	Crescent		412'	242'			25' 1940 C 234' 1946 C	434'	
15	28.46	Crescent		427'	155'			172' 1946 G	444'	
16	28.72	Crescent	South Boulder Canyon	684'	All			328' 1940 C 370' 1945 C	698'	
"Old 17"	29.00	Crescent		110' approx.	?				0	Caved in when partially complete, abandoned 1903. Partially daylighted prior to 1919 to secure fill for bridge 28.6 and for possible use of original alignment. Kink in by-pass gave Rio Grande engines trouble. Now replaced by cut which destroyed old tunnel.
17	29.50	Crescent		1725'	848'			853' 1945 C	1730'	
18	29.97	Crescent		249'	178'			98' 1944 C 84' 1953 G	238'	
19	32.11	Crescent		1045'	604'	West 1943		612' 1945 C	1055'	

No.	Mile post	Location or nearest siding		Length DNW&P	Timbering construction	New portal	Timber added (A) repaired (R)	Timber replaced by gunite (G) concrete (C)	D&RGW length	Remarks
20	32.45	Crescent	*South Boulder Canyon*	426'	All			260' 1947 C 95' 1950 G 105' 1950 C	460'	Fire, April 11, 1905
21	32.71	Crescent		633'	191'	West 1945		367' 1945 C	667'	
22	32.98	Crescent		177'	All			180' 1953 G	180'	
23	33.20	Crescent		1605'	214'	1950		65' 1951 G 100' 1951 C	1553'	
24	34.10	Crescent		815'	None				812'	Exists today as built.
25	34.61	Cliff		643'	80'			42' 1950 G 41' 1950 C	639'	
26	35.22	Cliff		286'				48' 1942 C 140' 1953 C 115' 1953 G	295'	
27	35.72	Cliff		646'	14'				643'	
28	35.02	Cliff		124'	124'				0	Daylighted 1951 due to sloughing of the sidewalls. Good view of site from Colorado 72 Highway.
29	36.38	Cliff		78'	39'			41' 1953 G	78'	Good view as above.
30	40.47	Rollins		254'	73'			90' 1953 C	257'	Sphinx Head Tunnel. Stream relocated at west portal, 1960.
31	53.93	Ladora	*Tunnels on Hill Line abandoned 1929*	550'	All				0	Caved in throughout after removal of timbering following abandonment.
32	63.47	Corona		170'	None				0	Needle's Eye Tunnel overlooking Yankee Doodle Lake. Used by present County Road.
33	69.45	Loop		412'	All				0	Riflesight Tunnel under Loop Trestle. Snowshed debris at both ends but clear throughout 1961.
	MOFFAT TUNNEL 50.18 to 56.39	East Portal Winter Park		6.21 miles	Timber 16,577' Gunite 9,078' Concrete 920' Unlined 5,400'		Yearly before concrete	65' 1932 C Entire tunnel lined 1935 except where rock solid	6.21 miles	See Moffat Tunnel chapter.
34	69.09	Elkdale	*Fraser Canyon*	361'	239'		162' 1936 A	146' 1950 G	372'	

No.	Mile post	Location or nearest siding		DNW&P Length	construction Timbering	New portal	Timber added (A) repaired (R)	Timber replaced by gunite (G) concrete (C)	D&RGW length	Remarks
35	108.64	Gore		150'	49'		27' 1930 A west	100' 1946 C	157'	
36	108.79	Gore		230'	None				230'	Exists today as built.
37	108.98	Azure		126'	66'			28' 1953 C / 86' 1953 G	134'	
38	110.05	Azure		111'	All	Both 1953		100' 1953 C	100'	
39	113.49	Azure		281'	All			294' 1944 C	294'	
40	113.79	Azure		54'	All	Both 1951		63' 1951 C	63'	
41	114.00	Azure		66'	All				0	Daylighted 1952 due cave-ins at end of tunnel.
42	115.78	Radium		450'	All			463' 1944 C	463'	

Gore Canyon — *"Little Gore"*

CRAIG BRANCH

No.	Mile post	Location or nearest siding		DNW&P Length	construction Timbering	New portal	Timber added (A) repaired (R)	Timber replaced by gunite (G) concrete (C)	D&RGW length	Remarks
43	130.69	Orestod		117'	All				117'	Exists today as built.
44	131.96	McCoy		702'	All				702'	Exists today as built.
45	140.51	Volcano		186'	All				186'	Exists today as built.
46	140.78	Volcano		622'	521'				622'	Exists today as built.
47	141.14	Volcano		173'	None				173'	Exists today as built.
48	141.33	Volcano		223'	All				223'	Exists today as built.
49	144.01	Volcano		293'	All				293'	Exists today as built.
50	144.72	Volcano		238'	All				238'	Exists today as built.
51	145.17	Volcano		255'	All				255'	Exists today as built.
52	145.92	Volcano		1316'	861'		10' 1930 A small portion repaired 1934		1316'	
53	146.34	Volcano		129'	All				129'	Exists today as built.
54	147.37	Egeria		1136'	516'		50' 1930 A		1136'	
55	148.12	Egeria		404'	All	Repaired 1932			404'	

Rock Creek Canyon — *Egeria Canyon*

DOTSERO CUTOFF

			D&RGW length	Remarks
Yarmony Tunnel	131.23	Bond	647'	Concrete lined when built.
Sweetwater Tunnel	159.17	Sweetwater	1115'	Concrete lined when built.

The Dotsero Cutoff. The westbound California Zephyr glides through Red Canyon near Burns about midway along the 41 mile link which created a new transcontinental route. *D.&R.G.W. photo.*

Rebuilding the Moffat. Work trains were busy replacing ballast, cleaning ditches, and doing a thousand other things to bring the sadly-neglected track up to mainline standards. War time traffic was soon to pound over these rails. Engine 213 and the other Moffat mallets were in the twilight of their era. *D.&R.G.W. photo.*

Mallet 200 leaving Utah Junction. Engine 200 is taken by fireman Allin Gillett in 1939. A water car is in tow as well as the 100 engine which is ready to double-head out of Utah Junction to Moffat Tunnel and Phippsburg. The rear helper is being cut in to help up to Moffat Tunnel. *Allin Gillett photo.*

Destruction at Tolland. At 4:12 A.M., September 16, 1934, D.&R.G.W. Extra 3413 West with helper 1162 passed Tolland station "throwing a large number of sparks." Shortly thereafter a fire was discovered in the roof of the eating house. Engine 1162 played steam on the fire, and the agent and telegrapher hooked up a garden hose, but the eating house could not be saved. A Moffat engine arrived later from Tabernash (most Moffat engines having fire hoses) in time to put out the fire on the water tank and save the depot. The roof of the tank collapsed. This view shows the brick chimney still standing, with the dancing pavillion in the background, and station at the left. Today all is gone. *D.&S.L. photo.*

Engine 121 pulls work train. Engine 121 is heading out with one of W. C. Jones's work trains that is cleaning up the right of way for better drainage and for a re-ballasting program with volcanic ash. *Allin Gillett photo.*

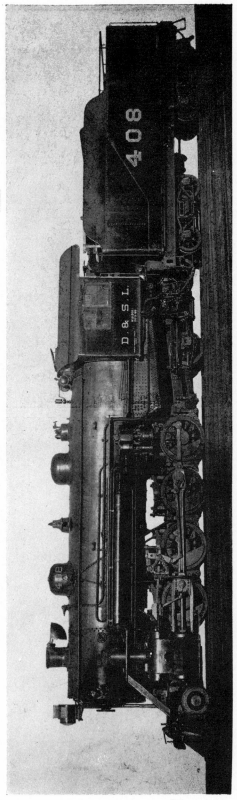

The 400-series, Lima built engines were designed by the very capable and likable Big Dan Cunningham for use west of Tabernash. They were too stiff for the hill, throwing the track out of place on the sharp curves. These engines were used to double-head the drags out of Phippsburg to Denver, making longer trains possible. So between the 200's and 400's the Moffat was ready with plenty of good power for the war. *Denver Public Library Western Collection.*

Cab interior of Engine 408.
Alco photo, Schenectady History Center.

Last freight over Rollins Pass. The opening of Moffat Tunnel released many fine 200 engines from hill-helper service. This last train over Rollins Pass had five mallets as she approached the Loop on the Western side and was shot by conductor L. J. Daly, who kept his camera on his cabin car. Little did anyone dream what the famous 200 engines would mean when the war came. Some would be leased to the Rio Grande. *L. J. Daly photo.*

Wrecks and the War Years

Just how well prepared was the D. & S. L. to take her part in World War II? The wrecks on any railroad reveal its weaknesses. Time and again Interstate Commerce Commission investigations of the road had concluded with recommendations for signals. These signals were installed as far as East Portal when the war broke out. The derailment of a football special at Hot Sulphur Springs warned of the need of a great tie renewal program, with new rail. New rail in the Moffat Tunnel was tragically corroded. Despite its welded joints, a serious derailment had taken the life of a helper crew backing out after shoving a drag up to Apex from the west. The continued rock slides in the several canyons warned that a costly program of relocation away from the canyon walls would be needed. The worst hazard of all was the fire hazard in the timbering of many of the tunnels. Come war, this could be serious.

Very fortunately the greatest asset the Denver and Salt Lake had was above average morale. An occasional violation of rules enabled the old timers to keep hammering away with pride that, "No passenger has ever lost his life on a Moffat passenger train." But the list of names of men who had died in the building and operating of the line was now totaling a cross per mile clear to Craig, Colorado.

The main line "Through the Rockies, Not Around Them" was fortunate in now being able to handle the fine modern mountain climbing locomotives of the D. and R.G.W. road. Indeed, the D. and S. L. was on the way to a first class road, but still haunted by the ghost of Bill Freeman's lack of maintenance.

Then there was the very live hand of the bondholders and those who had prevented the reorganization of the Rio Grande. The management could not move with as strong an initiative and enterprise as was needed to make up for so many lost years. Just let a great strain come. How would the line stand up?

We now turn to examples of what happened.

Mallet 206 at Utah Junction Enginehouse. One of Otto Perry's first railroad pictures was of mallet 206 and a sister standing at the coal chute beside the enginehouse in Denver. Perry was indeed a pioneer in railfan photography. *Otto Perry photo.*

Passenger Train 2 rammed rear of extra 209, at Tolland May 2, 1935. Extra 209, an eastbound freight with 35 cars, had climbed the two per cent to West Portal (today's Winter Park), where she received an order to run ahead of Number 2 until overtaken. This train proceeded through Moffat Tunnel. At East Portal the conductor went ahead to the engine and rode in the cab, so that when he would get to Tolland he could drop off and get immediate information regarding how close the passenger would be behind them. He instructed his flagman above all to take precautions to protect the rear of his train. He expected that the flagman would drop off the train before it stopped at Tolland and flag down the passenger and ride it on down to Pine Cliff. There it was the custom to run around the freight, which was usually short on the sixteen-hour-law out of Phippsburg. This would enable a meet to be made with Rio Grande 5 without delaying it.

At Tolland the conductor dropped off his train, went into the station to get the information, while the engineer and head brakeman picked up a car of ice. It was clearly seen that the flagman was back not more than several car lengths.

Passenger train Number 2 with two baggage mail and express cars, a coach and the parlor buffet car, was held at West Portal until Extra 209 had run through Moffat Tunnel. It then proceeded into the smoke-filled six-mile bore. After making the East Portal stop, both the engineman and fireman were on the lookout for the freight, which they knew could not go more than 25 m.p.h. But it was snowing and blowing slightly that afternoon. The flagman of the freight could have dropped two of the yellow fusees which the Moffat road used. He claims that he put down the torpedoes and then took them up when he saw his engine getting ready to take off.

The I.C.C. concluded that the flagman of the freight did not properly protect his train and that the engineman of the passenger did not have his train under proper control when he knew they were close to Extra 209. Passengers were jolted and the passenger enginemen injured when they unloaded. Another engine was able to take the passenger train on down to Denver. *F. A. VanVranken collection.*

Lloyd E. Parris collection.

Lloyd E. Parris collection.

Jesse Carrell photo.

The 215 ran away and piled up at Rollinsville, November 5, 1935. What may have been the fastest run of one of the small wheeled mallets is told thus. The dispatcher had phoned the operator at Tolland asking if he could see anything of the eastbound 215. Weather permitting, the trestle over South Boulder Creek two miles west would afford a good view before the train disappeared to the south. The operator started to say "Haven't seen a . . . hey, some damn fool just ran through without blowing for the board." This would mean no engineer and a runaway. Just then the agent at Rollinsville came on the phone, "Yes, he just piled up here."

The I.C.C. said she piled up at a speed in excess of 60 m.p.h. on the two per cent grade. Thirty-two cars were completely destroyed.

What happened? Extra 215 east had stopped in the middle of Moffat Tunnel to cut off helper-engine 200. Then she had proceeded out of the tunnel slowing to 5 m.p.h. at the east entrance and on down the main to stop near the east end of the passing track. Waiting until No. 1 came up the pass, Engineman Ohrns then pulled ahead with his water car and two cars of gravel preparing to put them on a spur of the passing track. The other thirty-nine cars were standing on the two per cent held by the air brakes. He looked up, and they were coming at him. So he prepared to outrun them two and sixty-seven hundredths miles to Tolland, hoping to get there ahead of them so that he could throw the switch and derail them. However, it was soon apparent that the thirty-nine cars of coal had no brakes at all. They were outrunning the mallet that was not supposed to run over 35 m.p.h. Ohrns put his engine in emergency and jumped, together with his fireman. The brakes on the locomotive, tender, water car, and two gravel cars could not hold the heavy train on the steep two per cent grade.

Officials had told crews to disregard the hand brake rule on the two per cent, if the cars were not supposed to be left more than ten minutes. The ICC declared that operating officers would have to share responsibility in this accident, since the cars were not properly secured. Only one man was injured—the engineer, as he unloaded.

Page 255

On September 27, 1938, there was a head-on collision between Denver & Rio Grande Western passenger train No. 5, the westbound Exposition Flyer with engine 1201, and eastbound Denver & Salt Lake freight First No. 72 (engine 201) at Lowell Boulevard, on Denver's northern outskirt. The collision caused the death of one trespasser and injury to sixteen passengers, one person carried under contract, four dining car employees, one employee off duty, and four employees on duty.

Sandhouse gossip said that the freight crew counted on Number 5 running a little late, as frequently occurred, and hoped to get in the clear at the beginning of the double track. Rules required that an inferior train must clear by five minutes. The engineer of the freight, with 41 cars and caboose, kept sounding short blasts on his whistle, trying to warn the crew of the passenger train, whose smoke he could see. The passenger engineer, however, relying on the rights of a superior class train, continued running. The ICC investigation concluded the speed of the freight was between eight and fifteen miles per hour at the time of impact. *L. J. Daly photo.*

Engine 201 before the head-on. *Alco photo, Schenectady History Center.*

The engine of the Exposition Flyer after the head-on meet with Engine 201. *L. J. Daly photo.*

On July 12, 1941, a large corrugated iron culvert just below East Portal gave way under the passage of D.& R.G.W. 3619 eastbound. After Office Engineer Sunergren's plans for a ninety-foot steel girder span across South Boulder Creek and the highway below had been rejected, his instructions for installing the culvert were disregarded with the result shown here. *L. J. Daly photo.*

D.&R.G.W. mallet 3619 on side. This photo was taken from the D.&R.-G.W. wrecker's crane just before it hooked on the head end. *L. J. Daly photo.*

D.&R.G.W. wrecker moves in. *L. J. Daly photo.*

Both wreckers prepare to pick up the 3619 above Tolland in July, 1941. The rail will hold the two engines in line as the mallet is righted. *L. J. Daly photo.*

This monstrous melee faced the wrecking crews as they began work. *L. J. Daly photo.*

Box cars in wash out. Rail fans to Moffat Tunnel drive through this underpass above Tolland. *L. J. Daly photo.*

Pile driver moves in to drive piling as culvert is repaired. *L. J. Daly photo.*

TOM WILLINGHAM RIDES TO GLORY

Tom Willingham was one of the most colorful men to operate a Rio Grande train over the Moffat. He was a licensed pilot who on occasion looked over his daily work from the air.

On February 24, 1941, he was called to run Rio Grande Freight Number 41, leaving Denver four hours and thirty-one minutes late because of its eastern connection. Time was lost cimbing up to Moffat Tunnel and braking down to Tabernash, where a message was handed up saying, "Account wet snow rocks reported falling in Gore and Byers canyons." Tom had the 3607 mallet of the Rio Grande, forty-three loaded cars, three empties, and the caboose, so that he was able to roll down the valleys and take precautions in Byers Canyon. By the time he had reached Kremmling he had made up twelve minutes time.

Tom, like all other men who made the fast schedules of the Rio Grande possible, had memorized the places where slides were in the habit of coming down. Section Foreman Gill patrolled the track by riding through the Gore fifty minutes ahead of Number 41. There was no sign of trouble on the cliffs. The freight speed limit was twenty-five miles per hour. Tom knew that no slide had ever occurred

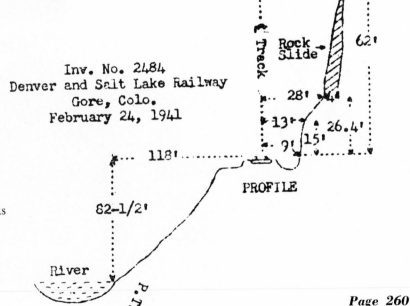

This photo was attached to the ICC report.

This drawing in the ICC report speaks eloquently for itself. *L. J. Daly photo.*

here. He was moving between ten and eighteen miles per hour with the cliff close to his face, so that he could not see more than 200 feet ahead. Right there on the track eighty-two and a half feet above the Colorado river (across the north rail) was a large rock weighing about twenty tons. Tom threw the train into emergency. The million pound mallet was derailed and hurled into the river with Tom riding to Glory. The pictures here show how impossible it was to see ahead. The map of the ICC. investigation is self explanatory. The tragedy had happened. Now, how was the big mallet to be lifted eighty-two and a half feet?

Both the Moffat and Rio Grande wreckers were brought. Men were sent down to dismantle the engine. The running gear was stripped from the engine and loaded on flats. Then came the big lift job with one man saying, "This is the biggest lift job in the world." Frequently the men were reminded that they could meet their Maker, as little rocks pelted down on the cabs of the wreckers.

So ended the last run of Tom Willingham. The ICC. investigation ends with these words, "CAUSE: It is found that this accident was caused by a rock slide."

One of the authors approached the roadmaster with the idea that an electric fence could be built here to give better warning. "The rocks would go over." But some years later he observed that the fence was stretched over the track. In the years that followed, dangerous rocks were scaled off and the right of way moved literally out into the river in most places, leaving room for boulders to fall into the borrow pit, if we dare use a highway term.

If you chanced to be in the dispatcher's office of the D.&S.L. on the morning of September 20, 1943, the scene would have looked routine: cigarette smoke curling up in vertical spirals, the train order ticker quietly busy, and, overlooking all, the stoic dispatcher's clock—impassive, but unforgetting. Dispatcher F. D. Stephenson glances up and beckons, "Want to see what's going on?" There on the train sheet can be seen the movement of all trains on the eastern end of the Moffat Road. Number 1 has just departed Denver at 9:50 A.M. headed for Craig, where it will arrive in late afternoon. Number 2 is coming the other way from Craig. A long D.&S.L. stock train is just leaving East Portal for the markets at Denver. Two D.&R.G.W. military specials are almost ready for departure at Denver Union Station,

L. J. Daly took this picture showing what Tom Willingham could see when he rounded the curve. There on the right lay a twenty-ton wedge of rock that frost had worked loose from the canyon wall above. The photograph proved that Tom was not at fault and should not be blamed for the wreck. *L. J. Daly photo.*

rushing via the Moffat Road and Rio Grande to Salt Lake City and the Coast. There are two freight

The end of Tom Willingham's last run was at the bottom of Gore Canyon, where mallet 3607 of the Rio Grande landed after being wedged off the Gore Canyon shelf by a twenty-ton boulder. *L. J. Daly photo.*

Extra 214 east is leaving Winter Park for the West Portal of Moffat Tunnel with the great tender of the Rio Grande mallet followed by the boiler of the 2-8-8-2 on flats. *E. T. Bollinger photo.*

The Rio Grande wrecker is to the left and the Denver and Salt Lake wrecker to the right at the moment of victory when the boiler of the 3607 had been lifted to the flat car. Most of the snow is gone by now. Men who worked at this location shiver to recall how little rocks fell like hail on several occasions during this job. *L. J. Daly photo.*

Hospital train with the 3607 on flats. This is a very characteristic shot of a Moffat mallet, cold air and steam. *L. J. Daly photo.*

The wheels of the 3607 headed east through Winter Park. *Ed Bollinger photo.*

extras and other light engines winding through the tunnel section northwest of Denver.

But behind this orderly atmosphere, and unknown to anyone in the room, is growing one of the greatest crises to face the Salt Lake. High in the mountains in the interior of Tunnel 10 a wisp of smoke appears, perhaps from the spark of a passing engine, smoldering gently at first, then faster, fanned by the cool, constant draft through the dark tunnel . . .

Meanwhile, engineer A. E. Vaughn on Number 1 was hammering through the reverse curves at Arena; then past Fireclay Siding, where many a Moffat head-end brakemen has dropped off, dashed up the two hundred foot hill, and bent the iron ahead of his train before it covered the half-mile circle of track. Number 1 was nearing the fill over Coal Creek, then curving to the left into the momentary darkness of Tunnel 1, and finally stopping for a few minutes at Plainview. Off again, it labored up the edge of the escarpment through Tunnels 2, 3, and 4 high over Eldorado Springs. Ahead, hidden from the early fall sunlight, lurked the smoldering fire.

Moffat men had to be keen. Fires were a constant dread and menace. As he passed through Tunnel 10 Vaughn thought he smelled wood smoke and so on arrival at Quartz, Conductor J. A. Pierson telephoned Denver, "Hello—hello, dispatcher. This is Pierson, first one, engine 302. We are at Quartz—that's it. Say, when we went through Tunnel 10 a few minutes ago, we smelled smoke, and it wasn't engine smoke. . . . Yeah, I know Schneitman. . . . you say he's got his B&B gang at Crescent? Yeah. . . . That's only two miles west of here. . . . O.K. . . . I'll tell him to get down there pronto. . . . Thought I had better play my hunch."

"All right, gun 'er, Vaughn. The DS wants us to meet Schneitman's B&B gang at Crescent and get 'em down to Tunnel 10 as soon as we can." Vaughn whistled off and started highballing his three-car train up the two per cent. Immediately the B&B supervisor and a bridge gang working nearby proceeded back to the tunnel. Dispatcher Stephenson alerted General Superintendent A. L. Johnson, whose office was just across the hall. Intending to go to lunch, Johnson nevertheless delayed his departure until a report could be received from the B&B gang. A Denver and Rio Grande engine returning light to Denver after having helped a freight up to the Moffat Tunnel was also dispatched to the scene. By 11:50 A.M. the men had reached the west portal of Tunnel 10 to find smoke and flame belching out of the tunnel mouth, making it impossible for them to approach closely.

At noon Johnson's phone rang: "Mr. Johnson, this is Burt Schneitman at Quartz. . . . Tunnel 10 is blazing like fury! . . . . Two engines with fire hoses at Crescent . . . . right away!" One was engine 121 with a work extra, the other had arrived light. Technologically, the D&SL was a progressive road. All engines were equipped with fire hoses to combat fires. Johnson at once ordered the dispatcher to move the two engines to the tunnel to lend immediate assistance.

Any semblance of quiet had been shattered in the dispatcher's office. The most urgent business at hand was to turn traffic back from the tunnel and to clear the tracks for fire fighting equipment. And thus, at midday, began the greatest traffic crisis in the Moffat history. The D.&S.L.-D.&R.G.W. joint line from Denver to Bond was carrying a wartime load of heavy traffic to and from the West Coast. Operation of the tunnel section by timetable and train order was a monumental task at any time, but the influx of the heaviest volume of traffic in its

Tunnel 10 was too hot to handle. The fire was of such intensity that rock flowed like lava. Before reconstruction was possible, fire hoses were played against the roof and walls to cool the bore and assist in scaling off faulted rock. *D.&R.G.W. photo.*

history found the Moffat with sidings too short, experienced people too few, and operating personnel fatigued.

Tunnel 10, 27.42 miles west of Denver on the single track line, in 1943 was not much different from what it was when originally constructed at the turn of the century. It was 1570 feet in length, straight except for 110 feet at the west end constructed on a very light spiral to the right. Entering the east portal there were first 198 feet of timber lining, then 103 feet unlined, then 41 more feet of timbers, then another 28 feet unlined, then 502 feet more of Moffat timber followed by 147 feet of rock, 45 feet of timber lining, 53 feet unlined, and finally 142 feet of timber lining. Judging by the conflagration at the west portal, the fire appeared to have started in the most westerly timbered section. Now, fanned with a natural draft which increased with every passing moment, the flames began to leap from section to section of the 12x12 timbers, creating a yellow inferno and sending columns of smoke into South Boulder Canyon.

Quickly the Denver Fire Department was consulted, and they advised that water would be the only effective means of fighting the flames. To combat the fire, a train was hastily organized at Utah Junction, consisting of several water cars with fire hoses, and dispatched with right over all trains to the Tunnel. Yardmaster Fenn at Utah Junction and

Storekeeper William Chappel assembled a relief train in two hours and sent it also on its way. When the engine had reached the east portal, they found the wind was blowing strongly from the east into the mouth of the tunnel, and they easily walked more than 850 feet into the tunnel with the fire hose to play water upon the burning timbers. It was impossible, however, to approach close enough to the burning section to cut through the lagging in order to play water on the packing, more than forty years old and burning furiously. Due to a difference in barometric pressure at the two ends of the tunnel, the winds would shift occasionally, driving the firefighters out.

Soon a stream of men and equipment was on the way from Denver. Some came from the Rio Grande because of the tremendous interest of that road in its trackage rights through the tunnel. A tarpaulin was placed over the east portal to end the draft through the tunnel and check the fire at the western end.

Immediately the closure of the tunnel began to effect a creeping paralysis throughout the D.&S.L.-D.&R.G.W system. Number 2 had to be turned back from Cliff. Rio Grande Number 6, the Exposition Flyer eastbound from Salt Lake City, was diverted via the Royal Gorge route when it reached

Engine 405 and collapsed trestle. Bill Freeman had been fired as president of the Denver and Salt Lake because he harrassed Bill Jones, the chief engineer, who was carrying out improvements on the line which would have prevented such accidents as this one in Egeria Canyon. Freeman made money by deferring maintenance. *L. J. Daly photo.*

Dotsero. Likewise, two Rio Grande long freights eastbound were detoured via the Gorge. The D.&-S.L. stock extra was also caught, turned around, and sent to Denver via the Cutoff and Salida. All westbound D.&S.L. trains, including the two D.&R.G.W. military specials, and such trains as the Mountaineer to Grand Junction and 5 and 6 to Salt Lake, were detoured via Pueblo and the Gorge route.

On the afternoon of September 20, 1943, and for nearly nine weeks thereafter, the D.&S.L. could operate only the western end of its trackage from Craig to Cliff, and every Rio Grande train normally using the tunnel was forced to be routed via Pueblo and Salida, 175 miles longer and over a line which included a maximum grade of three per cent on the west side of Tennessee Pass.

On the evening of the first day, a Denver Fire Department pumper and four firemen with respirators were brought to the scene. Three firemen, after removing the curtain from the east portal, entered the tunnel. One was forced to turn back after a few minutes because his mask was leaking. The other two had been inside the tunnel over an hour when the wind suddenly changed so that smoke was forced out the east portal. One of the remaining firemen started in to see if the two in the interior of the tunnel were still all right. Moments later G. E. Hamilton, D.&S.L. roadmaster, donned a respirator and entered the east portal, only to stumble over the body of the last of the firemen one hundred feet inside the portal. He attempted to drag the man out but was unsuccessful, and he in turn collapsed before he could stagger out of the tunnel. Fortunately, Hamilton was noticed by fellow workmen outside the tunnel, who rescued both men. Despite the fact that resuscitation was carried on for two hours, ef-

forts to revive the fireman were unsuccessful. The fierce fire, burning with the placement of the curtain over the east portal, had insufficient oxygen, resulting in the generation of tremendous amounts of carbon monoxide gas. The masks worn by the firemen were not effective against the concentration of this odorless gas, fatal in amounts as low as 0.025 per cent. The bodies of the other two firemen could not be reached and were not recovered until the tunnel was cleared nearly two months later.

Gradually the seriousness of the situation was coming home to the Moffat men and officials. Speculation as to the length of time the tunnel would be closed varied, depending upon whom one might ask. The bridge and building foreman, Schneitman, wanted to seal off the tunnel immediately at both ends, but A. L. Johnson, who had arrived on the scene, said, "What do you want to do, close the tunnel?" Even the most pessimistic felt that the tunnel could be cleared within several weeks, and some hoped for the opening within days. No one grasped the gravity of the situation or realized that nearly two-and-a-half months lay ahead before the tracks could be cleared. Already a rush was developing along the Rio Grande because of the sudden jump in traffic through Pueblo, amounting to nearly thirty-two per cent, and handled by the same number of men and amount of equipment as were in service before the fire.

Although part of the traffic was diverted to other transcontinental roads, these carriers had very nearly reached their own capacities. Enginemen were transferred the first night from Bond to Pueblo, and considerable numbers of D.&S.L. personnel were

Lining the tunnel. Some lining has been placed just inside the portal. It will be necessary to fill the large hole in the roof with cribbing before lining can proceed. Note the form outside the portal and the ventilation pipe against the tunnel wall. *D.&R.G.W. photo.*

sent to assist the Rio Grande at all points along the Gorge Route—Canon City, Salida, Tennessee Pass, and Minturn; rank-and-file and officials, as well, worked day and night through long hours of overtime to keep the traffic moving.

The delay in blocking off the ends of the tunnel had been a fatal one, for on the second day the fire continued to progress from the west end of the tun-

nel to the east. As it reached the next-to-the-last timbered section at the east end, the entire roof of the tunnel in this section collapsed, filling three hundred feet of the tunnel with huge granite boulders. Only the most easterly one hundred ninety-eight foot section of timber was not completely destroyed. Westward, spalling of the rock and collapse of the timbers resulted in progressive filling of the tunnel bore up to twenty feet in depth. The emergency job which had first been one of fire-fighting now took on an entirely different view—tunnel work, when the fire could be extinguished or would burn itself out. It had been nearly half a century since the original tunnels on the Denver, Northwestern and Pacific had been constructed, and D.&-S.L. President Wilson McCarthy said at the time, "We knew we would have to procure more trained tunnel workers and that such workers were employed on the Big Thompson Water Diversion Tunnel not far from the scene of the fire, at Granby." Thus, arrangements were made with the War Manpower Commission and the U. S. Reclamation Bureau to cease work on this project and move crews and equipment to Tunnel 10.

The morning of the third day, John Austin, general superintendent of the Stiers Brothers Construction Company, and one hundred men arrived on the job. The most immediate need was for an accurate estimate of the damage to the tunnel—in which the fire still raged. Caving began 306 feet inside the east portal, and the tunnel was completely filled at this point. It was not possible to estimate or determine the amount of rock which had fallen within the

mountain, but it was felt that this condition existed for 60 to 100 feet above the roof. It was evident that a "chimney" to the top might be created if any attempt was made to dig out the entire mass of debris from below. It was decided, therefore, to adopt tunneling methods through the fallen rock and to hold in place the rock above the tunnel by means of supporting timbers.

Re-drilling of the tunnel was complicated by the continued presence of carbon monoxide gas and the heat remaining in the rock. The carbon monoxide was released from crevices between the rock whenever the barometer dropped. Crews of men working within the tunnel were forced to abandon their tools repeatedly when warned of the presence of the deadly gas by means of detectors borrowed from the Bureau of Mines. Several hours would then be required for clearing the atmosphere. Heat in the tunnel during the fire and afterward was intense. In many places, solid rock had melted and flowed like lava. As late as November 2, forty-three days after the start of the fire, the heat inside the tunnel was such that work was stopped at times. Falling rock from the ceiling was a constant menace. "We were extremely fortunate in the matter of injuries," said A. E. Perlman, assistant to the president of the D.&.S.L. and chief engineer, D.&.R.G.W. "In only one case was a man hit by falling rock and injuries in this case were not serious," he continued . . .

After the tunnel cooled, a pioneer bore was used to begin the driving of the main railroad shaft. All this rock fell from a chimney above the old tunnel roof. *D.&R.G.W. photo.*

The boss at Tunnel 10 fire, A. E. Perlman, at right in hard hat, was chief engineer of the Rio Grande, and assistant to the president of the D.&S.L. on engineering matters at the time of the fire. He is now president of the New York Central. The *Marcia* waits in the left background. *D.&R.G.W. photo.*

"however, there were many narrow escapes."

Equipment was needed now. Ventilating fans, generators to drive them, mucking machines, and heavy equipment were rented from construction firms and mines in four states. Every B&B outfit car on the D.&S.L.—a total of twenty-four—was brought to the scene and a small city quickly grew up at Plainview, which had become headquarters for the men and work equipment. A small diesel switcher was borrowed from the Rio Grande and used to shuttle work cars in and out of the tunnel as work progressed. A siding was built for the outfit cars and steam crane at the east portal.

Because ventilation was a critical need, a carload of pipe was connected to two blowers outside the east portal to furnish fresh air to the men inside. Paul Guinn, of Draper, Utah, an expert at working through bad ground in tunnel construction, was flown to the scene to oversee the work of the muckers at the east end. Despite all precautions, on October 29, twelve men working on the open face of the tunnel, including A. J. Neff, supervisor of work equipment for the D.&S.L., were overcome by gas. Four collapsed. They were rushed to Denver in a bunk car using the diesel switcher. During this time, oxygen was administered from welding tanks. Physicians later stated this quick thinking on the part of Moffat men undoubtedly saved the lives of those most seriously affected.

A pioneer bore was being driven through the top of the muck pile from the east and lengths of 100 pound rails placed under tunnel timbers stabilizing the roof. The barometer was watched constantly, since falling pressure released more gas. Loose rock was scaled by hand, and gunite was applied to the tunnel walls to minimize the danger to personnel from spalling rock which occurred as the granite mass cooled. The expansion of the mica in the granite, due to the heat, created lines of cleavage and resulted in a very unstable rock structure. It was necessary to install a third rail to handle the narrow gauge mine dump cars used at the east end. On the west, however, such equipment was not used, with the result that a small diesel shovel could enter the tunnel and excavate down to sub-grade.

During the time necessary to open up the caved-in section, portable steel forms used in lining the 6.2 mile Moffat Tunnel were set up inside the west portal, whereupon the installation of reinforced concrete lining began. As work on the pioneer bore continued at the center of the tunnel, excavation and lining of the main tunnel was taking place at both ends. At many places the actual rock roof of the tunnel was high above the intended roof due to caving of the rock. In these sections steel I-beam arches were placed every three or five feet and 4x4 and 4x6 timbers were then packed between the arches and the sides and roof of the rock. Six carloads of timber were consumed in the 343 feet of tunnel in which steelwork was used. More than 590 feet of the tunnel had been lined with concrete before the caved-in portion was cleared. The pioneer bore was holed through on November 3, resulting in greatly improved working conditions because of the great acceleration in cooling of the tunnel and improved atmosphere within it. Likewise, the holing through of the pioneer bore obviated the need for the long and difficult trail around the mountain to get men and materials from one end to the other. Progress, however, was slow, averaging eight feet through the cave-in each two days.

Many of the engineers were apprehensive about rock conditions over the tunnel once traffic was resumed. This concern was due mainly to the effect of vibration from the Rio Grande mallets used to haul heavy drags through the tunnel. There was doubt regarding the ability of the 12x12 timbers to withstand the side pressure. It was decided to force fluid concrete (grout) into the area over the arch of the tunnel. This work, however, was carried on after traffic was resumed.

It was Indian summer when the fire started. Balmy days soon gave way to light snow and with it arrived the fall sheep marketing season. The D.&S.L. was maintaining passenger, mail, and express traffic by running Trains 1 and 2 between Craig and Rollinsville, fourteen miles west of Tunnel 10. By

Reopening Tunnel 10. Top mining men were sent by the army to reopen the tunnel when the rocks had cooled enough. *D.&R.G.W. photo.*

President Wilson McCarthy checks on the movement of sheep from Rollinsville to Denver by truck during Tunnel 10 trouble.

Wilson McCarthy was the last president of the Moffat Road. He was born in Utah, had ridden the range in Montana and Alberta, Canada. He went to school in Toronto. He legislated and sat on the bench in Salt Lake City. He served with the original Reconstruction Finance Corporation in Washington, then went across the continent to open a law office in Oakland, California. He became president of the Denver and Salt Lake Railway on December 21, 1934, and remained as such until it was merged with the Rio Grande, of which he was president.

Judge McCarthy, as he was called, won the affection of the veterans of both roads, so that confidence in his administration grew. Those in the general office who were intimately associated with him grew to hold him in the very highest esteem. It was his good judgment that brought the line from RFC control and Rio Grande bankruptcy to a sound, reorganized road owned and operated by Western men. *D.&R.G.W. photo.*

operating buses and trucks from that point to Denver the gap in the rails was bridged. To handle the sheep traffic, it was necessary for the railroad to build temporary sheep loading pens along the right of way at Rollinsville to effect the transfer of sheep from stock cars to doubledeck trucks for the remainder of the trip to Denver. A fleet of thirty-one trucks was rounded up for this operation by the Rio Grande Motorway, a subsidiary of the D.&R.G.W. These trucks averaged two round trips each day over the fifty-four mile Boulder Canyon Highway from Rollinsville to the Denver Union Stockyards. The pens built at Rollinsville were sufficient to handle 8500 sheep and lambs every twenty-four hours. Despite all handicaps, a total of 110,130 head originating on the D.&S.L. was delivered to market between September 28 and October 17.

Erection of steelwork and the building of concrete forms by the carpenters continued on a three-shift basis. Every possible effort was being made to complete the tunnel work at the earliest possible date.

It soon became necessary to give the transportation departments of both railroads a definite date for reopening of the tunnel—and to do this well in advance so that personnel transferred to the overtaxed Gorge Route could be recalled and others who had been furloughed from the Moffat Tunnel Route could be recalled to their jobs. In addition, motive power of the two roads would have to be reassigned. A. E. Perlman hopefully announced December 1 as the day, based on his estimates of the rate of progress being made through the big cave-in. As the day approached, however, the estimate appeared to be overly optimistic.

Efforts were redoubled.

Work equipment was still scattered at both ends of the tunnel when D.&S.L. Number 1—the last train through the tunnel on September 20—entered

The first train through Tunnel 10 after the fire was a Moffat coal drag. Coal was literally the blood of the railroad and industry during the war. The box cars have coal in them, as the Moffat had to press older box cars into coal service during the winter season. Little is seen in this picture of the nightmare activity that was still going on to finish the job. *D.&R.G.W. photo.*

the east portal at 4:53 P.M. on December 1, 1943, and cleared the west portal at 5:07 P.M. The first long train to move through the tunnel after its re-opening was a Moffat coal drag carrying the life-blood of the D.&S.L. Even after service was resumed, work continued to finish up placement of concrete grouting and lining. Tunnel 10 was finally reconstructed and is entirely fireproof, composed entirely of concrete-encased steelwork, solid rock, or gunite facing.

Old-time Moffat men would have smiled and regarded this nine-week interruption in service as not unusual and much less rigorous than the cold hell of the Hill during the years before the opening of the Moffat Tunnel. Nevertheless, the overcoming of this blockade in the more recent history of the Moffat Road can be regarded as a true milestone befitting the Moffat tradition of ingenuity, tenacity, and the spirit to get the job done—on time.

The need for new rail to handle the war effort demanded immediate action when the very first trains of troops hit the Moffat after Pearl Harbor. That day a train picked the switch at the west end of Rollinsville. But this was just the beginning. Ed Bollinger recalls replacing a broken rail at Hide-away Park curve one morning. Before the week was out, the third changeover occurred. The first rail taken out was put back on the curve, for there was no other rail to be had!

Then came the night in the Moffat Tunnel when the East Portal fan sucked forty below air into the hole that stood about sixty above and the sulphuric-acid-weakened rail snapped.

The line was plugged while weary section men were awakened to dress warmly and kick through the snow to the breezy shed that housed their motor cars. A cutting torch had to be loaded. The cars

D.&S.L. 207 renumbered 3367 rams freight in Tabernash yard. Human recklessness did not help the Rio Grande in the war effort. This engineman running much too fast on his return from a helper job up to Moffat Tunnel rammed the rear of a freight in the Tabernash yards. The same engineman had overrun his orders some months previously as he was running a helper engine down from Winter Park. In desperation the operator called the lumberjack pastor at Hideaway Park to flag down the same gentleman. The parson lost the race. Luckily the hogger sensed his mistake, turned out his lights, and tried to sneak back to the Winter Park siding only to find the parson holding the line unwilling to let anyone by unless he acknowledged his error. Having been roundly cussed out, the minister phoned the operator that he could notify Denver to cancel the call for the wrecker train. *Upper photo, L. J. Daly; lower, Allin Gillet.*

Under similar circumstances on an earlier occasion, engine 403 handles the wrecker in Tabernash yard, cleaning up the debris of a rear-ender caused by failure to have an engine under control inside yard limits during one of the area's frequent fogs. These pictures tell the story of careless men who made life nerve-wracking for the fine men of both railroads. *Allin Gillett photo.*

It was war time. Men were taking chances. And when you made a mistake you probably were kept in service, for you were badly needed. The miracle was that there were no more wrecks than there were, with thirty trains a day plus helper engines, on a single-track line—and no signals west of Winter Park at the beginning of the War. *Allin Gillett photo.*

On the line to Craig, some tunnels got by with almost no maintenance for forty years. Here in Egeria Canyon carpenters have unloaded some sand in the summer of 1959 where no work had been done for fifty years. But other tunnels were not so fortunate in withstanding fire hazards of locomotive sparks. *D.&R.G.W. photo.*

were slow starting, for their overhaul work was unsatisfactory. Then came the short piece of rail to be loaded and the run into the tunnel.

Here the soot had accumulated almost to the top of the rail, for the workers had only their trailer cars to haul it out on—when no train was in the tunnel and they had nothing else to do. But, anyway, it was warm inside. So a piece of rail the right length was cut out of the track and the new piece bolted in. By the time they got in the clear at East Portal, two hours and fifteen minutes had gone. Needed materials were on hot shots stranded all over the line. The newer men of the Rio Grande not used to the Moffat conditions had been attempting to run as far as they could without taking on water. In this delay they ran out of water and George Schryer, a Moffat engineer, had to run his 200 series mallet out to bring in several Rio Grande engines too low on water to run to the water tank.

At Fraser that night, a car of pigs froze to death.

Observe carefully this 3600 and the feedwater heater in front of the stack here and in the photo that follows, showing the trouble a much smaller rock brought about in Gore Canyon. L. J. Daly was trainmaster when he took this picture. He started as a water boy on the construction train, became a conductor, and outlived the Moffat Road. All the slides in Gore Canyon made him claim that he had heard every operating man say the road should have gone over Gore Pass. But then no Dotsero Cut-off would have enabled the Rio Grande to shorten its route by 175 miles. *L. J. Daly photo.*

Their squealing gradually died out. But the story ends with a miracle. When they finally got through the tunnel and were warmed up, they came to life again.

How cold was it at Fraser and Tabernash that night? Only fifty and sixty below. Trains froze to the rails and required hours to knock loose. The only diesel power on the road was the four unit 540 that had been stopped at Pine Cliff. The diesel fuel became slush and the 540 had no power until later the next morning. She proudly broke the freight loose from the rails at East Portal which had not been loosened by two 3600's.

Most unfortunate was the fact that in the weeks prior to the war a number of experienced and efficient men had been laid off at the shops. Those men had no trouble finding better-paying jobs in industries where the preparedness campaign had opened up. These men never returned to the D.&.S.L. No wonder the motor cars were frequently no better when they came out of the shops.

But the roadmaster who was to become the future president of the Rio Grande had a much tougher problem. Almost every maintenance-of-way man had gone to industries that were paying a reasonable wage. Only the section foremen stuck to their jobs. So the young roadmaster found his king-snipes going nuts trying to show lumberjacks and whoever came on the job, how to do the gandy dance. The exasperated king-snipe found that the language of the railroad was foreign to these men. This man's counsel to desperate foremen kept the track maintained under the heavy increase in business and won him undying respect from the men. Moffat service was resumed.

"Moffat Service" meant to the tourist spectacular scenery, but to the employees detested gas and soot in the tunnels. They were no steam fans. "Oh, if it were electrified or if they would get a diesel." These words were almost prayers. But one had a seat. An extra coach was down at the station hooked up ready to be carried along, if there was more

Picture puzzle is to find the largest type engine on the Rio Grande at Tunnel 38 in Gore Canyon. Note the feed-water heater, and compare with picture on page 277. *L. J. Daly photo.*

Wet snow or rain and freezing cold night brought rock slides time and again in the canyons. Rio Grande 3600 struck a boulder, rolled it into Tunnel 38, and then ground the props of the tunnel off leaving herself plugged tight in the collapsed bore. *L. J. Daly photo.*

business. And if this was not enough, train No. 1 just picked up all the equipment it needed at Utah Junction on the way out, even to a larger engine. The boys going to the YMCA camp out of Granby always had their own coach. They had fun, and the other passengers had peace. This train was the bad weather means of traveling for the local residents, and bad weather is bad. There was the little dinette with pop and food.

Moffat Service meant to the businessmen from one end of the line to the other that they could phone in the afternoon for parts, canned goods, or what not, and have it the next morning on the over-night mixed. Years later when l. c. l. business went by truck, Middle Park people moaned for the good old days of overnight service every night. That train was the sacred ox of the line. It was not to be delayed. To the gasoline dealer at Granby, who found a sudden flock of tourists emptying his bulk tanks, it

meant that a tank car of gas would be included on the train leaving Denver at night and be in Granby in the wee hours of the morning. To the cattlemen, it meant that the train was "hog and human." You did not have to wait for a cattle train. Your shipment went through when you wanted it to. To the Moffat County people, it meant a Pullman berth with a hogger who handled you as if you were on the Broadway Limited. The morale of the employees was good; they all worked for the success and business of the line.

The spirit of David Moffat was in the hearts of enough of the men that the ghost of Bill Freeman could not change it.

The war changed this service to some extent. The mixed train became tri-weekly, so that the main line could handle more war business. To the people in

D.&S.L. wrecker rescues D.&R.G.W. 1207. Number 19, the Mountaineer, served the Western Slope area. During the war this overnight mail and passenger plowed into a slide of great boulders in Gore Canyon. Later a slide fence was installed to set block signals when rocks came down. *L. J. Daly photo.*

Way car telescoped between engine and gondola. *Allin Gillett photo.*

guest ranch business, it meant that they stayed in business despite gasoline rationing, for the daily train brought their guests whom they could pick up at the station. The new ski area of Winter Park meant extra equipment that brought soldiers out of Denver for a day or weekend outing, or a ride up the mountains through the Moffat Tunnel and back on Train No. 2.

Moffat Service was a remarkable quality made possible by local, enterprising employees who were not handicapped by the size of great organization. This service neither the Rio Grande nor any other large system can equal, for it takes an act of Congress to get an extra car. The Moffat employees knew their people and how to give them good service. These men had seen the boys ride the train to college, calmed them down when they were too loud, and lived to see *their* sons go to college. It was the personal touch of real men for real men.

High Green

A part of the more recent history of the Moffat is the dismantling of the Hill line. After trains began operating through the Tunnel there was no service over the Hill whatsoever. The Moffat men understandably wanted to have no part of the Hill, and there was no nostalgia such as exists today. Records of the D.&S.L. show that trains were run over the top for a few days in 1929 when a small cave-in occurred in the Moffat Tunnel. Other than a brief mention in official reports, the authors can find no trace of any other use for regular train service. There was, of course, the case of the marooned snow-plow caught on the far side of the Tunnel which suffered unhappy fortune when brought over the Hill back to Denver. A photograph of this episode may be found elsewhere in this chapter.

The value of the Hill line property on June 29, 1934, was $1,220,000. Apparently the railroad had been holding the Rollins Pass branch in reserve, but this amount of investment demanded salvaging. On June 29, 1934, two section foremen were sent on foot to survey the entire Hill line. From the time it was submitted until the summer of 1961 their report lay buried until found by the authors, Bauer and Bollinger, in a railway equipment garage. The official photographs from this report are included in this chapter.

The ravages of time had brought a complete cave-in of the Loop Tunnel (Tunnel 33), but other than this, damage from the years of non-use was surprisingly small. There were a rock slide on the Ladder above Tolland, several small washouts, and a small slide at Tunnel 31 near Ladora which actually served to keep the water out of the Tunnel and protect it. The bridges were in fair condition, needing only minor repairs to permit work trains to be run.

It was evident that the line could be salvaged by using work trains. A large number of the snowsheds was still standing, although in some instances they were leaning and seemed destined to fall within the year. The section foremen recommended that they be burned to permit the sun to melt the three to six

Drawing by W. Steadman.

feet of snow found within them. There was fourteen feet of snow in the Corona sheds. Other than the cave-in of the Loop Tunnel, only a few boulders were found on the track throughout the entire length of the west side. Near Pacific a slide had moved the tracks about three feet, and even this would have been passable. The tail of the Spruce wye had heaved up nearly two feet.

Detailed estimates by A. L. Johnson showed that ten days work would clear the track from Newcomb to Dixie Lake; forty-five days of work would be required from Dixie through the worst sections near the top to Loop; and four days of work down to West Portal. It was estimated that a profit of $15,000 on the material could be realized beyond the cost of salvage. Railroad officials felt that about fifteen per cent of the rail and ten per cent of the ties could be reclaimed. Since the season was so late work was put off until the following year.

March 16, 1935, the D.&S.L. applied for permission to abandon 31.76 miles of track, and approval was granted by the ICC on May 14. Difficulty was experienced, however, in obtaining reputable contractors to undertake dismantling. In June, 1936, it was discovered that Tunnel 31 had caved in also, greatly increasing the amount of work required to re-open the line for a work train. It was decided

After completion of the Moffat Tunnel, it was found that the large rotary was on the west side. Since it was too large to be sent through the tunnel, a train was started up the west side from Idlewild (West Portal). But the deteriorating track spread, put Rotary 10200, consolidation, tender, and one reefer on the ground. Highway 40 crosses the old right of way at this point today and the Corona Pass road beckons fishermen and railfans to drive up. *A. Clarke photo.*

Tunnel 31 was still serviceable. The section foreman who took this picture said that 'two or three hours' work with a ditcher would clean up the mess. The slide served as a dam and kept water out of the tunnel, preserving it. Later it caved in, but today its course through the hill can be easily followed by a series of pockmarks on the surface. *D.&S.L. photo.*

The Hill line in 1934. This is a rock slide on the Ladder above Tolland. The slide came from the left and most of it rolled over the track without damage. A portion of the main track appears at the left of the photo. *D.&S.L. photo.*

Shed No. 2 at Dixie Lake. There was very little snow or ice in this shed. A few feet of the shed had fallen across the track. *D.&S.L. photo.*

Tunnel 33 was blocked. Collapse of the roof completely filled the tunnel. The main body of this cave-in was directly below the Loop Trestle and made it clear that operation of locomotives over the trestle would be very hazardous. In an early letter of H. A. Sumner a notation was made that native timbering was to be used in this tunnel to save the cost of Oregon fir. After all, the financing for the Main Range Tunnel was expected to be completed so that this Hill route could be by-passed. *D.&S.L. photo.*

Pressures on Tunnel 33 were severe. Timbering was beginning to collapse. When Moffat Tunnel was temporarily blocked, repairs had to be made in this tunnel before trains could be run. The same thing occurred two years later in Tunnel 31 near Ladora. *D.&S.L. photo.*

Shed No. 3 was flattened. This shed was near Dixie Lake and was completely demolished. *D.&S.L. photo.*

Sheds near Corona. Seven to nine feet of snow and ice still remained on June 30, 1934. *D.&S.L. photo.*

Trucks, not work trains, dismantled the Rollins Pass line. Faced with difficulty in securing a good contractor, one of the Moffat's best section bosses, Ed Harrison of Fraser, encouraged formation of a contracting firm by Fraser Valley men. Ed was in charge of this work. Among the ties taken out were some walnut ties that had been laid during World War I on curves below Arrow. Chief Engineer W. C. Jones had discovered that the ties deteriorated less as the elevation increased. Those at Corona had not rotted at all, although they had suffered from the hammering of the engines. *Bert Howell photo of the east side.*

Corona sheds looked like jackstraws. This official photo shows the conditions at the summit. Twelve feet of snow still remained in the shed. *D.&S.L. photo.*

Corona snowsheds— 1938. The Forest Service removed the planks on top so that the sun could melt the snow and permit the passage of fire fighting equipment through the sheds if required. In recent years this has become a most popular fishing road. *Ed Bollinger photo.*

October at Corona. If one flew over the hill as Gordon Rodgers did on October 7, 1951, one might see the Corona sheds blanketed with the winter's first hard snow. *Gordon Rodgers photo.*

In 1939 the Corona sheds looked like this after unsuccessful efforts to burn them down had failed. Guests of Ed Bollinger hear the story of "the Hill" in late July as they walk on snow drifts. *Ed Bollinger photo.*

Page 287

to handle the job by truck, and the first actual demolition occurred at Irvings July 18, 1936, all the work being performed by contract since the railroad was engaged in a heavy improvement program elsewhere.

By removing rails and ties at the bottom of the west side, the contractors were able to use the road-bed for a road with a minimum of construction.

The contractors had removed all rail as far as Corona by August 11, at which time they transferred their operations to the bottom of the East Side at Newcomb. August 25, 1936, saw fulfillment of a request by the Republic Steel Corporation. A two-foot section of rail, purchased in 1903 and laid September 3, 1904, was cut from the exact location of the Continental Divide. This was sent to Republic's Museum commemorating the highest point on any standard-gauge railroad in America, 11,660 feet.

The bridges were not destroyed, since the Forest Service desired that they be left in for roadway purposes. The old hotel at Corona was dismantled by the Forest Service, who reclaimed all the bricks. The coal tipple and other buildings at Arrow were given away to individuals who promised to demolish and remove them. Left almost in its entirety was the telegraph line from which only the wire was removed. This was done because it was uneconomical to salvage the poles; above 10,000 feet where the cold weather has preserved them, one may view cross arms silhouetted against the sky to this day.

By October 22, 1936, removal of the rails, water standpipes, and boilers at Corona was complete. A profit of $66,000 was actually realized from the operation. The snowsheds particularly presented a formidable problem. They were too large to remove and seemed impregnable to burning. In consideration of leaving them and certain other minor debris, the D.&S.L. deeded most of the right of way to the Forest Service. The following summer a minor amount of track material was brought down, bringing to a finish the Rollins Pass line, August 12, 1937.

One of the changes least noticed by passengers on the California Zephyr, but of great importance to the Operating Department, is the use of Centralized Traffic Control. With longer sidings this almost doubles the capacity of the single-track main line.

All trains between Denver and Bond (and beyond) are controlled by Centralized Traffic Control using coded carrier current transmitted over wayside telegraph wires. The finesse possible in arranging running meets intrigues even those people who are used to it. The engine crew has knowledge of what the dispatcher plans by means of the siding signals; "green over red" or "high green" indicates the train is to stay on the main. "Red over green" means that the train will take the siding. If "red over red" is encountered, rules permit the train to stop and proceed at reduced speed unless there is a metal letter "P" on the signal mast, in which case a positive stop must be made.

Many times the authors have ridden the cab of Rio Grande trains and have seen for themselves the utmost finesse with which running meets are accomplished under the supervision of the dispatcher in Denver who controls all the switches and signals as far as Bond. To illustrate the tremendous assistance of this device, the Rio Grande sent their photographer climbing up the frontal escarpment to take the accompanying pictures of trains on the Big Ten Curve. At this point from Rocky to Plain, Rio Grande's Little Ten Curve joins the Big Ten on the

Plow train at Ranch Creek Wye. Rotary 10200 and Mallet 211 pause for pictures before returning to the fight. This is a favorite picnic spot today for horseback parties from Winter Park ranches. *Allin Gillett photo.*

Long train nearly circles Big Ten, 2:08 P.M. The first train to greet the photographer on July 5, 1959, moving eastward, was WPD 20, photographed as it passed the narrowest point on the Big Ten Curve. It was here that oldtime trainmen were alleged to have dropped off their train, run uphill, shot their dinners, and thrown the siding switch before the ascending engine reached them. *Rio Grande Green Light photo.*

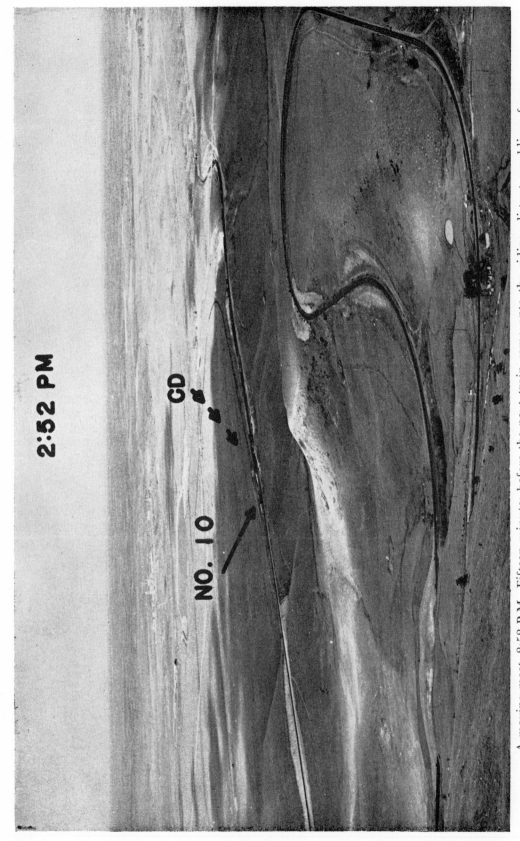

2:52 PM

CD

NO. 10

A moving meet, 2:52 P.M. Fifteen minutes before the next train came onto the siding, distant rumblings from the east told of the approach of the CD. At about the same time the Yampa Valley Mail No. 10, descending toward the east, made a moving meet at Rocky, with neither train stopping and control of all switches being handled in Denver, miles away by C.T.C. *Rio Grande Green Light photo.*

Modern mountain railroading, 2:59 P.M. Minutes later, completing an operation that might have taken an hour or more under train order operation, the CD headed out again without stopping, avoiding the attendant risk of broken drawbars. Meanwhile AD 17 from Ogden and Salt Lake was headed downhill through the Tunnel District. *Rio Grande Green Light photo.*

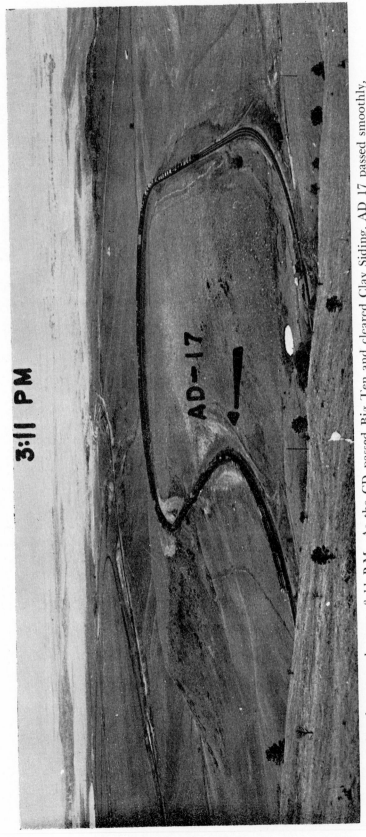

Another smooth meet, 3:11 P.M. As the CD passed Big Ten and cleared Clay Siding, AD 17 passed smoothly, bound for Denver over the tortuous track which had given Moffat men such headaches. *Rio Grande Green Light photo.*

Moffat Division, Timetable No. 1. This historic document signals the end of the Denver and Salt Lake as an operating entity. L. J. Daly was listed as Assistant to Superintendent at Denver; M. J. McGann, Trainmaster at Phippsburg; J. B. Culbertson, Chief Dispatcher, Denver. R. R. Marner and P. H. Foley, Road Foremen of Equipment, Denver and Utah Junction.

two per cent. Westbound trains after negotiating the Big S Curve head into the Tunnel District and on to the Moffat Tunnel.

April 10, 1947, the famous "Hog and Human," renamed the "Atomic Special" by the Pullman porter, left Craig with a handful of passengers as train No. 12 of the Denver and Salt Lake Railway. Next morning D.&S.L. Train No. 12 did not arrive in Denver, but Train No. 12 of the Denver and Rio Grande Western did come in. The Denver and Salt Lake Railway was no more. We should not weep for the D.&S.L. Railway, for it had been organized specifically to pull a fast one when its predecessor became entrapped in financial difficulties. The date to weep about is the day the Denver, Northwestern & Pacific went bankrupt—the fortune Dave Moffat and other pioneers had invested was sold for a penny.

This chapter is the story of the integration of the two railroads of which Dave Moffat had been President. The reorganization which brought them together was accomplished under the direction of President McCarthy and was a sound one. In integration there was no defeat for the Moffat. Physically the two roads were so entwined as to be one, regardless. This chapter is one of triumph for the ideas of Moffat as the road for which he dreamed continues to play its rightful competitive role in today's transportation picture.

The Moffat Road of today is not as it was years ago. It should not be, for progress needs change. Among the many changes wrought by the Rio Grande has been the use of two-way radio on moving trains. The authors have personally seen the tremendous assistance this can be in tieing on helpers at Tabernash, in stopping long freights to set out hot boxes, in reporting the train in the clear on a siding, and for many other uses.

One of the most spectacular engineering accomplishments on the Rio Grande in 1952 was the entire removal of Tunnel 41. This was remarkable because it was accomplished between trains by the use of high explosives and heavy-capacity work equipment.

The Tunnel was in need of constant maintenance since it cut through rock which was unstable. Careful geological investigation revealed a fault line right back of the Tunnel. It was determined that cautious use of modern high-explosive materials could completely disintegrate the top and one side along the fault cleavage line.

Late Troubles—Tunnel 41. The Rio Grande inherited the problem of licking canyon slides. These photographs show the hazard of cleaning up a little slide in 1951. The left photo shows the bulldozer operator pushing debris out of the way. Then some more ground gave way! When the dust had partly settled and a snapshot could be taken (right), it was found that the dozer operator had run to safety. *Ed Bollinger photos.*

Al Perlman as chief Engineer of the Rio Grande brought in off-the-track equipment, so that heavy traffic was not delayed. In this case a rock slide in Byers Canyon plugged the line, and Perlman quickly called in the nearest contractor's equipment to clear the tracks. During rainy seasons track walkers patrolled such places. Perlman pushed the removal of slide rock. *Clifford Miller photo.*

Page 294

Trouble with Tunnel 41. Cave-ins had been encountered at the west end of Tunnel 41 in Little Gore Canyon. This is the removal in 1951 of one such slide, seen from a vantage point across the river. Al Perlman was an advocate of off-track work equipment, and we see it working to great advantage here. A large volume of rock debris had to be cleaned up and removed from the track in a short time. This work, however, did not end the troubles with the unstable granite and more work had to be done the next year. This photo was the gift of Al Perlman to Ed Bollinger, both men being on the scene at this moment. *D.&R.G.W. photo*.

Drilling the holes for blasting Tunnel 41. Work equipment is assembling outside the portal as drilling takes place in the cliffs above. The charge was planned so carefully that the rock separated cleanly along a fault line just back of the tunnel. Note pole and insulated arm for overhead rock slide detector fence. *D.&R.G.W. photo.*

Ready for the shot. The last train through Tunnel 41 before it was demolished was the CZ, whose passengers never dreamed that right above their heads in the Vista Dome was planted ten thousand pounds of high explosives. *D.&R.G.W. photo.*

The blast obliterating Tunnel 41 took place exactly one-half hour after the California Zephyr had passed. Note the flying rocks captured in mid-air in this photograph taken from across the river. *D.&R.G.W. photo.*

Laying new rail past the daylighted Tunnel 41. So rapid was the work that new rail was laid up to the edge of the pile of debris. The entire demolition was planned to take a little over six hours. *D.&R.G.W. photo.*

By dusk the job is done. Tunnel 41 is gone and there is a clear track at nightfall. *D.&R.G.W. photo.*

Tunnel 41 is gone. Eastbound No. 18, the CZ, passes the scar on the wall of Gore Canyon, which is all that remains of Tunnel 41. *D.&R.G.W. photo.*

The Moffat Road

Ten thousand pounds of special formula dynamite did the trick. The blast holes were bored and the explosive placed before the last train through the Tunnel—the California Zephyr—passed at noon July 22, 1952. Little did the passengers realize what was placed immediately over their heads as they rode through. Before dark the same day the debris had been completely removed, trackage relocated, and the line reopened for traffic.

The Moffat Road has become a legend about a great empire builder of Colorado who gave to his state a ledge cut high on the south wall of South Boulder Canyon. Many places this ledge tunneled right through the mountains that literally breathed night and day. In fact this ledge is found over the Divide today as a fishing road. In Middle Park it has cut into the sides of several canyons that defied early travelers. It reaches on out into the northwestern part of the state. Between mountains and canyons it's not a ledge at all but a path through rich meadows or by coal and oil fields.

Now this gift has been appropriated by various groups of power and interest down the years. These men held to the wisdom of the business enterprise. They laid new ties and new rail on it. They fought battles against the same groups of interests that Uncle Dave defied. The slick deals and power.

Today the great battle for this pathway goes on. Faces and names change, but the right of way that he carved out of the mountains is still the much-fought-about bridge route.

The people of Middle Park and northwestern Colorado once felt that this was their battle. Now they are spectators and taxpayers for the privilege of watching the trains go by that haul from New York to the coast and industrial centers in between.

Moffat Tunnel to many newcomers is a tax that they pay with a growl and a curse, even thinking that David Moffat was the cause for the tax.

To others the Moffat Road was their life. They fought to build it, operate it, and make a living with and for it. Not many of these men are living as this story is written. Just what is a railroad? The stockholders? the gandy dancers? operators? clerks? the board of directors? To those fascinated with the soot the road left and the occasional rotting tie slipped down the canyon wall, it is the romance of a day gone by.

We must define a railroad as men, all kinds of men, engaged in transporting people and goods by rail. Some of these men hold the stock and think of it as their road. But someone buys them out, and someone else thinks of it as his road.

The Moffat was once the road of people who never owned stock, never worked on it, and sometimes shipped and traveled on it. It was a cause for them, their cause championed by a man who towered above them, to whom they were knit in affection. Over this road men's hopes and defeats traveled when the light was green, there were no slides, and the rail was plowed clean of snow. Today only ghost trains pass the California Zephyr, for the Number "30" has been flashed over the wire, and men ask, "Who was H. A. Sumner? Who was George Barnes?" But if you ask the authors, the ghost trains are very real; and H. A. Sumner is quite pleased as he sits in the parlor car, and George Barnes says, "We have a 'high green.'" Uncle Dave does not mind the time we lost as we waited for that long freight. He is going clear to Salt Lake, and he will ask Bob Bishop to have dinner with him again, when Skeeter takes the throttle at the end of the division.

In later days, Dick Kindig drove out to Utah Junction and photographed Engine 20 stored on a back track. But the daisies and sun flowers whisper the story of this engine's proud beginning. *R. H. Kindig photo.*

Only ghost plow trains turn here at Ranch Creek Wye today. But fishermen drive on the roadbed little aware of the significance of this spot. The train is on the main line which comes downhill from the left background. The train will back into the west leg of the wye in the foreground and then head uphill again. *Allin Gillett photo.*

Last Number 9 at Copper Spur, Jan. 31, 1950, pulled by a Rio Grande 800 (4-6-2) which replaced the Moffat 300's that were scrapped. Management turned down the plea of Harold Eno to build a new streamliner for Middle Park, Steamboat Springs, and Craig, saying that it might make money a while and then go in debt, when the same money could buy a four-unit freight diesel to earn big money. So the overnight tri-weekly mixed was taken off, together with day trains 9 and 10. Stub night trains were run to Craig out of Bond with a miserable layover. This proved so unpopular that an effort was made to cancel passenger service. The state commission, however, declared that good service should be restored with a day time train because the three counties deserved something for the Tunnel taxes that they paid. Rio Grande then restored No. 9 and gave it the name Yampa Valley Mail, with diesel power, excellent coaches, and a fast schedule. *Ed Bollinger photo.*

California Zephyr in Gore. When the California Zephyr glides through Gore Canyon, she is protected by the slide fence and slide "roof" on the right of the tracks in this photo. Rocks falling from the cliff and striking the wires break the signal circuit and set the block signals against the train. Meanwhile, oblivious of their safeguards, people in the Vista Domes look upward to see the glories of Sugar Loaf. This Rio Grande photograph speaks of all the pride held honestly by a modern railroad. *D.&R.G.W. photo.*

It's evening now. A little crowd of men gathers at the Kremmling station. Agent Chris Lomax has come down. The lights are on outside the station. "That's right, the Prospector is running as second No. 7 tonight. First No. 7 has Engine 300, Parlor Car 800, and the *Marcia*, and she is on time. Excuse me, I have to take a message."

Bob Bishop leans out of the cab of Engine 300 and calls out to his fireman, "High Green." They are soon rolling past the burner of the sawmill and now past the station. Bob asks his fireman, Skeeter, to reach for the hoop as the operator is ready with a message. There is also a message for the conductor.

George Barnes is reaching for the hoop himself. It's good to be running west tonight. He takes the message and reads "D. H. Moffat," so he walks back through the Parlor Car to the *Marcia*, knocks on the door, and steps on in.

"Mr. Moffat, there is a message for you."

Uncle Dave opens the message and says to Colonel Dodge, seated beside him, "Oh, I see it's from President Aydelott."

Colonel Dodge smiles. "I hear it's the old fight. Ogden Gateway and who is to have the Western Pacific."

Page 304

Mr. Moffat reads, "YOU AND MR. SUM-
NER HAVE GIVEN US A SUPERIOR ROUTE.
. . . OUR COMPETITORS HAVE TO FIGHT
HARD OR THROW IN THE TOWEL.
THANKS. HAVE A GOOD TRIP. G. B.
AYDELOTT, PRESIDENT."

Old Utah Junction yards and shops have made way for North
Yards. *Drawing by Don Johnson.*

Gone are the days of such wonderful sights as this. Mallets 200 and 216—first and last of the series—are doubleheaded into the afternoon sun at Arvada with 61 cars on November 27, 1947, glad to be using their power for
handling full tonnage rather than fighting the miseries of the Hill. *S. L. Logue photo.*

Joe Culbertson at sixtieth anniversary celebration. Sixty years before September 2, 1964, J.B.C. dispatched the first train to Corona. No other man began with the line and stayed to hear about this occasion. Even L. H. Bartholomew, who stands near the cab ladder, found no buddies of his Tabernash shop days. In removing the California Zephyr's photo from this page in the Second Edition we record the threat of its last run asked by the Western Pacific. But it's High Green for many short fast freights that anger the Union Pacific exceedingly and precipitate a new war front—the Rock Island Denver Gateway. *Photo by Mel Schieltz*, ROCKY MOUNTAIN NEWS.

U.S. Forest Service photo.

Appendices

I: TRAVEL GUIDE: ROLLINS PASS ROAD

This is a wonderful road to travel today. Although the four percent grade and sharp curves were killing for a railroad operation, they present to the tourist a highway of smooth curves and easy, steady ascent. There are broad views of Middle Park, and Hill Line romance galore. For the fisherman, the lakes high up in the mountains are just the thing. Because this trip is such a popular one, and the points of interest are so many, we think the automobile guide below will be of great help. You should drive first to East Portal. The tour starts at the end of the wye (which was Newcomb in the Moffat days) and is now the beginning of the Hill Line:

Miles from East Portal	Miles from Winter Park	
0	29.4	The county road starts in a sharp U turn as you head up the 2%.
1.6	27.8	Sharp jog around the site of trestle 51.24, now visible only as posts on either side of the gulley.
2.0	27.4	First view of Tolland in the valley; the site of the wye is plainly visible in the grass.
2.5	26.9	Ladora siding, called "Dora" in later years.
2.6	26.8	The railroad can no longer be followed by car because of bridge 52.27 just ahead, which has collapsed, and Tunnel 31, now caved in. A short hike will reach both with a good view of the square water tower next to

Miles from East Portal	Miles from Winter Park	
		Tunnel 31. This was used during construction days and abandoned while the Hill was still in operation. The county highway takes a sharp turn here and climbs to the second rung of the ladder, shortcircuiting both bridge and tunnel. Begin the four per cent.
2.9	26.5	Rejoin railroad grade.
3.5	25.9	Very short detour around bridge 54.08, now out.
4.0	25.4	Third rung of the Ladder.
5.1	24.3	Antelope siding. Ties plainly visible.
5.6	23.8	Bridge 56.07 out.
6.4	23.0	Site of old coal dock. Coal on ground.
6.6-7.0	22.8-22.4	Many evidences of extensive logging. Loading platforms remain on the uphill side of the track, and fields of stumps show the harvest which was removed.
7.4	22.0	Remains of log house
8.1	21.3	Spruce wye. Snowshed collapsed. From here plows operated every eight hours nine months of the year.
9.1	20.3	Another log loading platform.
9.8	19.6	Yankee Doodle Lake. Denver, Utah & Pacific tunnel burrows a short distance into the mountain, and the dump extends into the lake.

It remained for Fred Bauer of Dearborn, Michigan, to rediscover this square water tank back of Tunnel 31 above Tolland. It is just off the present fishing road, back of a hill, and not frequented by tourists who rush by. The tank had been hastily thrown together for construction engines. *Anne Bollinger photo.*

Back of the water tank were found these pony trucks dragged a thousand feet back near the water intake. There are many more mysteries to be figured out by railfans who can take the easily-traveled fishing road over the entire Hill grade. *Anne Bollinger photo.*

Miles from East Portal	*Miles from Winter Park*	
10.5	18.9	Dixie Lake is just a few steps from the tracks. Source of engine water.
10.7	18.7	Jenny Lake siding; passing track and stub siding, named for Jenny (later Dixie) Lake.
10.7	18.7	Collapsed log cabin.
12.3	17.1	Beginning of shelf road climb to Tunnel 32.
12.5	16.9	Wonderful views of Jenny (Dixie) Lake and the road up Jenny Creek Valley.
13.2	16.2	Tunnel 32, never timbered. (Needle's Eye).
13.3	16.1	Famous McClure view of Yankee Doodle Lake.
13.5	15.9	Cross old stage road. It can be seen most clearly downhill from the road at saddle next to Yankee Doodle Lake. It originally continued down the bottom of the valley to Tolland.
13.9-14.0	15.5-15.4	Twin bridges. A step off either would be sure death. Also known as Devil's Slide.
14.3	15.1	Remains of snowsheds east of Corona.
14.7	14.7	Pyramidal snowshed ventilators visible above road.
15.0	14.4	Moffat observation hut; part of the tourist attraction that was Corona.
15.2	14.2	Corona, elevation 11,660 feet, highest standard-gauge railroad in America. Past the wye the foundation for the brick hotel still remains. Similarly, a close observer can find the boiler house and water tank foundation. A good part of Corona village consisted of box car bodies which have long since been removed.
15.6	13.8	Magnificent view of Fraser in Middle Park.
16.0	13.4	Pump House Lake below the road.

Miles from East Portal	*Miles from Winter Park*	
		Here the pump operator and his wife spent the winter isolated except for the telegraph.
16.1	13.3	Stand of telegraph poles preserved by the frigid weather.
17.0	12.4	Ptarmigan Point.
17.1	12.3	Good view across Middle Fork Valley. The ramp on which the remains of the 210 were brought up can be seen below level of tracks at the Loop, and the ramp required to retrieve a snowplow 700 feet below the grade is directly across the valley.
17.7	11.7	Sunnyside. Marked today by a shelter hut when servicing the airway beacon at Rollins Pass.
18.5	10.9	Loop Trestle. Upper level of track. Tunnel and lower level of track are directly below. The drop is about 150 feet but seems far more. The bridge is unsafe because it rests directly upon the unsupported roof of Tunnel 33, which has caved in. Start a short detour.
18.6	10.8	Good view of Loop siding through the trees and excellent grasp of what a four per cent grade looks like.
18.8	10.6	Loop Tunnel. Closed by a cave-in. We now begin to ascend Loop siding in the reverse direction for about a quarter mile.
19.5	9.9	Because of the collapse of Tunnel 33 the county road avoids about two miles of the old roadbed. A steep sideroad here, however, leads down to the lower level of track. The ramp and remains of the 210 can be inspected at the bottom of the side road. A half mile

		downgrade from the end of the side road is the site of the disastrous avalanche which sent a trainload of coal down the mountainside, but left the mallets standing on the track.
19.8	9.6	A view of the Berthoud Pass ski slopes from the detour.
20.6	8.8	Rejoin railroad grade. The road up-grade from this point was passable to the Loop (1961) and connects with the side road mentioned above.
22.1	7.3	Ranch Creek wye. Another airway beacon shelter hut. The remains of bridge 72.83 still span Ranch Creek. This was the turn-around point for plow trains clearing the Hill.
22.8	6.6	Two lumber sidings are visible here, one upgrade, and the other down.
25.7	3.7	Arrow wye.

25.8	3.6	Site of Arrow. There was no passing track. The four per cent did not permit a convenient station stop and so a level stub was built above the main track to serve the station. There were a stockyard and a coal tipple. The eating house also fronted on the short level stub track. Foundations of buildings can be seen in all directions. A real ghost town.
26.2	3.2	Pacific siding, bordering Arrow on the north.
26.8	2.6	Excellent view of Winter Park, and log loading platforms.
29.4	0	U.S. 40 at Winter Park.

If you take this worthwhile trip, you'll have a much better appreciation of what operating the Hill must have been like. Allow four hours for the trip. No difficulty will be encountered in driving it in your car, but trailers are not advised, because of a sharp turn on the Ranch Creek wye.

Engine 391 at Utah Junction. Proud cadets used to ride behind the polished power of the Annapolis line. But this tea-kettle died at Utah Junction shorn of her high wheels and tailored with much smaller wheels for the grades of the Moffat. However, the fine Chesapeake Beach parlor-cars and coaches were the show pieces of the once-new line. Many a fine meal was served in the dining buffets. *Denver Public Library Western Collection.*

Page 309

The diesel came to Craig. Changes came after the war. The overnight mixed was canceled. On this day enough business demanded a freight run from Phippsburg. The work of switching is over. The crew has gone up town for their meals. Number 10 stands in front of the station ready to head for Denver as crew and passengers have eaten breakfast. *Ed Bollinger photo.*

Tower car for replacement of timber sets in tunnels. *Ed Sunergren photo.*

Denver and Salt Lake train at Craig, Colorado, in 1948. *Lloyd E. Parris collection.*

D.&.S.L. 213 renumbered 3372. Engine 213 died far away from home at Helper, Utah, where she had been taken for helper service. R. H. Kindig found her here on March 9, 1949, with a new number—D.&.R.G.W. 3372.

II: MOFFAT SNOWSHEDS

These sheds were located entirely on the Rollins Pass Branch. They were the protector and the scourge of enginemen, who feared their gas-laden atmosphere. Attempts to burn them have been unsuccessful, and for the most part they have merely been bull-dozed aside. All are visible from the County Road over Rollins Pass.

Number	Milepost	Location	Length*
--	58.5	East leg and stem of Spruce wye	600 feet
1	60.3	Yankee Doodle Lake upgrade side	340
2	61.1	Dixie Lake	1080
3	61.4	Dixie Lake	820
4	61.9	Dixie Lake	960
--	62.2	Dixie Lake	330
--	63.4	Tunnel 32, east end	105
5	63.4	Tunnel 32, west end	930
6	64.3	East of Corona	1530
--	65.3	Corona, main line	3650
--	65.3	Corona, wye	1100
--	69.5	Tunnel 33 (Loop), east end	150
--	69.5	Tunnel 33 (Loop), west end	90
		Total length of snowsheds	11,085 feet

*Lengths scaled from D.&S.L. track maps.

III: TRAVEL GUIDE: BY RAIL

Leaving Denver on a vacation trip, you have your choice of two ways to see the line by railroad. You could go as far as Bond (Orestod) and return in one day with a stop-over for lunch, or you might go the entire distance to Craig one day and return the next. The first trip is more convenient and hence more popular, but the second will afford an opportunity to see the "Switzerland of America" west of Orestod where even today the rails are in much the same condition as they were when the Hill line was operated. The western end of the line is completely different from the east, with its own set of surprises.

If a passenger trip cannot be for the length of the Moffat Road, a convenient daytime trip starts from Craig on No. 10 and takes one to Bond or Kremmling, depending upon

Page 311

The Moffat Road

how the train runs against schedule. This end of the Moffat is much less publicized, with the result that comparatively few railfans or tourists are acquainted with it. Yet on the west end are almost as many tunnels as in the "Tunnel District." The road passes through the "Switzerland of America" and crawls along the brinks of canyons in a thrilling manner.

From Craig to Steamboat Springs lie the fertile fields envisioned by Mr. Moffat. Anyone who has seen the wheat shimmering in the sun after a light rain can easily justify "Garden of Eden" as applied to the countryside. Nearby the cattle business is in full swing. Between Steamboat and Phippsburg the railroad follows the Canyon of the Yampa River. Here the once-prosperous coal mines, upon which the D.N.W.&P. counted for heavy traffic, now stand deserted. Numerous loading tracks are now missing. Piles of coal and slack remain to form the epitaph of deep mining. Only strip mining from the fields at the top of the canyon continues.

Between Toponas and Yampa, Finger Rock on the east side of the track dominates the Yampa Valley. The highway leaves the tracks at Egeria as the Moffat Road plunges into Egeria Canyon first and then moves on to Volcano where volcanic ash was obtained to serve as Moffat ballast for years. Winding on a ledge, the rails approach Rock Creek Canyon, formerly the site of the Moffat's longest and highest trestle.

If time limits you to a one-day trip, take the California Zephyr west from Denver in the morning. This luxury train is one of the most successful in the country due primarily to astute scheduling through scenic areas. By all means a seat in the Vista Dome is a necessity. If you're using color film, it's important to take along a CC-30R Color Compensating filter for daylight films to correct the blue tint in the Dome windows. For artificial light films, use a type A filter. Follow the exposure directions contained in booklets on the train. If you know what to watch for, it will be easier to see everything. To help, you might look for:

Approx. time from departure

From Denver	From Bond	
0:00	3:46	Denver
0:03		Prospect, a station at the edge of Denver. Train orders are hooped up on the lefthand side. The D.&R.G.W. tracks parallel the old D.N.W.&P. tracks from the Moffat station to Utah Junction.
0:07	3:39	Utah Junction, site of Moffat shops on a sweeping curve to the south side of the tracks at Pecos Street. The location can hardly be discerned today except for the metal water tower.
0:20	3:26	Leyden siding just before viaduct over State 72, and approximate beginning of two per cent grade to the Continental Divide.
0:25	3:10	Clay siding. Two tight "S" (the "Little Ten" and "Big Ten") curves.
0:35	3:00	Tunnel No. 1. The first of 27 tunnels in the next twenty-five miles. Tunnel numbers are shown on metal flags at the right side of the track, or cast into the concrete portals. Tunnels 9 and 17 were abandoned during construction due to earth pressures encountered, and Tunnel 28 has since been daylighted.
0:40	2:49	Tunnels 6-7-8. Last view of the plains. El Dorado directly below. One-fourth

One of the Devil's Slide trestles just east of Corona in August, 1952, before the County Road down the east side was completed. Today this road is opened sometime in July for sightseers and fishermen. *J. C. Thode photo.*

Page 312

of Colorado's area can be seen to the east.

0:41   2:48   Tunnel 10. Scene of disastrous tunnel fire in 1943 which blocked the line for three months, and caused the death of three Denver firemen. Notice the large dam across South Boulder Canyon in the vicinity of Tunnel 12. This is Gross Reservoir, part of Denver's water supply.

1:20   2:08   Tolland. Directly across the tracks to the north the three levels of old roadbed of the "Ladder" can easily be seen.

1:30   2:00   East Portal, Moffat Tunnel, 6.2 miles, second longest in the U. S. Notice the ventilation plant at East Portal where a canvas screen is lowered to blow all fumes to the west end. Apex 9239 ft. Continental Divide 2400 **feet** straight up. Reflector signs in tunnel each indicate a telephone. It's easy to get "lost" in smoke or fume laden conditions.

1:42   1:48   Winter Park, west portal of Moffat Tunnel. The four per cent descending from the Hill can be seen on the east side of the track just after leaving the tunnel. Several miles farther on is Fraser and after that Tabernash, which was a lively helper point in the days of the 200's climbing to Corona. A helper is still stationed there for use on eastbound tonnage trains.

2:20   1:05   Byers Canyon. Picturesque, narrow. U.S. 40 was built many years after the D.N.W.&P. The canyon is entered just after passing Hot Sulphur Springs.

3:00   0:24   Kremmling marks the beginning of Gore Canyon, deeper than the Royal Gorge. This is the site of the celebrated controversy regarding Gore Canyon vs. Gore Pass. Slide fences are wired into the signal circuit for rock fall protection.

3:48   0   Bond. The train stops just long enough for a crew change. Try eating in the railroad lunchroom between trains. Marvelous food, low cost, railroad atmosphere.

IV: TRAVEL GUIDE: BY AUTO

Good highways parallel almost the entire length of the line, and these can be used to see any historic and scenic points. To begin an automobile exploration, it is best to start in Denver. Pecos Steet running north from Denver on the west side of town goes through the heart of the old Utah Junction yards. Today there is not much to be seen, but even this fact is monumental in itself. The roundhouse and equipment buildings were to the east of Pecos for the most part. This, too, is the location of the famous interchange track where Bill Freeman outwitted the Rio Grande upon the opening of the Dotsero Cutoff.

Any Denver map will give the location of Colorado Highway 72 near Utah Junction. This should be the next objective, for it will lead very near the heart of the Tunnel District along South Boulder Canyon. Follow Colorado 72 through Arvada. Almost exactly five miles from the center of Arvada, the highway turns directly north and two-and-a-half miles on passes under the Rio Grande tracks beginning their 2% climb to the Moffat Tunnel. The next Rio Grande overpass is the site of the splendid Coal Creek Trestle (now a fill). To the right is Tunnel No. 1. A short distance before the viaduct is a short, bumpy sideroad which leads northward to Plainview, about a mile. From about the same location is a sideroad south through a pasture which gives a magnificent view of the serpentine curves at the Big and Little Ten. The sight of a long freight winding up the mountain here is something to be remembered.

As the highway continues up the valley of Coal Creek, it leaves the railroad and access to the track is difficult at all points except at Miramonte, where a road leads off to the right (north) giving a good view of the resort, formerly a station on the railroad. About 2½ miles beyond Miramonte, State 72 emerges on a mountainside high above the tracks. The location of daylighted Tunnel 28 can be seen almost directly below, and Tunnel 29 is visible upgrade as the tracks disappear from sight.

Pinecliff lies just beyond and State 72 ends at State 119. Two miles south of the junction lies Rollinsville, from which one may drive over the Hill in the summer, or take the longer route over Berthoud Pass to follow the Moffat farther west.

Across the Divide the trip should start at West Portal at Winter Park. This is the former location of Irvings, where helper engines were added to trains for the battle over the 4%. U. S. 40 is a fine highway leading through Fraser to Tabernash which was, and still is, the beginning of the helper district up to the Tunnel or Corona. By agreement with the brotherhoods, Moffat and Rio Grande crews alternate at Tabernash, but not all freights require helpers in these days of super-power diesel engines. Beyond Tabernash the Salt Lake tracks follow Fraser Canyon through more tunnels whereas the highway goes around,

The Moffat Road

rejoining the tracks at Granby. The two parallel to Hot Sulphur Springs, formerly the site of the CTC machine which is now located in Denver.

Byers Canyon (named for the first editor of *The Rocky Mountain News*) begins just past Sulphur. The close confines, the mountain stream, the bare rocky cliffs are all typical of mountain scenery at its best. It is a fine place for pictures if one can find a shoulder wide enough to park the car. Between Parshall and Kremmling, after the canyon is behind, it is of interest to note the extensive relocations made in the roadbed. It was here that Moffat's funds were running short and curving sidehill grading was adopted to save expensive bridging. Although U. S. 40 turns north at Kremmling, the railroad does not. This was the point of decision whether to go over Gore Pass or through Gore Canyon. It is easy to view Gore Pass be-cause the road to Toponas goes right over it. On the other hand, one of the most inspiring sights on the Moffat Road is Inspiration Point, high on the south wall of Gore Canyon.

To reach Gore Canyon one turns directly south in Kremmling on Colorado 9 and follows it for two miles to the junction with a dirt road (right). This is locally known as the "Trough Road" and leads to State Bridge and Bond, both on the railroad. The road climbs the mountains gradually and makes a breathtaking turn onto the precipice that is Gore Canyon. A clear view along the railroad for miles can be had, as well as one of the finest mountain views in the state. The real railroad enthusiast will not mind bumping along the gravel road to Yarmony (remember the "Black Year?" here when Moffat was broken financially and physically) and State Bridge. In addition, Bond lies just beyond, where the $1.95 steaks at the railroad dining room are something to write home about. The

Daylighting of Tunnel 28. The "28" still appears outside the portal as blasting and removal of the rock progress. *D.&R.G.W. photo.*

Engineering Office of D.&S.L. George Berry stands holding a transit just as he did in the locating of the road, thus measuring the stature of the quiet H. A. Sumner. G. S. Turner was division engineer under W. C. Jones and helped in rebuilding the Moffat. Ed Sunergren was the most capable office engineer and is seated with back to his desk. W. C. Jones has come over from his Rio Grande office to recall the rough days. Standing behind him is original locating engineer R. B. Parker. Seated at the table is Ed Graebing. Albert Peck holds in his hands an aging notebook of one of the chief engineers. Peck worked in the early days. So did Art Weston, who reads from the diary of J. J. Argo. The photograph above the desk is Rock Creek Canyon with its great trestle that had to be replaced with a fill. In this room history was made in the later days. *D.&R.G.W. photo.*

original D.N.W.&P. track climbs the hills in front of the hotel, while the Dotsero Cutoff follows the river.

Four miles past Bond is McCoy, the beginning of the side trip to Rock Creek Canyon. One should inquire locally for directions to McCoy station, about two miles from the town. Continuing on this road one comes to more serpentine 2% trackage while the county road follows a 4% grade for a short distance. Farther on the road takes several baffling right angle turns but ends up at Volcano, from whence came the fine Moffat ballast. It is from here that a short walk upgrade along the tracks leads directly into the heart of Rock Creek Canyon. Inquire locally relative to driving into the canyon bottom.

One now returns to McCoy. One mile beyond on State 131 the road along the Dotsero Cutoff branches to the south (left). This road is seldom out of sight of the railroad. It passes through a series of canyons. The main one is Ruby Canyon and it rivals the Glenwood Canyon of the Colorado River near Glenwood Springs in every aspect. Unlike Glenwood Canyon, the road at points climbs to the

The Moffat Road

canyon rim and gives thrilling views into the depths. In addition, there are two tunnels, one at either end of the cutoff.

Again one returns to Colorado 131 near McCoy. The road to Toponas by-passes Egeria Canyon through which the railroad passes. Between Toponas and Yampa one sees Finger Rock, a three-hundred-foot Moffat landmark of volcanic origin. Yampa itself is in Egeria Park. Phippsburg is the largest railroad town on the Craig extension. It is nicely nested in a valley and boasts a large yard which was

much busier years ago when coal business was at its height. Going through Oak Creek one comes to Haybro. This area is notable now for the large number of deserted and abandoned coal mines.

The journey through the beautiful fields near Steamboat Springs will revive Moffat's dream. Nowhere else is his dream so vividly portrayed. The green meadows with well-kept farm buildings and ranches survive to point out the basic soundness of his ideas. From here to the end of track at Craig the story is the same. Farther west, the Rangely oil field verifies the optimistic booklets fathered by Wm. Weston as he worked to sell the Road.

V: HISTORY: FROM D.&S.L. FILES

Denver, Northwestern & Pacific Railway Co. incorporated July 18, 1902. David H. Moffat was president until his death March 20, 1911. The line from Utah Junction to Arrow (via Rollins Pass) was started April, 1903, and completed September, 1904. Colorado-Utah Construction Company was the contractor.

The second phase, under the same construction company, ran from Arrow to Sulphur Springs, November, 1904, to June, 1905. From there the line was completed into Steam-

boat Springs during September, 1905, to January, 1909, and service inaugurated thereover January 20, 1909. The remaining 41 miles, Steamboat to Craig, were built during August to November, 1913, by the Denver and Salt Lake Construction Company.

Mr. W. G. Evans succeeded to the presidency after the death of Mr. Moffat and continued as such until the road went into Receivership on May 1, 1912. Col. D. C. Dodge and Mr. S. M. Perry were the Receivers of the road, which

Against the contract. There is a story behind this beautiful winter scene at Hideaway Park near Moffat Tunnel, and it shows the peculiarities of the contract between the D.&S.L. and D.&R.G.W. Neither railroad was permitted by union contract to use its engines to help the other. The engineer of D.&R.G.W. 1704 wasn't concerned with this obvious waste, he was just in a hurry to get back home during World War II. A Moffat coal drag with helper 206 had gotten ahead of him after he had helped a troop train up to the Moffat Tunnel and down to Tabernash. Although it was strictly against the rules, he had coupled into the Moffat train without orders. If he cracks his throttle a bit too much, the old D.&S.L. wood caboose will be in danger of folding up. Note the signal light box still mounted on the Moffat cupola. *Ed Bollinger photo.*

On this day the usual two-car consist of Train No. 9, the Yampa Valley Mail, is supplemented with a d d i t i o n a l coaches carrying passengers headed for a ranch school held every summer at S t e a m b o a t S p r i n g s. Two road-switcher freight units lead the trim 600 series Alco passenger diesel up the hill west of Orestod. *Fred Bauer photo.*

receivership continued for one year, ending April 30, 1913.

With the termination of the receivership, the name of the road was changed to The Denver and Salt Lake Railroad Co. with Newman Erb of New York as president. He remained as such until September 15, 1915, when he was succeeded by Charles Boettcher of Denver as president, who remained in this position until August 16, 1917, when the road again went into receivership with W. R. Freeman and Charles Boettcher as Receivers. This receivership terminated on December 31, 1926, with a reorganization as the Denver and Salt Lake Railway Company with W. R. Freeman as president, who remained as such until December 21, 1934.

On the latter date, Judge Wilson McCarthy of Salt Lake City, Utah, was elected president, in which position he continued until dissolution of the company on April 11, 1947, when it was merged into the corporate structure of The Denver and Rio Grande Western Railroad Company. Judge McCarthy, having previously been appointed co-

During the snow blockade of the Union Pacific's main line across Wyoming in February, 1949, much of their business was detoured over the railroad built by Dave Moffat. Here, Union Pacific diesel 1623, heading a re-routed eastbound manifest from Salt Lake City on February 22, 1949, drifts past the old D.&.S.L. water tank and shops at Utah Junction approaching the Denver yards, near the end of "Operation Snowbound." *George A. Trout photo.*

D.&S.L. Engine No. 401, photographed March 2, 1922, seven years after construction. The condition of this big engine (and also of the 200 series in background) indicates the road was short on money or had little traffic at that time. *J. C. Thode collection.*

Trustee of the latter road at the time it was thrown into bankruptcy on November 1, 1935, was elected president of the Rio Grande upon the reorganization of April 11, 1947, and continued as such until his death on February 12, 1956. He was ably succeeded as president on February 27, 1956, by the present incumbent and one-time D.&S.L. Roadmaster, Mr. G. B. Aydelott.

The mileage Denver to Craig, via the originally constructed line over Corona Pass, was 255 miles. The present mileage via the Moffat Tunnel is 232 miles. (231.46)

The road leases the main or railroad bore of the Moffat Tunnel, which was built as a municipal project during the years 1923-1928, at a total cost of almost $18,000,000. It is the second longest railroad tunnel in America, being 6.2 miles in length. The highest point on the now operated line of the railroad is 9,239 feet above sea level, located at approximately the center of the Moffat Tunnel.

Northwestern Terminal, Denver to Utah Junction, was constructed during October to December, 1905. East Denver Belt Line, Utah Junction to Union Pacific Connection and stockyards, constructed November, 1912, to early 1913.

About 70% of the railway's traffic consisted of high quality bituminous coal. It has been estimated by government geologists that there is enough coal located along this road to serve the entire United States for several hundred years. Following coal, livestock industry, agricultural products, and oil were the next most important commodities. The highest gross income of the road was achieved in 1926 when $4,268,447 was earned. The Company, along with other portions of the industry, suffered large declines in traffic and earnings and in 1938 had a gross income of only $2,264,605; however, because of increased operating efficiency and economies, it remained in good financial condition, and continued to earn its bond interest.

Acquisition of the Moffat Road's stocks and bonds was started by the Denver and Rio Grande Western Railroad in 1930; on September 15, 1931, the latter company was authorized by the Interstate Commerce Commission not only to acquire *stock control* of the Denver and Salt Lake, but also to construct the Dotsero Cutoff through the agency of the Denver and Salt Lake Western Railroad Company, which

had been organized in 1924 by the D. & S.L. for that same purpose.

Unable to secure by public means the financing necessary for such construction, because of the Great Depression of the early '30's, the Rio Grande borrowed money from the United States Reconstruction Finance Corporation, using its holdings of Denver and Salt Lake securities as collateral for the loan. Construction of the Cutoff, 38.1 miles long, between Dotsero on the Rio Grande's Tennessee Pass main line and Orestod (Dotsero spelled in reverse) on the D.&S.L. main line, began in November, 1932, with completion in June, 1934, when the D.&R.G.W. inaugurated service over D.&S.L. rails west of Denver under a joint trackage agreement.

Under the terms of the reorganization which was consummated April 11, 1947, the Denver and Salt Lake Railway Company was merged with The Denver and Rio Grande Western Railroad Company. Thus, while the corporate identity of David Moffat's brave little railroad was finally obliterated, its trains, its tracks, its tunnels, and its traditions continue to live and serve the purposes to which he gave his life.

Boilers from Moffat engines survive at an oil refinery in Denver. *Gordon Rodgers photo.*

The Moffat Station today. Rediscovery of the Moffat can begin at 15th Street and Delgany in downtown Denver, just a few blocks from the Union Station. Stripped of its former glory, with archways bricked up, it still retains some of the grace of former days. The old station tracks remain alongside and the freight shed back of the station is almost intact from Moffat days. Colorado Division office is seen beyond the station. *F. Bauer photo.*

Centralized Traffic Control Board, Daly, Barnes, Culbertson, Johnson. These four started with the Moffat road. L. J. Daly, as water boy, rose to trainman and trainmaster and assistant to superintendent. George Barnes was conductor extraordinary and a short time superintendent. J. B. Culbertson was the first and the last chief dispatcher. Nels Johnson was tunnel construction husky and number one engineer when the Moffat received "high green." It was a blustery winter's day when this photo was taken, keeping many Denverites at home. Nels Johnson picked up retired George Barnes, who declared that no blizzard would keep him home. Joe Culbertson sat at the CTC board. To make the story ring true a conductor came on the phone saying that his train had pulled a draw bar out at East Portal. Trainmaster Daly turned around and looked at the board, wondering if the freight was in the clear, so that Numbers 9 and 17 would not be laid out. George Barnes wanted to say, "Do you remember the day?" but he kept quiet. *D&R.G.W. photo.*

VI: CORPORATE PRESIDENTS OF THE MOFFAT ROAD WITH MANAGEMENT HISTORY

Denver, Northwestern & Pacific Railway Co.   (July 18, 1902 to April 30, 1913)

     David H. Moffat, Jr.   July 18, 1902 to March 20, 1911

     W. G. Evans   March 20, 1911 to May 1, 1912

     D. C. Dodge & S. M. Perry, Receivers   May 1, 1912 to April 30, 1913

The Denver and Salt Lake Railroad Co.   (April 30, 1913 to December 31, 1926)

     Newman Erb   April 30, 1913 to September 15, 1915

     Charles Boettcher   September 15, 1915 to August 16, 1917

     W. R. Freeman and Charles Boettcher, Receivers   August 16, 1917 to December 31, 1926

*The Denver and Salt Lake Railway Company   (January 1, 1927 to April 11, 1947)

     W. R. Freeman   January 1, 1927 to December 12, 1934

     Wilson McCarthy (R.F.C. held stock)   December 12, 1934 to April 11, 1947

*The D. & S. L. Railway was incorporated in Delaware on August 20, 1926, but did not take over the Railroad until January 1, 1927.

MANAGEMENT

7-30-1902	A. C. Ridgway	3-1-1905
3-1-1905	G. R. Simmons	5-4-1905
5-5-1905	W. A. Deuel	7-31-1910
8-19-1910	W. A. Beerbower, Gen. Supt.	1-13-1913
5-22-1911	D. C. Dodge	5-1-1912
4-1-1913	W. E. Morse	9-1-1917
9-1-1917	W. R. Freeman	6-30-1918
7-1-1918	W. F. Thufhoff	2-29-1920
3-1-1920	W. R. Freeman	12-31-1926
1-1-1927	A. L. Johnson	4-11-1947

7-2-1938 W. H. Sagstetter, Assistant to President, in charge of Mechanical Department.

9-8-1941 A. E. Perlman, Assistant to President, in charge of Engineering Department.

VII: LOCOMOTIVES OF THE DENVER AND SALT LAKE RAILWAY

Compiled by R. H. KINDIG of Denver; updated by J. C. THODE from Rio Grande files in 1961.

CLASS 28, 0-6-0

D&SL No.	Builder	Builder's No.	Date Built	Disposition and Date
20	Schenectady	29038	7-1903	Sc. 10-1939
21	Schenectady	29039	7-1903	Sc. 10-1939

Drivers Inches	Cylinders Inches	Wt. on Dr. Pounds	Total Wt. Pounds	Tractive Effort Pounds
51	19x26	132,000	132,000	28,160

CLASS 42, 2-8-0

D&SL No.	Builder	Builder's No.	Date Built	Disposition and Date
100	Schenectady	29204	2-1904	Sc. 5-1937
101	Schenectady	29205	2-1904	Sc. 5-1937
102	Schenectady	37709	5-1905	Sc. 5-1937

Drivers Inches	Cylinders Inches	Wt. on Dr. Pounds	Total Wt. Pounds	Tractive Effort Pounds
57	22x28	186,000	209,500	42,420

CLASS 44, 2-8-0

D&SL No.	Builder	Builder's No.	Date Built	Disposition and Date
103	Schenectady	39947	5-1906	Sc. 5-1937
104	Schenectady	39948	5-1906	Sc. 5-1937
105	Schenectady	39949	5-1906	Sc. 5-1937
106	Schenectady	41617	11-1906	Sc. 10-1939
107	Schenectady	41618	11-1906	Sc. 5-1937
108	Schenectady	45576	10-1908	Sc. 6-1942
109	Schenectady	45577	10-1908	Sc. 8-1943
110	Schenectady	45578	10-1908	Sc. 10-1947
111	Schenectady	45579	10-1908	Renumbered D&RGW 1031, 5-1949. Sc. 12-1951
112	Schenectady	48148	8-1910	Sc. 12-1948, without being renumbered D&RGW 1032
113	Schenectady	48149	8-1910	Renumbered D&RGW 1033, 5-1948. Sc. 7-1950
114	Schenectady	48150	8-1910	Sc. 6-1942
115	Schenectady	48242	8-1910	Sold, 9-1942, to Columbia Steel Corp., Geneva, Utah
116	Schenectady	48243	8-1910	Sold, 11-1942, to Columbia Steel Corp.
117	Schenectady	48244	8-1910	Sold, 10-1942, to Columbia Steel Corp.
118	Schenectady	48245	8-1910	Renumbered D&RGW 1034. 10-1948. Sc. 5-1955
119	Schenectady	48246	8-1910	Renumbered D&RGW 1035, 7-1948. Sc. 5-1955
120	Schenectady	48247	8-1910	Renumbered D&RGW 1036, 3-1948. Sc. 5-1951
121	Schenectady	48248	8-1910	Renumbered D&RGW 1037, 5-1948. Sc. 12-1951
122	Schenectady	48249	8-1910	Sc. 4-1948, without being renumbered D&RGW 1038
123	Schenectady	48250	8-1910	Renumbered D&RGW 1039, 5-1948. Sc. 3-1951

Drivers Inches	Cylinders Inches	Wt. on Dr. Pounds	Total Wt. Pounds	Tractive Effort Pounds
55	22x28	195,000	219,000	43,980

CLASS 76, 2-6-6-0

Engines 200-209 were built as 0-6-6-0, and rebuilt within a few years to the 2-6-6-0 type; 210-216 built originally as 2-6-6-0's.

D&SL No.	Builder	Builder's No.	Date Built	Disposition and Date
200	Schenectady	45604	10-1908	Renumbered D&RGW 3360, 6-1948, Sc. 6-1949
201	Schenectady	46560	10-1909	Renumbered D&RGW 3361, 12-1947. Sc. 6-1952
202	Schenectady	46561	10-1909	Sc. 12-1947, without being renumbered D&RGW 3362
203	Schenectady	48151	7-1910	Renumbered D&RGW 3363, 5-1948. Sc. 8-1949
204	Schenectady	48230	7-1910	Renumbered D&RGW 3364, 6-1948. Sc. 8-1949
205	Schenectady	48231	7-1910	Renumbered D&RGW 3365, 5-1948. Sc. 8-1949
206	Schenectady	48232	7-1910	Renumbered D&RGW 3366, 12-1947, Sc. 7-1951
207	Schenectady	48233	7-1910	Renumbered D&RGW 3367, 12-1947. Sc. 5-1950
208	Schenectady	48234	7-1910	Renumbered D&RGW 3368, 5-1948. Sc. 8-1950
209	Schenectady	48235	7-1910	Renumbered D&RGW 3369, 3-1948. Sc. 4-1951
210	Schenectady	53292	4-1913	Destroyed 12-5-1924 in derailment at Rifle Sight Notch.
211	Schenectady	53293	4-1913	Renumbered D&RGW 3370, 6-1948. Sc. 7-1951
212	Schenectady	55986	9-1916	Renumbered D&RGW 3371, 7-1948. Sc. 4-1951
213	Schenectady	55987	9-1916	Renumbered D&RGW 3372, 6-1948. Sc. 7-1949
214	Schenectady	55988	9-1916	Renumbered D&RGW 3373, 2-1948. Sc. 7-1950
215	Schenectady	55989	9-1916	Renumbered D&RGW 3374, 5-1948. Sc. 7-1949
216	Schenectady	56296	9-1916	Renumbered D&RGW 3375, 5-1948. Sc. 7-1951

Drivers Inches	Cylinders Inches	Wt. on Dr. Pounds	Total Wt. Pounds	Tractive Effort Pounds
55	21x32 & 33½x32	332,000	362,000	76,400

(Weight on drivers of engines 212-216 was 333,500 pounds, and total weight was 361,000 pounds.)

CLASS 30, 4-6-0

D&SL No.	Builder	Builder's No.	Date Built	Disposition and Date
300	Schenectady	29203	2-1904	Sc. 4-1947

Drivers Inches	Cylinders Inches	Wt. on Dr. Pounds	Total Wt. Pounds	Tractive Effort Pounds
63	20x28	142,000	186,000	30,220

CLASS 33, 4-6-0

D&SL No.	Builder	Builder's No.	Date Built	Disposition and Date
301	Schenectady	37708	5-1905	Sc. 6-1942
302	Schenectady	41616	11-1907	Renumbered D&RGW 795, 4-1948. Sc. 7-1948

Drivers Inches	Cylinders Inches	Wt. on Dr. Pounds	Total Wt. Pounds	Tractive Effort Pounds
57	20x28	301—138,500	182,000	33,405
		302—142,000	189,000	

CLASS 34, 4-6-0

D&SL No.	Builder	Builder's No.	Date Built	Disposition and Date
303	Schenectady	48147	7-1910	Sc. 7-1948, without being renumbered D&RGW 796

Drivers Inches	Cylinders Inches	Wt. on Dr. Pounds	Total Wt. Pounds	Tractive Effort Pounds
63	20x28	165,000	215,100	34,150

CLASS 19, 4-4-0

D&SL No.	Builder	Builder's No.	Date Built	Disposition and Date
390	Pittsburgh	1951	1899	Sc. 7-1937
391	Pittsburgh	1952	1899	Sc. 7-1937

Drivers Inches	Cylinders Inches	Wt. on Dr. Pounds	Total Wt. Pounds	Tractive Effort Pounds
60	18x24	70,000	108,000	19,280

D&SL 390-391 were originally Chesapeake Beach 3-4.

CLASS 63, 2-8-2

D&SL No.	Builder	Builder's No.	Date Built	Disposition and Date
400	Lima	5100	1915	Renumbered D&RGW 1220, 7-1948. Sc. 10-1953
401	Lima	5101	1915	Renumbered D&RGW 1221, 5-1948. Sc. 4-1949
402	Lima	5102	1915	Renumbered D&RGW 1222, 11-1948. Sc. 6-1954
403	Lima	5103	1915	Renumbered D&RGW 1223, 5-1948. Sc.. 12-1948
404	Lima	5104	1915	Renumbered D&RGW 1224, 12-1947. Sc. 9-1956
405	Lima	5105	1915	Renumbered D&RGW 1225, 1-1948. Sc. 1-1955
406	Lima	5106	1915	Renumbered D&RGW 1226, 12-1947. Sc. 4-1952
407	Lima	5107	1915	Renumbered D&RGW 1227, 2-1948. Sc. 10-1953
408	Schenectady	55984	8-1916	Renumbered D&RGW 1228, 5-1948. Sc. 5-1952
409	Schenectady	55985	8-1916	Renumbered D&RGW 1229, 3-1948. Sc. 10-1956

Drivers Inches	Cylinders Inches	Wt. on Dr. Pounds	Total Wt. Pounds	Tractive Effort Pounds
55	26x30	232,000	295,000	62,700

(Total weight of engines 408 and 409 was 306,000 pounds.)

VIII: ROTARY SNOW PLOWS OF THE DENVER AND SALT LAKE RAILWAY

D&SL 10200—All-steel, 36-foot rotary snow plow, scoop-wheel type, 12-foot cut, with 7,000 gallon tender; weight 172,000 pounds. Purchased by Colorado-Utah Construction Company. Built by American Locomotive Company at Patterson, New Jersey works, December, 1904. Retired February, 1950, by D.&R.G.W. Railroad.

D&SL 10201—All-steel, 33-foot rotary snow plow, scoop-wheel type, 12-foot cut, 14'6" wheel, with 7,000 gallon tender; weight not shown. Purchased by Colorado-Utah Construction Company. Built by American Locomotive Company at Patterson, New Jersey works, November, 1906. Retired 1938 by D.&S.L. Railway. (At time of I.C.C. Valuation Inventory, this snow plow was noted as being in wrecked condition at Denver on October 11, 1920.)

D&SL 10202—All-steel, 26-foot rotary snow plow, with 9,000 gallon tender; weight not shown. Purchased by U. S. Railroad Administration, September, 1918, from the Colorado, Wyoming and Eastern Railway (now Union Pacific line Laramie, Wyo., to Coalmont, Colo.), their No. 098. No record of builder or date built. Retired 1938 by D.&S.L. Railway.

From valuation records of Denver and Salt Lake Railway now on file in General Office of Denver and Rio Grande Western Railroad Company.

IX: DRAWINGS OF ROLLING STOCK

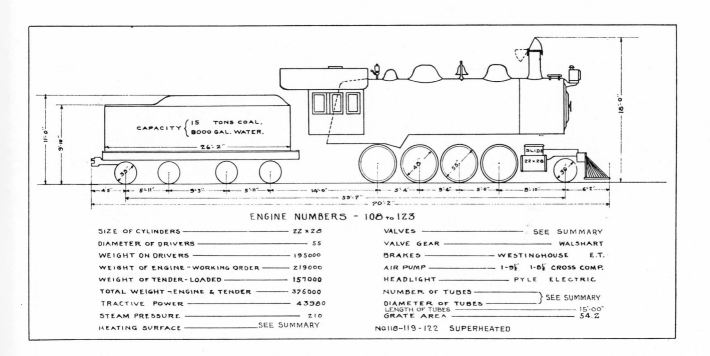

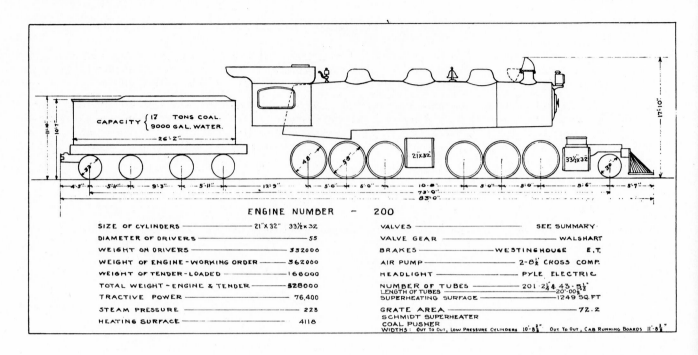

CAPACITY { 17 TONS COAL. 9000 GAL. WATER. }

ENGINE NUMBER — 200

SIZE OF CYLINDERS	21"X32" 33½"x32
DIAMETER OF DRIVERS	55
WEIGHT ON DRIVERS	332000
WEIGHT OF ENGINE - WORKING ORDER	562000
WEIGHT OF TENDER - LOADED	166000
TOTAL WEIGHT - ENGINE & TENDER	528000
TRACTIVE POWER	76,400
STEAM PRESSURE	223
HEATING SURFACE	4118

VALVES	SEE SUMMARY
VALVE GEAR	WALSHART
BRAKES	WESTINGHOUSE E.T.
AIR PUMP	2-8½ CROSS COMP.
HEADLIGHT	PYLE ELECTRIC
NUMBER OF TUBES	201 2¼ & 43 - 5½"
LENGTH OF TUBES	20'-00½"
SUPERHEATING SURFACE	1249 SQ. FT
GRATE AREA	72.2

SCHMIDT SUPERHEATER
COAL PUSHER
WIDTHS: OUT TO OUT, LOW PRESSURE CYLINDERS 10'-8½" OUT TO OUT, CAB RUNNING BOARDS 11'-8½"

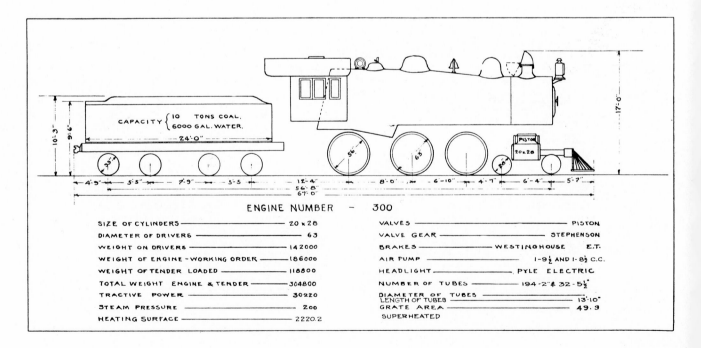

CAPACITY { 10 TONS COAL. 6000 GAL. WATER. }

ENGINE NUMBER — 300

SIZE OF CYLINDERS	20 x 28
DIAMETER OF DRIVERS	63
WEIGHT ON DRIVERS	142000
WEIGHT OF ENGINE - WORKING ORDER	186000
WEIGHT OF TENDER LOADED	118800
TOTAL WEIGHT ENGINE & TENDER	304800
TRACTIVE POWER	30220
STEAM PRESSURE	200
HEATING SURFACE	2220.2

VALVES	PISTON
VALVE GEAR	STEPHENSON
BRAKES	WESTINGHOUSE E.T.
AIR PUMP	1-9½ AND 1-8½ C.C.
HEADLIGHT	PYLE ELECTRIC
NUMBER OF TUBES	194-2" & 32 - 5½"
DIAMETER OF TUBES	
LENGTH OF TUBES	13'-10"
GRATE AREA	49.9

SUPERHEATED

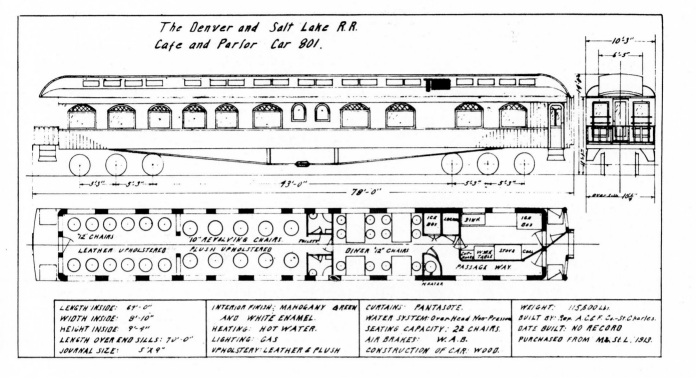

The Denver and Salt Lake R.R.
Cafe and Parlor Car 801.

LENGTH INSIDE: 69'-0"	INTERIOR FINISH: MAHOGANY GREEN AND WHITE ENAMEL.	CURTAINS: PANTASOTE.	WEIGHT: 115,600 Lbs.
WIDTH INSIDE: 8'-10"		WATER SYSTEM: Over Head Non-Pressure	BUILT BY: Rep A.C.&F. Co. St.Charles.
HEIGHT INSIDE: 9'-4"	HEATING: HOT WATER.	SEATING CAPACITY: 22 CHAIRS.	DATE BUILT: NO RECORD
LENGTH OVER END SILLS: 70'-0"	LIGHTING: GAS	AIR BRAKES: W.A.B.	PURCHASED FROM M.& St.L. 1913.
JOURNAL SIZE: 5"x 9"	UPHOLSTERY: LEATHER & PLUSH	CONSTRUCTION OF CAR: WOOD.	

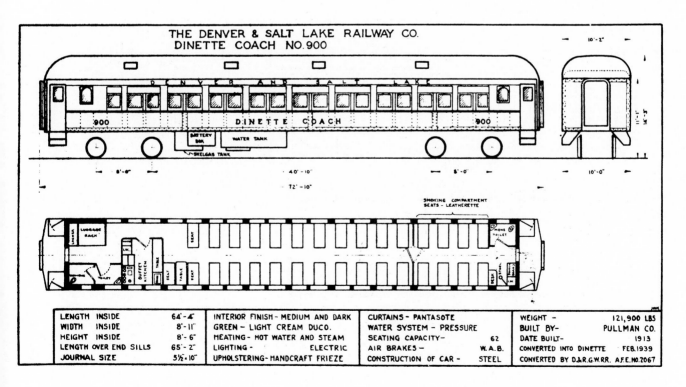

THE DENVER & SALT LAKE RAILWAY CO.
DINETTE COACH NO. 900

LENGTH INSIDE 64'-4"	INTERIOR FINISH - MEDIUM AND DARK GREEN - LIGHT CREAM DUCO.	CURTAINS - PANTASOTE	WEIGHT - 121,900 LBS
WIDTH INSIDE 8'-11"		WATER SYSTEM - PRESSURE	BUILT BY - PULLMAN CO.
HEIGHT INSIDE 8'-6"	HEATING - HOT WATER AND STEAM	SEATING CAPACITY - 62	DATE BUILT - 1913
LENGTH OVER END SILLS 65'-2"	LIGHTING - ELECTRIC	AIR BRAKES - W.A.B.	CONVERTED INTO DINETTE FEB.1939
JOURNAL SIZE 5½"x10"	UPHOLSTERING - HANDCRAFT FRIEZE	CONSTRUCTION OF CAR - STEEL	CONVERTED BY D.&R.G.W.RR. A.F.E.NO.2067

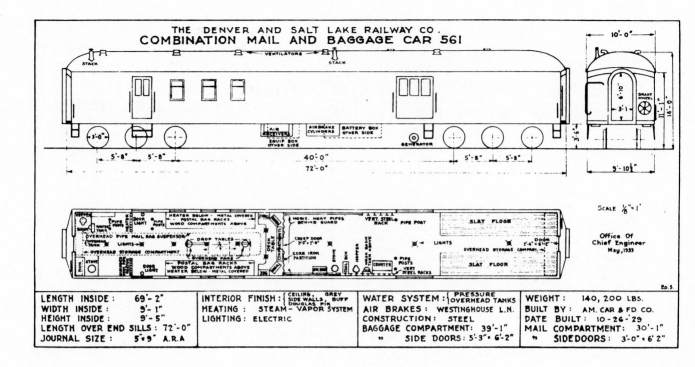

THE DENVER AND SALT LAKE RAILWAY CO.
COMBINATION MAIL AND BAGGAGE CAR 561

LENGTH INSIDE: 69'-2"	INTERIOR FINISH: {CEILING GREY SIDE WALLS, BUFF DOUGLAS FIR	WATER SYSTEM: {PRESSURE OVERHEAD TANKS	WEIGHT: 140, 200 LBS.
WIDTH INSIDE: 9'-1"	HEATING: STEAM-VAPOR SYSTEM	AIR BRAKES: WESTINGHOUSE L.N.	BUILT BY: AM. CAR & FD. CO.
HEIGHT INSIDE: 9'-5"	LIGHTING: ELECTRIC	CONSTRUCTION: STEEL	DATE BUILT: 10-26-'29
LENGTH OVER END SILLS: 72'-0"		BAGGAGE COMPARTMENT: 39'-1"	MAIL COMPARTMENT: 30'-1"
JOURNAL SIZE: 5"-9" A.R.A		" SIDE DOORS: 5'-3"x 6'-2"	" SIDEDOORS: 3'-0"x 6'2"

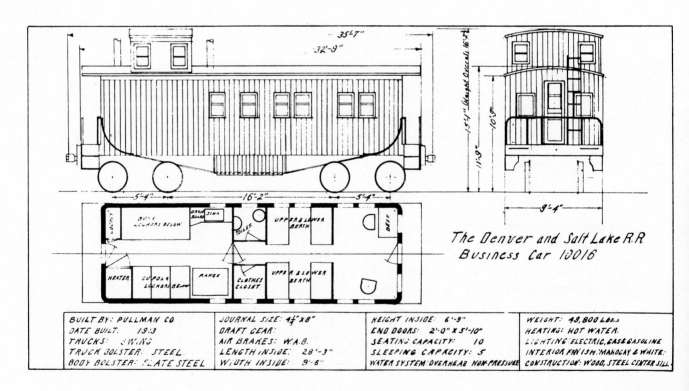

The Denver and Salt Lake R.R.
Business Car 10016

BUILT BY: PULLMAN CO	JOURNAL SIZE: 4¼"x8"	HEIGHT INSIDE: 6'-9"	WEIGHT: 43,800 Lbs.
DATE BUILT: 1913	DRAFT GEAR:	END DOORS: 2'-0"x 5'-10"	HEATING: HOT WATER.
TRUCKS: SWING	AIR BRAKES: W.A.B.	SEATING CAPACITY: 10	LIGHTING: ELECTRIC, GAS & GASOLINE
TRUCK BOLSTER: STEEL	LENGTH INSIDE: 28'-3"	SLEEPING CAPACITY: 5	INTERIOR FINISH: MAHOGAY & WHITE
BODY BOLSTER: PLATE STEEL	WIDTH INSIDE: 9'-6"	WATER SYSTEM: OVERHEAD NON-PRESSURE	CONSTRUCTION: WOOD, STEEL CENTER SILL

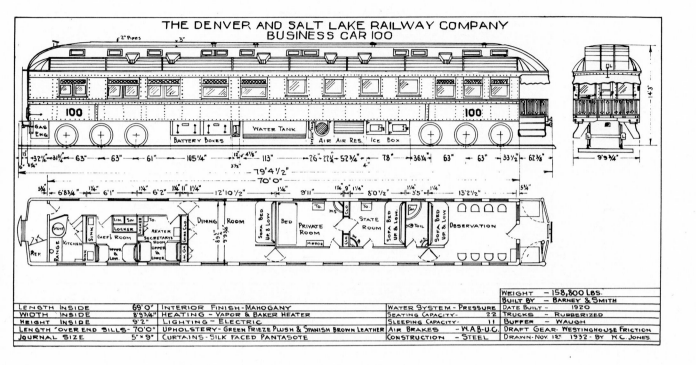

THE DENVER AND SALT LAKE RAILWAY COMPANY
BUSINESS CAR 100

LENGTH INSIDE	69'0"	INTERIOR FINISH-MAHOGANY		WATER SYSTEM - PRESSURE	WEIGHT - 158,800 LBS.		
WIDTH INSIDE	8'9¾"	HEATING - VAPOR & BAKER HEATER		SEATING CAPACITY- 22	BUILT BY - BARNEY & SMITH		
HEIGHT INSIDE	9'2"	LIGHTING - ELECTRIC		SLEEPING CAPACITY- 11	DATE BUILT - 1920		
LENGTH OVER END SILLS-70'0"		UPHOLSTERY- GREEN FRIEZE PLUSH & SPANISH BROWN LEATHER		AIR BRAKES - W.A.B-U.C.	TRUCKS - RUBBERIZED		
JOURNAL SIZE	5"x9"	CURTAINS- SILK FACED PANTASOTE		CONSTRUCTION - STEEL	BUFFER - WAUGH		
					DRAFT GEAR- WESTINGHOUSE FRICTION		
					DRAWN-NOV. 1ST 1932- BY H.C. JONES		

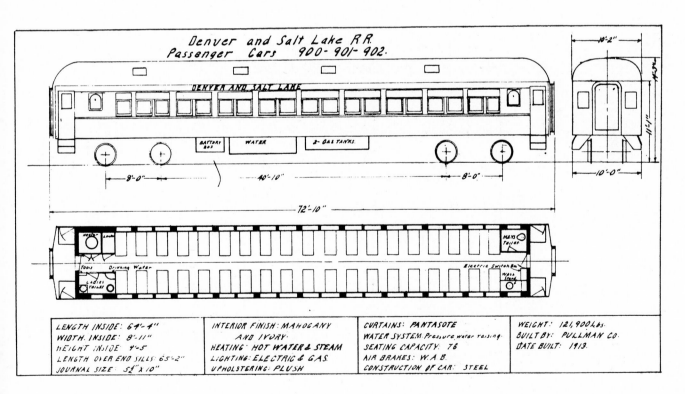

Denver and Salt Lake R.R.
Passenger Cars 900-901-902.

LENGTH INSIDE: 64'-4"		INTERIOR FINISH: MAHOGANY AND IVORY		CURTAINS: PANTASOTE	WEIGHT: 121,900 Lbs.	
WIDTH INSIDE: 8'-11"		HEATING: HOT WATER & STEAM		WATER SYSTEM: Pressure, water raising	BUILT BY: PULLMAN CO.	
HEIGHT INSIDE: 9'-5		LIGHTING: ELECTRIC & GAS.		SEATING CAPACITY: 76	DATE BUILT: 1913.	
LENGTH OVER END SILLS 65'-2"		UPHOLSTERING: PLUSH		AIR BRAKES: W.A.B.		
JOURNAL SIZE: 5¼"x 10"				CONSTRUCTION OF CAR: STEEL		

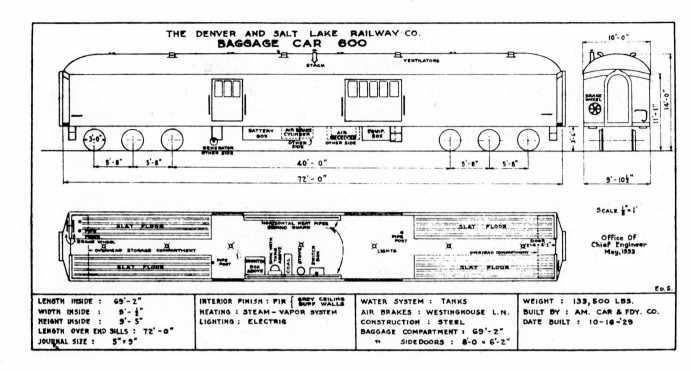

THE DENVER AND SALT LAKE RAILWAY CO.
BAGGAGE CAR 600

LENGTH INSIDE : 69'-2"	INTERIOR FINISH : FIR { GREY CEILING BUFF WALLS	WATER SYSTEM : TANKS	WEIGHT : 133,500 LBS.
WIDTH INSIDE : 9'-½"	HEATING : STEAM - VAPOR SYSTEM	AIR BRAKES : WESTINGHOUSE L.N.	BUILT BY : AM. CAR & FDY. CO.
HEIGHT INSIDE : 9'-5"	LIGHTING : ELECTRIC	CONSTRUCTION : STEEL	DATE BUILT : 10-16-'29
LENGTH OVER END SILLS : 72'-0"		BAGGAGE COMPARTMENT : 69'-2"	
JOURNAL SIZE : 5"x9"		" SIDEDOORS : 8'-0 x 6'-2"	

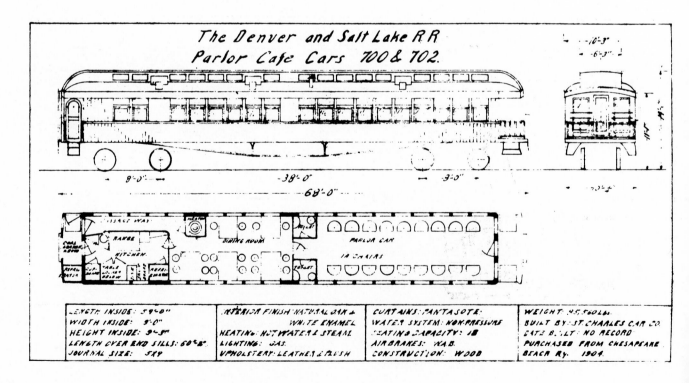

The Denver and Salt Lake R.R
Parlor Cafe Cars 700 & 702.

LENGTH INSIDE : 59'-0"	INTERIOR FINISH : NATURAL OAK & WHITE ENAMEL	CURTAINS : PANTASOTE	WEIGHT : 95,500 LBS.
WIDTH INSIDE : 9'-0"	HEATING : HOT WATER & STEAM	WATER SYSTEM : NON-PRESSURE	BUILT BY : ST. CHARLES CAR CO.
HEIGHT INSIDE : 9'-8"	LIGHTING : GAS	SEATING CAPACITY : 18	DATE BUILT : NO RECORD
LENGTH OVER END SILLS : 60'-8"	UPHOLSTERY : LEATHER & PLUSH	AIR BRAKES : X.A.B.	PURCHASED FROM CHESAPEAKE
JOURNAL SIZE : 5X9		CONSTRUCTION : WOOD	BEACH RY. 1904.

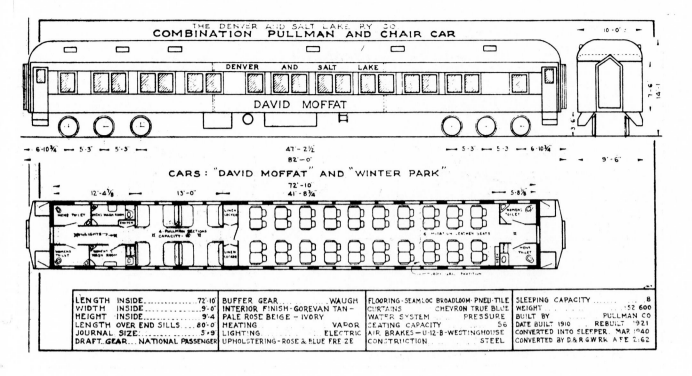

THE DENVER AND SALT LAKE RY CO
COMBINATION PULLMAN AND CHAIR CAR

DENVER AND SALT LAKE

DAVID MOFFAT

CARS: "DAVID MOFFAT" AND "WINTER PARK"

LENGTH INSIDE............72'-10"	BUFFER GEAR............WAUGH	FLOORING-SEAMLOC BROADLOOM-PNEU-TILE	SLEEPING CAPACITY............8
WIDTH INSIDE............9'-0"	INTERIOR FINISH-GOREVAN TAN-	CURTAINS............CHEVRON TRUE BLUE	WEIGHT............152 600
HEIGHT INSIDE............9'-4"	PALE ROSE BEIGE – IVORY	WATER SYSTEM............PRESSURE	BUILT BY............PULLMAN CO
LENGTH OVER END SILLS...80'-0"	HEATING............VAPOR	SEATING CAPACITY............56	DATE BUILT 1910 REBUILT '21
JOURNAL SIZE............5'-9"	LIGHTING............ELECTRIC	AIR BRAKES—U-12-B-WESTINGHOUSE	CONVERTED INTO SLEEPER. MAR. 1940
DRAFT GEAR...NATIONAL PASSENGER	UPHOLSTERING-ROSE & BLUE FREEZE	CONSTRUCTION............STEEL	CONVERTED BY D&RGW RR AFE 2:62

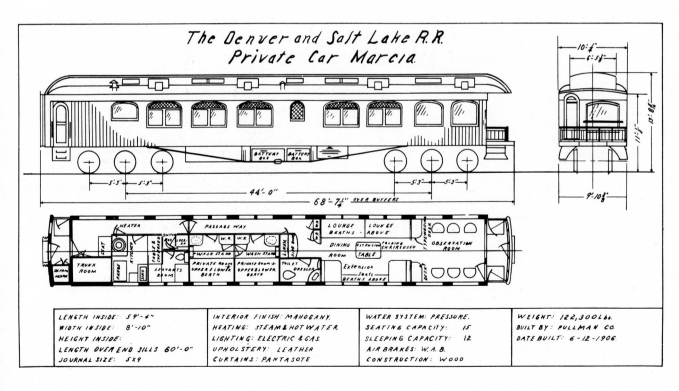

The Denver and Salt Lake R.R. Private Car Marcia.

LENGTH INSIDE: 59'-4"	INTERIOR FINISH: MAHOGANY.	WATER SYSTEM: PRESSURE.	WEIGHT: 122,300 Lbs.
WIDTH INSIDE: 8'-10"	HEATING: STEAM & HOT WATER.	SEATING CAPACITY: 15	BUILT BY: PULLMAN CO.
HEIGHT INSIDE:	LIGHTING: ELECTRIC & GAS.	SLEEPING CAPACITY: 12	DATE BUILT: 6-12-1906.
LENGTH OVER END SILLS 60'-0"	UPHOLSTERY: LEATHER	AIR BRAKES: W.A.B.	
JOURNAL SIZE: 5X9	CURTAINS: PANTASOTE	CONSTRUCTION: WOOD	

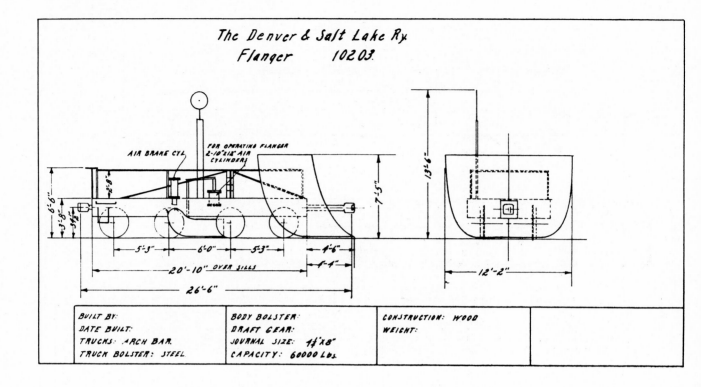

The Denver & Salt Lake Ry.
Flanger   10203.

AIR BRAKE CYL.
FOR OPERATING FLANGER
2-10"x12" AIR
CYLINDERS

BUILT BY:	BODY BOLSTER:	CONSTRUCTION: WOOD	
DATE BUILT:	DRAFT GEAR:	WEIGHT:	
TRUCKS: ARCH BAR.	JOURNAL SIZE: 4¾"x8"		
TRUCK BOLSTER: STEEL	CAPACITY: 60000 Lbs.		

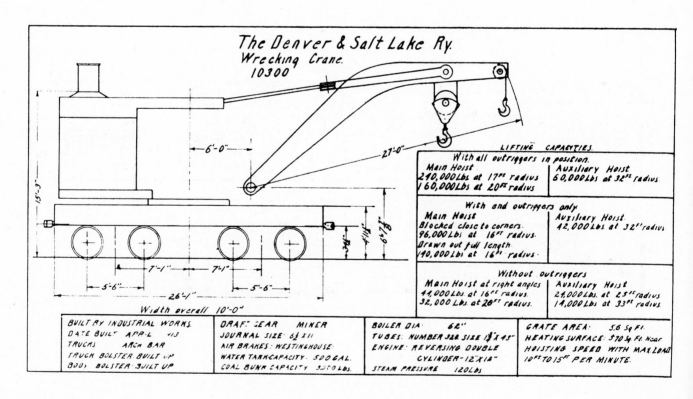

The Denver & Salt Lake Ry.
Wrecking Crane.
10300

LIFTING CAPACITIES.

With all outriggers in position.

Main Hoist
240,000 Lbs. at 17ᶠᵗ radius
160,000 Lbs. at 20ᶠᵗ radius

Auxiliary Hoist.
60,000 Lbs. at 32ᶠᵗ radius

With end outriggers only

Main Hoist
Blocked close to corners.
96,000 Lbs. at 16ᶠᵗ radius.
Drawn out full length
40,000 Lbs. at 16ᶠᵗ radius.

Auxiliary Hoist.
42,000 Lbs. at 32" radius.

Without outriggers

Main Hoist at right angles
44,000 Lbs. at 16ᶠᵗ radius.
32,000 Lbs. at 20ᶠᵗ radius.

Auxiliary Hoist
24,000 Lbs. at 25ᶠᵗ radius.
14,000 Lbs. at 33ᶠᵗ radius.

BUILT BY INDUSTRIAL WORKS.	DRAFT GEAR MINER	BOILER DIA 62"	GRATE AREA: 5.6 Sq.Ft.
DATE BUILT APRIL '13	JOURNAL SIZE: 6¼"x11	TUBES: NUMBER 328 SIZE 1¾"x45"	HEATING SURFACE: 570 Sq.Ft. Near
TRUCKS ARCH BAR	AIR BRAKES: WESTINGHOUSE	ENGINE: REVERSING DOUBLE	HOISTING SPEED WITH MAX LOAD
TRUCK BOLSTER BUILT UP	WATER TANK CAPACITY 500 GAL.	CYLINDER-12"x12"	10ᶠᵗ TO 15ᶠᵗ PER MINUTE.
BODY BOLSTER BUILT UP	COAL BUNK CAPACITY 3000 Lbs.	STEAM PRESSURE 120 Lbs	

X: EMPLOYEES TIME CARD NO. 49

| SUBDIVISION 1 | | EASTWARD | | | | | | | | |

Station Numbers	Ruling Grade Ascending Per Cent		TIME-TABLE No. 49 JANUARY 16, 1944 STATIONS	FIRST CLASS D. & S. L. 12 Mixed Arrive Daily	D.& R.G.W. 20 Mountaineer Arrive Daily	D.& R.G.W. 8 Advance Six Arrive Daily	D.& R.G.W. 6 Exposition Flyer Arrive Daily	D. & S. L. 2 Passenger Mail & Exp. Arrive Daily	SECOND CLASS 82 Freight Arrive Daily	74 Freight Arrive Daily	72 Freight Arrive Daily	78 Freight Arrive Daily
0	0.0	DN DB DI	DENVER (D&SL) DN	6 30 AM				3 00 PM				
1	0.0	CX	PROSPECT (D&RGW) DN —0.5—		6 38 AM	9 44 AM	12 44 PM					
2	0.3		FOX JCT. —0.91—	6 11	6 36	9 42	12 42	2 45				
3	0.4		ENDO —1.84—	6 05	6 33	9 39	12 39	2 41				
4	0.3	UJ	ZUNI DN —2.90—	5 52	6 30	9 36	12 36	f 2 38	5 10 AM	9 45 AM	3 35 PM	10 20 PM
7	0.0		RALSTON —4.82—	5 47	6 26	9 32	12 32	f 2 34	5 01	9 38	3 27	10 13
12	0.0	JN	LEYDEN DN —6.01—	5 32	6 17	9 25 (74)	12 25	f 2 27 (5)	4 48	9 25 (8)	3 14	10 00
18	0.0		ARENA —2.91—	5 16	6 07	9 17	12 17	2 12	4 31	9 01	2 56	9 42 (11)
21	0.0		CLAY —3.56—	5 06	5 57	9 10	12 10	f 2 05	4 21	8 51	2 46 (5)	9 19 (19)
24	0.0	PA	PLAIN DN —6.89—	s 4 55	5 48	9 01	12 01 PM	f 1 56	4 10	8 40	2 25	9 00
31	0.0		CRESCENT —5.70—	4 30	5 30	8 43	11 43	f 1 38	3 47	8 17	2 02	8 37
37	0.0	PC	CLIFF DN —4.69—	s 4 12	s 5 14	s 8 26	s 11 26 (1)	s 1 22	3 30	8 00	1 45	8 20
42	0.0	R	ROLLINS D —5.16—	s 3 57	5 02	8 10	11 10	s 1 10	3 05	7 35	1 20	7 55
47	0.0	MN	TOLLAND DN —3.20—	f 3 45	4 52	7 57	10 57	s 1 00 (12)	2 50	7 20	1 00 (3)	7 40
50	0.9		EAST PORTAL —6.77—	s 3 35	4 46	7 50	10 50	s 12 54	2 40	7 10	12 37	7 30
57	2.0	RV	WINTER PARK DN —2.33—	s 3 15	4 27	7 30	10 30	s 12 38	2 10	6 40	12 12 (1) PM	7 00
59	2.0		WOOD —2.97—	3 00	4 19	7 21	10 21	12 31	1 57	6 27	11 52	6 47
62	1.7	Z	FRASER D —3.82—	s 2 50	4 11	7 13	10 13	s 12 25 (1)	1 45	6 15	11 40	6 35
66	1.0	RN	TABERNASH DN —4.31—	s 2 40	4 04	7 05	10 05	s 12 16	1 35	6 05	11 30	6 25
70	1.0		DALE —5.48—	2 25	3 55	6 55	9 55	f 12 05 PM	1 15	5 45	11 10	6 03
76	0.9	B	GRANBY D —5.64—	s 2 10	3 46	6 46	9 46	s 11 55	1 00	5 30	10 55	5 48
81	0.8		WILLOWS —4.74—	1 55	3 39	6 38	9 38	f 11 42	12 46 (11)	5 15	10 40	5 33
86		GS NS	SULPHUR DN (86.15)	1 35 AM	3 33 AM	6 30 AM	9 30 AM	11 35 AM	12 30 AM	5 05 AM	10 30 AM	5 23 (9) PM
			Leave Daily	Leave Daily	Leave Daily	Leave Daily	Leave Daily	Leave Daily	Leave Daily	Leave Daily	Leave Daily
			Schedule Time Average Miles per Hour	(4'55") (17.5)	(3'05") (27.6)	(3'14") (26.3)	(3'14") (26.3)	(3'25") (25.2)	(4'40") (17.1)	(4'40") (17.1)	(5'05") (15.9)	(4'57") (16.5)

D. & S. L. Ry. Co.

XI: MAPS, PUEBLO DIVISION, D.&R.G.W.

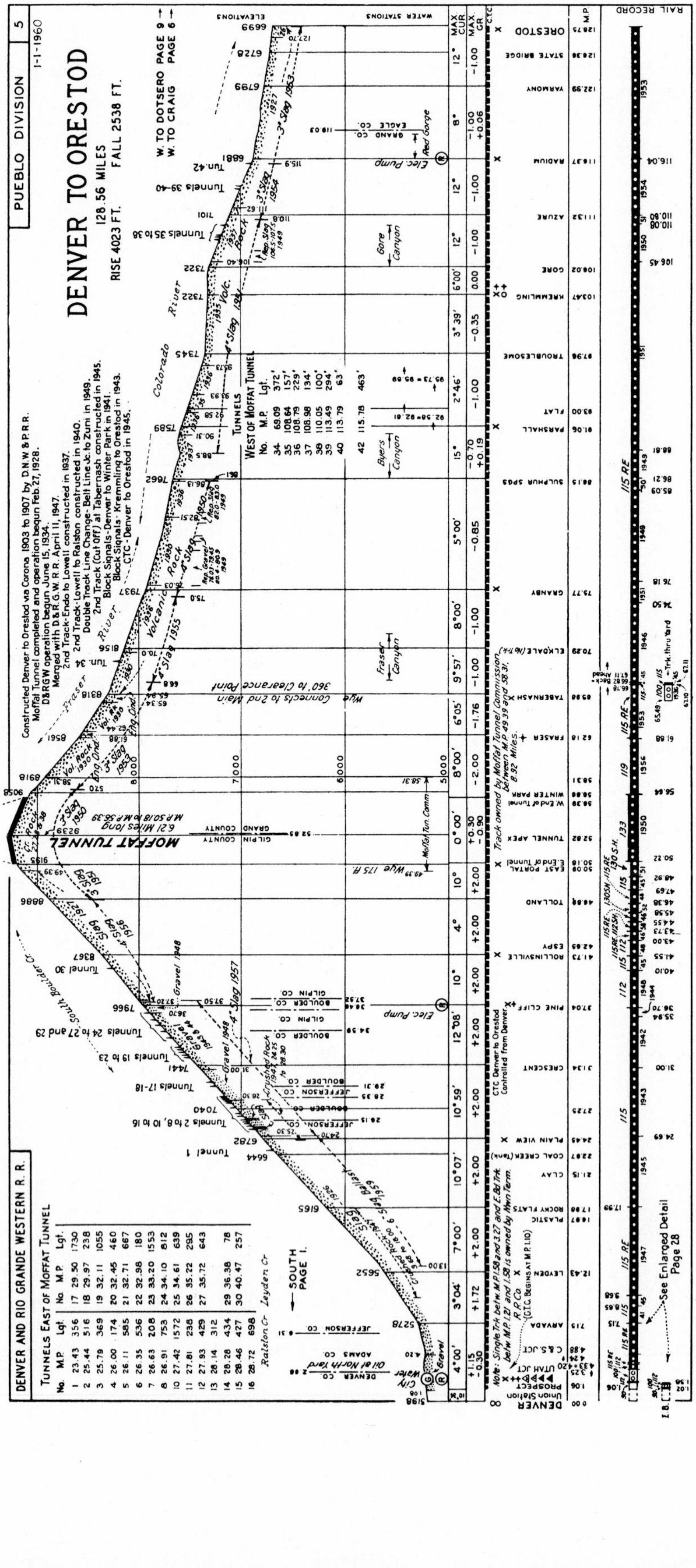

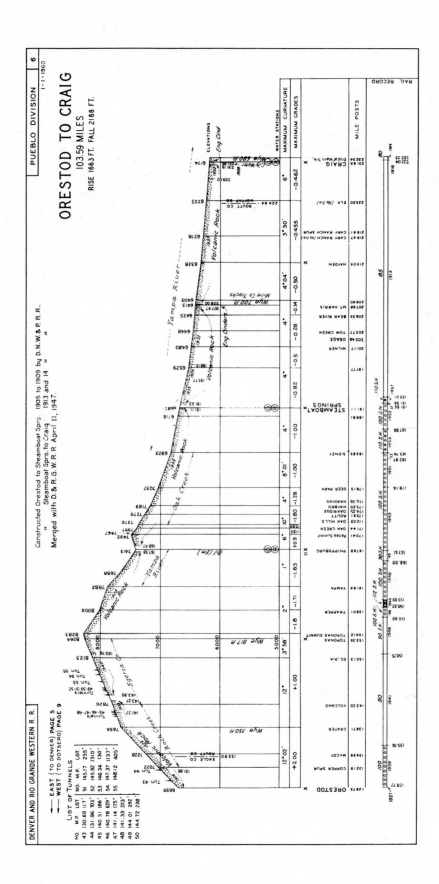

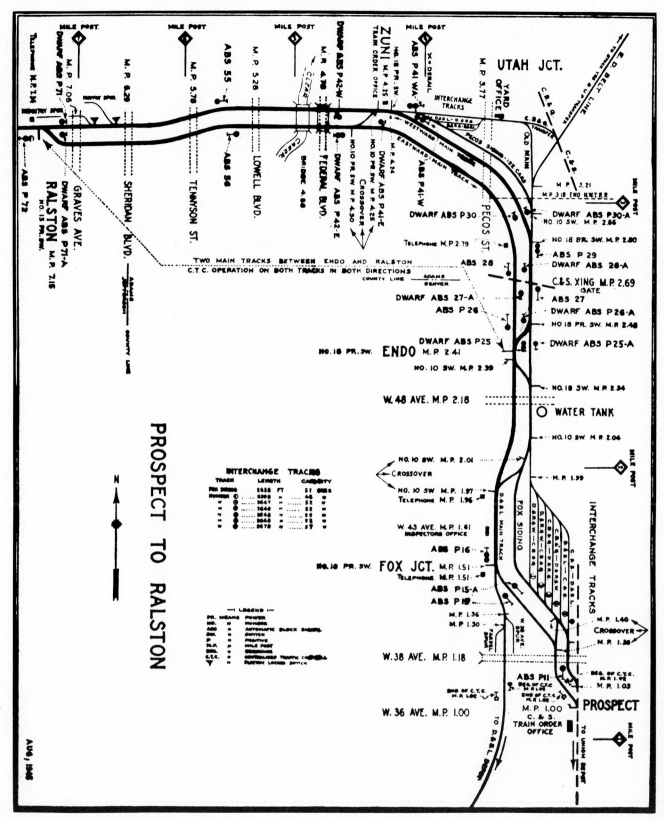

Appendices

XIII: ANNUAL PASSES, 1905 TO 1945

From E. S. Peyton collection.

1905
Denver, Northwestern & Pacific Railway.

Pass --: Mr. Robert Law, Jr. :--

Cashier, Colorado Midland Ry

UNTIL DECEMBER 31ST 1905 UNLESS OTHERWISE ORDERED.

N⁰ B 16

GENERAL MANAGER.

Not Good on Sundays, Holidays or on Special Excursion Trains between June 15th and September 30th.

Denver, Northwestern & Pacific Railway.
1908

Pass ---:Mr. John J. Harris:---

S t a t e   S e n a t o r.

UNTIL DECEMBER 31ST 1908, UNLESS OTHERWISE ORDERED.

N⁰ C 22

GENERAL MANAGER

1912

PASS ---:Mr. J. H. Waters:---

Pres.& G.M.,   F. & C. C. R.R.

GOOD ON ALL LINES UNTIL DECEMBER 31ST, 1912
UNLESS OTHERWISE ORDERED

COUNTERSIGNED BY
C.C. ANTHONY

GENERAL SUPERINTENDENT

1921   No. C 411
THE DENVER & SALT LAKE RAILROAD CO.
W. R. FREEMAN AND C. BOETTCHER, RECEIVERS

PASS   ----: Mr. J. Bruner :----
Chief Clerk, Vice Pres. and Gen. Mgr.,
ACCOUNT   The Colorado & Southern Railway Co.

BETWEEN ALL STATIONS
UNTIL DECEMBER 31ST, 1921 { UNLESS OTHERWISE ORDERED
SUBJECT TO CONDITIONS ON BACK

VALID WHEN COUNTERSIGNED BY MYSELF, G. R. SIMMONS OR R. A. RYAN

RECEIVER

THE DENVER & SALT LAKE RAILWAY CO.
1936-1937   NO. B 721

PASS Mr. A. E. Perlman,
Engineer – Maintenance of Way,
Denver & Rio Grande Western RR Co

BETWEEN ALL STATIONS DURING CURRENT YEAR { UNLESS OTHERWISE ORDERED AND
SUBJECT TO CONDITIONS ON BACK

ADDRESS Denver, Colo.   REQUEST OF   WMcC

VALID WHEN COUNTERSIGNED BY MYSELF, W. O. COLWELL, H. M. MOON OR J. T. URBAN.

COUNTERSIGNED BY

PRESIDENT

THE DENVER & SALT LAKE RAILWAY CO.
1945   No. B 569

PASS Mr. H. A. Clark,
Traveling Agent,
Chicago and North Western Railway Co.

BETWEEN ALL STATIONS DURING CURRENT YEAR { UNLESS OTHERWISE ORDERED AND
SUBJECT TO CONDITIONS ON BACK

ADDRESS Denver, Colo.   REQUEST OF   RLW

VALID WHEN COUNTERSIGNED BY W. O. COLWELL OR H. M. KIRKLEY.

COUNTERSIGNED BY

PRESIDENT

Page 335

XIV: MAP OF YAMPA VALLEY COAL FIELD, 1908

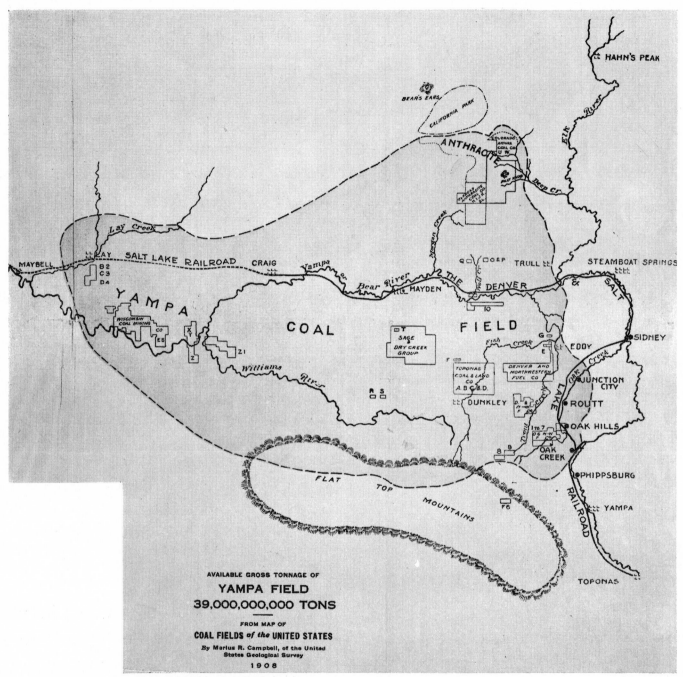

AVAILABLE GROSS TONNAGE OF
YAMPA FIELD
39,000,000,000 TONS

FROM MAP OF
COAL FIELDS *of the* UNITED STATES
By Marius R. Campbell, of the United
States Geological Survey
1 9 0 8

David Moffat sent out prospectors and used every means possible to evaluate the resources of this territory. Today we know he was right.

XV: MESSAGES AND WAY BILL

The Denver, Northwestern and Pacific
Railway Company.
DENVER, COLORADO.

Denver, Colo., June 5, 1909.

Mr D. H. Moffat:

5:00 P.M.

No. 1, 7 minutes late at Yampa, handled 31 Revenue, 15 complimentary and 5 Employes deadhead.

No. 2 On time by Plainview, handled 50 Revenue, 1 Complimentary and 4 employes passes.

No. 5 Arrived Arrow on time handled 59-1/2 Arrow, 3 Denver to Corona, 3 Denver to Tolland and 4 passes.

No. 6 On time should have had about same number passengers as No. 5.

Stock extra west with 29 cattle and 1 car emigrants passed

BILL. ACCOUNTANTS' ASSOCIATION STANDARD FORM No. 100.

STATION 1-29 1911

ATION VIA

To **Denver, Northwestern & Pacific Railway,** Dr. PRO.

FOR CHARGES ON ARTICLES WAYBILLED FROM VIA

DATE OF WAYBILL 19	No. of Pkgs.	ARTICLES AND MARKS	WEIGHT	RATE	FREIGHT	ADVANCES
SERIES AND NUMBER OF WAYBILL						
CAR INITIALS AND NUMBER						
CONSIGNOR						
CONNECTING LINE REFERENCE						
ORIGINAL CAR						
ORIGINAL WAYBILL NUMBER						
ORIGINAL POINT OF SHIPMENT						

RECEIVED PAYMENT _____ AGENT

PER _____ CASHIER

_____ 19

TOTAL TO COLLECT

DRAYAGE

THE DENVER, NORTHWESTERN & PACIFIC RAILWAY CO.
PAID
JAN 30 1911
C. L. ROBINSON
AGENT.
DENVER, COLO.

All carloads shall be subject to a minimum charge for trackage and rental of $1.00 per car for each 24 hours detention, or fractional part thereof, after the expiration of 48 hours from arrival at destination.

Original Paid Freight Bills should accompany all Claims for Overcharge, Loss or Damage.

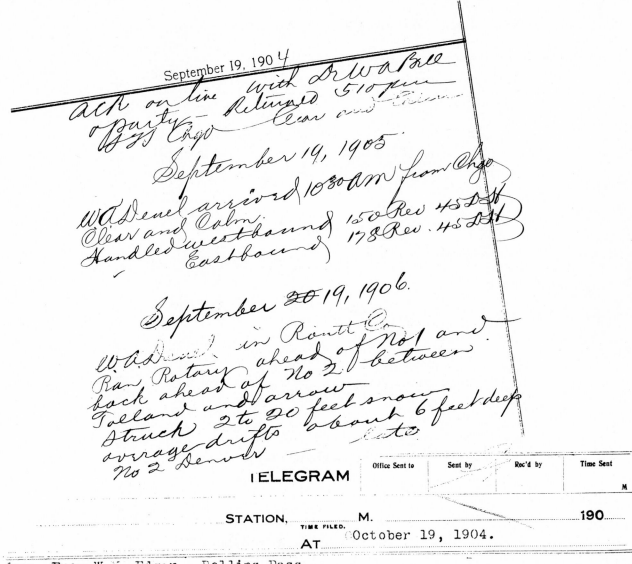

September 19, 190 **4**

ack on line with Dr W A Bee party. Returned 510 pm B G S Chgo   Clear and Calm

September 19, 1905.

W A Deuel arrived 1030 AM from Chgo Clear and Calm. Handled westbound 150 Rev 45 D H 178 Rev. 45 D H Eastbound

September ~~20~~ 19, 1906.

W A Deuel in Routt Co Ran Rotary ahead of No 1 and back ahead of No 2 between Tolland and arrow Struck 2 to 20 feet snow average drifts about 6 feet deep No 2 Denver   late.

TELEGRAM

Office Sent to	Sent by	Rec'd by	Time Sent
			M

STATION,_____ M._____ 190____

TIME FILED.

AT October 19, 1904.

Memo. From W. M. Edgar, Rollins Pass,
To Geo. R. Simmons, Denver.

Engines 179 and 20 are here headed east and coupled together and are just about ready to go to Sunnyside for water and to get McGovern's men who left loop and bring them to the pass.

Engine 101 with stock is standing in shed. Wind is not bad here but blowing hard at Jenny Lake and around tunnel No. 33, there are long and deep drifts between here and No. 2's train. Soon as engine 179 and 20 get back we will start for blockade with some grub for the passengers. We had to coal both engines 20 and 179. We started 10 or 15 of Dickson's gang on foot with shovels to go to No. 2's train.

Good many of Mike's men are leaving him and 10 of Dickson's gang quit also. It looks very bad and I fear we may not get 2's train out before late today, if at all.

I do not think it advisable to attempt to run No. 1 west of Tolland unless we have to with a way car to bring Tim Kennedy's men and another gang this side of Ladora up to help us out. We will pass on that later when we see what advance the force here can make.

8:15 A.M.

Finger Rock between Toponas and Yampa.. This 300 foot landmark is of volcanic origin and can be seen for miles. These diesels on the Craig extension are symbolic of the Rio Grande influence felt today. Although rail officials would deny it, the track and ballast have a branch line look about them. David Moffat's thorough research into the resources of northwestern Colorado is proved each year. The revival of this great bituminous coal field by strip mining has opened a new mine south of Milner at Energy, Colo. From Milner a twelve-mile spur is being built to serve the Energy mine of Morgan Coal Co. Together with the Pittsburg-Edna Mine of Oak Creek and the Osage Mine at Milner, a trainload of coal daily will be delivered to Denver area generating plants. *D.&R.G.W. photo.*

MAIN RANGE TUNNEL - COST VS. ALTITUDE

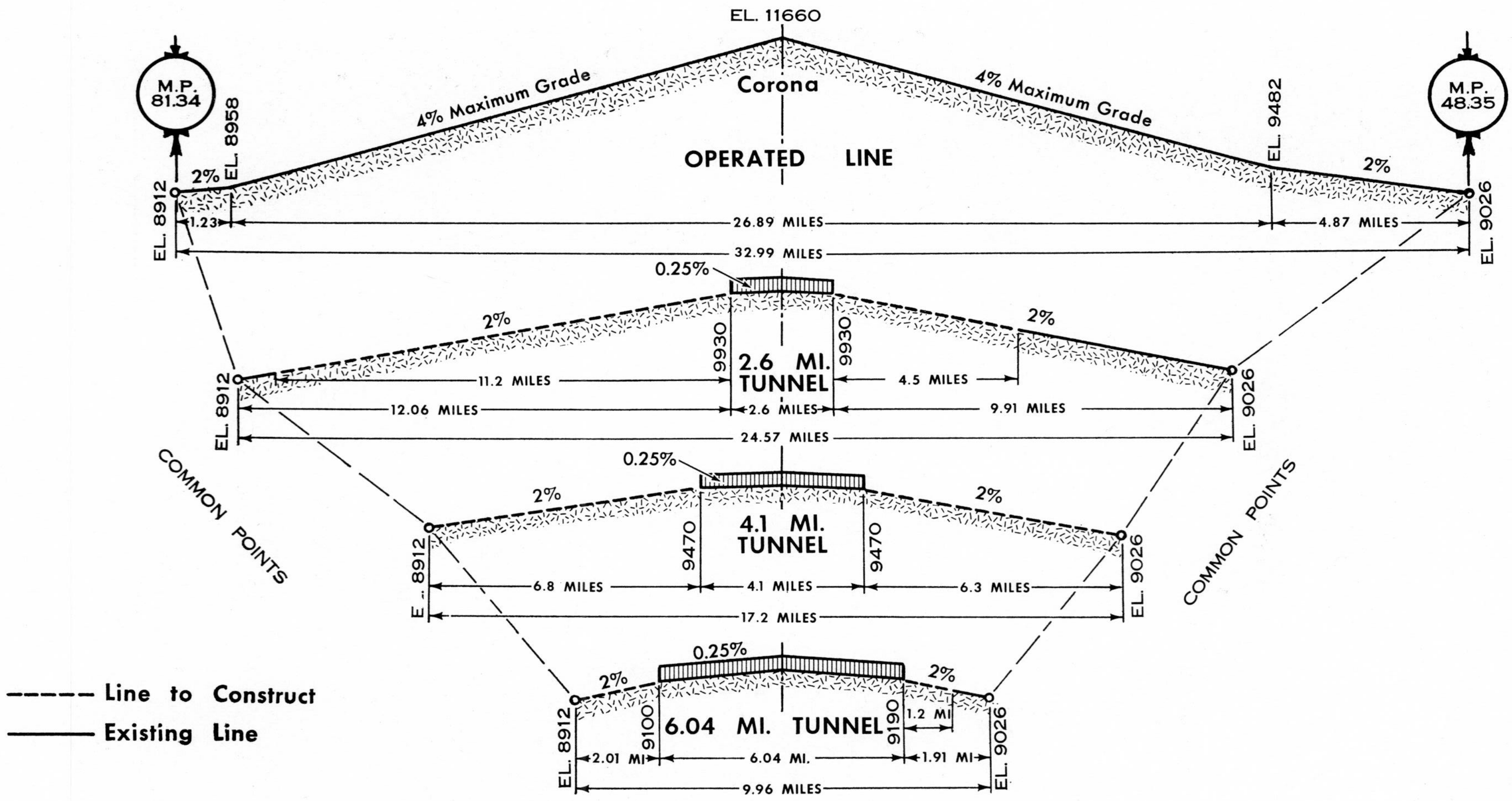

XVI: CHART

Drawn by F. Bauer

M.P. 48.35

EL. 9026

2%

EL. 9482

4.87 MILES

4% Maximum Grade

Corona

EL. 11660

OPERATED LINE

4% Maximum Grade

26.89 MILES

32.99 MILES

2%

EL. 8958

M.P. 81.34

2%

1.23

EL. 8912

COMMON POINTS

EL. 9026

2%

9.91 MILES

4.5 MILES

9930

0.25%

2.6 MI. TUNNEL

9930

2.6 MILES

24.57 MILES

2%

11.2 MILES

12.06 MILES

EL. 8912

EL. 9026

2%

6.3 MILES

9470

0.25%

4.1 MI. TUNNEL

9470

4.1 MILES

17.2 MILES

2%

6.8 MILES

E. 8912

COMMON POINTS

EL. 9026

2%

1.2 MI

1.91 MI

9190

0.25%

6.04 MI. TUNNEL

9100

6.04 MI.

9.96 MILES

2%

2.01 MI

EL. 8912

- - - Line to Construct

———— Existing Line

Notice how tunnel length increases greatly as tunnel altitude is decreased.

FORM 19	Standard	19

DENVER, NORTHWESTERN AND PACIFIC RAILWAY

TRAIN ORDER NO. 2

Stationer's Form 1237. 6-09. 400 Bks. 200 Lv.   11-17-19

To C & E Eng 105   At Sulphur Springs
                                          STATION

X _____ Opr. _____ M.

Eng 108 will run extra Arrow
to Tabernash eng 104 will run
extra Arrow to Vasquez. Eng 105
will run extra Sulphur Springs
to Arrow, meet extra 108 west
at Tabernash and extra 104 west
at Vasquez.

                                   SHB

CONDUCTOR AND ENGINEMAN MUST EACH HAVE A COPY OF THIS ORDER.

Made Complete Time 202g J Connett Opr.

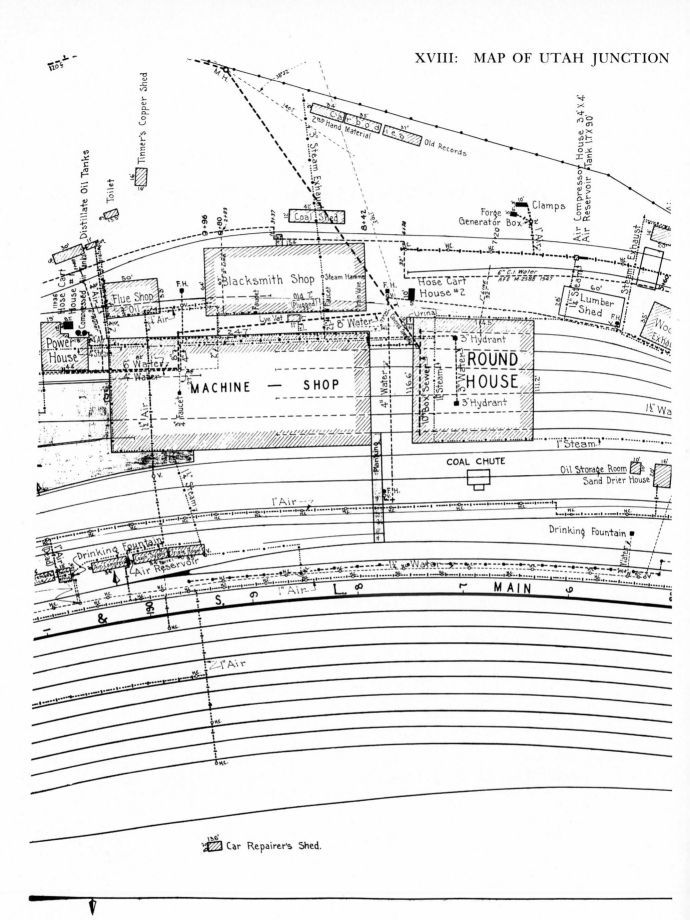

Car Repairer's Shed.

UTAH JUNCTION
WATER, AIR, STEAM, SEWER AND OIL LINES
THE DENVER AND SALT LAKE RAILWAY CO.
STATION 175 + 00 TO STATION 202 + 00

SCALE 1-IN = 50 FT.

Office of Chief Engineer
Denver, Colo.

P-2-2-1782.

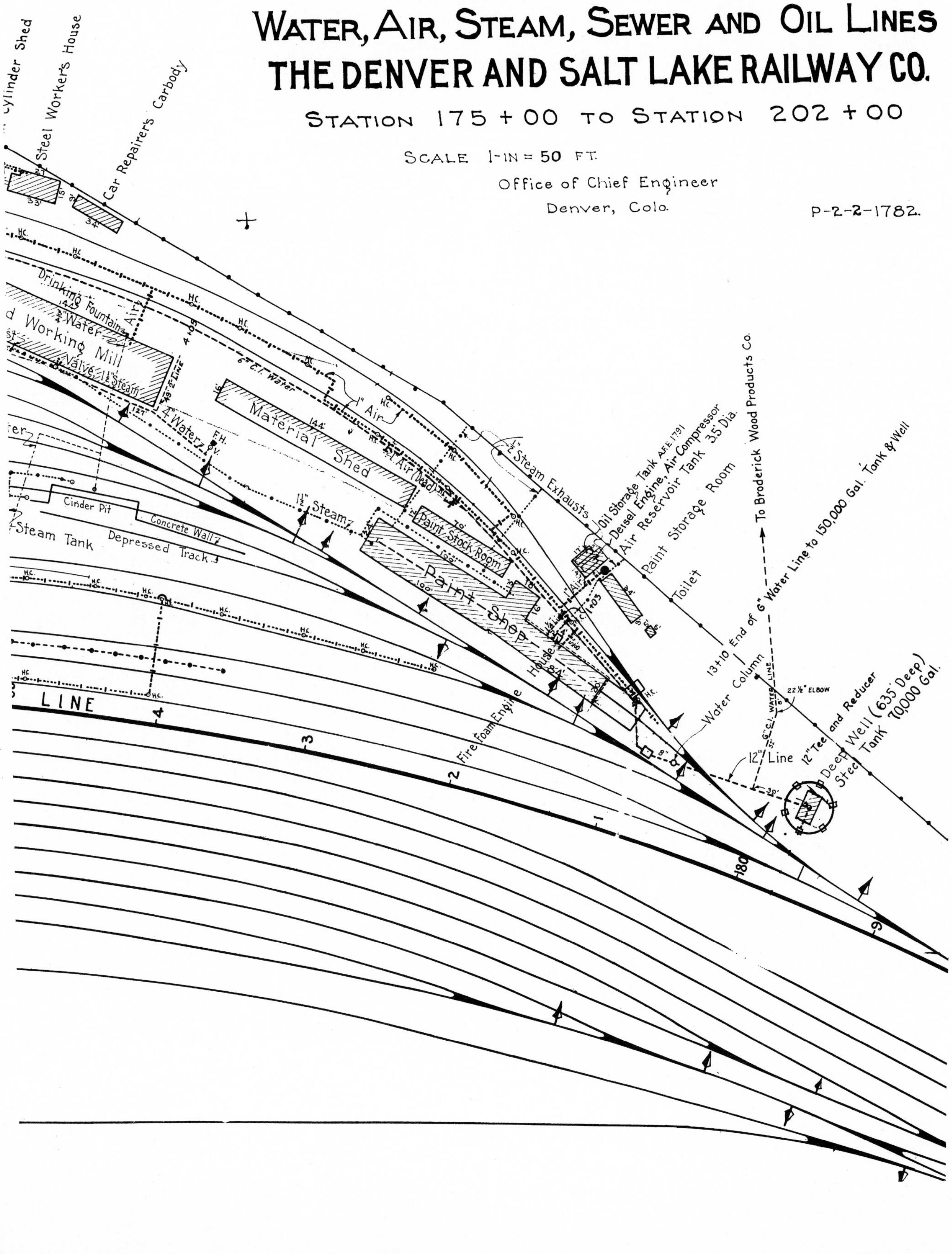

Cylinder Shed

Steel Workers House

Car Repairers Carbody

Drinking Fountains

¾" Water

d Working Mill

Valve 1" Steam

4" Water

F.H.

Material Shed

1" Air

1" Air

½" Steam Exhausts

Oil Storage Tank A.F.E. 1791

Diesel Engine, Air Compressor

Air Reservoir Tank 3.5 Dia.

Paint Storage Room

To Broderick Wood Products Co.

End of 6" Water Line to 150,000 Gal. Tank & Well

Cinder Pit

Concrete Wall

Depressed Track

Steam Tank

1½" Steam

1½" Steam

Paint Stock Room

Paint Shop

Fire Foam Engine House

Toilet

Water Column

13+10

6" C.I. WATER LINE

22½° ELBOW

12" Tee and Reducer

12" Line

Deep Well (635' Deep)
Steel Tank 70,000 Gal.

LINE

4

3

2

1

180

9

H.C.

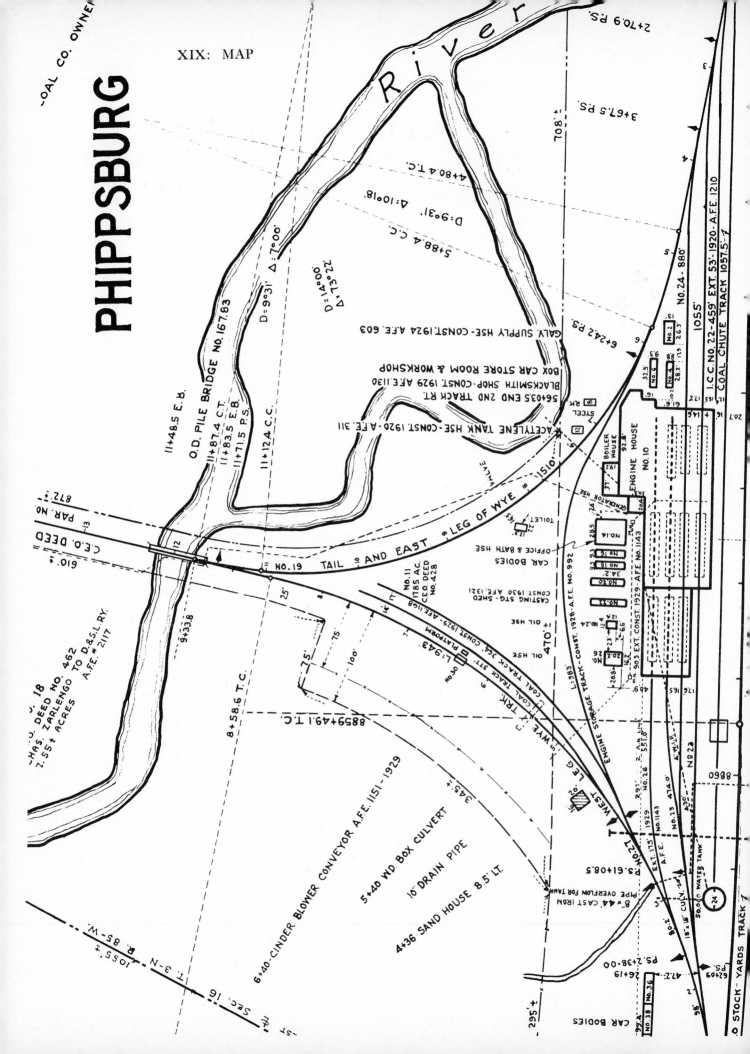

XIX: MAP

PHIPPSBURG

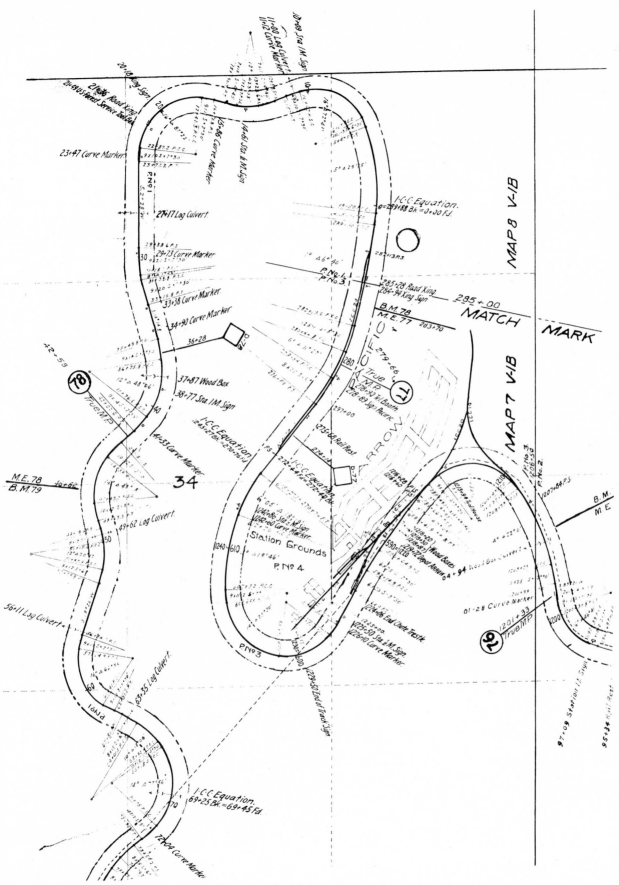

Western terminus for a short time of the line over Corona Pass, Arrow (head) provided eating facilities for passengers, and fuel, water, and turning facilities for engines. This map section, covering mile posts 76 to 78½, is from an original D.&S.L. tracing, and illustrates exceedingly well the almost complete lack of tangent track on the hill line. *Courtesy D.&R.G.W. Railroad.*

Bibliography

From the outset, the Moffat was a notable piece of construction. Attracting the attention it did, coverage in the public and technical press was quite complete. As a result, there exists today a wealth of material of absorbing interest available at most large libraries. Smaller libraries can always arrange for loans of the material you desire.

The authors have attempted to develop new facts through research and interviews. Moffat people are dwindling rapidly, however, and much reliance has been placed on the books and articles listed below. In order to assist in choosing articles of greatest interest, a short summary is included with most of the references.

DOCUMENTS

Found in Moffat vault:
> Twenty-seven volumes of letter press of H. A. Sumner's letters as Chief Engineer.
> General Manager's office diary for 1902-4 (in part), and for 1907-9 (in part).
> Operating Timetables complete.
> Maps with data concerning all lines run.
> Lesser papers too numerous to mention.
> Rock Island report on proposal to buy and complete the Moffat including the Moffat Tunnel.

Discovered in Castle Building debris:
> Two diaries of J. J. Argo in field work.

Discovered in Rio Grande garage building:
> Records principally from the mid-Twenties, but including much material from the original surveys, details of the brake tests, pictures of the Hill, Dotsero Cutoff, and many other items.

Court records:
> Grand and Routt County.

Libraries:
> Western Collection of the Denver Public Library completely searched as far as indexed.
> State Museum and Historical Society, completely searched as far as processed.
> Grand County.
> City Historian, History Center, City of Schenectady, New York.

Personal letters and interviews:
> Daisy Jenne Scrap Book—invaluable.
> W. I. Hoklas engineering office collection, Steamboat.
> Others as indicated in text or footnotes.

BOOKS

Campbell, Marius R., *Guidebook of the Western United States, Part E. The Denver and Rio Grande Western Route.* Washington: Government Printing Office, 1922. 266 pp. Brief description of the one-day trip to Corona.

Cunningham, Frank, *Big Dan.* Salt Lake City: The Deseret News Press, 1946. 350 pp. A biography of Dan Cunningham, noted D. & S. L. Superintendent of Motive Power.

McMechen, E. C., *The Moffat Tunnel of Colorado.* Denver: The Wahlgreen Publishing Co., 1927. 580 pp., two volumes. A prime source giving the complete history of the Moffat, construction details of the tunnel, and benefits derived.

Bollinger, E. T., *Rails that Climb.* Sante Fe: The Rydal Press, 1950. 402 pp.

ARTICLES (arranged chronologically)

"General Engineering Features of the D. N. W. & P.," *Engineering Record,* 51:223-4, February 25, 1905. Construction between Denver and Salt Lake City with good photographs and an explanation of the track laying machine in use.

"The Denver, Northwestern, & Pacific Ry.," *Engineering News,* 53:241-5, March 9, 1905. General description of resources, and detailed description of the new line which shortens the distance by rail between Denver and Salt Lake City and opens new territory. Excellent photos.

"The Denver, Northwestern, & Pacific Road," *Railroad Gazette,* 38:234-8, March 17, 1905. Road has reached Arrowhead. Excellent early photographs, construction specifications, details of topography, territory served, resources and outline of projected construction; success certain in tapping virgin territory.

"The Denver, Northwestern, & Pacific," *Railroad Gazette,* 40:503-8, May 18, 1906. Construction details with good photographs.

"The Rotary in the Rockies," *Railway and Locomotive Engineering,* 20:99-102, March, 1907. Description of snow removal on the Moffat Road; excellent photographs of scenery and rotaries in action.

"Articulated Compound of 0-6-6-0 Type," *American Engineer and Railroad Journal,* 83:61, February, 1909. Description of a Mallet engine recently delivered to the D. N. W. & P. patterned after a B. & O. engine.

"Railroad Tunnel Financing Proposed by Denver," *Engineering Record,* 67:310, March 22, 1913. Proposal for assistance of Denver to be submitted to electors May 20. Precedent found in Cincinnati Southern Railroad, and the Hoosac Tunnel (Massachusetts). Rights reserved for water tunnel, electric transmission, and minerals.

"The Moffat Tunnel as a Denver Municipal Project," *Engineering News,* 71:22-3, January 29, 1914. Railway and city to cooperate on venture. Report of geologist states solid gneiss rock expected throughout with cost estimated at $4,420,000 plus contingency. Special city election has amended city charter to permit municipal participation. Water tunnel included.

"Denver Municipal Bonds for Moffat Tunnel Declared Unconstitutional," *Engineering News,* 72:156, July 16, 1914. State

Bibliography

Supreme Court lists four reasons why municipal funds should not be used for this private enterprise; apparently the court failed to recognize the effort as a Public Work.

"State of Colorado Proposes Three Railway Tunnels," *Engineering News-Record*, 84:716, April 8, 1920. Description of James Peak Tunnel on D. & S. L.. 6.4 miles in length, together with Cumbres Tunnel on the Rio Grande Southern (sic), and Monarch Tunnel on the D. &. R. G. W.; the latter would by-pass Marshall Pass. L. D. Blauvelt proposes forty-two mile Dotsero Cutoff.

"Colorado Petitions for Tunnels," *Engineering News-Record*, 85:44, July 1, 1920. Initiative and referendum procedure petition used for vote on construction of three tunnels by issuance of state bonds; tunnels to be owned by the state.

"Colorado May Not Build Tunnels," *Engineering News-Record*, 85:1302, December 30, 1920. Proposal defeated at election. Proposal of new nature to be brought before the legislature authorizing "tunnel districts" and permitting them to issue bonds if desired.

"Colorado's Tri-Tunnel Project," *Universal Engineer*, Edgar C. McMechen, 32:23-9, December, 1920. Project provides for boring three transportation tunnels under the Continental Divide in Colorado.

"Successful Test of the Automatic Straight Air Brake on the Norfolk and Western Railway," *Railway and Locomotive Engineering*, 34:91-8, April, 1921. Details of Automatic Straight Air Brake Co. development later tried on D. & S. L.

"Physical and Operating Conditions on the Denver and Salt Lake Railroad," *Railway and Locomotive Engineering*, 34:233-8, September, 1921. The traffic hauled and results of a recent demonstration of the Automatic Straight Air Brake.

"D. & S. L. Presents Difficult Operating Problem," *Railway Review*, 69:357-61, September 17, 1921. Automatic straight air brakes assist in operation of heavy trains on 4% grades. Comparative tests with Westinghouse and Automatic Straight Air Brake Co. brakes involving the heaviest tonnage train ever operated downgrade.

Poor's Manual of Railroads, 1921:433. Three engineers appointed by the City of Denver have estimated the tunnel to cost $4,420,000 and require four years.

"Railway Tunnels as Public Work," *Engineering News-Record*, 88:811, May 18, 1922. Editorial comment that under certain conditions a railway may be considered a public improvement.

"Long Colorado Railway Tunnel To Be Built by Improvement Bonds," *Engineering News-Record*, 88:836, May 18, 1922. State law passed providing for improvement district to float bonds not in excess of $6,720,000. All property in certain counties to be assessed.

"Why Two Tunnels?" *Colorado Society of Engineers Bulletin*, December, 1922; Art Weston. Plans for use of tunnel pioneer bore as a water tunnel hidden since bill passed by legislature nowhere referred to "tunnels."

"Let First Contract on Moffat Main and Pilot Tunnels," *Engineering News-Record*, 91:77, July 12, 1923. $6,720,000 bonds sold for 5½% after U. S. Supreme Court validates by decision of June 11, 1923. Work hoped to be under contract by August 10.

Municipal Facts (Denver, Colorado), August-September, 1923. Moffat Tunnel issue. An exhaustive issue setting forth justification of the Tunnel and plans for its implementation.

"Moffat Tunnel Project Near Realization," *Railway Age*, 75:397-8, September 1, 1923. Moffat Tunnel Commission has prepared plans and invited bids. All indications point to early construction. Hill Line 27.63 miles of which 78% was on curves, and 31% on curves of 16°.

"Contract Awarded for Driving Moffat Tunnel," *Engineering News-Record*, 91:532, September 27, 1923. Contract price $5,2500,000 to be accomplished in forty-six months with penalty clause. Work to be performed by Hitchcock and Tinkler, builder of the eighteen mile Hetch-Hetchy Tunnel, and sixteen miles of the original D. & S. L. grade, including fifteen tunnels.

"Moffat Tunnel Bids Present Unusual Details," *Engineering News-Record*, 91:615, October 11, 1923. Particulars of bidding, including penalty clause, sharing of savings, extra work requested.

"Engineering Features of the Moffat Tunnel," *Colorado Scientific Society*, October, 1923, D. W. Brunton. Solid rock expected, no more than five percent timber; advantages of pioneer system, electric haulage a necessity. Bidders requested to take contingency funds out, since Tunnel Commission would absorb them because difficulty was so remote a possibility. The engineering outlook before construction began.

"Six Mile Tunnel Through the Rocky Mountains," *Engineering News-Record*, 91:962-5, December 13, 1923. History, outline of proposed construction, financing, grades, tunnel sections and sanitary requirements.

"Country's Longest Tunnel Project Well Under Way," *Railway Review*, 74:174-81, January 26, 1924. Construction details; work proceeding thirty feet per day. Excellent photographs, complete explanation of all operations.

Successful Methods, February, 1924.

"Progress on the Moffat Tunnel Through the Rockies," *Engineering News-Record*, 92:402, March 6, 1924. Daily average twelve feet.

Municipal Facts (Denver, Colorado), September-October, 1924.

"Driving the Moffat Tunnel," *Engineering & Mining Journal Press*, 118:765-9, November 15, 1924. Good equipment and organization expedite the work. Photographs of east portal pioneer tunnel, cross cuts, and drilling.

"Work on Moffat Tunnel Now in Full Progress," *Railway Age*, 77:889-94, November 15, 1924. Headings for America's longest railroad tunnel have been driven one-third through. Snow removal on the temporary line 40% of total cost of operation. Conditions on two ends of tunnel entirely different; solid rock at east, and shattered rock at west side requiring every foot to be timbered.

"Driving the Moffat Tunnel," *Explosives Engineer*, 3:51-8, 63, February, 1925. Drilling technique, history. Unusual photographs.

"Driving a Tunnel Through the Continental Divide," *Compressed Air Magazine*, 30:1133-8, February, 1925. What the Moffat Tunnel means to Colorado and the Country at large. Part I. History, unique aerial photographs of Corona and the Divide.

"Driving the First Tunnel Through the Continental Divide," *Compressed Air Magazine*, 30:1165-71, March 1925. General characteristics of the work with some details of work at West Portal. Part II. Tunnel drilling, techniques at West Portal; excellent photographs of the Hill Line.

The Moffat Road

"Driving the First Tunnel Through the Continental Divide," *Compressed Air Magazine,* 30:1205-13, April 1925. Part III. Methods of drilling at West Portal, blasting, mucking, timbering. Good photographs.

Municipal Facts (Denver, Colorado), March-April, 1925.

"Moffat Tunnel Heading Advances at Record Rate," *Engineering News-Record,* 94:830, May 14, 1925. Main heading progress 691 feet in one month.

"Driving the First Tunnel Through the Continental Divide," *Compressed Air Magazine,* 30:1237-44, May, 1925. Part IV. Methods at East Portal, good photographs.

"Modern Methods Speed Up Work on Moffat Tunnel," *Successful Methods,* 14-5, June, 1925. Up-to-date machinery used in drilling.

"Construction Methods on Six Mile Moffat Tunnel," *Engineering News-Record,* 94:966-71, June 11, 1925. Parallel tunnel with cross drifts to main tunnel takes care of haulage and other services. Squeezing rock calls for unusual timbering methods.

"A New Device for Tunnel Work," *Engineering and Contracting* (General Contracting), 64:173-5, July 15, 1925. The Lewis travelling cantilever beam as used at the Moffat Tunnel; a complete description with sketches and photographs in great detail. Basically a device for supporting the tunnel roof while enlarging and timbering proceed below it.

Municipal Facts (Denver, Colorado), September-October, 1925.

"The Moffat Tunnel in Colorado," *Mining and Metallurgy,* 6:554-9, November, 1925. History of needle bar, Lewis cantilever; progress to July, 1925.

"Electricity Driving Longest Railroad Tunnel in the United States," *Journal of Electricity,* 55:408-11, December 1, 1925. Synchronous motors, load factor, electric mucking machines, transmission line and photographs of electrical installations.

"Moffat Tunnel Leased," *Railway Age,* 80:246, January 16, 1926. Fifty year lease to D. & S. L. to retire and pay interest on two-thirds of the tunnel bonds aggregating $9,220,000. Annual payments $346,000 for the first six years, varying thereafter. D. & S. L. Ry. incorporated to take over the assets of the D. & S. L. R. R. in receivership.

"Soft Rock Conditions in Moffat Tunnel," *DuPont Magazine,* 20:11, 14-5, 23-4, February-March, 1926. Details of difficulty at west end climaxed by invention of the Lewis bar. Details of blasting. Good photographs.

"Will Hole Through Moffat Tunnel in July, 1926," *Engineering News-Record,* 96:284-5, February 18, 1926. Progress report; east heading 14,720 feet in solid gneiss, west heading 11,625 feet in shattered gneiss and schist, adding $100-$200 cost per foot.

"Mechanical Loading at the Moffat Tunnel," *Mining Congress Journal,* 12:210-12, March, 1926. Review of power mining machinery employed.

"Moffat Tunnel 75 Percent Complete," *Western Construction News,* 1:30-34, May 10, 1926, C. A. Betts. Status report, flow of water encountered, I-beam wall plates.

"The Moffat Tunnel, U. S. A.," *Engineer,* 142:4-12, July 2, 1926. History, complete description, unique photographs, open line vs. tunnel. Part I.

"The Moffat Railway Tunnel, U. S. A.," *Engineer,* 142:28-30, July 9, 1926. Part II. Pioneer bore, water tunnel, rock conditions, water troubles, enlarging headings, machine equip-ment.

"The Moffat Railway Tunnel, U. S. A.," *Engineer,* 142:54-6, July 16, 1926. Part III. Tunneling in bad material, enlargement, special roof supporting devices, electric supply, haulage, and ventilation.

"The Moffat Tunnel Through the Rocky Mountains," *The Railway Engineer,* 47:241, July, 1926. Brief description of mechanical methods used.

Moody's Investment Service, 17:339, October 15, 1926. Investment evaluation.

"Work on Moffat Tunnel Forging Ahead," *Railway Age,* 81:878-81, November 6, 1926. Completion in 1927 expected in spite of difficulties encountered—water flow and need for heavy timbering. Sale of D. & S. L. on August 16 concluded its receivership.

"The Moffat Six Mile Tunnel," *Western Construction News,* 2:37-40, March 10, 1927. Review of latest developments.

"The Moffat Tunnel," *Western Construction News,* 2:37-41, September 25, 1927. Further data on construction, methods of ventilation, mucking, transportation, and equipment.

"Speeding Up the Moffat Tunnel," *Scientific American,* 137:338-9, October, 1927. Cantilever beam cuts time in half, saves labor, and prevents slides.

"Mechanical Equipment Used in Driving Moffat Tunnel," *Mechanical Engineering,* 49:1181-86, November, 1927. History, methods, roof supports, drilling and firing. Consulting and construction engineers recommend electric locomotives to eliminate great fire risk; D. & S. L. will not consent but insist on steam locomotives and attempt to clear out gases by ventilation.

"Tunnel Ventilation," *Engineering News-Record,* 99:947, December 15, 1927. Editorial pointing out the danger of engine gases and noting that electric traction is increasing rapidly in long tunnels. Noting the decision to use steam in the Moffat, the position is taken that this becomes an isolated case hardly likely to be duplicated.

"Ventilation Experiments in Moffat Tunnel," *Engineering News-Record,* 99:956, December 15, 1927. Determination of air flow friction factors as basis for design of the plant for removing gas and smoke discharged by locomotives. Main railway bore had been holed through, but not enlarged when decision was made to use steam; ventilation counter to train movement decided upon although in winter fans must operate against natural draft and storm wind pressure.

"Construction of the Moffat Tunnel," *The Military Engineer,* 20:40-9, January-February, 1928. History, location, design, methods and timbering.

"Equipment Used In Driving the Moffat Tunnel," *Contractors' and Engineers' Monthly,* 16:87-91, February, 1928. Pioneer bore, air compressor equipment, drilling, mucking.

"The Moffat Tunnel," *Construction Methods,* 10:22-5, February, 1928. Methods, photographs of prominent persons.

"Will Moffat's Dream Be Realized?" *Railway Age,* 84:403-5, February 18, 1928. The case for and against the proposed Dotsero Cutoff. Why the D. & S. L. cannot build, because expense cannot be recovered through the volume of traffic it could handle as a bridge line. Effect on other roads. Excellent.

"The Moffat Tunnel, Hitchcock & Tinkler, Inc.," *Association American and Chinese Engineers Journal,* 9:3-22, March, 1928. Labor, geology, power, ventilation, air, transportation, muck-

Bibliography

ing, steels, and explosives.

"Steam Operation Through Long Tunnels," *Railway Age*, 84: 612, March 17, 1928. The true test of Moffat Tunnel ventilation (vs. electrification) can only come with greatly increased traffic.

"Ventilating the Moffat Tunnel," *Colorado School of Mines Magazine*, 17:11-13, March, 1928, A. F. Hewitt and R. F. Sopris. Ventilation plant at East Portal described and illustrated.

Engineering and Contracting, 67:214, March, 1928. Same as above.

"The Moffat Tunnel, Hitchcock & Tinkler, Inc.," *Association American and Chinese Engineers Journal*, 9:14-33, April, 1928. Procedure and methods, driving headings, holing through.

"Ventilation Control in the Moffat Tunnel," *Electrical World*, 91:1010, May 19, 1928. Two fan motors and a door at the East Portal vestibule ventilate the tunnel under all conditions of varying barometric pressures at the two ends.

"Moffat Tunnel Ventilation for Steam Locomotives," *Engineering News-Record*, 100:994-5, June 28, 1928. Due to the lack of western connection, ventilation is more economical than electrification. Excellent article with diagrams of operation under induced and forced draft conditions for west-, and east-bound trains, respectivley.

"Construction Methods on the Moffat Tunnel," *American Society of Civil Engineers*, Trans. 92:63-112, 1928, R. H. Keays. Probably the most scholarly work on the subject with every detail of all phases up to August, 1925.

"Finance Docket 4555, Proposed Construction by Denver and Salt Lake Western Railroad Co.," *Interstate Commerce Commission Reports*, 154:51-8, 585, submitted March 11, 1929, decided April 15, 1929. Historic Cutoff decision.

"Supercharging at Moffat Tunnel," *Oil Engine Power*, 7:553, October, 1929. Editorial pointing out the benefits to be obtained from a diesel-generator prime mover.

"Supercharged Diesel Ventilates Moffat Tunnel at 9200 Ft. Altitude," *Oil Engine Power*, 7:554-9, October, 1929. Since the peak load occurs only several hours during the day, local generation is used. House service and throw-over carried by utility.

"Steam Operation No Obstacle to Use of Moffat Tunnel," *Railway Age*, 87: 1423-7, December 21, 1929. The case against electrification; why air blown counter to train movement is used. Experience with trains held three hours in the tunnel. Investment of $250,000 with $1000 monthly operating cost results comparable to electrification at $100,000 yearly.

"Ventilating a Six Mile Tunnel," *Compressed Air Magazine*, 35:3031-6, February, 1930. Details of ventilating equipment, operation, and results. Excellent photos.

American Society of Civil Engineers, Proceedings, 56:679-716, April, 1930. Reprint of *Transactions* 92:1928.

"Rock Tunnel Methods," *Explosives Engineer*, 8:298-301, August, 1930. Drilling diagrams of tunnel blasting. Lewis bar.

"Completion of Moffat Tunnel of Colorado," *American Society of Civil Engineers, Proceedings*, 56:1741-4, September, 1930. Importance of D. & S.L. decision to use steam power requiring changing tunnel grade, thus leading to serious difficulties since tunnel was engineered to be electrified.

"Completion of Moffat Tunnel of Colorado," *American Society of Civil Engineers, Proceedings*, 56:2037-8, November, 1930. Discussion continued. Theory of pressure on tunnel timbering.

"Circuit Court Upholds Moffat Tunnel Lease," *Railway Age*, 89:1243, December 6, 1930. District Court of Appeals decides the lease within the letter and spirit of the Tunnel Law. Further, it rejected the contention that the actual purpose of the law was to lend the credit of the Tunnel District to the Railway.

"Completion of the Moffat Tunnel of Colorado," *American Society of Civil Engineers, Proceedings*, 57:307-8, January, 1931. Electrification assumed until the D. & S. L. exercised its option of steam operation. Deterioration of lining must be watched; concrete relining program recommended.

"Denver to Get New Line West Through Moffat Tunnel," *Engineering News-Record*, 107:213-4, August 6, 1931. Review of legal proceedings prior to, and subsequent to the Dotsero Cutoff; transfer of control of the Moffat Line to D. & R. G. W. assures construction of the Cutoff.

"Completion of the Moffat Tunnel of Colorado," *American Society of Civil Engineers, Transactions*, 95: 334-78. Story of the work from August, 1925, to completion. Continuation of the scholarly treatise in *Transactions* 92:1928.

"Bond Litigation Near End?" *Barron's*, 12:6, December, 1932. Colorado Court upholds the validity of $8,750,000 bonds of Moffat Tunnel Improvement District.

"Dotsero Cutoff Will Provide New and Shorter Traffic Route," *Railway Age*, 96:339-44, March 10, 1934. Character of country traversed, map.

"Denver's Dream Comes True—With Reservations!" *Forbes*, 33:14, May 15, 1934. Quarrel between the D. & R. G. W. and D. & S. L. (controlled by the former) delays through passenger service over the Dotsero Cutoff. Expected to be finished June 15, 1934.

"New American Railway Route," *Engineer*, 15:344, October 5, 1934. Detailed description of the Dotsero Cutoff.

"RFC Assumes Control of D. & S. L.," *Railway Age*, 97:872, December 29, 1934. Government body votes road's stock which had been pledged as security for a loan of $3,182,150 to Denver and Salt Lake Western (subsidiary of D. & R. G. W.). The loan had enabled the D. & R. G. W. to complete the purchase of the D. & S. L. stock at $155 per share.

" 'U. S. R. R.' May Be a Good Bet for the Government, But It's Hardly a Good 'Measuring Stick,' " *Business Week*, 18, February 2, 1935. U. S. takes over prosperous subsidiary of the D. & R. G. W. to prevent entanglement with heavily mortgaged parent. D. & S. L. could show profit without turning a wheel because of trackage right payments by D. & R. G. W. of $600-700,000 yearly. Questions proposed relative to labor policies, whether operation will be an experiment, and if tax payments under government ownership will continue.

"Denver Goes to West Slope for Additional Water Supply." *Engineering News-Record*, 115:357-8, September 12, 1935. Waters from Fraser River and tributaries to be diverted through Moffat Tunnel.

"Denver and Salt Lake Line Moffat Tunnel With Concrete," *Railway Age*, 99:626-3, November 16, 1935. Necessary adjustment of old timber lining and long haul pose many problems. Over 16,570 feet of old timber replaced because of $75,000 per year replacement cost. Old lining found out of line and irregular.

"D. & S. L. Ry. Admitted to Trusteeship," *Railway Age*, 99:738, November 30, 1935. Admitted to reorganization proceedings as court sought to prevent abandonment of D. & S. L. W. when unable to pay debts as they matured. RFC contended there was no need for bankruptcy since D. & S. L. W. could continue interest payments so long as D. & R. G. W. keeps its lease.

"Ingenious Relining Procedure in a Traffic Burdened Tunnel," *Engineering News-Record*, 115:774-9, December 5, 1935. Distorted and deteriorated timber lining of the Moffat Tunnel replaced with concrete between frequent train movements and in a cold and gas-filled atmosphere.

"Concreting Operations on the Moffat Water Tunnel," *Civil Engineering*, 6:758-60, November, 1936. Poor ground in the west half of the pioneer bore, coupled with the pressure needed to lift water over the Apex required concreting, begun in the Spring of 1935.

"Series Capacitor Proves Economical," *Electrical West*, 77:48-50, December, 1936. Voltage regulation of Moffat Tunnel power supply accomplished by capacitor on the line feeding 500 and 750 HP fan motors.

"Rebuilding the Moffat Railroad," *Engineering News-Record*, 119:381-7, September 2, 1937. Famous Rocky Mountain route has been transformed from a decrepit and bankrupt line into a first class profitable property by a complete rehabilitation program; designed to be used with the Moffat Tunnel and Dotsero Cutoff as part of a transcontinental route.

"D. & S. L. Ry.," *Commercial and Financial Chronicle*, 148:2739, May 6, 1939. Income account for years 1935-8; 150:3355, May 1940, Income account for 1936-9; 152:3180, May 17, 1941: Income account 1937-40.

Trains, 1:7, 13, 48, April, 1941.

"D. & R. G. W. R. R.—ICC Challenges Rail Stock Deal," *Commercial and Financial Chronicle*. 154:428, October 4, 1941. Misleading statements alleged in purchase of D. & S. L. Minority stockholders were paid $5 more per share than the $155 paid the majority.

"David Moffat's Dreams Came True," *Trains*, 2:28-36, January, 1942. The fiercest blizzards, the highest mountain pass, the longest tunnel; These things were conquered. History of the Moffat Road and Dotsero Cutoff.

"Six Miles of Rail and No Joint Anywhere," *Compressed Air Magazine*, 49:8-9, January, 1944. Thermit welded track in the Moffat Tunnel on the D. & S. L. Rails joined in 1000-foot

lengths outside east portal, then pulled into the tunnel.

"Reopening of Tunnel 10," *Trains*, 4:10-17, February, 1944. Swept by fire, extraordinary efforts were made to reopen the line to seasonal peak traffic. Good photos of reconstruction and traffic diversion.

"Fire in Long, Timber Lined Tunnel Presented Tough Problems," *Railway Age*, 116:450-3, March 4, 1944. Restoration of single track bore on the Moffat line after fire of September 20, 1943 at Tunnel 10. Line reopened December 1.

"D. & S. L. Renews Tunnel Rail," *Railway Age*, 117:108-11, July 15, 1944. Heavier welded rail laid, replacing original welded rail of 1938. Radium capsules used for weld examination. Tunnel ventilation changed because heavy traffic resulted in a "plug" of smoke being blown back and forth in middle of tunnel; severe corrosion and deposit of cinders.

"Denver and Salt Lake Steps Up Long Range Tunnel Relining Program," *Concrete*, 52:12-3. October, 1944. Satisfaction with Moffat Tunnel lining leads to acceleration in rehabilitation of many short tunnels. Photos of Tunnel 10 rebuilding after the fire.

"The Commission Says Yes," *Trains*, 5:30-1, May, 1945. The details of outstanding cases in which the ICC authorized the construction of new railroads. Dotsero Cutoff covered thoroughly.

"Old Railroad Folders," *Trains*, 5:22, July, 1945. Denver, Northwestern & Pacific advertising folder illustrated.

"Boat Train on the D. & R. G. W.," *Trains*, 7:30-1, November, 1946. Good photo of Gore Canyon.

"D. & S. L. Locos Renumbered," *Trains*, 9:11, March, 1948. Merged with the Rio Grande roster.

". . . Through the Rockies," *Trains*, 9:40-9, September, 1949. A cab ride from Denver to Bond.

"Rails That Climb," *Trains*, 11:56, January, 1951. Book review.

Trains, 11:50, March, 1951. Tunnel operation, ventilation procedure explained as revised in 1944.

"Under the Continental Divide," *Trains*, 13:60, October, 1953. Notable feats of engineering; the Moffat Tunnel.

ANNUAL REPORTS

Denver & Salt Lake Railway Company, for calendar years ending December 31, 1927, through 1946.

Denver & Rio Grande Western Railroad Co., for years ended December 31, 1930, through 1935; 1937-1938; 1940-1941; 1943 through 1947.

Index

Stations noted are those shown in the *Official Guide* of October, 1925. Other named on-line points, such as sidings and open telegraph offices, are indicated by an asterisk (*). Second Edition changes are indicated by a (†).

Index

Thanks to the *Rocky Mountain News* head photographer, Mel Schieltz, this picture of Ed Bollinger's lantern with its original frosted glass initials is reproduced. Note that the initials on the lantern show. All this and much more are thanks to a wonderful co-author, Fred Bauer.